SPANISH PRONUNCIATION:

Theory and Practice

SPANISH PRONUNCIATION:
Theory and Practice

An Introductory Manual of Spanish
Phonology and Remedial Drill

John B. Dalbor

PENNSYLVANIA STATE UNIVERSITY

HOLT, RINEHART AND WINSTON
New York   Toronto   London

Illustrations by Alan Moyler

Printed in the United States of America

Library of Congress Catalog Card Number: 68-13502
ISBN: 0-03-069120-6   456   038   98765

PREFACE TO THE TEACHER

Spanish Pronunciation: Theory and Practice has attempted to be several books at one and the same time: an introduction to phonetics and phonemics, an analysis of Spanish phonology, and, most important of all, a manual of oral drill for English-speakers seeking to acquire an authentic Spanish accent.

The book was written specifically for my own undergraduate course in Spanish phonology at the Pennsylvania State University and was used here for three successive years in typewritten form with extensive revisions each time. These materials, hopefully, will fulfill the needs of others who teach similar courses at the college level. The students in these courses, if they are like mine, have studied Spanish for at least three years—including high school—and need not only a solid grounding in Spanish phonology, but a systematic program for correcting their own pronunciation defects.

My analysis of the Spanish sound system is primarily structural and descriptive. The basic approach I have followed is quite similar in a general way to the one used by such linguists as Kenneth L. Pike, George L. Trager, Henry Lee Smith, Jr., and Archibald A. Hill for English and D. Lincoln Canfield, Frederick B. Agard, J. Donald Bowen, Robert P. Stockwell, Ismael Silva-Fuenzalida, and Daniel N. Cárdenas for Spanish. Perhaps the most important influence, though, has been that of the great Spanish phonetician, Tomás Navarro Tomás, whose extensive research has provided younger linguists with so much valuable raw data. I have, naturally, made many departures of my own in the linguistic analysis of Spanish, partly on pedagogical grounds and partly on the basis of my own research. I am well aware of the fact that the post-Bloomfieldean structuralist position has been challenged and attacked by the transformational-generative linguists. Nevertheless, I am convinced that Jakobsonian distinctive-feature analysis and Chomsky-Halle generative phonology, although perhaps superior on purely theoretical grounds, is less successful from a pedagogical point of view. The now classical place-and-manner-of-articulation approach to phonology is admirably suited to the needs of students whose primary and immediate goal is an active mastery of the sound system of the target language. These students with little difficulty can later make the transition to the transformational-generative approach as they advance in their linguistic studies.

The Spanish analyzed and presented here is American Spanish—particularly a group of dialects or sub-dialects spoken mainly in Central America and the South American highlands, which I chose to call "General American Spanish," just as linguists have talked about General American English (see Chapter 3 for details). Both concepts are unquestionably oversimplifications but extremely useful ones nonetheless. Whatever General American English is or is not, we can be certain that it is the dialect or dialect group with the greatest "acceptability" (if not prestige) in the United States. I submit that a rather similar situation exists in Latin America for what I call General American Spanish, the dialects spoken in Costa Rica, Colombia, Peru, and Ecuador, for example. This in no way implies that the Spanish of Cuba, Venezuela, Chile, or Argentina is in any respect inferior or less worthy of being learned by American students. I believe that one dialect (or dialect group)—the most "standard" one—had to be chosen to be taught in this book. Other attempts to present a "synthetic" (and non-existent, of course) American Spanish have proved less than satisfactory.

I have also discussed the most important dialectal variations of American Spanish, although they are not utilized in the drills, exercises, or tape recordings. As far as Castilian or peninsular Spanish is concerned, I have mentioned only the few features which distinguish it from American Spanish, such as the interdental [θ] and the retroflex apico-alveolar [ś]. Once again, what I have called General American Spanish is used exclusively in the drills, exercises, and tape recordings.

Most of the terminology used is standard in structural linguistics, although I have devised many of my own terms for features that pertain particularly to Spanish. For example, I have used "fused" to describe vowels in diphthongs, as opposed to "linked" for vowels in hiatus. Most of my phonetic symbols are the familiar ones. Many of them have been borrowed from Navarro Tomás, although I have made certain modifications. For example, since the voiced interdental slit fricative is the same sound whether in Spanish or English, I have used [ð] for Spanish rather than Navarro's [z̨].

Although my approach is structural-descriptive, I have taken the liberty of using one device originated by the transformational-generative phonologists —the generative "rule" or formula. Although some of these rules may seem rather complicated and mathematical at first (as much linguistic writing inevitably does), they are actually quite simple and turn out to be very handy economical summaries of the allophonic distribution of phonemes. The student, after having studied the data in conventional prose form or in a table or chart, will find that the rule is a simple, concise, and easily-grasped method of presenting it all once again. Perhaps the only omission in these rules, from the point of view of structural phonology at least, is the fact that, although they list all the phonetic realizations of phonemes in all possible environments, they do *not* assign these phonetic realizations to particular phonemes. For example, a rule like

$$/n/ \longrightarrow \begin{bmatrix} [m] \Big/ - \begin{cases} /p/ \\ /b/ \end{cases} \\ [\eta] \Big/ - \begin{cases} /k/ \\ /g/ \\ /x/ \\ /w/ \end{cases} \end{bmatrix}$$

simply means that the phoneme /n/ is realized as a bilabial [m] immediately preceding the phonemes /p/ and /b/, as in **un peso** and **un beso,** and as a velar [ŋ] immediately preceding the phonemes /k g x w/, as in **un coche, un gato, un juego,** and **un hueso.** However, nowhere in the rule is it stated that [m] belongs in strict structural procedure to the /m/ phoneme and [ŋ] to the /n/ phoneme. The rule does not inform the student, as I must do in the preceding analysis, that the phoneme /n/ is really being *replaced* by the phoneme /m/ in the first environment, i.e., before the bilabials /p/ and /b/. This, of course, is in the realm of what the transformational-generative linguists call "taxonomic" phonemics—an unnecessary and unproductive level for their methods of analysis. This may be so in pure linguistic theory, but the concept of taxonomic phonemics is symetrical and "elegant" (to borrow from transformationalist phraseology) from a theoretical point of view. More important, though, from a pedagogical point of view, it is quickly grasped and mastered by the student who is most interested in putting his linguistic knowledge to practical use.

This text has an abundance of phonetic and phonemic transcription exercises. Not only is transcription an essential technique for all serious students of linguistics, but it is one more force which can effectively be brought to bear in the student's efforts to learn to speak authentic-sounding Spanish. However, teachers who remain unconvinced of the value of phonetic transcription can easily omit these exercises if they wish.

The transcription taught is perhaps unconventional in that it shows syllabication. For example, **las habas** is written phonemically /la-sá-bas/ and phonetically [la-sá-bas]. Not only does this make the transcription easier to do and to read, but it continually points up such crucial facts of Spanish phonology as closed and open syllables, **enlace** or linking between words, and diphthongs or hiatus in vowel combinations.

The transcriptions make use of only the allophones of General American

Spanish. Although the suprasegmental features of stress, pitch, and juncture are phonemic rather than phonetic (at least as far as existing research has brought us in Spanish), they, too, have been marked in the phonetic transcriptions of the final chapters, i.e., those in which the suprasegmentals have been presented formally.

This book has several rather broad divisions. The first six chapters are introductory in nature and deal with basic concepts in linguistics, particularly as they pertain to Spanish phonology. The next seventeen chapters take up consonants, the next nine vowels, the next five suprasegmentals, the next one pronunciation problems in general, and the final one orthography. I am not convinced that such things as stress and intonation should not have been presented first. I simply felt that since they were somewhat more complex than the segmentals, at least in my own analysis, it would be better to follow a more conventional order of presentation.

Several of the above-mentioned divisions are preceded by a brief introductory chapter, such as 7, 24, and 33, and several are followed by a review chapter, such as 12, 17, 22, 32, and 37. Although repetition may not be the "soul" of learning, I believe that it is the "back-bone," and I, thus, have made very extensive use of review. In my own experience in teaching these materials, I have found that, as one might expect, students learn information much faster and retain it much longer if it is presented many times in slightly varied form. This explains what may seem to some excessive reiteration.

Most chapters have the following format: 1. a listing of all phonemes taken up in the chapter; 2. a listing of all allophones; 3. facial diagrams; 4. articulatory descriptions; 5. examples of allophonic distribution; 6. important dialectal variations; 7. the principal contrasts between the Spanish sounds and the corresponding English sounds or ones that interfere; 8. reading references; 9. oral drills; 10. written exercises.

Review chapters have a similar format: 1. a chart of the phonemes of the reviewed chapters; 2. a chart of their allophones; 3. a cross-reference to appropriate facial diagrams; 4. a table of the reviewed phonemes and their allophones; 5. a summary of their distribution with examples; 6. a summary of their dialectal variations; 7. a summary of the contrasts with English; 8. a reminder of previous reading references; 9. oral drills; 10. written exercises; 11. review questions.

The sections entitled "References" are divided in each case into two groups: works dealing principally with Spanish phonology and those dealing with English phonology or related general linguistic areas. "Phonology", as used here, includes both phonetics and phonemics. References marked with a * are relatively non-technical and are recommended for beginners in Spanish linguistics. Others are best consulted by teachers and students who have already had work in linguistics.

Many of the drills are designed to practice and test aural discrimination on the theory that students have a much better chance of producing a sound correctly when they are able to perceive it aurally. Most drills, of course, are for oral practice in the lab and classroom. I felt that far more than mere minimal pairs was needed; thus, many of these drills are in the form of answers to questions, phrases and sentences to be repeated, and paragraphs to be read aloud. It is essential that once the student's attention is focused squarely on the problem and he can handle the sound in isolation, he must practice it in the stream of speech. If he can reproduce it properly here, he has internalized the point.

Some of the drills make use of a technique rarely seen in textbooks but universally practiced by all imaginative teachers: the deliberate contrast of an incorrect form with a correct one. I believe there is no psychological justification for the fear that a student may be "contaminated" or "corrupted" simply by hearing his teacher pronounce an incorrect form—something that the student himself or his classmates have probably said many times before. If it is obvious that what the teacher has said is purposely incorrect, the "error" can dramatically or even humorously focus attention on the problem. Pronunciation mistakes are due principally to pressure and interference from the student's native language, and no advanced or even intermediate student of Spanish can be harmed by judicious use of the above-mentioned technique. Moreover, *at no time* are students ever called upon to utter an incorrect form themselves.

Many of the drills are specifically meant to be done with books open. Contrary to certain theories fashionable in recent years, many of these pronunciation problems are more readily solved with the aid of visual reinforcement. It is frequently very effective for students to see the graphic representation of the very sounds they are practicing. For example, seeing words spelled with **ge-** or **gi-** while pronouncing [x] or seeing words such as **comunica** and **teléfono** while working on difficult stress patterns can be most effective aids in the students' struggle to overcome their linguistic weaknesses.

The appendix is more than the term implies. Much of the material contained in it should be referred to frequently by the student as he prepares the lessons, practices in the laboratory, and reviews for tests. Section A contains the rules for allophonic distribution of all single segmental phonemes, plus examples. Section B has charts of the phonemes and allophones of Spanish and the phonemes of English. Section C has four dialogs for practice reading I have always followed the practice of having my students tape their own readings of dialogs at various points in the course and then submit them for correction and sometimes a grade. Not only is it effective for the students to be able to hear their own accents in Spanish, but it is enlightening for the teacher to compare a recording made at the very beginning of the course with one made at the end. Section D has the answers to all transcription exercises and review questions. Section E is an extensive bibliography on Spanish phonology, English phonology, and phonetics and phonemics in general, and also includes many general linguistic works which have sections pertinent to problems discussed here. All previous reading references are included with complete publication data. The vocabulary lists all Spanish words that occur in the text whose meanings a fourth-year Spanish student might not know. Finally there is a subject index.

Although this book can be used satisfactorily without a laboratory, the added advantage of having students hear the examples and practice the drills in the laboratory is obvious. The taped programs include all drills, including the so-called "live" transcriptions (taken by the students *viva voz*, so to speak, rather than from a written passage), and the practice dialogs of Appendix C. All readings are done by native-speakers of General American Spanish.

The Teacher's Manual has suggestions for handling various parts of the text, the passages for the "live" transcriptions in case the teacher prefers to read them in class himself, ideas for testing, and the timings for the entire tape program.

I would like to express my appreciation to all my students who so patiently put up with the constant revisions, the everpresent typographical errors, and the periodic flurries of loose pages when the book was being used in typewritten form in the Winter and Spring terms of 1966, 1967, and 1968. Many of them rendered valuable assistance, not only by calling errors to my attention, but by offering constructive criticisms.

Special thanks should also go to the following: Professor Joseph Kubica, of Marquette University, who taught other sections of the same Spanish phonology course at the Pennsylvania State University and suggested ways to improve the materials; Professor Rodrigo Solera, of the Pennsylvania State University and a native of Costa Rica, who served as the principal native-speaking informant and consultant and who also wrote the dialogs in Appendix C; Professor H. Tracy Sturcken, of the Pennsylvania State University, for reading sections of the manuscript and offering suggestions, particularly in Chapters 2 and 3; Mrs. Lucinda Wilder, formerly a graduate student in Spanish linguistics at the Pennsylvania State University and now at the University of Wisconsin, who performed various editorial and clerical tasks and typed almost all the manuscript in its final form, a particularly exacting chore with a text such as this; Mr. Enrique Grönlund, of the Pennsylvania State University (Ogontz Campus), who so kindly gave me permission to use one of his original poems in Spanish in one of the oral drills of Chapter 36; and Mr. Ronald Flores, of the Pennsylvania State University (Scranton Campus), who helped me find words and phrases for some of the oral drills.

I would also like to acknowledge my debt to Cynthia D. Buchanan's *A Programed Introduction to Linguistics: Phonetics and Phonemics*, an extremely valuable supplementary text in a course such as this and one which gave me the idea for the form and phrasing of the review questions.

I am also grateful for the generous financial assistance I received from Dr. Thomas F. Magner, Associate Dean for Research of the College of Liberal Arts, through the Central Fund for Research of the Pennsylvania State University.

J.B.D.

Pennsylvania State University
University Park, Pennsylvania

TABLE OF CONTENTS

SPANISH PRONUNCIATION:

Theory and Practice

1

~~~~~~

INTRODUCTION

A widespread misconception among Americans is that Spanish is the easiest of all foreign languages for them to learn. It is often compared favorably with French, German, Latin, Russian, etc. in this regard. This belief stems in part from the fact that Spanish has certain structural similarities to English and a large number of easily recognizable cognates. But Spanish is really considered to be such an easy language for Americans to learn mainly because it is reputed to be so easy to pronounce.

What people who say this really mean, without realizing it, is that Spanish is much easier to *spell* than these other languages. Unlike Russian or Japanese or many of the so-called "exotic" languages, Spanish uses the familiar Roman alphabet. The fact that a language like Russian uses an unfamiliar alphabet causes the average language-learner to place it automatically in the category of a difficult language. For example, the word for *already* is spelled **ya** and pronounced [yá] in Spanish, but the very same sounds in Russian (meaning *I*) are spelled Я. Even though the individual sounds are identical, the "strange" spelling or writing makes Russian seem intrinsically more difficult than Spanish. Perhaps Russian is really more difficult for Americans to learn than Spanish, but this writing difference is only a superficial and temporary obstacle, having little to do with the real difficulties.

Even with a more familiar language like French, which also uses the Roman alphabet, the problem is similar. One set of sounds—[dɔ-né], for example—is spelled **donner, donnez, donné, donnés, donnée,** or **données,** depending on their grammatical function and meaning. In Spanish, however, different spellings almost always represent different sounds, and, conversely, different sounds almost always are represented by different letters.

When the layman says that Spanish is a "phonetic" language, this is his imprecise way of saying that in Spanish orthography (the spelling system) there is a close and consistent correspondence between the written symbols and the sounds they stand for. This is not true of many other languages. In English, in fact, the spelling is so irregular that few native speakers ever learn it completely and must always rely on the dictionary for help. For example, the author, as he wrote these very lines, hesitated over whether the word *correspondence* has an *e* or an *a* at the beginning of the last syllable and was forced to consult his dictionary. An educated Spanish-speaker needs less such help in spelling his own language, and activities like spelling bees are not popular in the Hispanic countries because learning to spell is not the great accomplishment for these children that it is for English-speaking children. Also, because of Spanish orthography, most American students of Spanish who go beyond the basic courses learn to spell Spanish better than they do their own native language.

Despite all this, though, even the best of you make frequent and serious errors in your pronunciation of Spanish since the sounds of this language are really just as difficult for an American as are those of French or Russian or Japanese. A close comparison of the sound systems of English and Spanish reveals that very few sounds in one language are exactly the same as those in the other, and that most of the same or similar sounds are distributed in a different way in the two languages. Spanish is not unusual in this regard, but this fact is often ignored because of its relatively regular orthography.

Learning the sound system of Spanish well is undeniably difficult for most English-speaking students. A few of you, of course, have an excellent ear and can achieve a remarkably accurate pronunciation mainly through imitation. Most cannot, however. If you hope to master Spanish pronunciation, you must proceed systematically by trial and error, analysis, oral drill, correction, and constant practice.

Those of you who are prospective Spanish teachers, even if you may be fortunate enough to achieve good pronunciation of the language without such labor, will someday be faced with the problem of trying to get your own students to achieve an equally satisfactory pronunciation. Unless you are equipped to attack the problem soundly and systematically, you can only hope that your students will have the same good fortune to learn through imitation. With all this in mind, the present book has several purposes:

1. To teach you as English-speaking students the correct pronunciation of American Spanish—both through analysis and through imitation and practice.
2. To introduce you to the field of descriptive linguistics, mainly in the area of phonology.
3. To teach you some of the methods, techniques, and tools of descriptive linguistics, such as articulatory description, the facial diagram, and phonemic and phonetic transcription.

4. To point out and analyze the important contrasts between the sounds of American Spanish and those of English.
5. To acquaint you with the most important phonological differences between the various dialects of American Spanish. Included are the very few differences between American Spanish and Castilian or peninsular Spanish.

With regard to this last point, the sound differences between American and peninsular Spanish have been greatly exaggerated and are really fewer in number and much less important than those between American English and British English. American Spanish itself includes many dialects, and, although they are all included in this book, a so-called "general" American Spanish (found in most parts of Mexico, Central America, Colombia, Ecuador, and Peru) is presented as the standard dialect for you to learn. This dialect is described in detail and used in the oral drills and written exercises. This is comparable to presenting General American English rather than the Southern or Eastern dialects in a book on the pronunciation of American English for foreign students. Just as with English, all dialects of Spanish—both American and peninsular—are mutually comprehensible, and no speaker of any one of them has trouble communicating with speakers of another. This intriguing matter of dialect will be taken up in detail in Chapter 3.

Finally, a word should be said about the best way to use this book. You should read the theoretical and descriptive part of each chapter first, referring as directed to parts of other chapters and the Appendix. The reading references, which are gathered together in the end bibliography, pertain to the problems and points discussed in the chapter. The teacher may ask that some of them be read, but they are mainly for the student who is interested in pursuing more work in this area.

The drills, of course, are meant to be done orally in class. You should look at them carefully first to see how they are to be handled and to determine the purposes of each one. It is strongly recommended that you practice by reading them aloud. Although most of them are meant to be done with books closed, some are most effective when you can see the spelling as you practice the sounds. These drills are always indicated by the phrase "(books open)" after the heading of the drill. It is suggested that in class you keep your finger or a slip of paper in the place so that you can quickly open the book to the right place when such drills occur.

Next the written exercises should be done. The correct answers for almost all of them have been provided either in the chapter itself or in the Appendix, so you can easily check your work.

Although this book can be used satisfactorily without a laboratory, it is strongly recommended that the tape program be used for reinforcement and additional practice. When you have completed all your homework in the textbook chapter, you should take your book to the lab and listen to the examples and do the drills. Appropriate pauses are provided for your response, and, in certain drills, after the voice on the tape has given the correct answer, there is an additional pause for a second student repetition.

Practice readings for class or laboratory are found in the Appendix. Also included is a vocabulary. Although the words and phrases used as examples in the text are not as important for their lexical meaning as for the sounds they illustrate, you may want to know what they mean. Thus, the vocabulary includes all items that a fourth-year student of Spanish might not already know.

References

The reading references are divided into two groups: those dealing principally with Spanish phonology and those dealing with English phonology or related general linguistic areas. "Phonology," as used here, includes both phonetics and phonemics. There are works in both categories which deal with a great many linguistic areas, and, in this case, only chapters pertaining to the material under discussion in the present book are listed. References marked with an * are relatively non-technical and are recommended for beginners in Spanish linguistics. Others are best consulted by students who have already had work in linguistics.

With a few exceptions, works that treat specific dialects of Spanish have been omitted.

The references in each chapter are listed only by author's last name, title (sometimes shortened), and date of publication. Complete information is found in the bibliography in Appendix E.

SPANISH

* Delattre, " 'Spanish is a Phonetic Language' " (1945).
* Jones, "What Spanish Pronunciation Shall We Teach?" (1941).
* Lado, *Linguistics Across Cultures* (1957).

ENGLISH AND GENERAL

* Chreist, *Foreign Accent* (1964).
* Hall, *New Ways to Learn a Foreign Language* (1966).

2

LANGUAGE AND LINGUISTICS

Language is undoubtedly man's most important and at the same time most mysterious accomplishment. Everyone uses language and uses it quite adequately, but few people know much about this marvelous skill they possess. Physiologically and psychologically normal children are adept at speaking their own language by the age of five or six and many even before that. Very little is known about the exact process the child's brain and nervous system go through to attain this skill.

Even though animals have intelligence as well as a vocal mechanism—in some cases very similar to that of humans—none of them have language in the sense that human beings have it. Psychologists and linguists have theorized that this may be due to the fact that the human baby is the only young of any species that has a natural propensity for babbling, the only one that makes meaningless sounds just for the sheer joy of producing and hearing them. Other animals seem to make sounds mainly as a reaction to some stimulus— fear, hunger, pain, sex urge—rather than because of the desire to "express" themselves or to symbolize some mental concept.

The human baby's sounds cause a reaction in the individuals in his environment. These persons, in turn, respond vocally, and the baby is encouraged to continue his babbling and eventually to try to imitate the sounds he hears. A baby at first produces practically every sound capable of coming from the human vocal mechanism, but after a time he begins to discard the ones which he never hears, that is, the ones which are absent in the language of his companions. Gradually, he learns how to produce these sounds in some fairly consistent fashion, he becomes aware of certain meaningful contrasts, he begins to see how these sounds are related to objects in his environment, and he begins to understand how the production of these sounds can have a very practical value as well as provide a great deal of psychological satisfaction. But, above all, the baby never stops practicing. His parents, gladly fulfilling the role of proud language teachers, never stop trying to teach him. After a few years he has control over many, if not most of the basic patterns of sound, form, and arrangement in his language, and by the time he is five or six he has almost absolute mastery of the majority of them.

The child, as he learns to speak, also learns his own culture at the same time. Both elements—the language and the culture—are so closely related that it is sometimes difficult to tell which one has a greater influence on the other.

It should be pointed out that the term "culture" is used in the anthropological sense rather than the esthetic one. Here it means all the patterns of human behavior, patterns which differ markedly from one ethnic and linguistic group to another. It might be said that "culture" is the ways that men have developed to solve the problems of human existence—how to find food and shelter, how to cope with the realities of life and death, how to deal with hostile nature, how to interact with one another.

It is virtually impossible for anyone to learn a foreign culture well without knowing the language of that culture. When officials in charge of planning and administering programs in education, government, and the armed forces ignore this fact or pay lip-service to it, the programs, as we have seen, rarely attain real success. On the other hand, the relative success of some groups, like religious missionaries and businessmen, who devote a great deal of time and effort to learning the language of the culture they wish to understand and influence, is proof that knowing the language is one of the really indispensable factors.

For some, "knowing the language" means primarily being able to translate it into one's own native language and/or being able to read, understand, and appreciate the literature of that language. Some even deny or downgrade the importance of the spoken language. This attitude goes hand-in-hand with, and probably even stems from the commonly-held concept that language is primarily writing rather than sound. When the two conflict—as they usually do—many believe that sound should cede to writing. "Just pronounce it the way it's written!" is the rather impatient admonishment.

If one asks the average educated American how to make the plural of nouns in English, he usually talks about "adding -s if the word ends in a vowel or certain consonants, or -es in some cases like *watch–watches*, and changing the -y to -ie-, like *berry–berries*, etc." The individual may very well be surprised and perhaps even feel that his leg is being pulled if he is told that "you really add the sound /s/ after a final /p t k f θ/, /iz/ after a final /s z š ž č ǰ/ and /z/ everywhere else, as in *cat–cats*, *horse–horses*, and *dog–dogs*." He may object to the last part about /z/ and perhaps even cite something like *pen–pens* to prove that his rules are right. Obviously, both sets of rules are right in a sense, but they concern completely different things—the real language in the latter case and the way in which it is represented graphically in the former.

An educated person can hardly help thinking of language as the set of symbols which merely *represent* language. Yet writing cannot possibly be synonymous with language. The majority of the inhabitants of the earth can neither read nor write, yet they all speak languages as complicated, sophisticated, and logical as English or French or Spanish. We tend to think of an illiterate as a person who does not even know his own language, but this is not true. Illiterates cannot read or write their own language—many because they never learned to do it and many simply because they speak a language that has no written form.

"Written form" in this case refers to an alphabet or a system in which each graphic symbol purports to represent a sound. Some languages, like ancient Egyptian or certain American Indian languages, used hieroglyphics or pictographs to represent ideas and concepts. Other languages, like Chinese, have a system of ideographs which represent words or morphemes, that is, units of meaning. A few languages, like Japanese, have syllabic writing, in which the symbols, as the name implies, represent syllables rather than sounds or units of meaning. But the majority of the world's languages with writing systems use alphabetic or phonemic writing, as do English, Spanish, Russian, etc.

Most educated people have numerous and serious misconceptions about language and writing. These ideas permeate our educational system and are fostered in the very first days of school when pupils are told that English has five vowels—*a, e, i, o,* and *u*—that *bite* has a "long *i*," that *hot* has a "short *o*," etc. English has nine vowel sounds according to one system of analysis, *bite* does not have any kind of *i* sound, nor does *hot* have any *o* sound.

Another misconception that stems from this confusion between writing and language is the feeling held by most people—particularly educated people—that the written form is an inviolable standard to which all speakers of the language should adhere. They feel that there is only one really correct way of putting words together and that most of these words have only one unchanging meaning. The fact that these individuals themselves frequently depart from these standards does not mean that they feel that they are using acceptable variations within the system or that the system is actually changing because they occasionally make such "slips" as *gonna* instead of *going to*, *it's me* instead of *it's I*, *finalize* instead of *complete*. They simply admit that they, too, are human and sometimes make "mistakes." Yet, when put to the test, any two educated speakers are rarely in complete agreement as to what constitutes these "mistakes."

Language is a vital, evolving organism, which has its own internal system and whose speakers are at the same time the perpetrators and the victims of this evolution. What is correct in one time and place is incorrect in another, and what is correct and appropriate for one person in a given situation is completely incorrect and inappropriate for another person in another situation.

Many of the words we use in English or Spanish today were at one time considered incorrect or had a totally different meaning and connotation. If linguistic change is really corruption, English-speakers today must be speaking a most curious mixture of Anglo-Saxon and French and Spanish-speakers are speaking what might be called "bad" Latin.

Most educated speakers are well-meaning in their desire to "preserve" the language or at least its purity. They feel that it is the duty of the educational system to set and maintain linguistic standards and prevent the language from "degenerating," even though they may suspect in their hearts that the best efforts of teachers to keep the language from changing and to decide what is correct and incorrect will inevitably fail in the future as they have failed in the past. The speakers of the language in reality are the ones who quietly but most effectively set and maintain linguistic standards. They are the ones who cause and permit linguistic change, who determine whether *ain't* is correct or not, whether it is bad English to say "Who are you going with?" rather than "With whom are you going?," whether you can call an M.D. a *doctor* or whether you must call him a *physician*, whether the middle vowel in *pajama* rimes with *jam* or *job*.

Most people—and again particularly educated people—hold what is called the *prescriptive* approach to language. For them language teaching is a series of "do's" and "don'ts" (mostly "don'ts") where the student tries to learn to say things, many of which he rarely hears anywhere but in the confines of the classroom.

Educated people are, of course, becoming more liberal in these matters, but doubts still linger on. Many Americans still have a secret feeling of inferiority about their way of speaking the language and an often open admiration for the way the British speak it. Cultivated Spanish Americans, who are even more conservative in their approach to language than North Americans, usually defer to the Spanish *Real Academia* as the supreme authority in linguistic matters, and many harbor the notion that they are really speaking Spanish incorrectly as compared to the way it is spoken in Spain.

There is, however, another more modern approach to language—the *descriptive* approach. Here the individual who is analyzing the language is not interested—professionally, at least—in what is correct or incorrect, or what should or should not be said, but rather in what actually *is* said by the speakers of a given language or dialect. He makes no value judgments about what he hears, although he realizes full well that the speakers of that language make them all the time. He tries to describe as accurately, as consistently, and as economically as he can what the speakers of this language say. He includes in his analysis all sounds, forms, and structures he hears, regardless of how these are subjectively regarded by the speakers themselves.

This descriptive approach is the one that was used, for example, by the great American linguist, Charles C. Fries, in his study, *The Structure of English* (1952).[1] Every form and structure analyzed was drawn from a body of data, a corpus, which Professor Fries gathered from mechanically-recorded conversations amounting to something over 250,000 running words. Thus, his analysis is not his opinion on what people should or should not say in English, but rather his statement as to how people in one area of the United States were actually using the English language in the late 1940's.

The approach used in the present text is philosophically the same as that of linguists like Fries. We are interested in how Spanish-speakers actually speak their language today and what sounds you as an English-speaker studying Spanish must learn in order to sound like a native Spanish-speaker.

Unfortunately, many people mistakenly feel that *descriptive* means *permissive*. They accuse linguists of trying to tear down standards and promulgate the pernicious idea that "anything goes" in language. This attitude is the result of a fundamental misunderstanding. Linguists obviously have personal and private opinions on the way language is or should be spoken. But professionally their job is not to decide on which forms to use, but simply to record, describe, and analyze the forms that actually are heard in that language. They are content to leave the job of prescribing to others who are considered authorities on purity and correctness, but they know that the decisions on what should or should not be said are really made by the speakers themselves.

Some might pose the question that if linguists are supposed to be interested only in what is said and refuse to make value judgments on such matters as *you* vs. *youull*, *lie* vs. *lay*, *it's me* vs. *it's I*, or **Está para salir** vs. **Está por salir,** [ká-že] ([ž] as in *measure*) vs. [ká-ye] for **calle, Había tres** vs. **Habían tres,** why do they advocate the use of and even write foreign language texts literally crammed with rules that the students must expend great effort to master?

The answer is simply that linguists believe that almost anything a native speaker says (except for slips of the tongue and deliberate distortions for the sake of humor) is "correct" in a certain sense. They believe also that the so-called "errors" the native speaker makes in his own language are almost *never* the same real errors a foreigner makes when he learns to speak that language. What native speaker of English, no matter how uneducated or unintelligent, ever confuses *chocolate milk* with *milk chocolate,* or says *"Never he comes to our house"*[2] or *"He comes never to our house"* instead of "He never comes to our house," or says *two pens* with a final /s/ instead of /z/? What native speaker of Spanish ever mixes up **ser** with **estar,** or hesitates between the imperfect and the preterit, or forgets whether **toro** is pronounced

---

[1] See Bibliography, Appendix E, for complete publication information.

[2] In descriptive linguistics an asterisk * preceding any form indicates that it is hypothetical or non-existent in the language. In historical linguistics it indicates that the form is unattested, i.e., it has never actually been found in writing.

with the single tap /r/ or the trilled /r̄/? Yet these are all common errors made by foreigners learning these two languages.

You undeniably must learn many rules if you wish to speak Spanish "correctly," that is, the way a native speaker speaks it. You must learn rules which the native speaker knows unconsciously and never violates. In other words, you must avoid making mistakes no native would ever make, and when you make these mistakes you are "wrong" in a way that no native speaker is ever wrong. To the linguist the so-called errors committed by native speakers are really stylistic or usage variants which are determined for the most part by geographical, social, and educational factors.

The linguist feels that it is the job of the foreign language teacher to teach his students to speak the language the way it is spoken by educated native speakers, since the student is obviously trying to become educated regardless of what language he is speaking while he is doing it. Sometimes a choice must be made as to which region these educated speakers come from—in other words, which dialect to teach. But if the sounds, forms, and structures taught are used by these speakers in their own region, they are "correct" regardless of what any authority may proclaim about their validity.

A linguist is popularly thought of as one who speaks many languages. But a linguist is a scientist of language. A POLYGLOT is one who speaks many languages, even though he has little or no scientific knowledge of the structure of any one of them. Some linguists are also polyglots, but some do not even speak the languages which they study and analyze.

There are also differing degrees of emphasis and focus in linguistics. PURE or THEORETICAL linguists are interested in the study of languages or language primarily for its own sake and also in problems common to all languages. DIACHRONIC or HISTORICAL linguists are interested mainly in the process of linguistic change through time. In Spanish, for example, a historical linguist is interested in how Spanish has evolved from Latin, and he studies these changes down through the centuries. He works under certain handicaps since, although he may be mainly interested in sound, he must obviously rely on writing for his evidence and is often not absolutely sure as to what certain sounds were really like hundreds of years before. He must assume that pronunciation changes were reflected to a great extent by changes in spelling. He knows that certain forms existed at certain past times because he has found them in writing, and, by comparing these forms with modern forms, he formulates "laws" of linguistic change. Then by applying these laws, in reverse, so to speak, he can postulate certain past forms for which he has no actual evidence.

For example, the historical linguist knows that a /p/ between vowels in Latin often became /b/ in Spanish, since he has many examples of this. Latin **caput,** which he has seen in many documents, is now **cabo** in Spanish. He then presumes that Spanish **cabeza** must have come from a Latin word ***capitia** on the basis of the above sound change and many other considerations, such as meaning, constructions in other languages, semantic relationships, statements by people who actually observed these things, etc. The word *capitia must be written with an asterisk, however, since the linguist has never actually found the word anywhere—it is unattested. It probably existed at one time in the light of the /p/ > /b/ change and others, but it has never been found in writing.

COMPARATIVE linguists are interested in comparing two or more languages either down through the centuries (diachronically) or at one given point in time (synchronically). They study, for example, the evolution of one language family or the relationship of various languages to each other.

SYNCHRONIC linguists are interested in studying one language or dialect at a given point in time—usually the present since they can rely on living native speakers for their data. The following diagram shows the difference between the synchronic and the diachronic approaches in the case of Spanish:

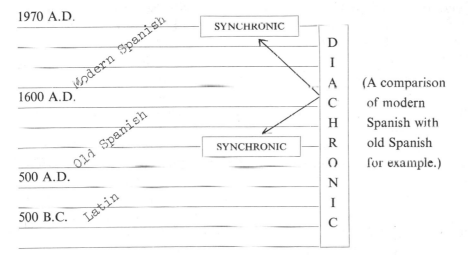

The DESCRIPTIVE or STRUCTURAL linguist, who is, of course, often synchronic in his approach, is mainly interested in describing the system of a given language and how it operates.

The APPLIED linguist is less theoretical in his approach. He utilizes his analysis or that of another linguist in some practical way, such as to compile a dictionary, to analyze the emotional state of mind of a speaker of a language, to teach a language to foreigners, or to create a writing system for a language without one.

The PSYCHOLINGUIST is interested mainly in the acquisition of language—not only children learning their own language but also students learning a foreign language.

These various branches of linguistics are usually not always neatly and clearly separated, and any given linguist is often really cultivating more than one of these approaches at the same time. For example, a linguist who writes a descriptive analysis of both Spanish and English and then compares the two languages in order to predict learning problems and prepare pedagogical materials to overcome them is at the same time concerned with STRUCTURAL (or DESCRIPTIVE), COMPARATIVE, APPLIED, and PSYCHO-linguistics.

Regardless of which type of linguistics he may cultivate, the linguist usually arbitrarily divides language into several main areas for study. These divisions are to a certain extent artificial because in reality the levels of a linguistic system are interdependent and inseparable.

Nevertheless, it is convenient for the beginner to view language in terms of pronunciation, grammar, and vocabulary—or phonology, morphology-syntax, and lexicology-semantics.[3] Phonology includes the study of the sounds of language, how they are produced, and how they function in the system. Morphology is the study of the form and organization of morphemes or the smallest units of meaning. Some morphemes are words like *boy* or **perro,** but others are only fragments like *-ness* or **-ción,** which carry meaning but are always connected or bound to other forms. Syntax is the study of the arrangement of these forms into larger constructions: "The man bit the dog" vs. "The dog bit the man," or **pobre hombre** vs. **hombre pobre.** Lexicology and semantics might include such matters as the choice and meaning of words—the many uses of *get* in English or the fact that **bravo** and **actual** do not really mean in Spanish what they seem to mean to the English-speaking learner.

Most linguists are interested more in form and structure than in content and meaning. They feel that words are quite meaningless out of the context of a given grammatical construction. You can think of the many different senses of the sound sequence /mæn/ in English: "Man is a rational animal", "Man is more logical than woman", "Take that man off the board—I just jumped him", "That's the man I saw last night", "My man Friday", "Give a man a chance" (said by one ten-year-old to another), "I now pronounce you man and wife", "Their fleet doesn't have a man-of-war", "The killing of the child was ruled manslaughter", "Man the lifeboats!", "Man, it's hot out!".

Linguists feel that content and meaning are determined by form and arrangement and that the latter aspects must be thoroughly analyzed before the former can hope to be determined satisfactorily. Thus, linguists are often able to analyze languages in which many of the words at first are unknown or unclear in their meaning. They are literally forced to base their analysis largely on form and structure and do it quite successfully.

The language learner is usually overly concerned with words and meaning and tends to equate the language with its vocabulary. Many linguists and

---

[3] Lexicology here includes such areas as lexicography (glossaries and dictionaries), lexicostatistics (method of dating languages), etymology (the history of words), and usage. Semantics is concerned with meaning.

language teachers believe that, particularly in the early stages of language learning, vocabulary is the *least* important element of language. They feel that it is much more essential for the learner to master first the patterns of sound, form, and arrangement, which are fixed and finite in number before he spends time trying to learn a large stock of lexical units, which are constantly changing in their meaning and infinite in number. The acquisition of a large vocabulary is valueless without control of the pronunciation and grammar of the language. When this control is achieved, new words are acquired rapidly and effortlessly by the learner as he needs them—duplicating the process he went through and is still going through in his own language.

Linguistics provides accurate and comprehensive knowledge of man's most important and wondrous activity. It also gives insights into the nature of man himself, his culture, and his way of viewing the world. Linguistic science provides the basis for the development of valuable techniques and materials for the teaching of one language to the speakers of another. After the descriptive linguist has described and analyzed the structures of both the native and the target language, the applied linguist (often the same person) or the language teacher can compare both languages and find points of similarity and contrast. By doing this, he can predict beforehand the learning problems and the most serious sources of error since most difficulties in language learning stem from the constant interference of the learner's native language.

You, as an English-speaking student, may have difficulties in mastering the pronunciation of Spanish not so much because of any intrinsic features of the Spanish sound system but because of the fact that many of the sounds of Spanish are different in form and are patterned and distributed differently from those of English. On the basis of this linguistic information, these pronunciation difficulties can be isolated, given special attention, and presented for practice and mastery.

References

SPANISH

* Bull, *Spanish for Teachers: Applied Linguistics* (1965).
* Politzer and Staubach, *Teaching Spanish: A Linguistic Orientation* (1965).

ENGLISH AND GENERAL

* Anderson and Stageberg, *Introductory Readings on Language* (1965).
* Belasco, "General Section," Part I, in *Manual and Anthology of Applied Linguistics* (1960).
* _____, "Introduction" to *Applied Linguistics: Spanish* (1961).
* Bolinger, *Aspects of Language* (1968), Chapters 1, 2, 7, 10, 11, 14.
* Fries, *The Structure of English* (1952), Preface, Chapter I.

* Gelb, *A Study of Writing* (1952).
* Gleason, *An Introduction to Descriptive Linguistics* (1961).
* Hall, *Introductory Linguistics* (1964).
* _____, *Linguistics and Your Language* (1962).
* Hockett, *A Course in Modern Linguistics* (1958).
  Hoenigswald, *Language Change and Linguistic Reconstruction* (1960), Chapters 8, 9.
  _____, "Phonetic Reconstruction" (1965).
* Hughes, *The Science of Language* (1962), Chapters I, II.
* Langacker, *Language and Its Structure* (1967), Chapters 1-3, 7-9.
* Lloyd and Warfel, *American English in Its Cultural Setting* (1957), Chapters 1–3, 28.
* Schlauch, *The Gift of Language* (1955), Chapters 1, 3.
* Waterman, *Perspectives in Linguistics* (1963).

3

~~~

LANGUAGES AND DIALECTS

Everyone knows that a New Yorker does not speak like a Texan and that someone from neither one of these places feels that the New Yorker and the Texan both have an "accent." The average person's ear is remarkably attuned to dialectal differences in speech—regardless of how little education and linguistic knowledge he may have. These differences and this general perceptiveness of them on the part of most of us provide a great source of humor, entertainment, and lively discussions. However, even though most speakers of a language can immediately pick out a speaker from a different geographical region solely on the basis of his speech, few of them really understand the nature of these dialectal features. Their knowledge of the production of speech sounds does not come close to matching their ability to perceive the corresponding auditory differences.

Not only is the average speaker of a language perceptive to dialectal variations, but he often has subjective, impressionistic, and erroneous opinions about different geographical dialects. Fact and fancy are mingled in such a way that widespread popular misconceptions abound in our thinking about not only the dialect but about the person who speaks it. Even though an American from Iowa knows better intellectually, when he hears a New York City dialect, he cannot help thinking of the city-slicker, the sophisticated, self-satisfied person who considers himself "in" and everyone rural or west of the Hudson River "out." To both the Iowan and the New Yorker, a typical Southern drawl (although there is really no such thing any more than there is a typical New York accent) can hardly keep from conjuring up images of magnolia trees, white-columned mansions, and charming belles or perhaps the contrasting concept of cotton fields, mountain cabins, and "red-necks" or sharecroppers. Regardless of how unrealistic or mistaken these images are, many Americans "see" them when they hear speakers of other dialects.

Spanish-speakers naturally have similar images of speakers from other dialect regions of the Hispanic world. The **madrileño** cannot help having certain subjective feelings about a man from Buenos Aires or Monterrey or San Juan. But it is interesting to note that such concepts are usually held only by speakers of the same language. The average American who learns Spanish at first experiences none or few of these associations when he hears different dialects of Spanish, and the average Spanish-speaker must know English quite well and have lived in the United States for a long time before he shares the feelings of Americans about dialectal differences in English.

The average American student of Spanish usually picks up the dialect of his first Spanish teacher—most often in high school—and from then on, all other dialects seem somewhat strange unless advanced study of Spanish enables him to approach the matter with some degree of sophistication. An unusually large proportion of American high-school students of Spanish until very recently have been exposed first to Castilian Spanish. When they hear such common features of American Spanish as the aspirated /s/ before consonants—**español** [ęh-pa-ñól]—or the palatal groove fricative [ž] (as in *measure*)—**yo** [žó] —their reaction is the expected one: that these pronunciations are wrong or represent uneducated speech. The students are usually surprised to find out that millions of Spanish-speakers (many of them cultured and educated) pronounce Spanish in this fashion. It is something akin to the reactions of many foreigners when they find out that Americans most of the time contract certain verb forms—*I'm*, *she's*, *he'd*, say *gonna* instead of *going to*, and say *chew* for the last part of *Don't you?*. It is even hard to convince them that they should imitate these features if they wish to speak correct and natural English.

Dialect is an extremely fascinating and important concept in linguistics, but one which is usually difficult to determine with great precision. Sometimes it is impossible to decide whether a linguistic form is merely a dialect or another language. There are many complex factors involved. One is mutual intelligibility. If speakers of two different linguistic forms can understand each other, even though with some difficulty and after some practice (and, of course, have never studied the form the other is speaking), they are usually considered to be speaking two dialects of the same language. For this reason, one speaks of German *dialects* where the situation described above exists, but of Chinese *languages* (Mandarin, Cantonese, etc.) because speakers of these forms cannot understand each other. Nevertheless, one also speaks of the various dialects of Italian (Piedmontese, Tuscan, Neapolitan, Calabrese, Sicilian, Venetian, etc.) although some of these are mutually incomprehensible (Neapolitan and Venetian, for example). This proves that there are other determining factors, such as political and cultural unity, which can distinguish dialects from languages.

Another case is that of Castilian and Catalan. Both are spoken by many of the same speakers in northeastern and eastern Spain and the Balearic Islands.

These people are politically and culturally united with the rest of Spain, yet Castilian and Catalan are definitely two different languages. They developed independently from Latin, they have great grammatical and phonological differences, they are mutually incomprehensible (relatively speaking), and they have different written forms. In this case political and cultural unity is not significant linguistically.

The case of forms of American English is quite different. A person from Boston and one from St. Paul both write *here* the same way, but the first person says /híh/ *heah* without any final *r* and the second one says /hír/ with his tongue curled back for a very prominent final *r*. Yet, each understands the other's pronunciation with no difficulty. Thus, partly because of the written forms and partly because of mutual intelligibility, we speak of New England and midwestern varieties of English as being two dialects of the same language but Castilian and Catalan as being two different languages.

When all is said and done, the definitive solution to the problem of language vs. dialect is perhaps one of quantity rather than quality. Catalan, Castilian Spanish, and Argentine Spanish all came originally from Latin, but the first two are considered separate languages and the last two different dialects of the same language partly because the differences between the first two are far greater than those between the last two. In some languages the determination of language vs. dialect is purely arbitrary, but fortunately in the cases of Spanish and English most everyone agrees on what dialects and different languages are.

Dialectal differences are usually of two main types: lexical and phonological. Grammatical differences are normally few and minor. If there are significant morphological and syntactic differences between the two forms, of course, we are dealing with different languages and not dialects. Naturally, in this text we are concerned only with dialectal differences in pronunciation.

So far dialect has been discussed on a strictly geographical basis. But everyone knows that in any language a bank president does not talk like an auto mechanic. There may even be a greater difference between the speech of a bank president and an auto mechanic from the same city than there is between the speech of a bank president from one city and one from another. Thus, one can talk about dialects based on social, educational, and even age differences—that is, "vertical" linguistic differences as opposed to "horizontal" or geographical differences.

In Spanish there are fewer *pronunciation* differences among educated speakers from various parts of the Hispanic world than there are among educated English-speakers from different parts of the United States. For example, a lawyer from Mexico City sounds more like a lawyer from Bogotá than he does like a factory worker from Mexico City. However, in the United States a lawyer from Boston often sounds more like a dockworker from Boston, at least as far as pronunciation goes, than he does a lawyer from Minneapolis. The reasons for this are complex and based on social, cultural, and educational factors.

Certain regional or geographical dialects in every linguistic community have greater prestige and "acceptability"[1] than others. A vastly over-simplified but convenient division shows three very general speech areas in the United States (although each can be further divided into important dialect regions): Eastern, Southern, and General. Eastern is New England and the New York City area. Southern is what is commonly referred to culturally and politically as the "South," plus West Virginia and eastern Texas. General is everywhere else, from the Atlantic to the Pacific coast. There is no doubt that General has the most prestige and acceptability in this country—probably because it is spoken by about four times as many Americans as the next most widespread dialect, Southern. A person born and raised in New York City cannot become an announcer on network television (the headquarters of which, of course, are located in Manhattan) no matter how correct his speech as long as he sounds like a "typical" New Yorker. A Southerner who still has his Southern accent cannot easily get a job as an announcer on a large Southern radio station with a wide reception area. These positions are almost all filled by people who speak General American, whether it is their natural dialect or not.

Further proof of the nationwide acceptability of General American is found in the critical attitude that so many Americans had about the speech of our last two presidents, John F. Kennedy and Lyndon B. Johnson, representatives of Eastern and Southern speech, respectively. Yet there was no such criticism of the previous president, Dwight D. Eisenhower, who is a speaker of General American.

The Hispanic world is also divided into various dialect areas, but the situation is even more complicated. Education is not nearly as widespread as it is in the United States, yet where it exists it is more uniform. In Spain there are great dialectal differences among the masses, but far fewer among educated speakers because of this uniformity of education and unanimity of linguistic standards.

There are four main languages on the Iberian peninsula: Portuguese, Catalan, Castilian, and Basque (see map on p. 19). The first three are Romance languages and the fourth, Basque (**vasco** or **vascuence**), is not known to be related to any other language spoken anywhere in the world today. Current theory holds that it is a descendant of one of the pre-Latin languages spoken on the Iberian peninsula. Galician (**gallego**), a language closely related to Portuguese, is spoken in the northwest corner of Spain. Catalan (**catalán**) and its dialects are spoken in northeastern Spain and in the Balearic Islands. Castilian is spoken by most inhabitants in these areas, too, and by all Spaniards

---

[1] "Acceptability" is best defined as the quality possessed by a dialect which calls little attention to itself and therefore causes in the listeners few subjective reactions toward the person speaking.

in the rest of Spain. There are, of course, many sub-dialects of Castilian itself. One of the most important of these groups, mentioned here because of its strong relationship to American Spanish, is spoken in southern Spain and is called Andalusian (**andaluz**). Two other Romance dialects, Leonese and Aragonese, are spoken by a small number of mainly rural inhabitants and are both gradually disappearing. Leonese is spoken in a small west central region of northern Spain and Aragonese in an even smaller east central region of northern Spain. Most inhabitants of these areas, however, speak Castilian. In the Middle Ages both these dialects of peninsular Romance (Hispanicized Latin) were spoken over a much wider region than Castilian, another dialect of peninsular Romance. But the speakers of Castilian were a particularly vital and aggressive group, and they led the reconquest of Spain from the Moors, advancing steadily southward. Their language and influence spread as they went until Castilian became the dominant dialect within the national boundaries of Spain and the term "Spanish" became synonymous with it. Thus, although Andalusian and American Spanish are both general dialects of Castilian, in this book the term "Castilian" will be reserved for the national and standard language of Spain today.

All over Spain Castilian is spoken by most people since it is the only official language of the country, taught in all the schools and used for business and social intercourse throughout the nation. Most people in the areas where Basque, Galician, and Catalan are spoken are bilingual and speak these latter languages at home and in other informal situations. Leonese and Aragonese are spoken only in remote rural regions and mainly by uneducated peasants who rarely use and sometimes do not even understand Castilian.

One other dialect of Spanish should be mentioned before passing to America. In 1492, along with the Moors, many Jews were expelled from Spain and fled to areas in the eastern Mediterranean, particularly in Asia Minor. There Sephardic Jews lived close together and maintained along with their religion and social customs the language they had brought from Spain. Although many foreign words have entered this dialect of medieval Spanish, it is considered to be phonologically quite similar to what it was in the days of Columbus. This is particularly interesting because it gives linguists a good idea of how all Spanish was pronounced at this time. Such a situation is a very fortuitous and practically unique one for linguists and scholars. This dialect of Spanish is, of course, archaic and quite different from modern Castilian because it did not participate in the great phonological changes of the 16th and 17th centuries. In the 20th century many of these Sephardic Jews migrated to other countries, and there are groups in the large Eastern cities of the United States. Nevertheless, Judeo-Spanish is now dying out since most of the younger generation speak only the languages of the country they are in.

By the time of the discovery of America and the expulsion of the Moors and Jews, Castilian was the dominant language throughout all Spain. Then, just as today, it had several dialects, including Andalusian spoken in southern Spain.

American Spanish today, as far as pronunciation is concerned, is closer to Andalusian than to other dialects of Castilian, and there are two theories to explain this fact. One holds that most of the Spanish **conquistadores** and settlers were from southern Spain and naturally carried their speech to America. However, there are weaknesses in this theory. Although a majority of settlers were from southern Spain, many were not, and certain features of southern Spanish pronunciation are not found in America today. The other theory holds that both the Spanish of Spain and that of America underwent certain similar sound changes at generally the same time in history and consequently are quite close today. In other words, the Spanish of America evolved in the same direction that the Spanish of southern Spain did.

At any rate, American Spanish itself now shows many dialectal variations just as peninsular Spanish does. Spanish America can be divided into six general dialect areas (see map on p. 22):

1. *Mexico* (most parts) and *Southwestern United States* (mainly New Mexico and Arizona).
2. *Central America* (southern Mexico and the Yucatan peninsula, Guatemala, Honduras, El Salvador, Nicaragua, and Costa Rica).
3. *Caribbean* (Panama, Cuba, Puerto Rico, Dominican Republic, and the northern coast of Colombia and Venezuela. We might also include the Puerto Ricans in New York and Cubans in Florida.)
4. *Highlands* (interior of Venezuela, most of Colombia, Ecuador, Peru, and Bolivia).
5. *Chile*.
6. *Southern* (Argentina, Uruguay, and Paraguay) [2]

In addition to Spanish and Portuguese in Brazil there are several important Indian languages spoken in America. In Mexico there are the Uto-Aztecan languages—Nahuatl being the most important—and in Mexico and Central America there are Mayan and the Mayan-related languages. Quechua, the language of the Indian peoples ruled by the Incas when the Spaniards first reached Peru, is still spoken by millions in Peru, Ecuador, and Bolivia. Guaraní is spoken by most inhabitants of Paraguay, who are bilingual. The governments of all these countries have made efforts to teach these Indians Spanish, but they have not been completely successful. The influence of these indigenous

[2] This simplified division is based for the most part on the one proposed by Pedro Henríquez Ureña in "Observaciones sobre el español de América" (1921). It is also partially based on the much more recent research published by D. Lincoln Canfield in his *La pronunciación del español en América* (1962) and personal observations and investigations of the present author. Some scholars, however, feel that this division is too broad. José Rona, for example, has proposed 23 dialect regions for Spanish America in "El problema de la división del español americano en zonas dialectales" (1964).

ESTADOS UNIDOS

MEXICO

CUBA HAITI
BR.   REPUBLICA DOMINICANA
HONDURAS
                    PUERTO RICO
HONDURAS
GUATEMALA
EL SALVADOR
NICARAGUA   VENEZUELA
COSTA RICA   GUAYANA BR.
PANAMA   SURINAM
COLOMBIA   GUAYANA FR.

ECUADOR

PERU   BRASIL

                                    BOLIVIA

CHILE   PARAGUAY

                                    URUGUAY

                    ARGENTINA

Area 1 of Spanish

Area 2 of Spanish

Area 3 of Spanish

Area 4 of Spanish

Area 5 of Spanish

Area 6 of Spanish

Countries where other European languages are official (areas in the
U.S. where there are many Spanish-speakers are also indicated).

languages on Spanish is negligible and consists mainly of specialized vocabulary —words like **canoa, chocolate, cóndor, llama, jaguar.**

Most speakers of American Spanish speak a Spanish which is quite uniform in its grammatical aspects. The principal differences are in vocabulary and pronunciation. Most of these various dialects and sub-dialects of Spanish are mentioned in this book, but the ones presented as standard General American Spanish are those spoken primarily in areas 2 and 4. Although this matter of dialect areas can certainly be debated, the brand of Spanish spoken in Central America (except Panama) and the Highlands of South America seems to have the greatest acceptability throughout Spanish America, just as General American does in the United States.

This in no way is meant to imply that this is the "best" dialect of American Spanish for an English-speaker to learn. None of these dialects has any more beauty or virtue than another—although the one we have chosen, as we said, seems to have more acceptability. A speaker from Lima, for example, will call less attention to himself in Mexico or Chile or Spain than will a speaker from Buenos Aires or Havana. Since American students learn Spanish as a foreign language it is most practical for them to start with the dialect with the greatest acceptability.

In the last analysis, the matter of dialects has perhaps been over-emphasized —certainly for the language student. The situation in Spanish is quite analogous to that of English. It should be asserted once more that any educated speaker of Spanish can be easily understood by any other educated Spanish-speaker anywhere in the world.

References

SPANISH

* Agard, "Present-Day Judaeo-Spanish in the United States" (1950).
  Alonso, Amado, *Estudios lingüísticos: Temas hispanoamericanos* (1953), Chapter 1.
  Alvar, "Estado actual de los atlas lingüísticos españoles" (1966).
* Besso, "Situación actual del judeo-español" (1964).
  Canfield, "The Diachronic Dimension of 'Synchronic' Hispanic Dialectology" (1964).
* ———, *La pronunciación del español en América* (1962).
* ———, "Trends in American Castilian" (1967).
* García de Diego, *Manual de dialectología española* (1959).
  Henríquez Ureña, "Observaciones sobre el español de América" (1921).
  Malmberg, "L'espagnol dans le Nouveau Monde—problème de linguistique générale" (1947, 1948).
  ———, *Estudios de fonética hispánica* (1965), Chapter 8.
* Navarro, *Manual de pronunciación española* (1957).

Rona, "El problema de la división del español americano en zonas dialectales" (1964).

Skelton, "Phonetics, Phonemics, and Pronunciation: Dialect and Standard Language" (1954).

* Zamora Vicente, *Dialectología española* (1960).

ENGLISH AND GENERAL

* Bolinger, *Aspects of Language* (1968), Chapter 9.
* Bronstein, *The Pronunciation of American English* (1960), Chapter 3.
* Buchanan, *A Programed Introduction to Linguistics: Phonetics and Phonemics* (1963), Chapter I.
* Chreist, *Foreign Accent* (1964), Chapters 1-3.
* Gleason, *An Introduction to Descriptive Linguistics* (1961), Chapters 24, 27, 28.
* Hall, *Linguistics and Your Language* (1962), Chapter 9.
* Hockett, *A Course in Modern Linguistics* (1958), Chapters 38, 40, 56.
* Hughes, *The Science of Language* (1962), Chapter II.
* Kenyon and Knott, *A Pronouncing Dictionary of American English* (1953).
* Langacker, *Language and Its Structure* (1967), Chapter 3.
* Lloyd and Warfel, *American English in Its Cultural Setting* (1957), Chapter 3.
* Marckwardt, "Regional and Social Variations" (1965).
* Martinet, "Dialect" (1954–55).
* Thomas, *An Introduction to the Phonetics of American English* (1958).
  Trager and Smith, *An Outline of English Structure* (1951), Part I.

4

~~~~~~

PRODUCTION OF SPEECH SOUNDS

Most parts of the human body used for speech are also there for other purposes, such as eating and breathing. Man alone, among all other animals, has developed the use of these organs and structures for systematic communication and expression.

Starting from the top and proceeding downward (the reverse of the way sound is produced), we have the nasal cavity, the mouth, the teeth and tongue, the throat, the vocal bands, the windpipe, the bronchial tubes, the lungs, and finally the diaphragm. These are precisely the parts of the body which man uses to breath and ingest food and liquid.

The production of sound begins with the DIAPHRAGM, which pushes upward forcing the air out of the LUNGS and up through the BRONCHIAL TUBES and the TRACHEA or windpipe (see diagram on p. 26). When the airstream gets to the LARYNX or voice box it must pass between bands of elastic tissue—the VOCAL BANDS, often referred to as vocal cords. The movement of the air causes these bands to vibrate. They can be tightened or relaxed, creating a somewhat triangular opening between them, called the GLOTTIS. If the bands are tightened, the resultant sound waves vibrate faster, i.e., at a higher frequency, and the sound is higher in musical pitch (see Diagram 1 on p. 27). This pitch is lowered when the bands are relaxed and the vibrations are slower. The size and thickness of these bands differ with age and sex and create a different sounding voice for men, women, and children. An infection (laryngitis) can also temporarily change the size and shape of these bands, making one hoarse or squeaky-voiced. Good singers have greater control than most people over the extent to which these bands can be tightened or relaxed.

The vocal bands vibrate for all vowel and many consonant sounds. This is called phonation or voicing. The bands are loose and do not vibrate for other consonants, like [t] and [s], which are unvoiced or voiceless. You can easily hear the difference by placing your hands tightly over

25

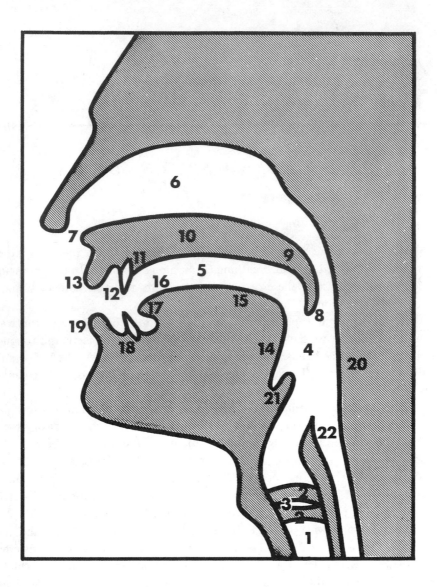

1 trachea
2 larynx
3 vocal bands
4 pharynx
5 oral cavity
6 nasal cavity
7 nostrils
8 uvula

9 velum
10 palate
11 alveolar ridge
12 upper front teeth
13 upper lip
14 root of the tongue
15 dorsum or back of
   the tongue

16 blade or front of the
   tongue
17 tip of the tongue
18 lower front teeth
19 lower lip
20 wall of the pharynx
21 epiglottis
22 esophagus

DIAGRAM 1

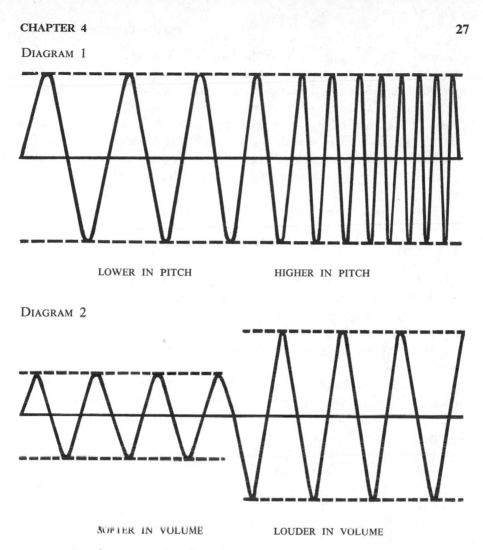

LOWER IN PITCH   HIGHER IN PITCH

DIAGRAM 2

SOFTER IN VOLUME   LOUDER IN VOLUME

your ears and pronouncing first the voiceless consonant [s] in a prolonged manner—s-s-s-s-s-s—and then the voiced consonant [z] in the same way—z-z-z-z-z-z.

The force with which the air is expelled from the lungs through the larynx controls the volume or loudness of the sound by increasing or decreasing the amplitude or size of the sound waves (see Diagram 2 above).

The airstream, now modified by the vocal bands, reaches the PHARYNX, a cavity formed by the root of the tongue and the wall of the throat. From there the air can be exhaled through one of two resonance chambers, the ORAL CAVITY or the NASAL CAVITY. If the VELUM is lowered (as it is in the diagram on p. 26), the air passes through the nasal cavity and out through the NOSTRILS. The resulting sound is a nasal like [m] or [n]. The size and shape of this passage are not subject to voluntary control although the passage can be blocked off deliberately by pinching or closing the nostrils. An infection (head cold) can cause the lining of the passage to swell and reduce the size of the passage or even completely block it off, thus modifying certain sounds. When this happens, nasal sounds cannot be made properly—[m] sounds like [b] (*Barry* instead of *Mary*), [n] sounds like [d] (*dough* instead of *no*), and [ŋ] sounds like [g] (*rig* instead of *ring*). This is actually the reverse of the popular notion that one sounds like he is talking through his nose when he has a bad cold. In reality, he *cannot* talk through his nose, and, consequently, the nasals do not sound right.

Most sounds, however, are produced by expiration of the air through the oral cavity or mouth. The lower or movable articulators—the LOWER LIP, LOWER FRONT TEETH, and TONGUE—move to make contact or come very close to the upper or fixed articulators—the UPPER LIP, UPPER FRONT TEETH, the ALVEOLAR RIDGE or gum ridge behind the upper front teeth, the hard PALATE, the VELUM or soft palate, the UVULA, and sometimes even the WALL OF THE PHARYNX. The tongue can be divided into four main parts—the TIP, the BLADE or front, the DORSUM or back, and the ROOT or extreme rear, which is not important in speaking Spanish or English, although it is for a language like Arabic.

In the front of the pharynx is the EPIGLOTTIS, which, although not functional in speech, is extremely important in the ingestion of food and liquid. It closes off the air passage to the larynx so the food and liquid will go down the ESOPHAGUS rather than the "Sunday" throat. Occasionally, however, the epiglottis does not close fast enough, and coughing, choking, and sometimes even strangulation can result.

In the production of sound, the exhaled air is modified or controlled in several important ways:

1. VOLUME—the force with which the diaphragm and lungs expel the air.
2. VOICING or LACK OF IT—whether or not the vocal bands vibrate.
3. PITCH—how loose or tight the vocal bands are.
4. RESONANCE—whether the sound resonates in only the oral cavity or in both the nasal and oral cavities.
5. PLACE OF ARTICULATION—which articulators approach or contact each other.
6. MANNER OF ARTICULATION—the type of approach or contact the articulators make.

Sounds are divided into two main groups: consonants, if the airstream is stopped or impeded, and vowels, if it is not. *Punto*

In Spanish there are ten places of articulation for consonants:

1. BILABIAL—lower lip against or near the upper lip: [m] as in **más.**

Mudo - consanents without vocal chords
Sonoro - consanents with vocal chords
CHAPTER 4   29

2. LABIODENTAL—lower lip against or near the edge of the upper front teeth: [f] as in **fuente.**

3. INTERDENTAL (only in Castilian)—tip of the tongue between the upper and lower front teeth: [θ] as in the Castilian pronunciation of **zapato.**

4. DENTAL—tip of the tongue against or near the edge or back of the upper front teeth: [d] as in **dar.** *(T)*

5. ALVEOLAR—tip of the tongue or blade against or near the alveolar ridge: [l] as in **luna.**

6. PALATAL—blade or dorsum of the tongue against or near the hard palate: [ĉ] as in **chico.**

7. VELAR—dorsum of the tongue against or near the velum: [k] as in **calor.**

8. BILABIO-VELAR—lower lip near the upper lip and dorsum of the tongue near the velum at the same time: [w] as in **hueso.**

9. UVULAR—dorsum of the tongue against the uvula: [R] as in **carro** in some dialects of Puerto Rico.

10. GLOTTAL—vocal bands: [h] as in **jardín** in many dialects of American Spanish.

Modo de articulación

In Spanish there are seven manners of articulation for consonants:

1. STOPS or OCCLUSIVES—airstream is stopped briefly and then abruptly released with a small explosion: [p] as in **pasar.** *OCLUSIVO - PTK BDG*

2. FRICATIVES or SPIRANTS—airstream, without being stopped, is forced through a narrow opening with friction. If the opening is wide (horizontal) and flat, the sound is a SLIT FRICATIVE: [f] as in **fuente.** If the opening (usually between the tongue and alveolar ridge or palate) is small and round, the sound is a GROOVE FRICATIVE: [s] as in **sol.** *Fricativo*

3. AFFRICATES (STOP + FRICATIVE)—airstream is stopped as with a stop, but instead of being released abruptly it is released with friction as with a fricative: [ĉ] as in **chico.** Some linguists, depending on the language, analyze affricates as combinations of two consonants: a stop and a fricative. *Africado -*

4. NASALS—the velum is lowered and the airstream passes out through the nasal cavity with great resonance: [m] as in **más.**

5. LATERALS—the oral cavity is closed off in the middle, but the airstream escapes on either or both sides of the place of articulation: [l] as in **luna.**

6. TAP or FLAP—tip of the tongue, under tension, strikes the alveolar ridge once as the airstream passes through: [r] as in **pero.** *toque*

7. TRILLS—the tip of the tongue, under tension, strikes the alveolar ridge several times in rapid succession: [r̄] as in **perro.** Sometimes the dorsum

VIBRATORIO

of the tongue strikes the velum or the uvula in this fashion: [R] as in **perro** in some dialects of Puerto Rico.

Thus the consonants can be classified and arranged on a chart, showing three of these meaningful ways of producing sounds: place or point of articulation, manner of articulation, and function of the vocal bands. In the chart below only the meaningful or distinctive consonants of Spanish are shown, thus many of the boxes are empty. The symbols in the upper part of the boxes represent voiceless sounds, those in the lower part, voiced ones.

SPANISH CONSONANT PHONEMES

POINTS OF ARTICULATION

MANNERS OF ARTICULATION	Bilabial	Labio-dental	Inter-dental	Dental	Alveolar	Palatal	Velar	Bilabio-velar	Glottal
STOPS	p / b			t / d			k / g		
SLIT FRICATIVES		f	θ			y	x	w	(h)
GROOVE FRICATIVES					s				
AFFRICATES						ĉ			
NASALS	m				n	ñ			
LATERALS					l	ḷ			
TAP					r				
TRILL					r̄				

Most dialects of American Spanish have only 18 consonant phonemes, lacking both /θ/ and /ḷ/. In some dialects /h/ replaces /x/, thus the parentheses on the chart.

With vowels, instead of place of articulation we talk about the position of the tongue and the shape of the resonance chamber (the mouth), both of which determine the quality or timbre of the vowels. Since the airstream is not blocked or impeded, there is no contact between the upper and lower articulators. Instead, the position of the tongue is significant since it changes the size and shape of the oral cavity. We speak of three vertical positions of the tongue which determine the degree of opening of the oral cavity (see diagrams on p. 32): HIGH, where the tongue is close to the palate; MID, where it is about halfway down in the mouth; and LOW, where it is very low in the mouth. There are also three tongue positions on a front-to-back axis: FRONT, where the highest part of the tongue, the blade, is fairly close to the alveolar ridge; CENTRAL, where the highest part of the tongue is in the center of the oral cavity; and BACK, where the highest part of the tongue, the dorsum, is fairly close to the velum.

Thus, we can classify vowels in this two-dimensional fashion. In Spanish there are five meaningful positions:

1. HIGH FRONT: [i] as in **piso.**
2. MID FRONT: [e] as in **peso.**
3. LOW CENTRAL: [a] as in **paso.**
4. MID BACK: [o] as in **poso.**
5. HIGH BACK: [u] as in **puso.**

SPANISH VOWEL PHONEMES

	Front	Central	Back
HIGH	i		u
MID	e		o
LOW		a	

There are three other features of vowel articulation which are important in many languages but not in Spanish or English since they happen automatically with the production of each vowel.

Lip-rounding vs. lip-spreading is important in German or French, for example, where it can determine the difference between the two high front vowels in **vie** [vi] *life* and **vu** [vü] *seen.* In both Spanish and English, however, the lips are automatically spread for the front vowels, rounded for the back vowels, and in an intermediate or neutral position for the central vowels.

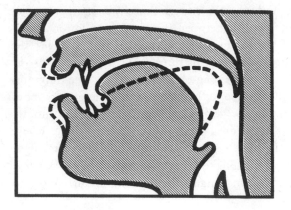

HIGH FRONT   HIGH BACK
[i] (solid line)   [u] (dotted line)

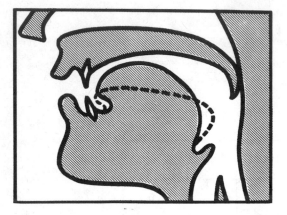

HIGH FRONT   LOW CENTRAL
[i] (solid line)   [a] (dotted line)

Nasalization is also important in some languages, such as Portuguese or French, where it can determine the difference between the two mid front vowels in **fin** [fɛ̃] *end* (˜ indicates a nasalized vowel in this case) and **fait** [fɛ] *made*. Although nasalization of vowels occurs in both English and Spanish, its presence depends entirely on the surrounding consonants and never distinguishes between two vowels articulated in the same place, as it does in French.

Time length or duration is also important in some languages, such as Latin or German, where it determines the difference between the two low central vowels in **Bann** [ban] *ban* and **Bahn** [baːn] *way, track* (: indicates a lengthened vowel). Lengthened and short vowels occur in English and to a lesser extent in Spanish, too, but they are never used to distinguish meaning, as they were in Latin and are in German.

In some languages certain sounds are considered neither consonants nor vowels, but semi-consonants, semi-vowels, or glides since they share the characteristics of both types of articulation. In English, for example, /y/ is a glide. Although it is essentially the same sound phonetically in either place, it functions as a consonant at the beginning of a syllable as in *yes* or as a vowel at the end of a syllable as in *say*. In Spanish the glides or semi-vowels [i̯] and [u̯] are only variants of the vowels /i/ and /u/, and there are similar sounds /y/ and /w/, which function as consonants.

Thus far, we have discussed speech sounds from a purely articulatory point of view, that is how they are produced in the vocal tract. Equally important in linguistic theory and analysis—although not as useful in language pedagogy—is acoustic phonetics, where the sounds are analyzed according to their acoustic properties. Vital to such work are machines, such as the spectograph, which make a graphic representation on paper of the sound waves and various modifications they undergo. This approach has led to a new and different way of classifying sounds, based in part on where and how they are produced in the vocal tract but also on how they are perceived and interpreted by the human ear. In this book, however, we confine our analysis to the more traditional manner of classifying the sounds, since it is not only much less complicated but also quickly mastered by the student as he learns a foreign language.

References

SPANISH

Alarcos Llorach, *Fonología española* (1965), Part I: Chapter III.
* Navarro, *Manual de pronunciación española* (1957), Sections 8–25.

ENGLISH AND GENERAL

* Belasco, "General Section," Part II, in *Manual and Anthology of Applied Linguistics* (1960).
* Bolinger, *Aspects of Language* (1968), Chapter 3.
* Bronstein (1960, Chapter 4.
* Buchanan (1963), Chapters II, III.
* Gleason, *An Introduction to Descriptive Linguistics* (1961), Chapter 15.
  Hala, "Apical, cacuminal, rétroflexe, coronal, dorsal" (1964).
* Heffner, *General Phonetics* (1949), Chapter II.
* Hockett, *A Course in Modern Linguistics* (1958), Chapters 7–9.
  ———, *A Manual of Phonology* (1955), Chapter 1.
  Kaiser, ed., *Manual of Phonetics* (1957).
* Malmberg, *Phonetics* (1963), Chapters II, III.

* Obrecht, "A Visual Aid to Pronunciation" (1956–57).
  Pike, *Phonetics* (1943), Part II.
* Shearer, *Illustrated Speech Anatomy* (1963).
* Smalley, *Manual of Articulatory Phonetics* (1964), Appendix: Lesson C.
* Wise, *Applied Phonetics* (1957), Chapter 3.

5

~~~~~~

PHONETICS AND PHONEMICS

The human speech apparatus can produce an infinite variety of sounds, most of which are never used in any one language. A baby makes a great number of these sounds but gradually learns to choose only those which it hears and which elicit desired responses. When the child finally has complete control over the sound system of his language, he has narrowed the range of important sounds considerably—to fewer than fifty.

The production of these sounds and the sounds themselves can be studied in several ways. In PHYSIOLOGICAL PHONETICS we can study the entire human speech mechanism, including the breathing and voicing apparatus. If we are mainly concerned with how the sounds are made by the vocal bands, the articulators, and the resonance chambers, we study ARTICULATORY PHONETICS. The facial diagrams presented in the previous chapter are called articulatory diagrams, and a description of a sound by its place and manner of articulation, function of the vocal bands, etc., is an articulatory description.

Sound is made up of waves which travel through the air at a speed of about 1100 feet per second. These waves are created by the vibrations caused by the movement of parts of the speech mechanism. Pitch is determined by the frequency of the waves and volume by the amplitude or size of the waves. The study of sound itself, its properties, its transmission, and also its reception by the human auditory mechanism is ACOUSTIC PHONETICS. This field, which utilizes machines to a great extent, is also important to musicians and singers, physicists, engineers, and medical men.

Linguists and particularly phoneticians are most interested in how and why these sounds are produced. They have created symbols to represent each individual sound, but unfortunately there is no one set of standard phonetic symbols used by all of them. Each phonetician or group of phoneticians uses his own system, and others who read their studies must constantly "translate" the new symbols into their own. Many of the symbols, however, are universally used. Usually regular letters of the alphabet and standard marks of punctuation are employed wherever possible for reasons of simplicity and economy. Square brackets [ ] indicate that the symbols enclosed are phonetic, i.e., they represent the sounds quite closely. Most of the small Roman letters, some capitals, and even some Greek letters are used. Capitals and punctuation marks, however, are never used *as such* in phonetic transcription. Such symbols as N R ' : , represent individual sounds or sound features and not sentence, clause, and word boundaries as they do in conventional writing. Beginning students of linguistics must make a great effort to avoid confusion on this count. Conventional letters of the alphabet when they indicate spelling, instead of being placed between brackets, are either printed in *italics* (underlined in handwriting and typescripts), or placed between single or double quotation marks, to call attention to them in a text.

When the phonetic symbols represent all or most of the sound differences perceived by the ear, they make up what is called a NARROW phonetic transcription. When many of these distinctions are ignored, it is called a BROAD phonetic transcription. The phonetic transcription used for Spanish in this book is for the most part narrow.

Some linguists in the early years of this century felt that although phonetic transcription of speech was useful and even essential for some types of work, it could at times be cumbersome and unnecessarily detailed. As they studied different languages, they came to the realization that many of these sound varieties in a given language were not as important as others and that certain similar sound varieties could be grouped into families or classifications. But, most important of all, they discovered that a relatively few sound groups in the language were really important and distinctive because they were the ones that determined meaning.

For example, in English *t* really represents several sounds, which we pronounce at different times, according to the position in the word. At the beginning of a word like *to* the *t* has a little puff of air after it. If you place the back of your hand a few inches from your lips as you pronounce this word, you can feel this breath. This aspirated *t*, then, can be represented with the phonetic symbol [t'].

If you pronounce the word *stew*, you notice that now there is not nearly as much breath with the *t*. This is because in English *t* after *s* is unaspirated. This unaspirated *t*, then, can be represented with [t].

If you pronounce the word *butter*, you notice that the *t* does not have the puff of air as in *to* nor does the tongue really stop the airstream as it does in both *to* and *stew*. The tip of the tongue quickly strikes the alveolar ridge and returns to its original position. This normally happens in English when *t* comes between vowels, the first one of which is stressed. This tap or flap *t*, then, can be represented with [t̂].

Finally, if you pronounce the word *lit*, you notice that the *t* has no aspiration like [t'] (unless you make a deliberate effort to give it some), the tongue does not return to its original position as it does with [t] and [t̂], but remains against the alveolar ridge. This unreleased *t*, then, can be represented with [t-].

Thus in English there are at least four distinct varieties of *t*, varieties which are not only articulated in different ways in the mouth but which sound different to us if we pay attention to them. Yet as we speak we rarely make any conscious effort to choose from among these *t* sounds. We pronounce them according to the surrounding sounds and their position in the word or sentence, that is, their PHONETIC ENVIRONMENT.

Let us return for a moment to the first word, *to*. If you place your tongue in the same position as you do for the first consonant in *to* but allow your vocal bands to start vibrating too soon, you produce a completely different consonant and a completely different word—*do*. The difference between *to* and *do* is enough to make all native speakers accept the fact that there is something fundamentally different between [t'] and [d']. This difference has caused the meaning to change, and we now use different letters of the alphabet in conventional writing to symbolize these two contrasting sounds. We begin to see that with [d'] we are now dealing with a sound that is "more different" from [t'] than [t], for example, is. To experiment, you can pronounce the unaspirated [t] (as in *stew*) instead of the aspirated [t'] at the beginning of *to*. The word sounds strange, but we all admit that it still means the same thing as *to* in the normal pronunciation. Now you can pronounce the word *lit* first with the aspirated [t'], then the unaspirated [t], and finally with the unreleased [t-], as is normal. All three words, however they may sound, still are the past tense of the verb *to light*. But if you pronounce *lit* with voicing in the final consonant —in other words, [d'] or [d] or [d-] instead of [t-], the resulting word, *lid*, certainly has a different meaning from *lit*, just as *do* is not *to*.

In this illustration we have been dealing with the most important concept in phonology, the PHONEME. In most positions in a word, no variety of *t* can be substituted for by any variety of *d* without changing the meaning (or creating a non-existent word like *dube for *tube*). Thus, all varieties of *t* belong to one family or class of *t* sounds called the PHONEME /t/, which is written between slash bars. All varieties of *d* likewise belong to the phoneme /d/. These two phonemes are distinctive sounds in English and many other languages as well because their use causes a change in meaning or creates a meaningless form. Pairs of words, that prove this—*to-do, till-dill, lit-lid*—are called MINIMAL PAIRS. By using this testing technique of minimal pairs we can begin to pick out the distinctive or meaningful sounds of English, i.e., the phonemes: *pill-bill* and other such pairs prove the existence of two phonemes /p/ and /b/; *kill-gill* and other such pairs prove the existence of two phonemes /k/ and /g/, and so on. The fact that the spelling in these examples is the same but for the one letter is pure coincidence. The words *rough* and *huff* form a minimal pair showing the phonemic status of /r/ and /h/. The fact that *-ough* and *-uff* are two different ways of spelling the sequence /əf/ is due to the English writing system. Such inconsistencies, which exist in the writing systems of most languages, cause linguists to resort to phonetic and phonemic transcription to indicate the sounds consistently and accurately.

All sounds can be referred to as PHONES. If they are contrasting and serve to distinguish meaning as /p b t d k g/, we call them PHONEMES and write them between slash bars. If they are mere variants of another sound and do not change the meaning (even though they may sound "funny") like [lit-], [lit], or [lit'] for *lit*, we place them between brackets [t- t' t t̂] and call them ALLO-PHONES, i.e., members of a phoneme family.

The phoneme is an abstraction and cannot really be pronounced except in terms of one of its allophones. Nevertheless, we find the phoneme a very convenient way of talking about meaningful sounds.

In any language the number of phonemes is obviously far lower than the number of phones or allophones. In most dialects of American English there are 33; General American Spanish has 23; French has 33; German has 28; Italian has 27; Russian has 41. These numbers, of course, vary slightly with the dialect.

Although the use of minimal pairs is usually the best and quickest way to determine whether two sounds in a language are phonemic or not, sometimes minimal pairs for certain phonemes are difficult to find because words containing these phonemes are very few in number or very uncommon. For example, in English /š/ (as in *she*) and /ž/ (as in *measure*) are phonemes, but there are very few minimal pairs to show this. One is *Aleutian-illusion*, but many people feel that the initial vowels in both words are or should be pronounced differently, and if a pair differs in more than one place, it is no longer a minimal pair. Another one is *tressure-treasure*, but the first word—a type of figure in a coat of arms—is unfamiliar to anyone but specialists in heraldry. In addition to these problems, it is often difficult or impossible to find minimal pairs in an unknown language when the linguist is first beginning his analysis.

Because of these difficulties linguists often rely on another technique for finding phonemes. They first find the phones which are phonetically similar. This usually means that two of the three factors—place of articulation, manner of articulation, and voicing or unvoicing—are the same. The next step is to chart the distribution of these phones to determine whether or not they are allophones of the same phoneme or different phonemes. Allophones are usually pronounced automatically by native speakers according to certain factors, the main one being phonetic environment. This has already been demonstrated for English with /t/ and [t' t t̂ t-]. The allophones the speaker chooses are most often the result of an obligatory choice, that is, an involuntary one. But the choice between /t/ and /d/ is an optional and voluntary choice. The English-speaker decides between an unreleased [d-] and an unreleased [t-], depending, for example, on whether he wants to say "I'm going to see the old sod" or "I'm going to see the old sot." The fact that phonemes are freely chosen but allophones are usually determined by other factors means that the linguist can determine the distribution of allophones by their phonetic environment.

In Spanish, for example, there is a phone [d], a voiced dental stop, and another one [đ], a voiced dental or interdental fricative. In a language like English, these two phones function as phonemes and occur frequently in the SAME ENVIRONMENT. In this case, we can never substitute one for the other without changing the meaning: *dough-though*, or destroying it: *dew-*thew*. But in Spanish [d] and [đ] rarely occur in the same environment. [d] occurs at the beginning of a breath group or phrase and after /l/ and /n/, and [đ] occurs everywhere else. Thus, we can set up the following table to show the distributional pattern of the [d đ] phones in Spanish:

	PHRASE-INITIAL	AFTER /l/	AFTER /n/	ELSEWHERE
[d]	x	x	x	——
[đ]	——	——	——	x

Such a pattern of distribution leads the linguist to suspect that [d] and [đ], since they do not occur in the same environment, are merely allophones of the same phoneme /d/. He can find no minimal pairs where the two sounds contrast or where a meaningless word is produced. In other words, even though the Spanish-speaker might not say [lá-do] for **lado,** he accepts it and usually hears no difference between [lá-do] and [lá-đo], the normal pronunciation. [đ] never occurs where [d] does, and, if one pronounces it unnaturally in such a position, there is still no contrast.

This pattern of non-occurrence in the same position or the same phonetic environment is called COMPLEMENTARY DISTRIBUTION. The varieties of /t/ in English can be set up similarly in a table of complementary distribution:

	WORD-INITIAL OR BEFORE STRESSED VOWEL	AFTER /s/	INTERVOCALIC AFTER STRESSED VOWEL	WORD-FINAL
[tʰ]	x	——	——	——
[t]	——	x	——	——
[t̂]	——	——	x	——
[t-]	——	——	——	x

Other possibilities, of course, exist for /t/ in English but are not shown here.

In all languages there are certain allophones which, while they obviously do not change or destroy meaning, can and do occur in the same environment. In Spanish, for example, at the beginning of a word either [y] (as in *yoke*) or [ŷ] (as in *joke*) occurs. The same speaker may say either [yó] or [ŷó] with no change in meaning. When this happens, we say that these allophones, rather than being in complementary distribution, are in FREE or NON-FUNCTIONAL VARIATION. Their occurrence is either random or determined by unknown or unimportant factors rather than by phonetic environment.

Any two allophones of the same phoneme can be substituted one for the other without changing the meaning, although the resulting word may sound "funny." Such a case is English *to* with [t] instead of [t'] or Spanish **lado** with [d] instead of [đ]. But the point is that most native speakers usually do not make these substitutions. When they do with great frequency, as Spanish [ŷó] for [yó], we then talk about real free variation. In English, for example, some people feel that aspirated final voiceless stop allophones sound more "elegant" and "educated" than their unreleased counterparts as in *stop*, *light*, *walk*. Thus, the use of these allophones in these positions is a type of free variation. In natural and rapid speech, however, the use of allophones is determined most often by phonetic environment; that is, the allophones occur in complementary distribution.

When one learns a foreign language, he must, of course, learn to make all the *phonemic* distinctions in the new language. If he does not, communication is often severely hampered. The learner will not perceive certain sounds and sound contrasts and will, in turn, be misunderstood when he tries to pronounce them. If the American does not make a distinction between the Spanish tap /r/ and the trilled /ř/, he will not distinguish between **caro** and **carro** and he might make such errors as saying **Está enterrado** ("He's buried") when he really means **Está enterado** ("He's informed").

Thus the unquestionable goals for the language learner with regard to pronunciation must be complete mastery of all the phonemes of the target language, both in hearing and speaking.

But what about the allophones? Must you use the fricative [đ] between vowels as Spanish speakers do, or will the stop [d] be good enough? Since they are allophones and do not change meaning, is it necessary to try to choose the right one? We are now talking about much more than mere comprehension or the lack of it. We are now concerned with the task of trying to learn to speak the new language with a native or near-native accent. If the Spanish-speaker wants to sound like an American, he must aspirate his word-initial [t'], even though *to* with an initial unaspirated [t] (the most common Spanish variety) is still the same word. If you want to sound like a Spanish-speaker, you must use the fricative [đ] between vowels as in **lado** even though the use of the stop [d] would not change the meaning of the word.

Thus, a complete mastery over the allophones, as well as the phonemes, of the language is essential if the learner is to pronounce the language as native speakers do.

The whole matter is complicated by the fact that the phonemes and allophones of two languages are never the same in either quality or distribution. Spanish [ŷ] and English [j] are almost the same sounds from an articulatory and auditory point of view, but they pattern in a completely different fashion in the two languages. In English /j/ and /y/ are phonemes, as in *joke-yoke*. But in Spanish the corresponding [ŷ] and [y] sounds are allophones as in the two acceptable pronunciations of the word **yo**. Thus, when the Spanish-speaker learns English, he must learn to make a meaningful distinction, which in his own language is unimportant and happens unpredictably (free variation) or automatically according to phonetic environment (complementary distribution), if he wishes to be sure he is saying "He went to Yale" and not "He went to jail." Conversely, you must learn to accept either sound in a word like *yo* and not attach any special significance to one pronunciation or the other just because the two acceptable Spanish sounds happen to be phonemes in English.

References

SPANISH

Alarcos Llorach, *Fonología española* (1965), Part I: Chapters I, II.
* Gili Gaya, *Elementos de fonética general* (1950).
* Navarro, *Manual de pronunciación española* (1957).
* Quilis and Fernández, *Curso de fonética y fonología españolas para estudiantes angloamericanos* (1966), Chapter IV.
Skelton, "Phonetics, Phonemics, and Pronunciation: Dialect and Standard Language" (1954).

ENGLISH AND GENERAL

* Albright, *The International Phonetic Alphabet: Its Backgrounds and Development* (1958).
* Belasco, "General Section," Part II, in *Manual and Anthology of Applied Linguistics* (1960).
* ———, "Introduction" to *Applied Linguistics: Spanish* (1961).
* Bolinger, *Aspects of Language* (1968), Chapter 4.
* Bronstein (1960), Chapter 2.
Cohen, "On the Value of Experimental Phonetics for the Linguist" (1962).
Delattre, *Comparing the Phonetic Features of English, French, German, and Spanish* (1965).
* ———, "The Physiological Interpretation of Sound Spectograms" (1951).
Denison, "Phonetics and Phonemics in Foreign Language Teaching" (1962).
* Gleason, *An Introduction to Descriptive Linguistics* (1961), Chapters 15–22.
Halle, "On the Bases of Phonology" (1964).
——— , "Phonology in Generative Grammar" (1962).
* Heffner, *General Phonetics* (1949).
Hill, *Introduction to Linguistic Structures* (1958), Chapter 4.

* Hockett, *A Course in Modern Linguistics* (1958), Chapters 10–13.
———, *A Manual of Phonology* (1955), Chapters 3–5.
* International Phonetic Association, *The Principles of the International Phonetic Association* (1957).
Jakobson and Halle, *Fundamentals of Language* (1956).
———, Fant, and ———, *Preliminaries to Speech Analysis* (1963).
Jones, *The Phoneme: Its Nature and Use* (1950).
Kaiser, ed. *Manual of Phonetics* (1957).
Ladefoged, *Elements of Acoustic Phonetics* (1962).
Langacker, *Language and Its Structure* (1967), Chapter 6.
Malmberg, "Análisis estructural y análisis instrumental de los sonidos del lenguaje" (1963).
* ———, *Phonetics* (1963).
Mol, "The Relation Between Phonetics and Phonemics" (1963, 1964).
Pierce, "Spectographical Study of Vowel Nuclei" (1962).
Pike, *Phonetics* (1943), Part I.
* Potter, Kopp, and Green, *Visible Speech* (1947).
Pulgram, *Introduction to the Spectography of Speech* (1964).
* Quilis Morales, "El método espectográfico" (1960).
* Sebeok, comp. "Selected Readings in General Phonemics (1925–1964)".
* Smalley, *Manual of Articulatory Phonetics* (1964).
Stetson, *Motor Phonetics* (1951).
* Wise, *Applied Phonetics* (1957), Chapter 3.

6

~~~~~~

SYLLABLES AND THE PHONEMIC PHRASE

When we talk about "letters," "sentences," and "paragraphs," we are, of course, talking about graphic symbols rather than sounds. These writing groups often do not coincide with sound groups. This is particularly true of a language like Spanish where most word boundaries cannot normally be distinguished in the stream of speech as they can be on the printed page. This is one of the reasons rapid conversational Spanish is so difficult for the beginning student to understand. It also causes even an advanced student some difficulty when he first reads phonetic or phonemic transcription. He looks for familiar graphic indicators of letter groups, such as capitals, spaces between letters, and punctuation marks, but finds instead new symbols and unfamiliar groups. Instead of **El hombre vive en España** he sees /elómbrebíbenespáña/ or [e lóm bre bí be nes pá ña] or [e-lóm-bre-bí-be-nes-pá-ña] (as we write it phonetically in this book), all of which, despite their unfamiliar look, are more accurate indications of the sounds than conventional letters are.

The first and most basic group in phonetics is the SYLLABLE. It is difficult to define precisely, and its nature varies from one language to the next. Nevertheless, most native speakers of any language seem to know intuitively how many syllables a given sequence in their language has even if they do not know exactly where the syllable boundaries are and have little idea of what a syllable really is.

Approaching the problem from a physiological point of view, we might say that the syllable is the sound produced between two successive occurrences of muscular tension in the vocal tract and breathing apparatus. It might be regarded as a type of "pulse." From an acoustic point of view, the syllable is the stretch of sound which occurs between two successive depressions in the perceptibility of the stream of sound. But the easiest way to determine syllables in Spanish is to approach the matter from the point of view of the nature of the sounds themselves and how they pattern. Certain combinations or sequences of segmental phonemes—vowels and consonants—are possible in Spanish and others are not. Some of these sequences can begin a syllable, others can end one, and still others must be divided to form the end of one syllable and the beginning of the next. Consonants in the *same* syllable are also referred to as clusters. A handy rule-of-thumb for the placement of consonants is that any consonant sequence that cannot cluster to begin a word in Spanish cannot begin a syllable either. Thus, such words as **isla, perla,** and **palma,** must be divided **is-la, per-la,** and **pal-ma** because no Spanish word starts with *sl-* or *rl-* or *lm-*.

In reality, of course, these combinations cannot begin words because they cannot begin syllables. However, you are probably more familiar with the form of words than with syllables, so it is best to begin by identifying the sequences that cannot begin words.

The correct division of words into syllables—SYLLABICATION (**silabeo**)—is important in Spanish since it often determines the phonetic environment, which, in turn, determines the quality of individual sounds. Before giving the statements for Spanish syllabication, let us present a few definitions.

An OPEN SYLLABLE is one which ends in a vowel (including the letter *y*, which sometimes represents the sound /i/ at the end of a word): **no, ma-no, re-ve-la, hoy.** A CLOSED SYLLABLE is one which ends in one or two consonants (excluding the letter *y*): **más, már-tir, im-por-tan-tes, trans-por-tan.**

A DIPHTHONG is a cluster of two vowels, one of which must be an unstressed /i/ or /u/, *fused* into a single syllable: **seis, hay, cau-sa, deu-da, sie-te, pio-jo, bue-no, muy.** If either the /í/ or /ú/ is stressed, the sequence is *not* a diphthong but is composed of separate syllables: **mí-o, le-ís-te, ba-úl, con-ti-nú-a.**[1]

A TRIPHTHONG is a group of three vowels *fused* into a single syllable. Both the first and third vowels must be an unstressed /i/ or /u/: **es-tu-diáis, cam-biéis, a-ve-ri-guáis.**

A SEMI-VOWEL is an unstressed [i̯] or [u̯], which fuses with any vowel (except itself) to form a diphthong or triphthong. It may come first: **sie-te, bue-no,** or second: **seis, deu-da.**

Syllables are formed in Spanish in the following ways. Notice that since Spanish writing is fairly regular, virtually the same statements can be used for both writing and sound.

　　1. A single consonant SOUND between two vowels always starts a syllable with the next vowel: **o-ro, ma-no, re-ve-la.** The combinations **ch, ll,** and **rr** are DIGRAPHS or pairs of letters which each represent only *one* sound and therefore are not separated: **ha-cha, ca-lle, pe-rro.**

---

[1] Since verbs, nouns, and adjectives are stressed in the stream of speech, such a combination as **Vi animales** does not start with a diphthong because the /i/ of **vi** is stressed even though it does not bear a written accent. See pp. 214-15 for a listing of all parts of speech which are ordinarily stressed in the stream of speech in Spanish.

2. Two consonant sounds between vowels form a *cluster* and start the syllable if they are **pl, pr, bl, br, tr, dr, cl** (representing /kl/), **cr** (representing /kr/), **gl, gr, fl, fr: a-pli-ca-do, a-gra-da-ble, a-fli-gi-do.** Otherwise they are merely a sequence and must be divided, one with each syllable: **per-la, ac-to, gran-de, lec-ción.** These twelve clusters are not too difficult to remember since they represent the six stop phonemes (see chart on p. 30) + /l/ or /r/ (except **dl** and **tl**) and the fricative /f/ + /l/ or /r/. Since these twelve clusters are the only ones that can begin a syllable they are also the only ones that can begin a word, and no Spanish word begins with such combinations as **tl-, *dl, *sl-, *mr-,* etc.

3. Three consonants between vowels are always divided. If the second two are one of the twelve clusters in statement 2 above, **pl, pr, bl, br,** etc., the first consonant goes with the preceding vowel and the second pair of consonants cluster with the following vowel: **hom-bre, siem-pre, a-sam-ble-a.** If one of these twelve clusters is *not* involved, the first two consonants go with the preceding vowel and the third one with the following vowel: **trans-por-te, ins-tan-te.**

4. Four consonants between vowels is a very rare combination in Spanish, and they are always divided in the middle: **obs-truc-ción, trans-plan-tar.** Many speakers, however, do not even pronounce the first consonant in these groups, thus reducing them to three-consonant groups.

5. Two vowels together are always divided unless one is an *unstressed* /i/ or /u/ in which case they form a diphthong: **ca-er, le-ón, cre-er, pa-se-ar, mí-o, dí-a, a-cen-tú-a, ba-úl,** but **seis, sie-te, cau-sa, ciu-dad.**

There are some exceptions to these five statements. For example, there are some words with internal consonant groups that some speakers regard as compounds and divide that way: **sub-le-var.** Other speakers, however, in both speech and writing, follow the normal patterns: **su-ble-var.** A word like **sub-rayar** (*to underline*) is really not an exception of this type since the first **r** represents the phoneme /r̄/ of the word **rayar,** and this trilled /r̄/ never goes with another consonant to form an indivisible cluster as the simple /r/ does.

Another area of exceptions—vowel combinations—is quite complex and depends to a great extent on stress patterns and style of speech. This is taken up in detail in Chapter 30, "Vowel Combinations." *is second in importance to syllables*

After the syllable the next most important sound group is not the word or the clause or the sentence, but rather the PHONEMIC PHRASE. This is the stream of sounds which are produced between two pauses no matter how slight. Every speaker makes frequent pauses in his speech—to separate grammatical groupings, to emphasize certain words, to think, to remember, to breathe, to swallow. In Spanish the sounds in these phonemic phrases or "breath groups" are run together and are pronounced *just as though they were in one single word.* Spanish-speakers do not normally observe word boundaries when they speak, as we often do in English. The sounds within the phonemic phrase in Spanish are just as intimately related to each other as are those within a single word.

The first sound in the phonemic phrase, i.e., the first sound after a pause, is called ABSOLUTE-INITIAL, as opposed to word-initial or syllable-initial. This position is extremely important because several Spanish phonemes have different allophones, whose occurrence depends on whether the phoneme occurs *within* the phonemic phrase or at the beginning in this initial position. For example, /b/ has a stop allophone [b], which is used in the absolute-initial position, and a fricative allophone [ƀ], which is used between vowels. This has nothing to do with word boundaries since the /b/ of **voy** has the stop allophone in the phrase **Voy a casa** [bó-ya-ká-sa] but the fricative allophone in the phrase **Yo voy a casa** [yó-ƀó-ya-ká-sa], where it is no longer absolute-initial, although still word-initial and syllable-initial.

Another important concept is LINKING (**enlace**). The last consonant of a word followed by another word beginning with a vowel goes with that next vowel to form a single syllable, exactly as described in statement 1 of syllabication. Although the letters for the phrase *gold* are arranged **el oro** on paper, the sounds are really [e-ló-ro], **el hombre** is pronounced [e-lóm-bre], **con estos amigos** [ko-nés-to-sa-mí-gos], etc., because of this phenomenon of linking within the phonemic phrase.

DIPHTHONGS also occur across word boundaries as long as the /i/ and /u/ are *unstressed*: **me imagino** [me̦i-ma-xí-no], **hable usted** [á-ƀle̦us-té̦d], **su ave** [su̦á-ƀe]. But if the /í/ or /ú/ is stressed, just as within a word, the vowels form separate syllables: **me iba** [me-í-ƀa], **se une** [se-ú-ne], **tú hablabas** [tú-a-ƀlá-ƀas]. Notice that the stressed /í/ and /ú/ often do not carry written accents: **iba, une.**

The letter *h* (except in the digraph **ch**) represents silence and has no effect on any of the combinations: **airoso** [ai̦-ró-so] and also **ahijado** [ai̦-xá-do], **esta islita** [és-tai̦s-lí-ta] and also **esta hijita** [és-tai̦-xí-ta]. But **esta isla** is [és-ta-ís-la] and **esta hija** is [és-ta-í-xa] because the /í/ is now stressed even though it does not have a written accent.

Except for **ll** and **rr** two identical consonants are usually divided into separate syllables: **innato** is [in-ná-to], **más suave** is [más-su̦á-ƀe], **en el libro** is [e-ne̦l-lí-ƀro]. This happens both within a word and between words.

The native speaker pauses naturally without thinking about it, and these pauses form the boundaries of the phonemic phrases. If you are transcribing his speech, you should have no problem deciding where the phonemic phrases are. The native speaker decides this for you and reveals it by pausing. But if you are speaking Spanish or transcribing a written passage for practice, you yourself must make the decisions as to where to make the pauses. In writing, punctuation is a fairly good indication of phonemic phrase boundaries. To be sure, native speakers often make pauses where there would be no written punctuation, and conversely they often do *not* make pauses where there would be written punctuation. But when working with a written text and having no one to listen to, you can assume that almost every punctuation mark (except quotation marks and apostrophes) indicates a pause of some sort and thus the end of a phonemic phrase.

There are other pauses, however, which are not marked by punctuation. The native speaker usually places them between relatively long syntactical elements, such as between a subject and its predicate or between two clauses: **El hombre que les habló ayer | es el jefe de la nueva compañía petrolera** or **Vuelva usted a casa | y la encontrará en la sala.**

In summation, here are the different ways in which the sounds of Spanish will be divided into syllables and phonemic phrases in the transcription exercises in this book. For the exercises in this chapter conventional letters of the alphabet will be used, but when the transcription exercises start, the answers will be written entirely in phonemic and phonetic transcription, with only the sounds analyzed up to that point underlined: /bá-na-bér/ or [bá-na-bér]. Obviously, you must use conventional letters for the sounds not yet taken up, and check only the underlined symbols for which you are responsible. All syllables, including those between words, will be indicated with hyphens: [mé-nos], [me-mos-tró], [le-a-bla-ré], [tú-a-blá-ba-sa-mi-pá-dre]. Until we see how phonemic phrase boundaries are marked according to their intonation, spaces will be used to indicate them: [buél-baus-té-da-ká-sa i-la-en-kon-tra-rá-en-la-sá-la]. Words that are linked together because of **enlace,** or because the last vowel of one forms a diphthong with the first vowel of the next, are shown just as any other syllables: [e-ló-ro], [e-nes-pá-ña], [mei-ma-xí-no], [á-blçus-ted].

References

SPANISH

* Bäckvall, "¿Es únicamente francés el fenómeno llamado *liaison*?" (1967).
* Cárdenas, *Applied Linguistics: Spanish* (1961), Chapter III.
  Delattre, *Comparing the Phonetic Features of English, French, German, and Spanish* (1965), Chapter II.
* Gili Gaya, *Elementos de fonética general* (1950), Chapter VII.
  Kahane and Beym, "Syntactical Juncture in Colloquial Mexican Spanish" (1948).
  Malmberg, "La structure syllabique de l'espagnol" (1948).
* Navarro, *Manual de pronunciación española* (1957), Sections 26–30, 153–156.
  Quilis, "La juntura en español" (1964).
* _____ and Fernández, *Curso de fonética y fonología españolas para estudiantes angloamericanos* (1966), Chapter XII.

ENGLISH AND GENERAL

* Albright, *The International Phonetic Alphabet: Its Backgrounds and Development* (1958).

Hala, "La syllable, sa nature, son origine et ses transformations" (1961).
* Harms, "Programed Learning for Phonetic Transcription" (1963).
Hockett, *A Manual of Phonology* (1955), Chapter 2.
* International Phonetic Association, *The Principles of the International Phonetic Association* (1957).
* Lado, *Linguistics Across Cultures* (1957), Chapter 2.
* Malmberg, *Phonetics* (1963), Chapter VII.
Pulgram, "Consonant Cluster, Consonant Sequence, and the Syllable" (1965).
Stetson, *Motor Phonetics* (1951), Chapter I, Appendix X.

Exercises   (Correct answers for all exercises are found in Appendix D.)

A

Using regular orthography, divide the following words into syllables:

1. homenaje	15. quebrar	29. ahí
2. día	16. ciudad	30. embaular
3. vereda	17. pantalla	31. espalda
4. baúl	18. caos	32. hombre
5. agradable	19. hoyuelo	33. paisano
6. tranquilizar	20. deuda	34. permitir
7. caudillo	21. hay	35. león
8. desastroso	22. pasear	36. reina
9. país	23. ahogar	37. transplante
10. durante	24. perla	38. poesía
11. oído	25. ahumado	39. construcción
12. habituarse	26. lechero	40. extraordinario
13. caer	27. relatar	41. loar
14. subrayar	28. amarrar	42. espontaneidad

B

Using regular orthography, divide the following phrases into syllables. Ignore word boundaries within these phrases:

1. el oro	12. con este hombre
2. hablar francés	13. para este hijo
3. las hijas	14. la odio
4. hablas español	15. hable usted
5. su ave	16. el honor
6. esta hija	17. la honra
7. para este hijito	18. por el amor a España
8. lo vi ayer	19. en el lomo
9. se une	20. la isla
10. se veía muy bien	21. tan negro
11. en España	22. los suizos

7

INTRODUCING THE CONSONANTS OF SPANISH

Consonants are sounded when the airstream is stopped or impeded in some way in the upper vocal tract or supraglottal cavities, i.e., from the vocal bands up and out to the lips. There are three meaningful ways of classifying consonant phonemes in Spanish: PLACE OF ARTICULATION—bilabial, labio-dental, interdental, dental, alveolar, palatal, velar, bilabio-velar, glottal; MANNER OF ARTICULATION—stops, fricatives, affricates, nasals, laterals, tap, trill; and FUNCTION OF VOCAL BANDS—voicing or the lack of it.

Although General American Spanish has only 18 consonant phonemes, it is quite rich in consonant phones. These phones play a much more important role in determining pronunciation differences in Spanish dialects than they do in English, where the vowels and vowel nuclei perform a similar role. For example, in Spanish the digraph **ll** represents a palatal [l̦] in peninsular Spanish and certain dialects in the highlands of South America, either a palatal fricative [y] or a palatal affricate [ŷ] in most American Spanish dialects, and a fricative [ž] (as in *measure*) in Argentina and Uruguay. Spanish vowels, however, are quite uniform from dialect to dialect.

Many consonantal modifications occur in one particular position—syllable-final. Using V to represent any vowel, C any consonant, and # pause or the end of a word or group, we can show this syllable-final position as V̱C-C or V̱C#. Of course, these symbols represent only the immediate environment of the last consonant. The entire syllable might be CVC-CV, as in **costa,** or CCVC-CV, as in **pronto,** etc.

A consonant in syllable-final position naturally occurs either before another consonant in a sequence or before silence since if it occurs before a vowel, it goes with that vowel and is syllable-initial rather than syllable-final.

The speech organs, getting ready for the next consonant, often pronounce a syllable-final consonant differently than when it begins a syllable. For example, /s/ is not modified when it is absolute-initial (beginning of a phonemic phrase) or intervocalic (between vowels), but it is frequently modified or even eliminated in syllable-final position. It can voice to [z] before another voiced consonant, as in **mismo** [míz-mo], it can change to glottal aspiration before any consonant, as in **esperar** [ęh-pe-rár], and it can even disappear, as in **está** [ę-tá].

The voicing of [s] to [z] before another voiced consonant is an example of a type of consonant modification which is very widespread in language: ASSIMILATION. One sound undergoes a change when it comes in contact with another; it assimilates to or becomes more like the neighboring sound. The most common form in Spanish is REGRESSIVE ASSIMILATION, in which the assimilated sound *precedes* the conditioning sound, as in [míz-mo], where [s] becomes [z] because of the following voiced consonant /m/. A less common form in Spanish is PROGRESSIVE ASSIMILATION, in which the conditioning sound comes first, as in the phrase **un día** [uŋ-dí-a], where the preceding nasal [ŋ] causes the /d/ to be realized as a stop [d] rather than a fricative [đ], as it is in other phrases in which **día** occurs, such as **los días** [loz-đí-as], **este día** [és-te-đí-a], etc.

The distribution of Spanish consonants is somewhat more restricted than that of English consonants. Three- and four-consonant sequences, very common in English, as in *glimpsed* /glímpst/, *lengths* /léŋθs/, *texts*, /téksts/, etc. are very rare in Spanish, and they never occur in the same syllable, i.e., they do not form clusters as they do in English. Also, certain consonants, such as /p t k b g/ do not end words, and others like /ĉ/, /y/, and /x/ (in most dialects) do not even end syllables. Spanish-speakers occasionally pronounce these consonants in these positions in foreign words, but more often they eliminate them, as in **Nueva York** [nųé-ƀa-yór] or **vermut** [bęr-mú].

There are other important differences between the consonant systems of Spanish and English, all of which are taken up in detail in succeeding chapters. In addition to the distributional limitations just mentioned, Spanish stops are not aspirated as are English stops. Spanish has just as great a variety of fricative sounds as English but only five of them are phonemes /f y w x s/, whereas nine are in English /f v θ ð s z š ž h/. Spanish consonants assimilate very readily— even across word boundaries—whereas adjoining or contiguous English consonants in different words are often separated by a pause-like feature called plus juncture /+/, which prevents assimilation. For example, in Spanish /n/ is always velar [ŋ] before a velar consonant, whether in the same word or not: **encantar** [ęŋ-kaŋ-tár] or **en casa** [ęŋ-ká-sa]. But in English, although we find the same phenomenon within a word: *inky* /íŋkĭy/, there is usually a lack of assimilation between words: *inn key* /ín+kìy/.

Before passing to the individual consonant phonemes a word should be said about the "rules" or "formulas" used to indicate or summarize the allophonic distribution. Although somewhat complicated in appearance at first, they are quite simple when you become familiar with the use of each symbol.

/ /, of course, represents "phoneme."

→ means "is realized as" or "becomes."

[ ] represents "allophone."

/ means "in the environment of."

{ } to the left of the diagonal enclose allophones and { } to the right of the diagonal enclose the phonemes that form the phonetic environment.

represents silence, i.e., the pause before or after a phonemic phrase.

___ shows where the allophone in question occurs.

$\left[\right]$ enclose the entire "rule" or "statement" of the distribution. Other symbols will be explained as they occur. Thus, the rule

$$/d/ \longrightarrow \left[\begin{array}{l} [d] \ / \left\{ \begin{array}{l} \# \\ /n/ \\ /l/ \end{array} \right\} - \\ \left\{ \begin{array}{l} [đ] \\ [\text{Ø}] \end{array} \right\} / \text{word-final} \\ [đ] \ \text{elsewhere} \end{array} \right]$$

means that the phoneme /d/ is realized as the stop allophone [d] in the following environments: after a pause as in **Démelo** [dé-me-lo], after /n/, as in **grande** [grán-de], and after /l/, as in **aldea** [al-dé-a]. It is realized either as the fricative allophone [đ] or as silence [Ø] at the end of a word, as in **verdad** [ber-dáđ) or [ber-dá]. It is realized as the fricative [đ] everywhere else, as in **lado** [lá-đo], **verde** [bér-de], **Va a dármelo** [bá-dár-me-lo], etc.

Remember that the braces to the left of the diagonal indicate free variation, i.e., *either* or *any* allophone in the braces may be used in the environment indicated to the right of the diagonal. But the braces to the right of the diagonal indicate that the allophones to the left occur in ALL the environments in these braces to the right. Thus, EITHER [đ] or [Ø] ("silence") may occur in word-final position, but [d] occurs in absolute-initial position (after a pause) *and* after /n/ *and* after /l/, i.e., in all three environments. This usage will be followed in all such rules in the book.

Once the symbols are learned, you can see that the rule is not only a concise description of the behavior of the phoneme, but also a convenient device for quick review of the allophonic distribution. It should be emphasized that these "rules" are really statements of the allophonic distribution for General American Spanish, the dialect used as a standard in this book.

References

SPANISH

Alarcos Llorach, *Fonología española* (1965), Part I: Chapter II, Part II: Chapter III.

Allen, "Tense/Lax in Castilian Spanish" (1964).

Delattre, *Comparing the Phonetic Features of English, French, German, and Spanish* (1965).

Malmberg, *Estudios de fonética hispánica* (1965), Chapter I, III.

Martin, "Distinctive-Feature Systems of English and Spanish" (1965).

* Navarro, *Manual de pronunciación española* (1957), Sections 71–78.

* Politzer and Staubach, *Teaching Spanish: A Linguistic Orientation* (1965), Chapter VI.

Predmore, "Notes on Spanish Consonant Phonemes" (1946).

Rabanales, "Las siglas: un problema de fonología española " (1963).

* Stockwell and Bowen, *The Sounds of English and Spanish* (1965), Chapter V.

ENGLISH AND GENERAL

* Bronstein (1960), Chapter 11.

* Gleason, *An Introduction to Descriptive Linguistics* (1961), Chapter 2.

* Heffner, *General Phonetics* (1949), Chapters VI, VII.

* Malmberg, *Phonetics* (1963), Chapters V–VII.

Stetson, *Motor Phonetics* (1951), Chapters III–IV.

* Thomas, "Phonetic Change: Assimilation" (1965).

8

/ p t k /

8.1 Phonemes

/p/ is a voiceless, bilabial stop.
/t/ is a voiceless, dental stop.
/k/ is a voiceless, velar stop.

8.2 Allophones

[p] is a voiceless, bilabial stop.
[t] is a voiceless, dental stop.
[k] is a voiceless, velar stop.

8.3 Facial Diagrams

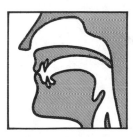   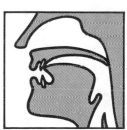   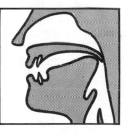

    [p]   [t]   [k]

8.4 Articulation

For [p] the two lips press together to stop the airstream, which is then released abruptly *without* aspiration.

For [t] the tongue tip presses against the back of the upper front teeth to stop the airstream, which is then released abruptly *without* aspiration.

For [k] the tongue dorsum presses against the velum to stop the airstream, which is then released abruptly *without* aspiration.

8.5 Allophonic Distribution

Although these consonants each have only one allophone, they all undergo certain modifications. /p/, since it is implosive or unreleased in syllable-final position, rather than explosive, weakens and sometimes disappears before /t/ in certain words, such as **séptimo** [sé-ti-mo]. In one common word, **se(p)tiembre,** the alternate spelling reflects this common pronunciation. The few words in Spanish that start with the letters **ps-** have no /p/ sound: **psicología** [si-ko-lo-xí-a.]

/t/ in syllable-final position before a voiced consonant is sometimes voiced to a fricative [đ]: **ritmo** [ř íd-mo], **Atlántico** [ađ-láṇ-ti-ko]. In a few words where **t** is written, such as **istmo** [ís-mo], there is no [t] sound.

/k/ in syllable-final position before any consonant is sometimes voiced to a fricative [g]: **actor** [ag-tór], **técnico** [tég-ni-ko]. It is often eliminated in rapid speech: **doctor** [do-tór], **exacto** [e-sák-to]. It is often eliminated in word-final position of foreign words: **coñac** [ko-ñá], **Nueva York** [nu̯é-ba-yór].

The following rules summarize the allophonic distribution of these three consonant phonemes in General American Spanish.

$$/p/ \longrightarrow \left[\begin{array}{l} \left\{ \begin{array}{l} [p] \\ [\text{Ø}] \end{array} \right\} \Big/ \begin{array}{l} \text{in } \textbf{séptimo,} \\ \textbf{se(p)tiembre} \end{array} \\ [p] \text{ elsewhere} \end{array} \right]$$

$$/t/ \longrightarrow \left[\begin{array}{l} \left\{ \begin{array}{l} [t] \\ [đ] \end{array} \right\} \Big/ \underline{\quad}/C_v/ \\ [t] \text{ elsewhere} \end{array} \right]$$

$/C_v/$ is any voiced consonant.

$$/k/ \longrightarrow \left[\begin{array}{l} \left\{ \begin{array}{l} [k] \\ [g] \end{array} \right\} \Big/ \underline{\quad}/C/ \\ [k] \text{ elsewhere} \end{array} \right]$$

8.6 Dialectal Variations

The above modifications occur in rapid speech in all dialects of Spanish.

8.7 Contrasts with English

The most important contrast is the fact that /p t k/ are always unaspirated in Spanish, but they are aspirated in English in word-initial position or at the beginning of a heavy-stressed syllable: *part, till, cur, apart, until, occur.* Although the aspiration of these consonants does not affect meaning in Spanish, it sounds strange and helps to create a "foreign accent."

/t/ is dental in Spanish but alveolar in English. Sometimes in English /t/ in an intervocalic position is realized as a tap or flap, as in *water, butter,* etc. Spanish also has this tap sound, but it is the /r/. Thus, you must be careful to make a dental stop for Spanish /t/ even in an intervocalic position. If you carry over your English habit of articulation, such words as **moto, foto, meta** will sound like **moro, foro, mera.**

The lack of aspiration with Spanish/ p t k/ may also make them difficult for you to distinguish from /b d g/ in such pairs as **paño-baño, tomar-domar, callo-gallo.** You tend to "hear" voicing in these non-aspirated voiceless stops and may sometimes even produce the voiced stops when attempting to imitate the voiceless ones.

8.8 References

SPANISH

Allen, "Tense/Lax in Castilian Spanish" (1964).
* Bowen and Stockwell, *Patterns of Spanish Pronunciation* (1960), Chapter 3.
* Gili Gaya, *Elementos de fonética general* (1950), Chapter IX.
Malmberg, *"Obtativo y sujuntivo:* A propósito de dos grafías" (1965).
* Navarro, *Manual de pronunciación española* (1957), Sections 79, 83, 98, 125, 128.

ENGLISH AND GENERAL

* Bronstein (1960), Chapter 4.
* Buchanan (1963), Chapter IV.

8.9 Drills

A   Recognition

Your teacher will pronounce a series of words, some of which begin with /p t k/ *and some of which begin with the voiced counterparts* /b d g/.

*Identify the voiceless phonemes by saying "one" if the word begins with
/p t k/ and identify the voiced phonemes by saying "two" if the word
begins with /b d g/.*

1. cama	11. tanza	21. pelar
2. bala	12. domar	22. domar
3. dato	13. paz	23. cama
4. tomar	14. gata	24. gola
5. ganso	15. vender	25. canso
6. vino	16. teja	26. taba
7. pista	17. pender	27. cola
8. panal	18. pino	28. penado
9. callo	19. vista	29. palón
10. gama	20. panal	30. venado

B Recognition

*Your teacher will pronounce a series of three-word groups. After each
group, pick out the one word which is* different *from the other two by
saying "first," "second," or "third," as the case may be. For example,
if he says* **pan van pan,** *say "second." However, say "All are the same"
if he says* **pan pan pan.**

1. paca paca vaca	11. di ti ti
2. daba taba taba	12. ganas canas ganas
3. gala gala cala	13. vez vez pez
4. pan pan pan	14. teja deja teja
5. danza tanza danza	15. goza cosa goza
6. cordura gordura cordura	16. poca boca boca
7. prisa prisa prisa	17. tomar tomar tomar
8. té té dé	18. codo codo godo
9. coma coma coma	19. besar pesar pesar
10. beca peca beca	20. tan dan dan

C Repetition

Repeat the word after your teacher.

1. paño	9. tato	17. teja
2. vino	10. dan	18. camba
3. teja	11. cana	19. pelar
4. domar	12. godo	20. penado
5. cancho	13. vender	21. ti
6. gasa	14. deja	22. calesa
7. panal	15. gamba	23. cola
8. borra	16. pender	24. pista
	25. pagar	

D Recognition-Production

After your teacher says a word beginning with a voiceless stop, say the corresponding word beginning with a voiced stop, and vice versa. For example, for **pino** *say* **vino**; *for* **domar** *say* **tomar**; *for* **casa** *say* **gasa**.

1. penado	7. pega	13. dan
2. boca	8. brisa	14. daba
3. dé	9. gallo	15. pino
4. gasa	10. té	16. pista
5. deja	11. cordura	17. besar
6. gancho	12. cama	18. cata
	19. gala 20. tonar	

E Repetition

Repeat the minimal pairs after your teacher.

1. pagar-vagar	8. pelar-velar	15. tan-dan
2. té-dé	9. tomar-domar	16. canso-ganso
3. cama-gama	10. cota-gota	17. panal-banal
4. pasar-basar	11. paño-baño	18. tato-dato
5. y cuál-igual	12. ti-di	19. cosa-goza
6. palón-balón	13. coma-goma	20. pega-vega
7. taba-daba	14. porra-borra	21. cola-gola

F Repetition

Repeat the phrases and sentences after your teacher.

1. Tomarlo es necesario.
2. Me canso mucho.
3. Pásame la sal.
4. Té helado, por favor.
5. ¿Cómo se dice eso en español?
6. ¡Pégale fuerte, hombre!
7. ¿Tan rico él?
8. Coca cola, por favor.
9. Págalo en seguida.
10. ¿Qué quieres, Carlos?
11. Papá, permíteme pelar las papas.
12. Teodoro, no tomas té con tenedor.
13. Quico, no comes carne con cuchara.
14. Pablo, no pelas papas con pala.

G Question-Answer

Answer the questions in the affirmative with a complete sentence.

1. ¿Pasará usted las vacaciones en Panamá?
2. ¿Toma usted mucho té?

3. ¿Quiere usted coca cola?
4. ¿Paga usted con esta plata?
5. ¿Tienes que ir a Tejas mañana?
6. ¿Come Carlos con usted?
7. ¿Podemos jugar en esa pista?
8. ¿Su tío tenía tanta plata?
9. ¿Cuestan mucho esas cosas?
10. ¿Metió usted la pata?

H   Read Aloud (books open)

Read the sentences aloud.

1. Pablo, quiero tomar una taza de café.
2. Tomás, ¿a ti te gusta más el té o la coca cola?
3. Carlos, ¿cuándo te vas para la tierra de Tejas?
4. Papá, quisiera tener tanta ropa como tu tío, Teófilo.
5. Pepe, no puedes pasar por su casa tan temprano.
6. ¡Caramba, Quico, cuando comes carne con cuchara, te creen loco!
7. Camilo, no permitas que Paco te pague con esas pesetas. Mejor que te pague con esos pesos.

8.10 Exercises

A

Give an articulatory description for /p/, for /t/, for /k/. Then check your answers in section 8.2.

B

Sketch a facial diagram for /p/, for /t/, for /k/. Then check the diagrams in section 8.3. Notice that the velum is closed for all of these sounds since they are oral rather than nasal.

9

~~~~~~

/ b /

9.1 Phonemes

/b/ is a voiced, bilabial stop.

9.2 Allophones

[b] is a voiced, bilabial stop.
[ƀ] is a voiced, bilabial slit fricative.
[v] is a voiced, labio-dental slit fricative.

9.3 Facial Diagrams

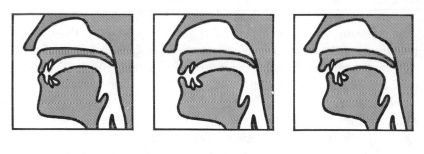

[b]   [ƀ]   [v]

9.4 Articulation

For [b] the two lips press together to stop the airstream, which is then
released abruptly without aspiration. The vocal bands vibrate, distinguishing

[b] from [p].

For [ƀ] the two lips almost touch, and the airstream, without stopping, passes through the slit formed between them. The vocal bands vibrate.

For [v] the lower lip lightly touches the edge of the upper front teeth, and the airstream, without stopping, passes through the slit formed by the lip and teeth. The vocal bands vibrate.

9.5 Allophonic Distribution

The phoneme /b/ has two main allophones, the stop [b] and the fricative [ƀ]. The stop occurs in absolute-initial position, i.e., after a pause at the beginning of the phonemic phrase, and also after [m]. The fricative occurs everywhere else. Thus, the two are in complementary distribution. **Voy a casa** is [bó-ya-ká-sa] but **Yo voy a casa** is [yó-ƀó-ya-ká-sa]. The fricative occurs here since the phoneme is no longer in the absolute-initial position. Also **el vaso** is [ęl-ƀá-so] but **un vaso** is [um-bá-so]. The stop is used since the phoneme follows [m].

Regardless of word boundaries and spelling— **-mb-, -n b-, -nv-** —the sequence of nasal + /b/ is always [mb]: **hombre** [óm-bre], **un buen día** [um-bu̯ę́ṇ-dí-a], **enviar** [ęm-bi̯ár]. Regressive assimilation to /b/ causes the nasal to be realized as [m], and progressive assimilation to the nasal causes /b/ to be realized as [b].

There are two reasons for the occurrence of labio-dental [v]. It is either in free variation with [ƀ] and occurs sporadically, or it is a hyper-corrected pronunciation used principally in words spelled with *v*. However, [v] is *not* phonemic in any dialect or idiolect of Spanish and is never contrasted with [ƀ] in the stream of speech. Even the speakers who use it because they feel it is more cultured and "correct" rarely do so consistently. This shows up when they attempt to learn a foreign language such as English or French where /v/ and /b/ are phonemic. A Spanish-speaker inevitably confuses the two sounds at first, showing that they have no contrastive function in Spanish.

Speakers who occasionally use [v] for [ƀ] unintentionally and sporadically never correlate their pronunciation with the written form. **Haber** and **a ver** might both be pronounced [a-vę́r] at one time and [a-ƀę́r] at another.

The fricative [ƀ] also disappears in certain sequences, particularly /ob-/ and /sub-/ at the beginning of words: **obstáculo** [os-tá-ku-lo], **subjetivo** [su-xe-tí-ƀo]. In many words which begin with /obs-/ and /subs-/, such as **o(b)scuro, su(b)scribir, su(b)stituir,** the alternate spellings reflect the disappearance of the [ƀ] in pronunciation.

Sometimes /b/ before another consonant, particularly /t/, is pronounced [p] due to regressive assimilation: **obtener** [op-te-nę́r].

The rule for /b/:

$$/b/ \longrightarrow \begin{bmatrix} [b] \Big/ \left\{ \begin{matrix} \# \\ /m/ \end{matrix} \right\} - \\[2ex] [\text{Ø}] \Big/ \left\{ \begin{matrix} /\text{o}\underline{\text{b}}\text{-}/ \\ /\text{su}\underline{\text{b}}\text{-}/ \end{matrix} \right\} \\[2ex] [\text{ƀ}] \text{ elsewhere} \end{bmatrix}$$

9.6 Dialectal Variations

With many speakers of Spanish, [v] is rarely heard. Its occasional use seems to be purely a matter of idiolect and speech level (hyper-correction with certain educated speakers) rather than of dialect.

All over the Spanish-speaking world speakers often use [b] in place of [ƀ] in careful speech, particularly in word-initial position. Thus, while a phrase like **la vaca** is [la-ƀá-ka] in rapid speech, it is often [la-bá-ka] in careful speech. **Es bueno** is either [éz-ƀu̯é-no] or [éz-bu̯é-no]. However, you should make an effort to produce the fricative [b] in these cases since it is always correct while sometimes the stop [b] might sound unnatural.

9.7 Contrasts with English

The most important contrast is the fact that [v] is not phonemic in Spanish and that the spelling **v** most often represents either [b] or [ƀ]. Because of such contrasts in English as *TB-TV*, *berry-very*, etc., you may feel that the same contrast should be made in Spanish between **tubo** and **tuvo**—really both [tú-ƀo] —or between **la sabes** and **las aves**—both [la-sá-ƀes]. But such groups are *not* minimal pairs in Spanish and are pronounced exactly the same by all speakers in natural speech. You tend to equate [ƀ] with your own [v], partly because the two sounds are acoustically similar and partly because [ƀ] is often spelled with **v**.

The sound [v] has never been used consistently and contrastively in modern Spanish anywhere in the world, as far as dialectologists know. The Spanish Academy long ago gave up in its efforts to convince Spanish-speakers that there was an important difference between [v] and [b] or [ƀ]. The fact that a word like **bien** is spelled with a **b** and **viene** with **v** is merely an orthographic tradition carried down from Latin (where there was a phonemic difference) and in no way reflects a contrast today. Thus, it is best for you to avoid [v] in Spanish.

9.8 References

SPANISH

* Bowen and Stockwell, *Patterns of Spanish Pronunciation* (1960), Chapter 3.
* Gili Gaya, *Elementos de fonética general* (1950), Chapters IX, X.

Malmberg, "*Obtativo* y *sujuntivo:* A propósito de dos grafías" (1965).
* Navarro, *Manual de pronunciación española* (1957), Sections 80–84, 90, 91.

ENGLISH AND GENERAL

* Bronstein (1960), Chapter 4.
* Buchanan (1963), Chapter IV.

9.9 Drills

A   Recognition

Your teacher will pronounce a series of words and phrases, some of which have the correct and most natural allophone of /b/ and some of which do not. Identify the best use of the stop [b] and the fricative [b̵] by saying "correct" or "incorrect."

1. baile [b]	11. la vuelta [b̵]	21. el baile [b̵]
2. Venga aquí [v]	12. Venga aquí [b]	22. la vuelta [v]
3. este vaso [v]	13. baile [b̵]	23. este vaso [b̵]
4. la última vez [b̵]	14. un vaso [b̵]	24. Bótalo [b̵]
5. el baile [b]	15. viejo [v]	25. una visita [v]
6. vamos [b]	16. el vino [b̵]	26. un vaso [b]
7. enviar [v]	17. la última vez [b]	27. el vino [b]
8. Bótalo [b]	18. enviar [b]	28. una visita [b̵]
9. un vaso [v]	19. ambos [b]	29. Buenos días [b]
10. ambos [b̵]	20. Buenos días [b̵]	30. viejo [b]

B   Recognition

Your teacher will pronounce a series of three-word groups. After each group, pick out the one word which is different *from the other two by saying "first," "second," or "third," as the case may be. However, if they are all different or all the same, say so.*

1. baile [b] baile [b] baile [b]	11. el buzón [b] —[b̵] —[b̵]
2. la voz [b̵] —[b] —[v]	12. una broma [b] —[b̵] —[b̵]
3. labio [b] —[b] —[b̵]	13. Véalo [b] —[b] —[v]
4. ambos [b] —[b] —[b]	14. Me voy [b̵] —[b] —[b̵]
5. tuvo [v] —[b̵] —[b̵]	15. un vuelo [b] —[b] —[v]
6. vuelta [b̵] —[b] —[b̵]	16. la boda [v] —[v] —[b̵]
7. también [b] —[b̵] —[b]	17. Bébalo [b b̵] —[b b] —[b b]
8. salvar [v] —[b̵] —[b]	18. un bocadillo [b] —[b] —[b]
9. estuviste [b̵] —[b̵] —[b̵]	19. este bocadillo [b̵] —[b̵] —[b̵]
10. un vapor [b] —[b] —[b]	20. las uvas [b̵] —[v] —[v]

C   Transformation

After your teacher says a word with the definite article, say the word with the indefinite article and vice versa. For example, for **el vaso,** *say* **un vaso;** *for* **una vez,** *say* **la vez.**

1. el baile	7. un barrio	13. el bebé
2. la voz	8. una viuda	14. la bala
3. un boleto	9. el verano	15. un bastón
4. una vela	10. la vuelta	16. una broma
5. el banco	11. un vago	17. el bulto
6. la vista	12. una vida	18. la vaca

19. un viaje   20. una botella

D   Repetition

Repeat the word or phrase after your teacher.

1. vuelve	10. lo vende	19. el banco
2. no vuelve	11. vale mucho	20. un banco
3. va	12. esto vale mucho	21. boleto
4. no va	13. bebe leche	22. el boleto
5. vamos	14. no bebe leche	23. un boleto
6. no vamos	15. vaso	24. bocadillo
7. viene	16. el vaso	25. el bocadillo
8. Juan viene	17. un vaso	26. un bocadillo
9. vende	18. banco	27. viejo

28. el viejo   29. un viejo

E   Repetition

Repeat the phrase after your teacher.

1. Voy al baile.	6. Lo envié cuando estaba en Venezuela.
2. Volvemos al banco.	
3. Me levanto temprano en el invierno.	7. Ven acá, Benito.
	8. Ese vago está borracho.
4. Tuve que comer las uvas.	9. Venda usted ambos.
5. Esta vaca no vale nada.	10. Suba con otro vaso.

11. Hay que botar esas botellas.

F   Transformation

Transform the following affirmative commands into negative commands. For example, after **Véndalo,** *say* **No lo venda.**

1. Bébalo.
2. Baile aquí.
3. Bótelo.
4. Véalo.
5. Vuelva mañana.

6. Viaje en tren.
7. Vuele a México.
8. Viva en el campo.
9. Vaya a casa.
10. Venga aquí.

G   "Live" Transcription

Your teacher will read a brief passage in Spanish. Just listen the first time. Then he will read the passage, one phonemic phrase at a time. Take each phrase down in phonetic *transcription, using conventional letters for the sounds you have not studied yet. Each phrase will be repeated several times. Then the entire passage will be read once more; and you can check your transcription a final time. The correct transcription is found in* Appendix D. *The allophones you have studied so far and are expected to know are underlined.*

9.10 Exercises

A

Give an articulatory description for [b], *for* [ƀ]. *Then check your answers in Section 9.2.*

B

Sketch a facial diagram for [b], *for* [ƀ]. *Be sure the velum is closed. Indicate voicing by drawing a few zig-zag lines for the vocal bands. Then check your diagrams in Section 9.3.*

C

Make a PHONEMIC *transcription of the following passage. Use spaces, as usual, to indicate pauses. Remember that you are transcribing only the phonemes. Here and in all future transcription exercises, consider that the speaker is speaking General American Spanish. Then check your transcription in* Appendix D. *The phonemes you have studied so far are underlined.*

—¿Viene Benito a verte el sábado?
—No, ¡qué va! Va a visitar a Pablo, que vive en Venezuela.
—¿Va a volar?
—Sí, fue al banco a cambiar un cheque para sacar el boleto.

D

Now make a PHONETIC *transcription of the same passage in Exercise C, but this time indicate* allophones *instead of phonemes. Of the allophones you have studied so far, use only the following standard ones:* [p t k b ƀ]. *Use conventional letters for the sounds you have not studied yet. Then check your transcription in* Appendix D. *The allophones studied so far are under-lined.*

10

/ d /

10.1 Phonemes

/d/ is a voiced, dental stop.

10.2 Allophones

[d] is a voiced, dental stop.
[đ] is a voiced, dental slit fricative.

10.3 Facial Diagrams

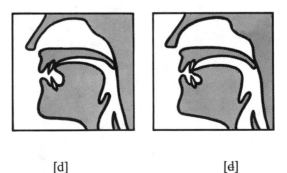

[d]   [đ]

10.4 Articulation

For [d] the tip of the tongue presses against the back of the upper front teeth, thus stopping the airstream, which is released with a slight explosion.

The vocal bands vibrate, distinguishing [d] from [t]. For [đ] the tip of the tongue is placed very lightly against either the back or the edges of the upper front teeth. The airstream, rather than being stopped, passes through the slit formed by the tongue and teeth. Sometimes [đ] is interdental, since the tongue can touch both the upper and lower teeth at the same time, like the English /ð/ in *this*.

10.5 Allophonic Distribution

The phoneme /d/ has two principal allophones, the stop [d] and the fricative [đ]. The stop occurs in absolute-initial position, after /n/, and after /l/. The fricative occurs everywhere else. Thus, the two are in complementary distribution. **Dámelo** is [dá-me-lo], **mandar** is [maṇ-dár], **aldea** is [al-dé-a], but **Va a dármelo** is [bá-dár-me-lo], **cada** is [ká-đa], **es de aquí** is [éz-đe-a-kí].

The sequence of nasal + /d/ is always [ṇd]: **mundo** [múṇ-do]. Regressive assimilation to /d/ causes the nasal to be realized as a dental [ṇ], and progressive assimilation to the nasal causes /d/ to be realized as the stop [d].

The intervocalic [đ] in all dialects of Spanish is usually quite soft and weak and sometimes disappears completely. Most Spanish-speakers, including educated ones, occasionally eliminate it in words ending in **-ado,** such as **tomado** [to-má-o], and usually eliminate it in word-final position, such as **usted** [us-té]. In fact, a prominent [đ] in these cases can even sound affected. However, the elimination of [đ] in other combinations, such as **nada** [ná-a] or [ná], **tomada** [to-má-a], or **boda** [bó-a] is considered sub-standard, even in rapid speech.

The rule for /d/:

$$
/d/ \longrightarrow \begin{bmatrix} [d] \Big/ \begin{Bmatrix} \# \\ /n/ \\ /l/ \end{Bmatrix} — \\[2ex] \begin{Bmatrix} [đ] \\ [\varnothing] \end{Bmatrix} \Big/ \begin{Bmatrix} \text{word-final} \\ /\text{-ado}/ \end{Bmatrix} \\[2ex] [đ] \text{ elsewhere} \end{bmatrix}
$$

10.6 Dialectal Variations

All over the Spanish-speaking world speakers often use [d] in place of [đ] in careful speech, particularly in word-initial position (just as they do with [b]). Thus, while a phrase like **las damas** is [laz-đá-mas] in rapid speech, it is often [laz-dá-mas] in careful speech. However, you should make an effort to produce the fricative [đ] in these cases since it is always correct while sometimes the stop [d] might sound unnatural.

10.7 Contrasts with English

You must be careful to articulate /d/ as a *dental* rather than as an alveolar as it is in English. /d/ in English has a tap allophone [đ] in a post-tonic (after the stress) intervocalic position, as in *muddy, ladder*, etc. But this sound is just like the Spanish tap /r/. Thus, if you use this [đ] for the Spanish [đ] in such words as **modo, todo, mida,** they will sound like **moro, toro, mira.** It is best for you, at first at least, to exaggerate the Spanish [đ] and pronounce it as interdentally as the English /ð/ of *father*. Even though English /ð/ is more forceful and more interdental than Spanish [đ], its conscious use will keep you from your tendency to pronounce the tap [đ], which will always be confused with Spanish /r/.

Also, you must avoid aspirating the Spanish /d/ in word-initial position or at the beginning of accented syllables as you do in English. Just as with /t/ this aspiration does not affect meaning in Spanish, but it sounds strange. Usually this aspiration can be avoided simply by making the /d/ dental instead of alveolar.

10.8 References

SPANISH

* Bowen and Stockwell, *Patterns of Spanish Pronunciation* (1960), Chapter 3.
* Gili Gaya, *Elementos de fonética general* (1950), Chapters IX, X.
* Navarro, *Manual de pronunciación española* (1957), Sections 99, 102.

ENGLISH AND GENERAL

* Bronstein (1960), Chapter 4.
* Buchanan (1963), Chapter IV.

10.9 Drills

A   Recognition

Your teacher will pronounce a series of minimal pairs, containing the /r/-/d/ contrast. Identify these phonemes by saying **ere-de** *or* **de-ere**, *depending on which order they occur in the pair.*

1. moro-modo	5. duro-dudo	9. miro-mido
2. toro-todo	6. hablada-hablara	10. seda-sera
3. estados-estaros	7. cada-cara	11. amada-amara
4. lloro-yodo	8. oda-ora	12. loro-lodo

B   Repetition

Repeat the word after your teacher.

1. moro	7. cara	13. duro
2. lodo	8. mida	14. oda
3. hablada	9. todo	15. modo
4. jugara	10. tomada	16. estados
5. muro	11. sera	17. uniros
6. lloro	12. amada	18. coro

19. seda   20. yodo

C   Recognition-Production

Say the "opposite" word. If your teacher says **moro,** *say* **modo.** *If he says* **dudo,** *say* **duro.**

1. mira	6. hablara	11. loro
2. toro	7. miro	12. amara
3. mido	8. hora	13. mudo
4. codo	9. cada	14. tomara
5. dudo	10. unidos	15. estaros

16. jugara

D   Repetition

Repeat the word after your teacher.

1. dar	12. estado	23. pidan
2. dado	13. dónde	24. hablado
3. día	14. dormir	25. guardando
4. oda	15. diente	26. podría
5. quedan	16. divertir	27. dolor
6. aldea	17. barbudo	28. ponderar
7. yendo	18. alrededor	29. desayuno
8. hablando	19. pidiendo	30. derecho
9. despertador	20. doctor	31. indio
10. falda	21. ido	32. tomado
11. despacio	22. andando	33. grande

34. poder   35. dormido

E Repetition

Repeat the words and phrases after your teacher.

1. día	16. doctor	31. docena
2. el día	17. el doctor	32. la docena
3. este día	18. este doctor	33. las docenas
4. buenos días	19. los doctores	34. una docena
5. en días	20. buscan doctores	35. en docenas
6. dulce	21. dónde	36. duerme
7. el dulce	22. adónde	37. no duerme
8. los dulces	23. de dónde	38. él duerme
9. este dulce	24. para dónde	39. ellos duermen
10. con dulces	25. por dónde	40. Juan duerme
11. dolor	26. el dedo	41. dueña
12. el dolor	27. este dedo	42. la dueña
13. con dolor	28. los dedos	43. las dueñas
14. este dolor	29. ese dedo	44. tienen dueña
15. los dolores	30. esos dedos	45. tiene dueña

F Repetition

Repeat the words after your teacher.

1. verdad	9. amistad	17. pared
2. la verdad	10. la amistad	18. la pared
3. bondad	11. usted	19. red
4. la bondad	12. con usted	20. la red
5. ciudad	13. Madrid	21. habilidad
6. la ciudad	14. en Madrid	22. con habilidad
7. tempestad	15. Valladolid	23. virtud
8. la tempestad	16. a Valladolid	24. una virtud

G Question-Answer

Answer the question in the affirmative with a complete sentence.

1. ¿Pide usted más tiempo?
2. ¿Guarda usted este libro?
3. ¿Mide usted la caja?
4. ¿Puede usted hacerlo?
5. ¿Se queda usted?
6. ¿Nadan ustedes mucho?
7. ¿Recuerdan ustedes el nombre?
8. ¿Reducen ustedes la cantidad?
9. ¿Tardan ustedes mucho tiempo en llegar?
10. ¿Tienen ustedes mucho cuidado?

H Transformation

Transform the affirmative statement to a negative one. For example, after **Duerme ocho horas,** *say* **No duerme ocho horas.**

1. Debe mucho dinero.
2. Dice esas cosas.
3. Desayuna con jamón.

4. Divierte a sus compañeros.
5. Da dinero a los pobres.
6. Despierta a sus padres.

I   Transformation

Transform the statement in present tense to one in the present perfect. For example, after **Habla,** *say* **Ha hablado.**

1. Toma mucho vino.
2. Vive en España.
3. Come mucho.

4. Juega al fútbol.
5. Sale a la calle.
6. Entiende todo.

J   Read Aloud (books open)

Read the following passage aloud.

El doctor le dijo que no podía quedarse en este clima y que tendría que dormir más y comer menos.

—Pero, doctor, ¿adónde iré para vivir de este modo? Y no puedo dormir más si me despiertan tan temprano todos los días. Me gusta demasiado divertirme con deportes, con dulces y con discos.

K   "Live" Transcription

Your teacher will read a brief passage in Spanish. Just listen the first time. Then he will read the passage, one phonemic phrase at a time. Take each phrase down in phonetic *transcription, using conventional letters for the sounds you have not studied yet. Each phrase will be repeated several times. Then the entire passage will be read once more, and you can check your transcription a final time. The correct transcription is found in* Appendix D. *The allophones you have studied so far and are expected to know are underlined.*

10.10 Exercises

A

Give an articulatory description for [d], *for* [đ]. *Then check your answers in Section* 10.2.

B

Sketch a facial diagram for [d], *for* [d̶]. *Be sure the velum is closed. Indicate voicing by drawing a few zig-zag lines for the vocal bands. Then check your diagrams in Section* 10.3.

C

Make a PHONEMIC *transcription of the following passage. Use spaces, as usual, to indicate pauses. Remember that you are transcribing only the phonemes. Here and in all future transcription exercises, consider that the speaker is speaking General American Spanish. Then check your transcription in* Appendix D. *The phonemes you have studied so far are underlined.*

—Eduardo me dijo que Renaldo todavía le debía mucho dinero. Cuando me vio, me preguntó dónde andaba Renaldo en estos días.

Y le respondí que no sabía nada.

D

Now make a PHONETIC *transcription of the same passage in Exercise C. But this time indicate* allophones *instead of phonemes. Of the allophones you have studied so far, use only the following standard ones:* [p t k b b̶ d d̶]. *Use conventional letters for the sounds you have not studied yet. Then check your transcription in* Appendix D. *The allophones studied so far are underlined.*

11

/ g / *AND* / w /

11.1 Phonemes

/g/ is a voiced, velar stop.
/w/ is a voiced, bilabio-velar slit fricative.

11.2 Allophones

[g] is a voiced, velar stop, allophone of /g/.
[g] is a voiced, velar slit fricative, allophone of /g/.
[w] is a voiced, bilabio-velar slit fricative, allophone of /w/.

11.3 Facial Diagrams

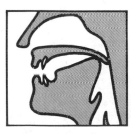
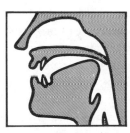
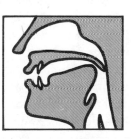

[g]   [g]   [w]

II.4 Articulation

For [g] the dorsum or back of the tongue presses against the velum, thus stopping the airstream, which is released with a slight explosion. The vocal bands vibrate, distinguishing [g] from [k]. For [g̵] the back of the tongue is placed very lightly against or very close to the velum. The airstream, rather than being stopped, passes through the slit formed by the tongue and the velum. It is practically the same sound as is heard in the rapid pronunciation of *sugar* and *beggar* in English.

For [w] the back of the tongue comes almost as close to the velum as it does for [g̵], but at the same time the lips are rounded as for the vowel /u/. [w] is almost the same as [u] and [u̯], except that phonetically the closure is greater for [w] and phonemically [w] functions as a consonant while [u] and [u̯] are both vowels.

II.5 Allophonic Distribution

The phoneme /g/ has two principal allophones, the stop [g] and the fricative [g̵]. The stop occurs in absolute-initial position and after /n/. The fricative occurs everywhere else. Thus, the two are in complementary distribution. **Grande** is [grán-de], **tengo** is [téŋ-go], but **qué grande** is [ké-grán-de], **hago** is [á-go̵], **los gatos** is [loz-gá-tos].

The sequence of nasal + /g/ is always [ŋg]: **pongo** [póŋ-go]. Regressive assimilation to /g/ causes the nasal to be realized as a velar [ŋ], and progressive assimilation to the nasal causes /g/ to be realized as the stop [g].

The intervocalic [g̵] in all dialects of Spanish is usually quite soft and weak, and the sequence [g̵u̯] is often replaced by [w], as in **agua,** which is [á-g̵u̯a] or [á-wa].

Sometimes syllable-final [g̵] disappears, such as **indigno** [in-dí-no]. In the same position [g̵] often replaces [k]: **actor** [ag̵-tór].

Bilabio-velar [w] is phonetically very close to [g̵], except that the lips are rounded as they are for [u] or [u̯]. In most dialects of Spanish [w] and [g̵u̯] alternate in such words as **hueso** [wé-so] or [g̵u̯é-so], **la huerta** [la-wȩ́r-ta] or [la-g̵u̯ȩ́r-ta]. The stop [g] is also heard in these combinations in absolute-initial position and after /n/, as in **huele bien** [gu̯é-le-bi̯ȩ́n] and **un hueso** [uŋ-gu̯é-so]. The words in which [w] and [g̵u̯] alternate are spelled with **hu-, gu-,** or **gü-,** as in **hueso, huidizo, guardar, antiguo, vergüenza,** in addition to a few foreign words that begin with **w-: Wáshington, wáter.** It would really make no difference whether these words were spelled with **g-** or **h-** as in *güeso, *ahua, etc. However, a distinction can be made in careful speech between such pairs as **de huellas** [de-wé-yas] *from tracks* and **degüellas** [de-gu̯é-yas] *you behead*, thus proving the existence of two phonemic sequences /w/ and /gu/.

The rules for /g/ and /w/:

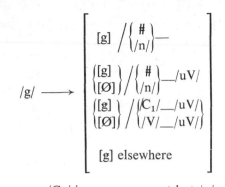

/C₁/ is any consonant but /n/.

The second and third parts of the rule refer to the alternation of /gu/ with /w/. In absolute-initial position or after /n/ the sequence is either [gu̯] plus vowel or /w/ plus vowel as in **Huele bien** [gu̯é-le-b̞i̯én] or [wé-le-b̞i̯én] or **un huerto** [uŋ-gu̯ér-to] or [uŋ-wér-to]. In other cases the sequence is either [gu̯] plus vowel or /w/ plus vowel as in **no huele bien** [nó-gu̯é-le-b̞i̯én] or [nó-wé-le-b̞i̯én], or **el huerto** [el̞-gu̯ér-to] or [el̞-wér-to].

$$/w/ \longrightarrow \begin{bmatrix} \begin{Bmatrix} [w] \\ [gu̯] \end{Bmatrix} / \begin{Bmatrix} \# \\ /n/ \end{Bmatrix} \underline{\hphantom{xx}} \\[2ex] \begin{Bmatrix} [w] \\ [gu̯] \end{Bmatrix} \text{ elsewhere} \end{bmatrix}$$

11.6 Dialectal Variations

In the speech of many uneducated or rural Spanish-speakers [w], [gu̯], and [gu̯] not only alternate with each other but often replace [bu̯] or [b̞u̯] in such words as **bueno** [wé-no], [gu̯é-no], [gu̯é-no], **abuela** [a-wé-la] or [a-gu̯é-la]. These variations, however, are considered sub-standard by educated speakers, and authors often indicate this regional or rustic speech by such spellings as "**agücla**", "**guesos**", "**güenos días**", etc. The alternation of [w] and [gu̯], as in **agua** and **hueso,** however, is common among educated speakers.

11.7 Contrasts with English

Just like /b/ and /d/, /g/ is not aspirated in Spanish as it is in English in word-initial position or at the beginning of an accented syllable. However, because /g/ is pronounced farther back in the mouth, such aspiration will be less noticeable than with /b/ and /d/.

Fricative [g], although not nearly as common in English as in Spanish, does exist in rapid speech in such words as *sugar* and *beggar*.

In Spanish /w/ the velar element is the most important while in the English /w/, as a consonant, the bilabial element is most important. However, this fact seems to trouble Spanish-speakers learning English more than it does you as English-speakers learning Spanish. Substituting an English consonantal /w/ for the Spanish /w/ has no effect on meaning and does not sound strange, but when Spanish-speakers use their /w/ in place of English consonantal /w/, it always sounds to English-speakers like they are saying /g/ first, as in *will* */gwil/ or *would* */gwud/.

11.8 References

SPANISH

* Bowen and Stockwell, *Patterns of Spanish Pronunciation* (1960), Chapter 3.
* Gili Gaya, *Elementos de fonética general* (1950), Chapters IX, X.
  Malmberg, *Estudios de fonética hispánica* (1965), Chapter IV.
  ——, "Phonèmes labio-vélaires en espagnol?" (1961).
* Navarro, *Manual de pronunciación española* (1957), Sections 126, 127.

ENGLISH AND GENERAL

* Bronstein (1960), Chapters, 4, 6.
* Buchanan (1963), Chapter IV.

11.9 Drills

A   Recognition

Your teacher will pronounce a series of words and phrases, some of which have the correct and most natural allophone of /g/ and some of which do not. Identify the best use of the stop [g] and the fricative [g] by saying "correct" *or* "incorrect."

1. gafas [g]	11. la gota [g]	21. llega [g]
2. gota [g]	12. guardia [g]	22. la guerra [g]
3. pongo [g]	13. gallo [g]	23. es gordo [g]
4. es grande [g]	14. tengo [g]	24. jugo [g]
5. gordo [g]	15. muchas gracias [g]	25. agradable [g]
6. la gana [g]	16. guerra [g]	26. hago [g]
7. aguardar [g]	17. la guardia [g]	27. no gana [g]
8. gritar [g]	18. juego [g]	29. negro [g]
9. gracias [g]	19. angustia [g]	29. gusto [g]
10. vengo [g]	20. me gusta [g]	30. con mucho gusto [g]

B   Transformation

After your teacher says a word with the definite article, say the word with the indefinite article and vice versa. For example, for **el gato,** *say* **un gato;** *for* **un grito,** *say* **el grito.**

1. el gato	6. un gabán	11. el gancho
2. un gallo	7. el golpe	12. un gato
3. el gordo	8. un gorrión	13. el gallo
4. un grupo	9. el grado	14. un gordo
5. el guante	10. un guardia	15. el grupo

C   Repetition (books open)

Repeat the word or phrase after your teacher, following along in the book as you do.

1. gusto	12. traigo	22. voy a jugar
2. el gusto	13. ángulo	23. vamos a jugar en este lugar
3. gato	14. agrio	24. ¿cuándo llega?
4. un gato	15. igual	25. es una ganga
5. este gato	16. engaña	26. es una gran ganga
6. digo	17. me gusta	27. golpe
7. pongo	18. no me gusta	28. le di un golpe
8. hago	19. me gusta este	29. le di unos golpes
9. tengo	color negro	30. guía
10. salgo	20. trágueselo	31. un guía
11. vengo	21. juego	32. es un buen guía

D   Repetition (books open)

Repeat the word or phrase after your teacher, following along in the book as you do.

1. hueco	9. hueso	17. jamón con huevos fritos
2. es hueco	10. este hueso	18. huelo algo
3. huelga	11. estos huesos	19. huele
4. una huelga	12. un hueso	20. huele bien
5. huella	13. huésped	21. el jardín huele bien
6. las huellas	14. es mi huésped	22. esos huevos huelen mal
7. huerto	15. huevo	23. huir
8. un huerto	16. huevos fritos	24. tuvo que huir

E   Question-Answer

Answer the following questions in the affirmative with a complete sentence.

1. ¿Le gusta esta universidad?
2. ¿Llega usted temprano a clase?
3. ¿Juega usted al golf?
4. ¿Sigue usted trabajando después de clase?
5. ¿Lo hace usted de buena gana?
6. ¿Le gustan los huevos fritos?
7. ¿Trabaja usted en la huerta?
8. ¿Usa usted huaraches?
9. ¿Tiene usted un huerto?
10. ¿Huele usted las flores?

F   "Live" Transcription

Your teacher will read a brief passage in Spanish. Just listen the first time. Then he will read the passage, one phonemic phrase at a time. Take each phrase down in PHONETIC *transcription, using conventional letters for the sounds you have not studied yet. Each phrase will be repeated several times. Then the entire passage will be read once more, and you can check your transcription a final time. The correct transcription is found in* Appendix D. *The allophones you have studied so far and are expected to know are underlined.*

11.10 Exercises

A

Give an articulatory description for [g], *for* [g], *for* [w]. *Check your answers in Section* 11.2.

B

Sketch a facial diagram for [g], *for* [g], *for* [w]. *Be sure the velum is closed. Indicate voicing by drawing a few zig-zag lines for the vocal bands. Then check your diagrams in Section* 11.3.

C

Make a PHONEMIC *transcription of the following passage. Use spaces, as usual, to indicate pauses. Remember that you are transcribing* only *the phonemes. Here and in all future transcription exercises, consider that the speaker is speaking General American Spanish. Use* /g/ *when the spelling is* **g** *and* /w/ *when it is* **hu** + vowel. *Then check your transcription in* Appendix D. *The phonemes you have studied so far are underlined.*

Sentía el frío hasta en los huesos. Llevaba puestos los antiguos huaraches y tenía ganas de poner los pies cerca del fuego para calentárselos. Hacía varios días que los obreros estaban de huelga. Se confesaba interiormente que había querido huir, pero sabía que lo necesitaban de guardia. ¡Guardia! De repente, le gritaron:
—¡Venga!

D

Now make a PHONETIC *transcription of the same passage in Exercise C. But this time indicate* allophones *instead of phonemes. Of the allophones you have studied so far, use only the following standard ones:* [p t k b ƀ d đ g g w]. *Use conventional letters for the sounds we have not studied yet. Then check your transcription in* Appendix D. *The allophones studied so far are underlined.*

12

~~~~~~

REVIEW OF STOPS / p t k b d g / *AND FRICATIVE* / w /

12.1 Phonemes

	Bilabial			Dental		Velar	Bilabio-velar
STOPS	p b			t d		k g	
SLIT FRICATIVES							w

12.2 Allophones

	Bilabial	Labio-dental		Dental		Velar	Bilabio-velar
STOPS	p b			t d		k g	
SLIT FRICATIVES	ƀ	v		đ		g	w

12.3 Facial Diagrams

See Sections 8.3, 9.3, 10.3, and 11.3.

12.4 Articulation

/p/ {[p] voiceless, bilabial stop

/t/ {[t] voiceless, dental stop

/k/ {[k] voiceless, velar stop

/b/ ⎰[b] voiced, bilabial stop
⎱[ƀ] voiced, bilabial slit fricative
⎰[v] voiced, labio-dental slit fricative

/d/ ⎰[d] voiced, dental stop
⎱[ð] voiced, dental slit fricative

/g/ ⎰[g] voiced, velar stop
⎱[ɣ] voiced, velar slit fricative

/w/ {[w] voiced, bilabio-velar slit fricative

12.5 Allophonic Distribution

/p t k/ each have only one principal allophone, an unaspirated stop. All of these weaken and sometimes disappear in syllable-final position, and they never occur at the end of native Spanish words.

/b d g/ each have a stop allophone and a fricative allophone, which are more or less in complementary distribution with each other. The stops occur in absolute-initial position and after a nasal. The nasal always assimilates to the following stop and takes on its point of articulation: bilabial [m] precedes [b], dental [n̪] precedes [d], and velar [ŋ] precedes [g]. Stop [d] also occurs after /l/. The fricatives occur everywhere else.

[ƀ] has a variant [v], which is not nearly as common and is often the result of hypercorrection.

[d] weakens and often disappears in /-ado/ endings and word-final position.

[ɣ] weakens when followed by [u̯], and the sequence [ɣu̯] varies with [w] in intervocalic position.

/w/ has one principal allophone [w], which varies with the sequence [ɣu̯] or [gu̯]. However, [w], [ɣu̯] or [gu̯] for [bu̯] or [ƀu̯] (as in **"agüela"**) is considered sub-standard.

See Appendix A for the rules for allophonic distribution and corresponding examples.

12.6 Dialectal Variations

/p t k b/ have few important dialectal variations.

In the case of /d/ the fricative allophone [ð] tends to disappear in the intervocalic position in rapid speech of most dialects of Spanish.

12.7 Contrasts with English

All stops in Spanish are unaspirated just as they are in English after /s/, as in *spill*, *still*, and *skill*.

Intervocalic /d/ and /t/ have tap allophones in English, which are equivalents of Spanish /r/. If you use them instead of the dental stop [t] and the dental fricative [đ], such words as **cata** and **cada** will be confused with **cara.**

12.8 References

See Sections 8.8, 9.8, 10.8, and 11.8

12.9 Drills

 Recognition

Your teacher will pronounce a series of words and phrases, some of which have the correct and most natural allophones of /b d g/ and some of which do not. Identify the best use of the stops [b d g] *and the fricatives* [b đ g] *by saying "correct" or "incorrect."*

1. baile [b]	9. un gato [g]	17. guárdalo [g]
2. gallo [g]	10. este baile [b]	18. no lo guardes [g]
3. dólar [d]	11. este dicho [đ]	19. buenos días [b]
4. el baile [b]	12. este gato [g]	20. un buen día [b]
5. el gallo [g]	13. venga [b]	21. me gusta [g]
6. el dólar [d]	14. no venga [b]	22. un grupo [g]
7. un vaso [b]	15. dámelo [đ]	23. el dato [d]
8. un dicho [d]	16. no me lo des [đ]	24. aldea [đ]

B   Recognition

Your teacher will pronounce a series of words and phrases, some of which have the correct sequences of /w b g/ and some of which do not. Identify them by saying "correct" or "incorrect."

1. abuela [gu̯]	5. la huerta [w]	9. bueno [gu̯]
2. agua [w]	6. con huevos [gu̯]	10. antiguo [w]
3. hueso [gu̯]	7. aguardar [w]	11. guardar [bu̯]
4. buenos días [bu̯]	8. buey [gu̯]	12. hueso [w]

C Transformation

After your teacher says a word with the definite article, say the word with the indefinite article and vice versa. For example, for **el vaso,** *say* **un vaso;** *for* **una gota,** *say* **la gota.**

1. el baile	11. el verano	21. el deber
2. un dicho	12. el dato	22. un grito
3. el gallo	13. un gabán	23. el barrio
4. la vaca	14. un viaje	24. la danza
5. el diablo	15. un duque	25. un gato
6. un grupo	16. el golpe	26. el bulto
7. un boleto	17. el banco	27. un decano
8. un deseo	18. el dedo	28. el guante
9. una botella	19. un gordo	29. una viuda
10. el dolor	20. la bala	30. el dicho

D Repetition (books open)

Repeat the word or phrase after your teacher, following along in the book as you do.

1. vuelve	7. no vale mucho	12. vivía en los
2. no vuelve	8. déme un boleto	Estados Unidos
3. dámelo	9. vamos a tomar la	13. no hago nada
4. no me lo dé	guagua	14. no digo nada
5. gusta	10. ya le ha hablado	15. no salgo
6. me gusta	11. ya lo he tomado	16. es un engaño

17. es un bobo   18. es un dedo

E Transformation

Transform the affirmative commands into negative commands. For example, after **Véndalo,** *say* **No lo venda.**

1. Bébalo.	5. Déjelo.	9 Grite.
2. Dígalo.	6. Gástelo.	10. Vuelva.
3. Guárdelo.	7. Venga.	11. Dedique.
4. Bótelo.	8. Duerma.	12. Golpee.

F Composition

Make up short original sentences with these verbs.

1. volver	5. poder	9. pagar
2. dejar	6. llegar	10. beber
3. gastar	7. vender	11. nadar
4. venir	8. estudiar	12. gustar

    G   "Live" Transcription

12.10 Exercises

A

Give an articulatory description for [t], *for* [d̪], *for* [b̪], *for* [w]. *Then check your answers in Section* 12.4.

B

Sketch a facial diagram for [p], *for* [k], *for* [g]. *Remember to have the velum closed and to indicate voicing. Then check your diagrams in Sections* 8.3 *and* 11.3.

C

Make a PHONEMIC *transcription of the following passage. Then check your transcription in* Appendix D.

    —Víctor dice que ya votaron en Bolivia y que no le gustan nada los resultados. Esperaba que todos hubieran declarado una huelga general. Pero averiguamos que todo salió bien y que el gobierno sigue rigiendo de una manera muy estable.

D

Now make a PHONETIC *transcription of the same passage in Exercise C. Use only the following allophones* [p t k b b̪ d d̪ g g̪ w] *and conventional letters for the sounds you have not studied yet. Then check your transcription in* Appendix D.

12.11 Questions

Write your answers on a separate sheet of paper and check them in Appendix D.

1. Three meaningful ways of classifying consonant phonemes in Spanish are ____, ____, and ____.
2. CONSONANTS/VOWELS play the more important role in determining pronunciation differences in dialects of Spanish.
3. Many consonantal modifications in Spanish occur in ____ position.
4. One sound changing to become more like the following sound is called ____ ____.

5. Two Spanish sounds which do not exist in English are ___ and ___.
6. /p/ has ___ (the number) allophone(s) in Spanish.
7. The major difference between Spanish /t/ and English /t/ is that in English it is ___ in ___ position.
8. A typical mispronunciation by an English-speaker of /t/ makes **pata** sound like ___.
9. The letter **p** is written but represents no sound in the Spanish word ___.
10. The lack of aspiration with Spanish /p t k/ often makes them sound like ___ to the English-speaker.
11. [b] is a GROOVE/SLIT fricative.
12. Even though we see the letter combinations **n b** or **nv** in written Spanish, these spellings always represent [___] (phones).
13. [v] is sometimes pronounced instead of [b] because it is in ___ with it and because of ___.
14. TRUE/FALSE /v/ exists as a phoneme in some dialects of Spanish.
15. If [v] is not regularly heard in all dialects of Spanish, why are so many words spelled with **v**?
16. [d] resembles the English sound [___], as in ___.
17. In some Spanish dialects it is quite normal to eliminate [d] in words that ___.
18. If you are not careful to use [ ] instead of your own ___ allophone of /d/, **cada** will sound like **cara**.
19. In Spanish /n/ assimilates to /d/ and is realized as [___].
20. In Spanish /n/ assimilates to /g/ and is realized as [___].
21. [w] often alternates with the sequence [___] in such words as **agua** and **antiguo**.
22. [g] is in FREE VARIATION/COMPLEMENTARY DISTRIBUTION with [g] in Spanish.
23. [gu] for [bu] or [bu] is considered ___ by most speakers of Spanish.
24. One of the main articulatory differences between /g/ and /w/ is that for /w/ ___.

13

$$/\,\hat{c}\,f\,/$$

13.1 Phonemes

/ĉ/ is a voiceless, palatal affricate.
/f/ is a voiceless, labiodental slit fricative.

13.2 Allophones

[ĉ] is a voiceless, palatal affricate, allophone of /ĉ/.
[š] is a voiceless, palatal groove fricative, allophone of /ĉ/.
[f] is a voiceless, labiodental slit fricative, allophone of /f/.
[ƥ] is a voiceless, bilabial slit fricative, allophone of /f/.

13.3 Facial Diagrams

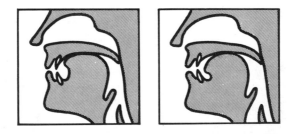

[ĉ]   [š]

The diagram for [f] is the same as that for [v], except that there is no voicing (see Section 9.3).

The diagram for [ɸ] is the same as that for [b], except that there is no voicing (see Section 9.3).

13.4 Articulation

For [ĉ] the blade and tip of the tongue raise and touch the alveolar ridge and the front part of the palate. The sides of the tongue dorsum touch the sides of the palate and the upper back teeth, leaving an opening in the middle. The contact of the tongue blade with the front palate momentarily stops the airstream, as with a stop. But the blade then quickly relaxes its contact, forming a round opening between itself and the front palate, and the airstream passes through this groove as in a fricative. [ĉ], like any affricate then, is a stop + fricative, pronounced at almost the same time.

For [š] the tongue assumes almost the same position as for [ĉ], except that the tongue blade never touches the front palate. The airstream keeps passing through the groove formed between the tongue dorsum and the front palate. [š] is completely fricative where [ĉ] has a slight stop first, making it an affricate.

For [f] the lower lip lightly touches the edge of the upper front teeth. The airstream, without stopping, passes through the slit formed by the lip and teeth. For [ɸ] the two lips almost touch, and the airstream, without stopping, passes through the slit formed between them. The place and manner of articulation are the same as for [b], but there is no voicing.

13.5 Allophonic Distribution

In most dialects of Spanish /ĉ/ has only one allophone. This sound is always represented by the digraph **ch: chico** [ĉí-ko], **muchacho** [mu-ĉá-ĉo], **salchicha** [sal̪-ĉí-ĉa].

/f/ also has only one allophone in most dialects of Spanish. This sound is always represented by the letter **f: fuerte** [fу̯ér-te], **gafas** [gá-fas]. Regardless of the fact that nasal + /f/ is spelled **nf** or **n f** (across word-boundaries), the phonetic sequence is always [ɱf]. Regressive assimilation to /f/ causes the nasal to be realized as a labiodental [ɱ].

The rules for /ĉ/ and /f/:

$$/ĉ/ \rightarrow [ĉ]$$
$$/f/ \rightarrow [f]$$

13.6 Dialectal Variations

The fricative [š] is used in free variation with [ĉ] in areas in some countries of the Caribbean region, such as in Panama, Cuba, and the Dominican Republic.

Some dialects in America have another allophone, the bilabial [ɸ], the voiceless counterpart of [ƀ], which is in free variation with [f], particularly after /m/, which drops out and nasalizes the previous vowel, as in **enfermo** [ẽ-ɸér-mo], and before /ue/, as in **fuerte** [ɸu̯ér-te].

13.7 Contrasts with English

The sounds [ĉ] and [f] represent no problem for you since they both are almost exactly the same in English, except that there is slightly less aspiration for Spanish [ĉ].

13.8 References

SPANISH

Dykstra, "Spectographic Analysis of Spanish Sibilants" (1955).
* Gili Gaya, *Elementos de fonética general* (1950), Chapters X, XI.
* Navarro, *Manual de pronunciación española* (1957), Sections 88, 118.
* Zamora Vicente, *Dialectología española* (1960), "Español de América".

ENGLISH AND GENERAL

* Bronstein (1960), Chapter 5.
* Buchanan (1963), Chapter VI.

13.9 Drills

A   Repetition

Repeat the word or phrase after your teacher.

1. fuerte	8. fui	15. la estufa
2. fofo	9. se fue	16. la filología
3. frío	10. es fuerte	17. la fonética
4. flemático	11. hace frío	18. la fonología
5. finca	12. prende el fuego	19. viene Francisco
6. fuego	13. está fuera	20. se llama Federico
7. fuera	14. las gafas	21. aquí se vende nafta
	22. no blasfemes	

B   Repetition

Repeat the word or phrase after your teacher.

1. chico
2. chancho
3. chorizo
4. chiquitito
5. charlatán
6. charlar
7. chamaco

8. chavalito
9. es un chico
10. es un chancho
11. ¿comes chocolate?
12. es tan chiquitito
13. ¿vas a dar una charla?
14. es un chamaco
22. trabaja de noche

15. son chinos
16. es ancho
17. ¿qué anchura tiene?
18. ¿comes salchicha?
19. ¡qué muchacho!
20. ¡qué muchachito!
21. ¡qué facha!

C   "Live" Transcription

13.10 Exercises

A

Give an articulatory description for [ĉ], *for* [f]. *Then check your answers in Section* 13.2.

B

Sketch a facial diagram for [ĉ], *for* [f]. *Since these sounds are voiceless, leave out the zig-zag lines for the vocal bands. Then check your diagrams in Sections* 13.3 *and* 9.3.

C

Make a PHONEMIC *transcription of the following passage. Then check your transcription in* Appendix D.

Chalito y Francisco iban a dar una charla sobre Francia, pero los muchachos rechazaron la idea. En vez de eso, se fueron todos a tomar chocolate frío y salchichas fuertes.

D

Now make a PHONETIC *transcription of the same passage. Use only* [p t k b ƀ d đ g g w ĉ f]. *Then check your transcription in* Appendix D.

14

/ s / (*AND* / θ /)

14.1 Phonemes

/s/ is a voiceless, alveolar groove fricative.
/θ/ is a voiceless, interdental slit fricative.

14.2 Allophones

[s] is a voiceless, alveolar groove fricative, allophone of /s/.
[z] is a voiced, alveolar groove fricative, allophone of /s/.
[ś] is a voiceless, alveolar groove fricative, allophone of /s/.
[ż] is a voiced, alveolar groove fricative, allophone of /s/.
[h] is a voiceless, glottal slit fricative, allophone of /s/, and also of /x/.
[θ] is a voiceless, interdental slit fricative, allophone of /θ/.
[ð] is a voiced, interdental slit fricative, allophone of /θ/.

14.3 Facial Diagrams

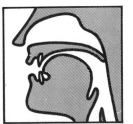
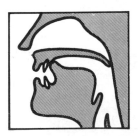

[s]   [s]   [ś]

The diagrams for [z] and [ż] are the same as for [s] and [ś], respectively, plus voicing in each case.

14.4 Articulation

/s/ has several allophones and dialectal varieties. There are two common articulations for [s] and [z]. For one the tip of the tongue rests against the alveolar ridge, and the groove through which the airstream passes is formed in the tongue tip. The tongue is rather flat on top. (See the first diagram in Section 14.3.) For the other the tip of the tongue rests against or near the lower front teeth. The groove is in the tongue blade or sometimes the front dorsum as it presses against the alveolar ridge. The tongue has a convex shape. (See the second diagram in Section 14.3.)

For [ś] and [ż] the tip of the tongue is retroflexed or turned back as it touches the alveolar ridge. The groove through which the airstream passes is also formed in the tongue tip, but the tongue has a concave shape. (See the third diagram in Section 14.3.) The acoustic effect is similar to English /š/ (as in *shell*), but not quite as "full," i.e., not as much accompanying noise.

[h], also an allophone of the velar fricative /x/, is a glottal aspiration. The tongue is relaxed with the tip resting against the lower front teeth.

For [θ] and [ð] the tip of the tongue is placed between the upper and lower front teeth or sometimes lightly against the back of the upper front teeth, just as it is for these sounds in English. [θ] and [ð] are more interdental than [đ].

14.5 Allophonic Distribution and 14.6 Dialectal Variations

Most dialects of American Spanish use [s] with its principal allophones [z] and [h]. One of the main differences between American Spanish and Castilian (or standard peninsular Spanish) is the fact that the former has no /θ/ phoneme. /s/ is heard instead and is represented in writing by s, z, c + e, and c + i, as in **sol** [sól], **zapato** [sa-pá-to], **cena** [sé-na], and **cinta** [síṇ-ta]. This usage is called **seseo** and characterizes not only all Spanish-speakers in America, but many in southern Spain as well.

[s] varies with [z] because of regressive assimilation when it precedes a voiced consonant: **mismo** [mís-mo] or [míz-mo], **isla** [ís-la] or [íz-la]. With many speakers [s] and [z] are in complementary distribution, but with others they are in free variation. [z] is usually heard before /d/, however: **desde** [déz-đe].

Many dialects of Spanish, particularly in the coastal areas of America— Cuba, Puerto Rico, Dominican Republic, Venezuela, the River Plata areas of Argentina and Uruguay, Chile—have the allophone [h] for both [s] and [z] in syllable-final position, as in **esperar** [ęh-pę-rár], **los chicos** [loh-ĉí-koh], **desde** [dęh-đe], **las muchachas** [lah-mu-ĉá-ĉah]. This pronunciation is common among educated speakers, particularly in rapid conversation, and a prominent [s] in this position can even sound affected and exaggerated. These speakers sometimes even pronounce [h] for [s] in any word-final position even though it is intervocalic as in **los he visto** [lo-hé-ƀíh-to].

In many dialects of Castilian or peninsular Spanish and also in the highland area of Colombia, the retroflex [ṡ] is heard, with its corresponding allophone [ż]: **sol** [ṡól], **mismo** [míż-mo]. This [ṡ] has a pronounced hissing quality which often causes it to be mistaken for [š].

/θ/ is, of course, used only in standard Castilian Spanish and is represented in writing with **z, c + e,** and **c + i,** as in **zapato** [θa-pá-to], **cena** [θé-na], and **cinta** [θíṇ-ta]. Its voiced counterpart [ð] is heard before voiced consonants: **juzgar** [xuð-gár], **en vez de** [ęm-bęð-đe]. /θ/ is not used in American Spanish and in parts of Andalusia—in other words, the **seseo** areas.

Most speakers of Spanish, both **seseo** and Castilian dialects, either use [h] in place of /s/ or eliminate /s/ completely when it precedes the trilled /r̄/: **los ricos** [loh-r̄í-kos] or [lo-r̄í-kos].

The rule for /s/:

$$/s/ \longrightarrow \begin{bmatrix} \left.\begin{Bmatrix} [s] \\ [z] \end{Bmatrix}\right/ \_/C_l/ \\ [z]\Big/ \_/d/ \\ \left.\begin{Bmatrix} [s] \\ [h] \\ [\varnothing] \end{Bmatrix}\right/ \_/r̄/ \\ [s] \text{ elsewhere} \end{bmatrix}$$

/C$_l$/ is any voiced consonant but /d/ and /r̄/.

14.7 Contrasts with English

Since English has the same two articulations for [s] as Spanish does, you have no trouble pronouncing it. However, you may mistakenly substitute [z] for it in word-initial and intervocalic position, as in **zapato** *[za-pá-to] or **rosa** *[r̄ó-za]. This is because the letters *z, zz,* and even *s* in certain positions often represent /z/ in English, as in *zeal, fuzzy, busy, houses,* etc. Spanish-speakers never use [z] in word-initial position and rarely in intervocalic position. Thus, you should avoid it in all but syllable-final position where it can help to distinguish between such pairs as **este** [és-te] and **es de** [éz-đe] or **rascar** [r̄as-kár] and **rasgar** [r̄az-gár]. Although this is useful for you as an English-speaker, it should be remembered that for Spanish-speakers these pairs are really distinguished because of the phonemic contrasts between /t/ and /d/ in the first case and /k/ and /g/ in the second. The [z] occurs simply as an allophone of /s/ before voiced consonants.

The other difficulty for you concerns /s/ and /θ/. American students are often taught Castilian Spanish, but for some reason they rarely master the correct use of /θ/. They confuse /s/ with it and say such things as **En esta ciudad hace mucho frío** [e-nés-ta-siu-dá-dá-0e-mú-ĉo-frí-o]. Unless you can be completely consistent and use /s/ and /θ/ as Spaniards do, it is best to drop /θ/ completely and use the **seseo** pronunciation. This may make spelling a little more difficult at first—you may forget whether the word is **oficio** or ***ofisio**— but this is a minor problem which most Spanish-American school children face and overcome without too much trouble.

14.8 References

SPANISH

Bès, "Examen del concepto de rehilamiento" (1964).
Beym, "*Porteño* /s/ and [h] [ȟ] [s] [x] [Ø] as Variants" (1963).
* Bowen and Stockwell, *Patterns of Spanish Pronunciation* (1960), Chapter 3.
Dykstra, "Spectographic Analysis of Spanish Sibilants" (1955).
* Gili Gaya, *Elementos de fonética general* (1950), Chapter 10.
* Hefler and Thompson, "Seseo vs. θ in the Classroom" (1943).
Lapesa, "Sobre el ceceo y el seseo en Hispanoamérica" (1956).
* Lundeberg, "What is *ceceo*? Inquiry and Proposal" (1947).
* Navarro, *Manual de pronunciación española* (1957), Sections 92–94, 106–09.
* Zamora Vicente, *Dialectología española* (1960), "Español de América".

ENGLISH AND GENERAL

* Bronstein (1960), Chapter 5.
* Buchanan (1963), Chapter VI.

14.9 Drills

A   Recognition

> *Your teacher will pronounce a series of words and phrases containing the phoneme /s/ + a voiced or a voiceless consonant. The* [s] *or* [z] *allophone of /s/ will help you to identify the following consonant, which you should name. For example, if you hear* **rascar** [r̄as-kár], *say* **ka**. *If you hear* **desde** [déz-de], *say* **de**.

1. rasgar	4. los huevos	7. rascar
2. esposo	5. es vaca	8. esbozo
3. de este	6. tienes pecas	9. es de

10. ¿quieres pesarlo?	15. los codos	20. no es gordura
11. es paca	16. tienes becas	21. los baños
12. es gancho	17. desde	22. ¿dices "boca"?
13. no es cordura	18. ¿quieres besarlo?	23. los godos
14. ¿dices "poca"?	19. los suevos	24. los paños

B   Recognition-Production

After your teacher says a word or phrase containing /s/ + *voiceless consonant, say the "opposite" word or phrase, i.e., the one containing* /s/ + *the corresponding voiced consonant, and vice versa. For example, if he says* **rascar** *[r̄as-kár], say* **rasgar** *[r̄az-gár]. If he says* **los godos** *[loz-gó-đos], say* **los codos** *[los-kó-đos].*

1. es de	8. ¿quieres besarlo?	15. tienes becas
2. los codos	9. los paños	16. los suevos
3. no es gordura	10. rasgar	17. es cancho
4. los baños	11. de este	18. los godos
5. ¿dices "boca"?	12. esposo	19. esbozo
6. tienes pecas	13. este	20. es vaca
7. es gancho	14. ¿quieres pesarlo?	21. los huevos
	22. desde	

C   Repetition

Repeat the words and phrases after your teacher.

1. es de aquí	7. no es cordura	13. los codos
2. éste aquí no vale	8. es un esposo	14. los godos
3. muchas gracias	9. tienes pecas	15. los dramas
4. ¿dónde están los baños?	10. tienes becas	16. las tramas
5. es un esbozo	11. rascar	17. ¿quieres pelarlo?
6. las vacas	12. rasgar	18. ¿quieres velarlo?
	19. ¿dónde están los paños?	

D   Repetition

Repeat the words and phrases after your teacher.

1. presidente	7. Kánsas	13. esbozo
2. residencia	8. reserva	14. mozo
3. rosa	9. observa	15. taza
4. propósito	10. preservación	16. zeta
5. zapato	11. cazador	17. chorizo
6. presente	12. manzana	18. belleza

19. zafar	22. posar	25. caza
20. zurdo	23. Isabel	26. lechuza
21. zapoteca	24. raza	27. vez

28. voz   29. capaz

E   Read Aloud (books open)

Read the words aloud. Remember that [z] in Spanish occurs only before a voiced consonant.

1. presidente	10. observa	19. voz
2. esbozo	11. chorizo	20. vos
3. esposo	12. belleza	21. posar
4. taza	13. zeta	22. Isabel
5. tasa	14. seta	23. raza
6. reserva	15. vez	24. caza
7. zapato	16. ves	25. casa
8. zurdo	17. capaz	26. presente
9. roza	18. rosa	27. residencia

28. lechuza   29. Kánsas

F   Read Aloud (books open)

Read the phrases and sentences aloud.

1. Fuimos a la casa del presidente.
2. ¿Aquí se caza, señor?
3. Oímos una voz misteriosa en la residencia.
4. ¿Lo ves esta vez?
5. ¿Vos no tenés voz?
6. Esta raza no usa zapatos.
7. No soy capaz de coger esas rosas.
8. Esta taza está reservada para mí.
9. Obsérvese que no hay zeta.
10. Algo me rozó el brazo.

G   "Live" Transcription

14.10 Exercises

A

Give an articulatory description for [s], for [ṡ], for [θ]. Then check your answers in Section 14.2.

B

Sketch a facial diagram for [s], *for* [ṡ]. *Then check your diagrams in Section* 14.3.

C

Make a PHONEMIC *transcription of the following passage. The passage, of course, represents* **seseo** *speech. Then check your transcription in* Appendix D.

El mozo dijo en voz alta que no era capaz de robar los zapatos. Volvió a la residencia, oyendo las lechuzas, los tiros de los cazadores y las voces de las cigarreras. Desde donde estaba, husmeaba las rosas y pensaba en los días cuando llegaron los godos a esas regiones.

D

Now make a PHONETIC *transcription of the same passage. Use only* [p t k b ƀ d đ g g w ĉ f s z h]. *Then check your transcription in* Appendix D.

15

~~~~~~

/ y /

15.1 Phonemes

/y/ is a voiced, palatal slit fricative.

15.2 Allophones

[y] is a voiced, palatal slit fricative.
[ŷ] is a voiced, palatal affricate.
[ž] is a voiced, palatal groove fricative.

15.3 Facial Diagrams

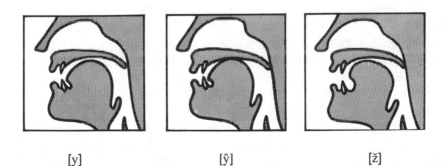

[y]   [ŷ]   [ž]

15.4 Articulation

For [y] the tip of the tongue rests against the lower front teeth. The dorsum humps up and almost touches the palate. The airstream keeps passing through the slit formed by the tongue and palate. There is more friction, actual and audible, than the English /y/ of *yes*.

Although [ŷ] is the voiced counterpart of [ĉ], the articulation is somewhat different. For [ŷ] the tongue tip rests against the lower front teeth. The dorsum humps up and makes extensive contact with the palate—more so than with [ĉ]. The contact of the dorsum with the palate momentarily stops the airstream, as with a stop. But the dorsum then quickly relaxes its contact, forming a round opening between itself and the palate, and the airstream passes through the groove as in a fricative. Spanish [ŷ] is very similar to English /ǰ/, but for the latter sound the tongue tip and blade raise and touch the alveolar ridge and the front part of the palate. Spanish [ŷ], less "full" in its acoustic effect, is like any affricate, a stop + fricative, pronounced at almost the same time.

Spanish [ž] is the same as the English /ž/ as in *measure*. To articulate it, the tongue assumes almost the same position as for [š] and [y], except that the sides of the tongue dorsum touch the sides of the palate and the upper back teeth, leaving an opening in the middle. The tongue blade never touches the alveolar ridge. The airstream keeps passing through the groove formed between the tongue dorsum and the front palate. [ž] is completely fricative, like a prolongation of the second part of the affricate [ŷ] or the English /ǰ/.

15.5 Allophonic Distribution

In most dialects of Spanish /y/ has only two allophones. The affricate [ŷ] often occurs in absolute-initial position and sometimes after /n/ and /l/, as in **Yo no voy** [ŷó-nó-bói̯], **inyección** [iñ-ŷęk-si̯ón], **el hielo** [ęl-ŷé-lo]. The fricative [y] usually occurs everywhere else. In other dialects these two sounds are in free variation: **Va a llamar** [bá-ya-már] or [bá-ŷa-már].

The sequence of nasal + /y/, then, is often [ñ-ŷ]: **en hielo** [ęñ-ŷé-lo]. Regressive assimilation to /y/ causes the palatal /ñ/ to be used instead of the alveolar /n/, and progressive assimilation to the nasal causes /y/ to be realized as the affricate [ŷ]. The sequence of lateral + /y/ is often [l̦-ŷ]: **el hielo** [ęl̦-ŷé-lo]. In these dialects regressive assimilation to /y/ causes the palatal [l̦] to be used instead of the alveolar [l], and progressive assimilation to the lateral causes /y/ to be realized as the affricate [ŷ].

One frequent exception to [ŷ] in the absolute initial position is the word **y** when it precedes a word beginning with a vowel. If it is unstressed, it is pronounced [y] and forms the beginning of the syllable: **Y eso** [yé-so]. However, if it is stressed, it is a vowel [í], and forms its own syllable: **Y eso** [í-é-so].

Some dialects of Spanish use the palatal groove fricative [ž] in place of [y] and [ŷ]: **yo** [žó], **llamar** [ža-már].

The rule for /y/:

$$/y/ \longrightarrow \left[\begin{array}{l} \begin{Bmatrix} [y] \\ [\hat{y}] \end{Bmatrix} \Big/ \begin{Bmatrix} \# \\ /n/ \\ /l/ \end{Bmatrix} \text{---} \\[2ex] [y] \text{ elsewhere} \end{array} \right]$$

15.6 Dialectal Variations

In most dialects of Spanish /y/ and its allophones are represented in spelling by **y, hi + e,** and **ll,** as in **yo, hielo, llamar.** In these dialects the palatal lateral/l̥/ is absent as a phoneme (although it occurs as a pre-palatal allophone of /l/), and such pairs as **haya-halla** [á-ya] and **cayó-calló** [ka-yó] are identical in sound. This usage is called **yeísmo** and extends throughout most of Spanish America and much of Spain.

Other speakers of Spanish, however, have this palatal lateral /l̥/ as a phoneme and make a distinction between **haya** [á-ya] and **halla** [á-l̥a]. This usage, sometimes called **lleísmo** [l̥e-íz-mo], is often mistakenly considered to be one of the features that distinguishes peninsular Spanish from American Spanish. But it is not found everywhere in Spain and, on the other hand, exists in some areas of America—mainly in the highlands, such as the inland areas of Colombia and Argentina, southern Peru, parts of Chile and Bolivia, and most of Paraguay.

The substitution of [ž] for [y] and [ŷ] is common in eastern Argentina, Uruguay and central Colombia. Some speakers vary [š] with [ž], as in **calle:** [ká-že] or [ká-še]. Among educated speakers in Argentina this usage occurs in words spelled with **y** and **ll,** but not **hie-.** Thus, the word **yerba** is pronounced [žér-ba], but **hierba** is [yér-ba]. This is one of the few cases in Spanish where speakers consciously choose their pronunciation according to the orthography.

15.7 Contrasts with English

Both Spanish [y] and [ž] have close equivalents in English, as in *yoke* and *measure.* Spanish [ŷ], although not the same, is similar enough to the initial sound of *joke* that you can easily learn it or even use the English /ǰ/. However, these three sounds are all phonemes in English and cannot be interchanged as they can be in Spanish. Thus, you may have a tendency to overdifferentiate between the three and even feel reluctant to imitate the use of [ŷ] and [ž] when you hear it. But since [ŷ] and [ž] are perfectly acceptable varieties of /y/ in many dialects, you should be able to use them with no difficulty.

I5.8 References

SPANISH

Alonso, Amado, *Estudios lingüísticos: Temas hispanoamericanos* (1953), Chapter
    II: Section 2.
* Beberfall, " 'Y' and 'll' in Relaxed Spanish Speech" (1961).
Bès, "Examen del concepto de rehilamiento" (1964).
Bowen and Stockwell, *Patterns of Spanish Pronunciation* (1960), Chapter 3.
* Foster, "A Note on the /ŷ/ Phoneme of *Porteño* Spanish" (1967).
* Gili Gaya, *Elementos de fonética general* (1950), Chapter X.
* Navarro, *Manual de pronunciación española* (1957), Sections 119–21, 124.

ENGLISH AND GENERAL

* Bronstein (1960), Chapter 6.
* Buchanan (1963), Chapter VII.

I5.9 Drills

A   Recognition

*Your teacher will pronounce a series of words, some of which have an
intervocalic /y/, such as* **villa,** *and some of which have two contiguous
vowels, such as* **vía.** *Identify the words with /y/ by saying* "consonant"
and those without it by saying "two vowels."

1. bello	8. sella	15. trillo
2. leyes	9. mía	16. lees
3. brío	10. bella	17. trío
4. vea	11. ea	18. brillo
5. pía	12. lío	19. milla
6. tilla	13. veo	20. tía
7. Lillo	14. pilla	21. ella
	22. sea	

B   Recognition-Production

Say the "opposite" *word. If your teacher says* **bello,** *say* **veo.** *If he says*
mía, *say* **milla.**

1. bello	6. tilla	11. bella
2. leyes	7. Lillo	12. pilla
3. brío	8. mía	13. trillo
4. vea	9. sella	14. ea
5. pía	10. veo	15. lío

16. lees   18. milla   20. tía
17. brillo   19. trío   21. ella
              22. sea

C   Repetition

Repeat the word after your teacher. (NOTE: In this drill /y/ in word-initial position may be pronounced [y] or [ŷ].)

1. hielo	18. arrollo	35. yodo
2. joya	19. yunque	36. llave
3. llama	20. mallo	37. allá
4. callar	21. hierba	38. humillar
5. yeso	22. hoyo	39. llama
6. gallina	23. yacer	40. allí
7. yegua	24. desarrollar	41. llano
8. callo	25. yuyo	42. haya
9. llorar	26. silla	43. yugo
10. cayó	27. ya	44. halla
11. llevar	28. bello	45. yerma
12. calló	29. yerno	46. vaya
13. lleno	30. villa	47. llegada
14. arroyo	31. llegar	48. valle
15. yerba	32. cayó	49. lluvia
16. capilla	33. yo	50. camilla
17. llover	34. mayo	51. llaga

52. gallo   53. yema

D   Repetition

Repeat the phrase after the teacher. (NOTE: In this drill /y/ in absolute-initial position may be pronounced [y] or [ŷ].)

1. Llámame después.
2. Ya no puede caminar.
3. Es bellísimo.
4. Se calló.
5. Yo no voy.
6. Se cayó.
7. Estaba en una camilla.
8. Llénala de agua.
9. Tiene dos hoyuelos.
10. Llega a las seis.
11. El cinco de mayo.
12. Llora cuando se siente triste.
13. Vive en el llano.
14. Llueve mucho allí.
15. Con hielo, por favor.
16. Yerba mate.

E   Read Aloud (books open)

Say each word or phrase two times, first with [y], *then with* [ŷ].

1. llamar	11. llave	21. Así se llama.
2. callar	12. llevar	22. No se calla nunca.
3. villa	13. llorar	23. Es una gallina.
4. gallina	14. llover	24. Es completamente llano.
5. bello	15. capilla	25. No llegará a tiempo.
6. desarrollar	16. halla	26. Dame esa silla.
7. llano	17. valle	27. Está lleno de agua.
8. llegar	18. camilla	28. ¿Dónde está la llave?
9. silla	19. gallo	29. Llévatelo.
10. lleno	20. arrollar	30. Está llorando.

F   "Live" Transcription

15.10 Exercises

A

Give an articulatory description for [y], *for* [ŷ], *for* [ž]. *Then check your answers in Section* 15.2.

B

Sketch a facial diagram for [y], *for* [ŷ], *for* [ž]. *Then check your diagrams in Section* 15.3.

C

Make a PHONEMIC *transcription of the following passage. The passage, of course, represents* **yeísta** *speech. Then check your transcription in* Appendix D.

Mi yerno estaba trabajando con hierro y yeso, se cayó en el hielo, y se dañó mucho. Y he llamado al doctor Gallardo. Va a llegar muy pronto para ponerle una inyección.

D

Now make a PHONETIC *transcription of the same passage. Use only* [p t k b ƀ d đ g g w ĉ f s z h y ŷ]. *Then check your transcription in* Appendix D.

16

/ x (h) /

16.1 Phonemes

/x/ is a voiceless, velar slit fricative.
/h/ is a voiceless, glottal slit fricative.

16.2 Allophones

[x] is a voiceless, velar slit fricative, allophone of /x/.
[ç] is a voiceless, palatal slit fricative, allophone of /x/.
[h] is a voiceless, glottal slit fricative, allophone of /h/.

16.3 Facial Diagrams

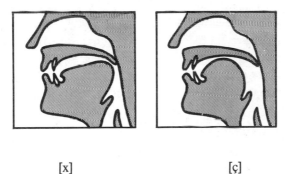

[x]   [ç]

[h] cannot be represented with a facial diagram since there is no contact or closure anywhere above the larynx.

16.4 Articulation

For [x] the back of the tongue is placed lightly against or very close to the velum. The airstream, rather than being stopped, passes between the tongue and the velum. The tongue dorsum sometimes vibrates very audibly, making the sound almost a trill like [R] (see Section 20.4) rather than a fricative. This velar fricative does not exist in English, but is heard in German, as in **machen** [má-xən], and in Russian, as in **хорошо** [xa-rə-šó].

The articulation of [ç] is almost the same as that of [y] except that there is more friction and no voicing. The tongue dorsum humps up and almost touches the palate, and the airstream keeps passing through the slit. Many speakers of English have this sound in some words that begin with *hu-*: *Hugh*, *humility*, *Huron*, etc. The sound also exists in German, as in **ich** [íç].

[h] is actually articulated more like a vowel than a consonant. The speech organs are "neutral," that is to say, they assume the position of the next sound, usually a vowel. However, since [h] is voiceless, the airstream passes through the glottis with friction but without creating vibration. The vocal bands begin vibrating for the following vowel, which is always voiced, of course.

16.5 Allophonic Distribution and 16.6 Dialectal Variations

In many dialects of American Spanish /x/ has two allophones, depending on the following vowel. [ç], farthest forward in the mouth, often precedes the front vowels /i/ and /e/: **girar** [çi-rár], **gente** [çę́ṇ-te]. [x], farther back in the mouth, usually precedes the central and back vowels /a/, /o/, and /u/: **jardín** [xar-dín], **joya** [xó-ya], **jugar** [xu-gár].

In other dialects of American Spanish, such as Central America, the Caribbean area, Colombia, and Venezuela, both [ç] and [x] are replaced by glottal [h]: **girar** [hi-rár], **jugar** [hu-gár], etc. Thus, in these dialects the phoneme is best analyzed as /h/ rather than /x/.

/x/ and /h/ are represented in spelling by **j**, **g + e**, and **g + i**, as in **mujer**, **gente**, and **girar**. A few Indian words and names with these sounds are spelled with **x**: **México, Oaxaca, xococo**. In one common word **j** usually represents silence rather than /x/: **reloj** [r̄e-ló], although some speakers say [r̄e-lóx].

In some dialects of American Spanish [h] also occurs as a syllable-final allophone of /s/: **esperar** [ęh-pe-rár] (see Sections 14.5 and 14.6).

The rules for /x/ and /h/:

$$/x/ \longrightarrow \begin{bmatrix} \begin{Bmatrix} [x] \\ [ç] \end{Bmatrix} / \_\begin{Bmatrix} /i/ \\ /e/ \end{Bmatrix} \\ [x] \text{ elsewhere} \end{bmatrix}$$

$$/h/ \longrightarrow [h]$$

Remember that any dialect of American Spanish has *either* the phoneme /x/ *or* the phoneme /h/.

16.7 Contrasts with English

You probably had difficulty at first with [x]. This is partly because it does not exist in English and partly because it strikes many English-speakers as being a somewhat unpleasant sound. Sometimes they take the closest English sound—the velar /k/—and pronounce **baja,** for example, as [bá-ka], which, of course, is another word in Spanish. Many of you, thus, prefer [ç] and [h], both common sounds in English and acceptable Spanish substitutes for [x].

16.8 References

SPANISH

* Bowen and Stockwell, *Patterns of Spanish Pronunciation* (1960), Chapter 3.
* Gili Gaya, *Elementos de fonética general* (1950), Chapter X.
* Navarro, *Manual de pronunciación española* (1957), Section 131.
* _____, "The Old Aspirated *h* in Spain and in the Spanish of America" (1949).
* Zamora Vicente, *Dialectología española* (1960), "Español de América".

ENGLISH AND GENERAL

* Bronstein (1960), Chapter 5.

16.9 Drills

A   Recognition

Your teacher will pronounce a series of words, some of which have /x/ and some of which have /k/. Identify them by saying **jota** *for /x/ and* **ka** *for /k/.*

1. baja	12. cota	23. bajo
2. jama	13. jurar	24. jema
3. jarro	14. faca	25. laca
4. cama	15. paja	26. joya
5. vaca	16. curar	27. faja
6. toco	17. moco	28. loca
7. Baco	18. bajo	29. laja
8. jareta	19. jornada	30. teca
9. jara	20. teja	31. careta
10. laja	21. cornada	32. ceja
11. quema	22. mojo	33. cota

34. carro	35. tojo	36. paca

37. loja   38. cara

B   Recognition-Production

Say the "opposite" word. If your teacher says **baja** *(with /x/), say* **vaca** *(with /k/). If he says* **curar** *(with /k/), say* **jurar** *(with /x/).*

1. baja	13. curar	25. loca
2. jama	14. moco	26. loja
3. vaca	15. Baco	27. ceja
4. toco	16. jornada	28. cota
5. bajo	17. careta	29. carro
6. jareta	18. mojo	30. tojo
7. jara	19. bajo	31. paca
8. quema	20. cornada	32. loja
9. cota	21. jema	33. cara
10. jurar	22. laca	34. jarro
11. faca	23. joya	35. jema
12. paja	24. faja	36. curar

C   Repetition

Repeat the word after your teacher.

1. baja	10. gimnasio	19. elegir
2. pijama	11. cajón	20. gente
3. jalar	12. dirigir	21. flojo
4. queja	13. jardín	22. gemir
5. genial	14. geología	23. mujer
6. jurar	15. reja	24. eje
7. digerir	16. escoger	25. general
8. relojes	17. jarro	26. jota
9. genio	18. gitano	27. afligido
	28. congelado	

D   Read Aloud (books open)

Read the phrases and sentences aloud.

1. Es una vaca.
2. Mis pijamas.
3. No recoja esas flores.
4. El general fue a Ginebra.
5. Es un poco flojo.
6. Los gitanos viven allí.
7. ¿Cuándo fue elegido?
8. Hay una reja alrededor del jardín.
9. Diríjase a un guardia.
10. Oh, ¡es genial!
11. Está muy afligido.
12. Gerardo estudia geología.
13. Su mujer se queja mucho.
14. La gente jura que sí.

E   Read Aloud (books open)

Read each word or phrase twice first with [x] *or* [ç], *depending on the following vowel, then with* [h].

1. baja	8. gimnasio	15. escoger
2. jalar	9. relojes	16. gitano
3. pijama	10. jardín	17. elegir
4. genial	11. cajón	18. gente
5. queja	12. geología	19. flojo
6. jurar	13. reja	20. general
7. digerir	14. jarro	21. mujer

F   "Live" Transcription

16.10 Exercises

A

Give an articulatory description for [x], *for* [ç], *for* [h]. *Then check your answers in Section* 16.2.

B

Sketch a facial diagram for [x], *for* [ç]. *Then check your diagrams in Section* 16.3.

C

Make a PHONEMIC *transcription of the following passage. Then check your transcription in* Appendix D.

El general juró que respetaría las quejas de la mujer, quien estaba tan afligida porque la gente había recogido todo el ajo en su jardín. Los gitanos dijeron que no sabían ni jota. El general por fin eligió hacer construir una reja para proteger el jardín.

D

Now make a PHONETIC *transcription of the same passage. Use only* [p t k b ɓ d ɗ g g w ĉ f s z h y ŷ x]. *Then check your transcription in* Appendix D.

17

~~~~~~

REVIEW OF AFFRICATE /ĉ/ *AND FRICATIVES* /f s y x (h)/

17.1 Phonemes

		Labio-dental	Inter-dental	Alveolar	Palatal	Velar	Glottal
SLIT FRICATIVES		f	θ			x	(h)
					y		
GROOVE FRICATIVE				s			
AFFRICATE					ĉ		

17.2 Allophones

	Bilabial	Labio-dental	Inter-dental	Alveolar	Palatal	Velar	Glottal
SLIT FRICATIVES	ƥ	f	θ		ç	x	h
					y		
GROOVE FRICATIVES				s ś	š		
				z ż	ž		
AFFRICATES					ĉ		
					ŷ		

17.3 Facial Diagrams

See Sections 13.3, 14.3, 15.3, and 16.3.

17.4 Articulation

/ĉ/ $\begin{cases} \text{[ĉ] voiceless, palatal affricate} \\ \text{[š] voiceless, palatal groove fricative} \end{cases}$

/f/ $\begin{cases} \text{[f] voiceless, labio-dental slit fricative} \\ \text{[ɸ] voiceless, bilabial slit fricative} \end{cases}$

/s/ $\begin{cases} \text{[s] voiceless, alveolar groove fricative} \\ \text{[z] voiced counterpart of [s]} \\ \text{[ṡ] voiceless, alveolar groove fricative. The tongue tip is slightly} \\ \qquad \text{retroflexed.} \\ \text{[ż] voiced counterpart of [ṡ]} \\ \text{[h] voiceless, glottal slit fricative} \end{cases}$

/θ/ $\begin{cases} \text{[θ] voiceless, interdental slit fricative} \\ \text{[ð] voiced counterpart of [θ]} \end{cases}$

/y/ $\begin{cases} \text{[y] voiced, palatal slit fricative} \\ \text{[ŷ] voiced, palatal affricate} \\ \text{[ž] voiced, palatal groove fricative} \end{cases}$

/h/ {[h] voiceless, glottal slit fricative.

/x/ $\begin{cases} \text{[ç] voiceless, palatal slit fricative} \\ \text{[x] voiceless, velar slit fricative} \end{cases}$

17.5 Allophonic Distribution

/ĉ/ has only one principal allophone [ĉ]. Some speakers have [š] in free variation with it.

/f/ has only one principal allophone [f]. Some speakers have [ɸ] in certain sequences.

/s/ has several allophones: [z] or [ż] before voiced consonants, [s], [h] or [Ø] (silence) before /r̄/, and [s] or [ṡ] everywhere else. Many speakers have [h] in any syllable-final position.

/θ/, heard only in peninsular Spanish, has two principal allophones: [ð] before voiced consonants and [θ] everywhere else.

/y/ has two principal allophones: some speakers have [ŷ] in absolute-initial position and after [ñ] and [l̦], and [y] everywhere else, other speakers have [y] everywhere, and some vary between [y] and [ŷ] in absolute-initial position and after [ñ] and [l̦].

/x/ has two principal allophones [x] and [ç]. /h/ has one main allophone [h]. Remember that the parentheses around /h/ in the chart in Section 17.1 mean that any given dialect of American Spanish has EITHER a /x/ phoneme OR a /h/ phoneme. See Appendix A for the rules for allophonic distribution and corresponding examples.

17.6 Dialectal Variations

Most dialects of Spanish have only [ĉ] for /ĉ/, but some use [š] in free variation with [ĉ].

[ɸ] is primarily a rural variant of /f/ in many parts of the Spanish-speaking world.

All American Spanish-speakers use **seseo,** that is, the pronunciation of /s/ where Castilian has the phoneme /θ/. Many dialects—particularly in the coastal areas of America and the Caribbean—have [h] for /s/ in syllable-final position.

Most Spanish-speakers use **yeísmo,** that is, the pronunciation of /y/ where some dialects of Castilian and American Spanish have palatal /ļ/. These latter dialects are called **lleísta** in contrast to **yeísta** speech.

The substitution of [ž] for /y/ is common in Argentina, Uruguay, and central Colombia.

The phoneme /x/ is used in many dialects of American Spanish and /h/ is used in the others.

17.7 Contrasts with English

English-speakers have no trouble with /ĉ/ and /f/.

The main mispronunciation of /s/ is the use of the voiced allophone [z] in the wrong place—often when **z** is found in spelling, as in **azul,** or for inter-vocalic /s/ in cognate words: **presidente, rosa,** etc.

Most English-speakers do not use the Castilian /θ/ consistently and confuse it with /s/.

Many English-speakers feel that there must be a significant difference between the various allophones of /y/ and are reluctant to use [ŷ] in the places where it is naturally used in Spanish.

/x/ is a difficult sound for many English-speakers, who prefer to use the acceptable variety /h/ instead.

17.8 References

See Sections 13.8, 14.8, 15.8, and 16.8.

17.9 Drills

A Recognition

Your teacher will pronounce a series of words and phrases, some of which are pronounced correctly and some incorrectly. Identify the correct pronunciation by saying "correct" or "incorrect."

1. fuerte [f]	7. bello [y]	13. mujer [x]
2. rosa [z]	8. jardín [k]	14. se fueron [f]
3. llamar [ŷ]	9. calle [l̦]	15. yo me voy [ŷ]
4. desde [z]	10. esperar [h]	16. gitano [ç]
5. gente [h]	11. hielo [ŷ]	17. inyección [ŷ]
6. presidente [s]	12. isla [z]	18. se fue [x]

19. cazador [z]   20. gente [k]

B Recognition-Production

Your teacher will pronounce a series of words and phrases, some of which are pronounced correctly and some incorrectly. If the word or phrase is correctly pronounced, simply repeat it. If it is incorrect, say "incorrect" and then pronounce it correctly.

1. fuerte [x]	7. se calló [ŷ]	13. caja [h]
2. rosa [s]	8. jota [x]	14. se fue [x]
3. llamar [l̦]	9. calle [y]	15. yo me voy [y]
4. desde [θ]	10. esperar [z]	16. gitano [ŷ]
5. gente [x]	11. hierba [hi̦e]	17. el yerno [ŷ]
6. presidente [z]	12. isla [s]	18. se fueron [f]

19. zapato [z]   20. general [x]

C Read Aloud (books open)

Read the words and phrases aloud.

1. salchicha	10. conllevar	19. hígado
2. hierro	11. Santa Rosa	20. ancho
3. jorobado	12. hielas	21. hidalguía
4. el yerno	13. influenza	22. juzgar
5. congelar	14. esfuerzo	23. homólogo
6. hazlo	15. callejuela	24. visitar
7. desgana	16. hojarasca	25. inyección
8. yodo	17. lechuza	26. Venezuela
9. frambuesa	18. digerir	27. hacha

28. humillar	35. rasgar	42. fofo
29. presentar	36. hijuela	43. hojaldrado
30. homónimo	37. escoger	44. rascar
31. chisme	38. razón	45. hondijo
32. gafas	39. caja	46. hoyuelo
33. esbozo	40. ahijado	47. hiena
34. hijastro	41. esposo	48. propósito

49. Mallea   50. huérfano

D   Read Aloud (books open)

Read the sentences aloud.

1. El hijo hizo un esfuerzo.
2. Tuvo razón en escogerlo.
3. El presidente va a visitar a Venezuela.
4. Si te hielas así, coges influenza.
5. El esposo hizo un esbozo que era completamente fofo.
6. Si no estás muy desganado, hazlo.
7. Mi ahijado rasgó la hoja.
8. Sí, el yerno va a comprar un congelador.
9. No se digiere bien por el hígado.
10. Para defenderse de la hiena, sacó una barra de hierro de la caja.
11. La hidalguía no se juzga así.
12. A propósito, haz un esfuerzo para evitar esa callejuela.

E   "Live" Transcription

17.10 Exercises

A

Give an articulatory description for [ĉ], *for* [ṡ], *for* [y], *for* [x]. *Then check your answers in Section* 17.4.

B

Sketch a facial diagram for [f], *for* [z], *for* [θ], *for* [ŷ]. *Then check your diagrams in Sections* 13.3, 14.3, 14.4, *and* 15.3, *respectively.*

C

Make a PHONEMIC *transcription of the following passage. Then check your transcription in* Appendix D.

El muchacho rasgó la hoja de papel y la tiró a la alfombra. Se le llenaron los ojos de lágrimas, y empezó a llorar. Todas las damas fueron a solazarlo, pero, ahora el chico se yergue, se dirige al yerno, y le dice: —¡Voy a llamar al presidente!

D

Now make a PHONETIC *transcription of the same passage. Use only* [p t k b ɓ d̚ d g g w ĉ f s z h y ŷ x]. *Then check your transcription in* Appendix D.

17.11 Questions   *Idiolect - personal manner of speech.*

Write your answers on a separate sheet of paper and check them in Appendix D.

1. The second part of the affricate [ĉ] is almost exactly like [___].
2. [f] is labio-dental. This means that the ___ lip touches the ___ teeth.
3. [š] is a voiceless, palatal ___ fricative.
4. Labio-dental [m̩] before [f] shows that ___ consonants always assimilate to the following consonants in Spanish.
5. How is the substitution of [x] for [f] before [u̯], as in **fue,** regarded in the Spanish-speaking world?
6. **Seseo** is the use of /s/ to the exclusion of /___/.
7. The use of both /s/ and /θ/ characterizes CERTAIN DIALECTS OF AMERICAN SPANISH/PENINSULAR SPANISH.
8. In some Spanish dialects /s/ is realized as [h] in ___ position.
9. If [s] and [š] are both voiceless, alveolar groove fricatives, what are the articulatory features that distinguish them?
10. Word-initial letter **z-** ALWAYS/SOMETIMES/NEVER represents [z] in Spanish.
11. [ŷ] is the voiced counterpart of [___].
12. The use of /y/ to the exclusion of /l̦/ in Spanish is called ___.
13. TRUE/FALSE Palatal /l̦/ is not phonemic in any dialect of American Spanish.
14. Why do Spanish-speakers often have trouble distinguishing the words in such English pairs as *Yale-jail* and *yellow-jello?*
15. Why are some English-speakers reluctant to use [ŷ] in Spanish?
16. Why is [x] a difficult sound for some English-speakers?
17. In English [ç] IS NEVER USED/OCCURS IN SOME IDIOLECTS AND DIALECTS.
18. TRUE/FALSE Some dialects of American Spanish have both /x/ and /h/ as phonemes.
19. Why is [h] in a certain sense articulated like a vowel?
20. What letters represent /x/ (or /h/) in most Spanish words?

18

/ m n ñ /

18.1 Phonemes

/m/ is a voiced, bilabial nasal.
/n/ is a voiced, alveolar nasal.
/ñ/ is a voiced, palatal nasal.

18.2 Allophones

[m] is a voiced, bilabial nasal, allophone of /m/.
[m̪] is a voiced, labiodental nasal, allophone of /m/.
[n̪] is a voiced, dental nasal, allophone of /n/.
[n] is a voiced, alveolar nasal, allophone of /n/.
[ñ] is a voiced, palatal nasal, allophone of /ñ/.
[ŋ] is a voiced, velar nasal, allophone of /n/.

18.3 Facial Diagrams

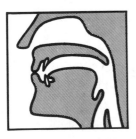
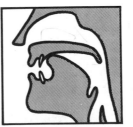
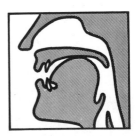

[m]   [n]   [ñ]

Diagram for [m̩] is the same as for [v] in Section 9.3, except that velum is open.

Diagram for [n̪] is the same as for [d] in Section 10.3, except that the velum is open.

Diagram for [ŋ] is the same as for [g] in Section 11.3, except that the velum is open.

18.4 Articulation

Each of the nasals is homorganic with a non-nasal, that is, they are articulated in the same place. The only functional difference in each case is that the velum is open and the airstream passes through and resonates in the nasal cavity as well as the oral cavity.

For [m] the lips press together as they do for [b].

For [m̩] the lower lip touches the edge of the upper front teeth as it does for [v] and [f]. However, since these last two sounds are fricative, the lip touches lightly, but for [m̩] it presses against the teeth.

For [n̪] the tip of the tongue is placed against the back of the upper front teeth as it is for [d].

For [n] the tip of the tongue is placed against the alveolar ridge.

For [ñ] the tongue dorsum humps up and makes extensive contact with the palate as it does for the first part of [ŷ]. But since this last sound is an affricate, the tongue is quickly released but for [ñ] it presses against the palate.

For [ŋ] the tongue dorsum presses against the velum as it does for [g].

18.5 Allophonic Distribution

The most important characteristic of the nasals in Spanish is that in syllable-final position they always assimilate to the following consonant. Not only does the following consonant determine which nasal allophone will be used, but also which nasal phoneme. For example, a following alveolar consonant [s] causes the preceding /n/ to be realized as the alveolar [n] as in **mensual** [men̩-suál]. A following velar consonant [k] causes the preceding /n/ to be realized as the velar [ŋ] as in **blanco** [bláŋ-ko]. But a following bilabial consonant [b] causes the phoneme /ñ/ to REPLACE /n/, since [m] is an allophone of /m/ rather than /n/, as in **enviar** [em̩-bi̯ár]. A following palatal consonant [ĉ] causes the phoneme /ñ/ to REPLACE /n/, since [ñ] is an allophone of /ñ/ rather than /n/, as in **ancho** [áñ-ĉo]. Only three nasals in Spanish contrast in syllable-initial position, thus there are only three nasal phonemes /m/, /n/, and /ñ/, as in **rama** *branch*, **rana** *frog*, and **raña** *lowland*.

The bilabial [m] always precedes the bilabials [p b], regardless of spelling:

un peso [um-pé-so], **un beso** [um-bé-so], **enviar** [ẹm-bi̯ár]. It usually precedes [m], too: **conmigo** [kom-mí-go]. /m/ is restricted in its distribution and never occurs in word-final position, where it is replaced by /n/, regardless of spelling: **máximum** [mák-si-mun], **álbum** [ál-bun]. [m] is also one of the only three nasals that can begin a syllable: **más** [más], **como** [kó-mo].

The labio-dental [m̩] always precedes the labio-dental [f], regardless of spelling: **enfermo** [ẹm̩-fẹ́r-mo]. Notice that the phonemic transcription of this word is /em-fér-mo/.

The dental [n] always precedes the dentals [t d]: **antes** [án̪-tes], **dónde** [dón̪-de].

The alveolar [n] always precedes the alveolars [s r̄ l]: **mensual** [mẹn-su̯ál], **enredar** [ẹn-r̄e-dár], **enlazar** [ẹn-la-sár]. /r̄/ replaces /r/ after /n/, as in **enredar** above. The alveolar [n] sometimes precedes [m] in certain words, as **inmediato** [in-me-d̯i̯á-to], but [im-me-d̯i̯á-to] is also heard. Like [m], alveolar [n] can begin a syllable: **no** [nó], **fino** [fí-no]. But, unlike [m], it can end a word: **van** [bán].

The palatal [ñ] always precedes the palatals [ĉ y ŷ l̮] (but not [ç]): **ancho** [áñ-ĉo], **en hielo** [ẹñ-yé-lo] or [ẹñ-ŷé-lo], **con llave** [koñ-l̮a-be]. Notice that the phonemic transcription of these words and phrases has /ñ/: /áñ-ĉo/. Like [m] the [ñ] never ends a word, but like both [m] and [n], it can begin a syllable: **ñato** [ñá-to], **paño** [pá-ño].

The velar [ŋ] always precedes the velars [k g x]: **encantar** [ẹŋ-kaṇ-tár], **tengo** [tẹ́ŋ-go], **monja** [móŋ-xa], and bilabio-velar [w]: **con huevos** [koŋ-wé-bos]. Velar [ŋ] also alternates with [n] in word-final position in many dialects of Spanish, including General American Spanish: **van** [bán] or [báŋ]. With some speakers it occurs exclusively in word-final position, thus creating such contrasts as **enaguas** [e-ná-gu̯as] *petticoats* vs. **en aguas** [e-ŋá-gu̯as] *in waters*. In these dialects, thus, some linguists analyze /ŋ/ as another nasal phoneme since it causes a change in meaning in this position.

The rules for /m n ñ/:

$$
/m/ \longrightarrow
\begin{bmatrix}
[\underset{\smile}{m}]\!\!\Big/\underline{} /f/ \\[2mm]
\begin{Bmatrix} [n] \\ [ŋ] \end{Bmatrix} \Big/ \text{word-final} \\[2mm]
[m] \text{ elsewhere}
\end{bmatrix}
$$

$$/n/ \longrightarrow \begin{bmatrix} [m] & /\!\!-\!\!\begin{Bmatrix} /p/ \\ /b/ \end{Bmatrix} \\[10pt] [\underset{\sim}{m}] & /\_\ /f/ \\[10pt] \begin{Bmatrix} [n] \\ [m] \end{Bmatrix} & /\!\!-\!\!/m/ \\[10pt] [\underset{.}{n}] & /\!\!-\!\!\begin{Bmatrix} /t/ \\ /d/ \end{Bmatrix} \\[10pt] [\tilde{n}] & /\!\!-\!\!\begin{Bmatrix} /\hat{c}/ \\ /y/ \end{Bmatrix} \\[10pt] [\eta] & /\!\!-\!\!\begin{Bmatrix} /k/ \\ /g/ \\ /x/ \\ /w/ \end{Bmatrix} \\[16pt] \begin{Bmatrix} [n] \\ [\eta] \end{Bmatrix} & /\ \text{word-final} \\[10pt] [n] & \text{elsewhere} \end{bmatrix}$$

$$/\tilde{n}/ \longrightarrow [\tilde{n}]$$

18.6 Dialectal Variations

In most dialects of Spanish the distributions discussed in the previous section are typical. In some dialects, particularly in the Caribbean region and Central America, velar [ŋ] either occurs exclusively in word-final position or alternates freely with [n].

18.7 Contrasts with English

Although English has no palatal /ñ/, the sequence of /ny/, as in *onion*, is close enough to make /ñ/ in Spanish quite easy for you.

The main problem stems from the fact that in English a pause feature called plus juncture /+/ prevents assimilation from taking place in many sequences of nasal + consonant: *tango* /tǽŋgo/, but *tan goat* /tǽn+gówt/. Thus, English-speakers say things like **enfermo** [ẹn-fẹr-mo], instead of [ẹm-fẹr-mo], **en casa** [ẹn-ká-sa], instead of [ẹŋ-ká-sa], etc. While not really wrong, since phonemic contrasts between the nasals in Spanish disappear or are neutralized in this syllable-final position, it is not native pronunciation and can sound strange in many cases.

Also, since /n/ and /ŋ/ are phonemic in English—*sin-sing*—you may be reluctant to imitate the use of the velar [ŋ] in word-final position when you hear it, even though meaning is not affected in Spanish by [n] or [ŋ] at the end of a word.

18.8 References

SPANISH

Allen, "Tense/Lax in Castilian Spanish" (1964).
* Bowen and Stockwell, *Patterns of Spanish Pronunciation* (1960), Chapter 3.
* Hyman, "[ŋ] as an Allophone Denoting Open Juncture in Several Spanish-American Dialects" (1956).
* Kiddle, "On Phonemes and Allophones" (1956).
* Navarro, *Manual de pronunciación española* (1957), Sections 86, 87, 89, 103, 110, 122, 130.
* Sawyer, "The Distribution of Some Consonant Allophones in Spanish" (1956–57).
* Stockwell, "On Phonemes and Allophones" (1956).

ENGLISH AND GENERAL

Bronstein (1960), Chapter 6.
Buchanan (1963), Chapter VI.

18.9 Drills

A Recognition

Your teacher will pronounce a series of words and phrases with nasal consonants. Identify the nasal by saying "bilabial" for [m], "labio-dental" for [m̩], "alveolar" for [n], "palatal" for [ñ], and "velar" for [ŋ].

1. pongo	12. enviar	23. con hielo
2. enfático	13. en casa	24. confiar
3. enfocar	14. enredar	25. un vaso
4. con huevos	15. un fósforo	26. ingerir
5. convertir	16. un palo	27. hablan vasco
6. son	17. hinchar	28. infiel
7. lana	18. un coche	29. un cheque
8. enfilar	19. hablan	30. un gato
9. un lobo	20. invitar	31. en Brasil
10. un jarro	21. mensual	32. gancho
11. ancho	22. en Filadelfia	33. estanco

34. ganso   35. hablan ruso

B Repetition

Your teacher will pronounce a series of words and phrases with nasal consonants. Repeat each one, being careful to pronounce the correct nasal allophone.

1. hablan ruso
2. ganso
3. estanco
4. gancho
5. en Bogotá
6. un kilo
7. un chico
8. infiel
9. hablan vasco
10. ingerir
11. un vaso
12. confiar
13. con hielo
14. en Filadelfia
15. constar
16. invierno
17. ven
18. un carro
19. henchir
20. un peso
21. un foco
22. con riqueza
23. en Cuba
24. enviar
25. chancho
26. con generales
27. un lado
28. ancho
29. fino
30. se van
31. convertir
32. con huesos
33. enfocar
34. el nabo
35. énfasis
36. tengo

C   Read Aloud (books open)

Read the words and phrases aloud, being careful to pronounce the correct nasal consonants.

1. un peso
2. en Francia
3. antes
4. insistir
5. ancho
6. ángulo
7. un vaso
8. enfermo
9. andar
10. consecuencia
11. cónyuge
12. encantado
13. un beso
14. un fósforo
15. un techo
16. un litro
17. un chico
18. un gato
19. invierno
20. enfrentar
21. condenar
22. enredar
23. hinchar
24. monje
25. enviar
26. con furor
27. un dedo
28. un saco
29. un yerno
30. engendrar
31. hembra
32. confianza
33. interno
34. enlatado
35. con yeso
36. un huevo

 D   Read Aloud (books open)

Read the phrases and sentences aloud, being careful to pronounce the correct nasal consonants.

1. Se lo envié el año pasado.
2. Cantan canciones a sus santos.
3. Hay que enfrentarse con la verdad de vez en cuando.
4. Un señor con sus hijos pudieron terminar su trabajo en el jardín.
5. Un chico enyesó el muro con pala.
6. Buscan huevos de gallina en un huerto lleno de naranjos.

E   "Live" Transcription

18.10 Exercises

A

Give an articulatory description for [m], *for* [ŋ̊], *for* [ŋ]. *Then check your answers in Section* 18.2.

B

Sketch a facial diagram for [m̥], *for* [n], *for* [ñ]. *Remember that the velum must be open for all nasal sounds. Then check your diagrams in Sections* 9.3 *and* 18.3, *respectively.*

C

Make a PHONEMIC *transcription of the following passage. Then check your transcription in* Appendix D.

En frente del convento de San Benito había un jardín lleno de naranjos. Un monje paseaba rezando sus oraciones en voz baja. Un chico estaba jugando con un gatito que un padre le había enviado.

D

Now make a PHONETIC *transcription of the same passage. Use only* [p t k b ƀ d đ g g w ĉ f s z h y ŷ m m̥ ŋ̊ n ñ ŋ]. *Then check your transcription in* Appendix D.

19

/ 1 ļ /

19.1 Phonemes

/l/ is a voiced, alveolar lateral.
/ļ/ is a voiced, palatal lateral.

19.2 Allophones

[ḻ] is a voiced, dental lateral, allophone of /l/.
[l] is a voiced, alveolar lateral, allophone of /l/.
[ļ] is a voiced, palatal lateral, allophone of /l/ or /ļ/.

19.3 Facial Diagrams

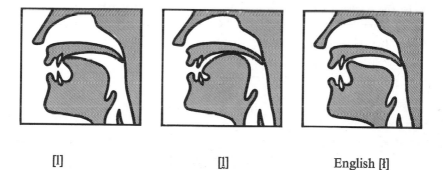

[l]   [l]   English [ɫ]

    Diagram for [ḻ] is the same as for [d] in section 10.3. For [l] and [ļ] the openings on either or both sides of the tongue cannot be shown on a facial diagram.

19.4 Articulation

For all laterals the vocal bands vibrate, and the airstream escapes on one or both sides of the tongue, hence the name "lateral."

For dental [l̪] the tip of the tongue presses against the inside of the upper front teeth.

For alveolar [l] the tip of the tongue presses against the alveolar ridge. For palatal [ļ] the tongue tip rests against the lower front teeth. The dorsum humps up and makes extensive contact with the palate. Palatal [ļ] is similar to the sequence [li̯], but there is an articulatory difference since [l] is alveolar and a functional difference since a distinction can be made in some dialects between **hallar** [a-ļár] *to find* and **aliar** [a-li̯ár] *to ally*. This palatal [ļ] exists in other languages, such as Italian, as in **figlio** [fíl-ļo], and Portuguese, as in **filho** [fí-ļu].

19.5 Allophonic Distribution

/l/, like the nasals, assimilates to the following consonant. Dental [l̪] precedes the dentals [t d]: **alto** [ál̪-to], **aldea** [al̪-dé-a].

Alveolar [l] is the most widely used lateral and precedes the bilabials [p ƀ m]: **salpicar** [sal-pi-kár], **alba** [ál-ƀa], **calma** [kál-ma]; the labiodental [f]: **alfombra** [al-fóm-bra]; the alveolars [s n r̄]: **falso** [fál-so], **el niño** [ęl-ní-ño], **alrededor** [al-r̄e-đe-đór]; the velars [k g x]: **alcoba** [al-kó-ƀa], **algo** [ál-go], **álgebra** [ál-xe-ƀra]; and the bilabio-velar [w]: **el hueso** [ęl-wé-so].

Alveolar [l] can also begin a word: **lana** [lá-na] and a syllable: **malo** [má-lo], and it can end a word: **mal** [mál].

Palatal [ļ] in the dialects where it exists as a phoneme can begin a word: **llamar** [ļa-már], and a syllable: **calle** [ká-ļe], but it never ends a word. Palatal [ļ] also precedes the palatals [y ŷ ĉ ñ ļ] (but not [ç]) in all dialects of Spanish: **el hielo** [ęl-yé-lo] or [ęl-ŷé-lo], **salchicha** [saļ-ĉí-ĉa], **el ñoño** [ęl-ñó-ño], **el llano** [ęl-ļá-no].

In these cases, if the dialect is **yeísta,** as General American Spanish is, [ļ] functions merely as an allophone of /l/, but if the dialect distinguishes /l/ from /ļ/, then the /ļ/ is really replacing /l/ phonemically.

The rule for /l/:

$$
/l/ \longrightarrow
\begin{bmatrix}
[l̪] & \Big/ - \begin{Bmatrix} /t/ \\ /d/ \end{Bmatrix} \\[2em]
[ļ] & \Big/ - \begin{Bmatrix} /ĉ/ \\ /y/ \\ /ñ/ \end{Bmatrix} \\[2em]
[l] \text{ elsewhere}
\end{bmatrix}
$$

19.6 Dialectal Variations

Most dialects of Spanish—both in America and in Spain—are characterized by **yeísmo;** that is, the palatal lateral /l̬/ phoneme is replaced by /y/. **Halla** and **haya** are pronounced exactly alike: [á-ya]. Some speakers of American Spanish, however, have a palatal lateral /l̬/ phoneme and distinguish between **halla** [á-l̬a] and **haya** [á-ya]. This usage, called **lleísmo,** exists in some parts of Colombia, Chile, Argentina, Peru, Bolivia, and in most of Paraguay. It, of course, also characterizes some dialects of peninsular Castilian.

[l] in syllable-final position is sometimes replaced by [r] and vice-versa: **bolsillo** [bor-sí-yo], **enfermo** [ęm̯-fę́l-mo]. The replacement of [l] by [r], as in the first case, is heard mainly among uneducated speakers in the Caribbean area, the coast of Colombia, and parts of Chile. The replacement of [r] by [l], as in the second case, is common, however, in these areas even among educated speakers.

19.7 Contrasts with English

English [l] in syllable-initial position is not too different from Spanish alveolar [l], but English [ł] in syllable-final or pre-consonantal position, as in *bell, wheel, build,* or *halt,* is quite different. This [ł] is called "dark" whereas the Spanish [l] is called "light." In Spanish, regardless of the position in the word or the phonemic phrase, the alveolar [l] is pronounced with the tongue relatively flat. The English "dark" [ł] is pronounced with the front of the tongue dorsum lowered or concave and the back of the dorsum raised nearer the velum, giving it a vocalic sound (see the diagrams in Section 19.3). In such words as **hotel, mal, tal, sol,** etc., the use of English [ł],while it does not change the meaning, causes a "foreign-sounding" accent.

19.8 References

SPANISH

Alonso, Amado, *Estudios lingüísticos: Temas hispanoamericanos* (1953), Chapter II: Sections 2, 3.

Bès, "Examen del concepto de rehilamiento" (1964).

* Bowen and Stockwell, *Patterns of Spanish Pronunciation* (1960), Chapter 3.

Gili Gaya, *Elementos de fonética general* (1950), Chapter XI.

* Navarro, *Manual de pronunciación española* (1957), Sections 104, 111, 123.

Skelton, "Phonetics, Phonemics, and Pronunciation: Dialect and Standard Language" (1954).

ENGLISH AND GENERAL

* Bronstein (1960), Chapter 6.
* Buchanan (1963), Chapter VI.

19.9 Drills

A　Recognition

Your teacher will pronounce a series of Spanish words and phrases, mixed in with phonetically similar English words and phrases. Identify each by saying "Spanish" or "English."

1. *dell*	21. al	41. *feel*
2. *la*	22. *Lita*	42. *"lotta"*
3. fil	23. balsa	43. cal
4. *lock a*	24. lo	44. laca
5. sol	25. bol	45. lira
6. Lara	26. *loco*	46. loco
7. *call*	26. *goal*	47. *bowl*
8. lama	28. *loan a*	48. gol
9. *tall*	29. *Lucas*	49. lona
10. *Lana*	30. *loose*	50. *Lisa*
11. *Oh, tell*	31. tal	51. *all*
12. les	32. *low*	52. Lucas
13. mal	33. lana	53. *balsa*
14. lid	34. *lace*	54. *coal*
15. sal	35. *mall*	55. *llama*
16. *Lima*	36. del	56. hotel
17. col	37. la	57. luz
18. *Linda*	38. *soul*	58. *lead*
19. *tool*	39. Linda	59. Lima
20. lisa	40. tul	60. *Saul*

B　Recognition-Production

Your teacher will pronounce a series of Spanish words and phrases, mixed in with phonetically-similar English words and phrases. If the word or phrase is Spanish, say "Spanish" and repeat it, but if it is English, say "English" and pronounce the corresponding Spanish word or phrase correctly.

1. del	9. *bowl*	17. *loan a*
2. *soul*	10. *goal*	18. al
3. *tall*	11. lira	19. *Saul*
4. *mall*	12. hotel	20. *Lita*
5. col	13. *Linda*	21. sol
6. *Lisa*	14. la	22. *lace*
7. *Oh, tell*	15. *low*	23. gol
8. lo	16. tul	24. *la*

25. Lucas	35. *tool*	45. *"lotta"*
26. *coal*	36. lona	46. *balsa*
27. linda	37. loco	47. *all*
28. *Lima*	38. luz	48. lama
29. cal	39. lisa	49. *call*
30. *Lucas*	40. *lead*	50. Lima
31. balsa	41. *Lana*	51. lid
32. laca	42. *llama*	52. *dell*
33. Lara	43. les	53. *feel*
34. *loose*	44. *lock a*	54. *call*

C   Repetition

Repeat the word or phrase after your teacher.

1. lana	10. lijar	19. levantarse
2. pelo	11. el gato	20. elevar
3. falta	12. él	21. volver
4. loro	13. la muchacha	22. lavarse
5. mala	14. a la muchacha	23. ilegal
6. altura	15. esmalte	24. mal
7. leche	16. lo hizo	25. lechuza
8. solo	17. no lo hizo	26. alcoba
9. sol	18. no lo hizo él	27. alcohol

D   Question-Answer

Answer the questions in the affirmative with a complete sentence.

1. ¿Va usted al hotel?
2. ¿Usa usted mucha sal?
3. ¿Vive usted en el distrito federal?
4. ¿Es esto confidencial?
5. ¿Es alto su hermano?
6. ¿Compra usted muchos (-as) calcetines (faldas)?
7. ¿Es usted sentimental?

E   Read Aloud (books open)

Read the sentences aloud.

1. Este valle no vale mucho.
2. El loro lo cantó luego.
3. Voy a lavarme el pelo.
4. Voy a levantarme a la una.
5. Luis la alaba a la luz de la luna.
6. La llama que se llamaba Lola se lamía el lodo.

7. El general es genial.
8. En el hotel vamos a pedir sal, col y alcohol.
9. Leonardo le regaló al niño un real.

F   "Live" Transcription

19.10 Exercises

A

Give an articulatory description for [l̮], *for* [l], *for* [l̪]. *Then check your
answers in Section* 19.2.

B

Sketch a facial diagram for [l], *for* [l̪]. *Then check your diagrams in Section*
19.3.

C

Make a PHONETIC *transcription of the following passage. Remember that
the speaker is* **yeísta.** *Then check your transcription in* Appendix D.

El general llamó al soldado y le dijo que fuera al edificio federal que
estaba en la parte central de la aldea para ver si había llegado la carga de
sal. Cuando llegó al portal del edificio, el guardia le gritó, —¡Alto!

D

Now make a PHONETIC *transcription of the same passage. Use only* [p t k b
b̶ d d̶ g g w ĉ f s z h y ŷ x m m̩ n̩ n ñ ŋ l̮ l l̪]. *Then check your transcription
in* Appendix D.

20

/ r r̄ /

20.1 Phonemes

/r/ is a voiced, alveolar tap.
/r̄/ is a voiced, alveolar trill.

20.2 Allophones

[r] is a voiced, alveolar tap, allophone of /r/.
[ɹ] is a voiced, alveolar slit fricative, allophone of /r/.
[ɹ̥] is a voiceless, alveolar slit fricative, allophone of /r/.
[r̄] is a voiced, alveolar trill, allophone of /r̄/.
[r̥̄] is a voiceless, alveolar trill, allophone of /r̄/.
[R] is a voiced, velar or uvular trill, allophone of /r̄/.
[R̥] is a voiceless, velar or uvular trill, allophone of /r̄/.

20.3 Facial Diagrams

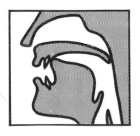

[r]

[r̄]

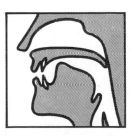

English [ɹ]

Diagrams for [ɹ] and [ɹ̥] are the same as for [r] above, except that for [ɹ̥] there is no voicing.

Diagram for [r̥] is the same as for [r̄] above, except that there is no voicing.

Diagrams for [R] and [R̥] are the same as for [g] in Section 11.3, except that for [R̥] there is no voicing. Sometimes the tongue dorsum touches the uvula instead of the velum for both [R] and [R̥].

20.4 Articulation

For [r] the tongue tip quickly strikes the alveolar ridge once as the airstream passes through. [r], because it is a tap, is like a very short stop.

For [ɹ] the tongue tip touches the alveolar ridge, and the airstream passes through the slit formed by the two. It sounds something like [ż] or [ž], but these two sounds are groove fricatives.

For [ɹ̥] the tongue does the same as for [ɹ], but the vocal bands do not vibrate. It sounds something like [ṡ] or [š], but these two sounds are groove fricatives.

For [r̄] the tongue tip, under tension, strikes the alveolar ridge several times in rapid succession. The articulation for [r̥] is the same as for [r̄] except that there is no voicing.

Both [ɹ] and [ɹ̥] can be lengthened or doubled to function as allophones of the trilled /r̄/ as in **tierra**]ti̯ę́ɹ-ɹa] or [ti̯ę́ɹ-ɹa].

For [R] and [R̥] the tongue dorsum, under tension, strikes either the velum or the uvula several times in rapid succession. They are similar to [g] and [x] respectively, except that these latter sounds are slit fricatives rather than trills as the former. [R] exists in other languages, such as French, as in **rouge** [Rúž] *red*, and German, as in **rot** [Ró:t] *red*.

20.5 Allophonic Distribution

Although /r/ and /r̄/ are phonemes in all dialects of Spanish, they contrast in only one position—syllable-initial in the middle of a word: **caro** [ká-ro] vs. **carro** [ká-r̄o]. In word-initial position only /r̄/ occurs: **rico** [r̄í-ko], although a single **r-** is used to represent it in writing. In the other positions—syllable- and word-final—either one can occur: **puerta** [pu̯ę́r-ta] or [pu̯ę́r̄-ta], **hablar** [a-ɓlár] or [a-ɓlár̄], with no change in meaning. /r/, however, is more common than /r̄/ in these latter positions.

In addition [r̄] occurs after [n] and [l]: **enredar** [ęn-r̄e-dár], **alrededor** [al-r̄e-ɗe-ɗór].

In writing, /r̄/ in word-initial position is represented by **r-**, but intervocalically by **-rr-**. In compounds containing a word beginning with **r-** as the second element, **-rr-** is used to indicate the trilled phoneme if the first element ends in a vowel: **pelirrojo, Monterrey, carirredondo.** Single **-r-** is used if the first element ends in a consonant: **subrayar, subrogar.**

The rules for /r/ and /r̄/:

$$
\text{/r/} \longrightarrow
\begin{bmatrix}
\begin{Bmatrix} [\text{r}] \\ [\bar{\text{r}}] \end{Bmatrix} \ / \ - \begin{Bmatrix} /C/ \\ \# \end{Bmatrix} \\[2ex]
[\bar{\text{r}}] \ \ / \begin{Bmatrix} /\text{n}/ \\ /\text{l}/ \end{Bmatrix} - \\[2ex]
[\text{r}] \ \text{elsewhere}
\end{bmatrix}
$$

$$
\text{/r̄/} \longrightarrow \begin{Bmatrix} [\bar{\text{r}}] \\ [\bar{\text{r}}] \end{Bmatrix}
$$

20.6 Dialectal Variations

In much of Spanish America the single voiced fricative [ɹ] and the single voiceless fricative [ɹ̥] alternate with or replace the tap [r] and the lengthened or doubled varieties do the same with the trilled [r̄]. In the case of [ɹ] and [ɹ̥] this happens mainly in word-final position: **comer** [ko-méɹ] or [ko-méɹ̥]. Lengthened or doubled they replace [r̄] as in **rico** [ɹɹí-ko] or [ɹ̥ɹ̥í-ko]. These fricatives are heard in Chile, western and northern Argentina, Paraguay, western Bolivia, central Ecuador and central Colombia, Costa Rica, and parts of Guatemala and Mexico.

In these areas—particularly in Costa Rica—[ɹ̥] also occurs as the second consonant of a two-consonant cluster, particularly when the first consonant is [t]: **otro** [ó-tɹ̥o]. This [tɹ̥] sequence sounds something like [č], although **otro** still contrasts with **ocho, potro** with **pocho,** etc.

In most of the Spanish-speaking world, however, including the area of General American Spanish, the tap [r] and trilled [r̄] are more widely used and enjoy greater acceptability and prestige. Sometimes speakers in these areas use the voiceless trill [r̥̄] in place of the more standard voiced variety [r̄].

In the Caribbean area, coastal Colombia, and parts of Chile, [l] and [r] are often interchanged in syllable-final position: **enfermo** [ęm-fę́l-mo], **bolsillo** [bor-sí-yo] (see Section 19.6).

In parts of Puerto Rico, Dominican Republic, Cuba, Panama, and coastal Colombia the velar or uvular [R] and [R̩] replaces [r̄]: **carro** [ká-Ro] or [ká-R̩o].

20.7 Contrasts with English

Americans usually have trouble with the trilled /r̄/ since this sound does not exist in American English, although it does in some dialects of British English, such as Scottish.

You also may have difficulty with the tap [r] at first until you become aware of the fact that it is practically the same sound as the English tap or flap [ṱ] and [ḓ] which exist in post-tonic (after the stress) intervocalic position in so many words: *butter, water, muddy, bidder,* etc. Knowing this, you may then be able to convert the single tap into a multiple trill for [r̄].

In any case, the typical English retroflex [r] sounds very strange to the Spanish ear and can even impede communication. It is, incidentally, one of the last sounds mastered by Spanish-speakers, foreigners in general, and even English-speaking children themselves. English [r] is actually almost vocalic (see diagram in Section 20.3) in its articulation and is often analyzed as a semi-vowel, a glide, a liquid, or even a lateral. But the Spanish /r/ and /r̄/ are purely consonantal.

English also has a voiceless fricative [ɹ̊], as in *try, crash.* This is practically the same sound as the Spanish [ɹ], but stands out as foreign-sounding in such words as **tres, otro** to the majority of Spanish-speakers, who use the tap [r] rather than the fricative varieties.

When you use the intervocalic [ṱ] or [ḓ] in such words as **cada, moto, todo, meta,** these sounds are heard by Spanish-speakers as [r], and, thus, these words become **cara, moro, toro, mera.** Therefore, you must be sure to use the dentals [t] or [ḓ] rather than the alveolar taps in these words.

20.8 References

SPANISH

Allen, "Tense/Lax in Castilian Spanish" (1964).
Alonso, Amado, *Estudios lingüísticos: Temas hispanoamericanos* (1953), Chapter II: Sections 1, 3.
* Bowen and Stockwell, *Patterns of Spanish Pronunciation* (1960), Chapter 3.
* Cárdenas, "The Geographic Distribution of the Assibilated *R, RR* in Spanish America" (1958).
* Gili Gaya, *Elementos de fonética general* (1950), Chapter XI.
* Navarro, *Manual de pronunciación española* (1957), Sections 112–17.
* Sawyer, "The Distribution of Some Consonant Allophones in Spanish" (1956–57).
Skelton, "Phonetics, Phonemics, and Pronunciation: Dialect and Standard Language" (1954).
* Wright, "Five Spanish *R*'s: How to Approach Them" (1962).
Zamora Vicente, *Dialectología española* (1960), "Español de América".

ENGLISH AND GENERAL

* Bronstein (1960), Chapters 6, 9.
* Smalley, *Manual of Articulatory Phonetics* (1964), Chapter 17.

20.9 Drills

A   Recognition

Your teacher will pronounce a series of words, some containing /r/ and others /d/. Identify each by saying **ere** *or* **de.**

1. moro	9. mido	17. toro
2. toro	10. sera	18. yodo
3. lloro	11. amada	19. hablada
4. dudo	12. loro	20. hora
5. estaros	13. mira	21. sera
6. hablada	14. jugara	22. seda
7. cara	15. tomada	23. costada
8. hora	16. modo	24. mira

B   Recognition

Your teacher will pronounce a series of words, some containing /r/ and some /r̄/. Identify each by saying "one" for /r/ and "two" for /r̄/.

1. ahora	11. amarra	21. parra
2. barrios	12. torrero	22. barra
3. perro	13. moro	23. cerro
4. caro	14. enterrado	24. cero
5. para	15. cerrado	25. hierro
6. vara	16. deriva	26. forro
7. coro	17. ahora	27. amara
8. cerro	18. varios	28. torero
9. hiero	19. pero	29. morro
10. foro	20. carro	30. enterado

C   Recognition-Production

After your teacher says a word with /r/, say the corresponding word with /d/, and vice versa. For example, for **moro,** *say* **modo;** *for* **todo,** *say* **toro.**

1. modo	9. miro	17. todo
2. todo	10. seda	18. lloro
3. yodo	11. amara	19. hablara
4. duro	12. lodo	20. oda
5. estados	13. mida	21. seda
6. hablara	14. jugada	22. sera
7. cada	15. tomara	23. costara
8. oda	16. moro	24. mida

D   Recognition-Production

After your teacher says a word with /r/, *say the corresponding word with* /r̄/, *and vice versa. For example, for* **ahora,** *say* **ahorra;** *for* **barrios,** *say* **varios.**

1. ahorra	11. amara	21. para
2. varios	12. torero	22. vara
3. pero	13. morro	23. coro
4. carro	14. enterado	24. cerro
5. parra	15. serado	25. hiero
6. barra	16. derriba	26. foro
7. corro	17. ahorra	27. amarra
8. cero	18. barrios	28. torrero
9. hierro	19. perro	29. moro
10. forro	20. caro	30. enterrado

E   Repetition

First repeat after your teacher the English word or phrase, which may have no meaning. Then repeat after him the Spanish word, which in each case does have a common meaning.

1. *eat a* —ira	8. *"a blottah"*	14. *dew dough* —duro
2. *lot o'* —Lara	—hablara	15. *moo dough* —muro
3. *eight o'* —era	9. *"who gotta"*	16. *who dough* —juro
4. *moto* —moro	—jugara	17. *Joe dough* —lloro
5. *pot o'* —para	10. *cot a* —cara	18. *bay dáh* —verá
6. *"oughta"*	11. *photo* —foro	19. *say dáh* —será
—hora (*or* ara)	12. *lead a* —lira	20. *a motta* —amara
7. *meet a* —mira	13. *toto* —toro	21. *Coe dough* —coro

F   Repetition

Repeat the word or phrase after your teacher.

1. espero	11. irá	21. verde
2. hablara	12. será	22. parte
3. toro	13. verá	23. cuerpo
4. para	14. hablará	24. muerdo
5. pero	15. jugará	25. arde
6. ira	16. comerá	26. tordo
7. fuera	17. venderá	27. muerte
8. Miura	18. entenderá	28. cuerno
9. hora	19. comprenderá	29. tuerzo
10. juro	20. lisonjeará	30. perla

31. ir	34. comer	37. jugar
32. dar	35. hablar	38. entender
33. ser	36. salir	39. pasear
	40. enfrentar	

G   Repetition

Repeat the word or phrase after your teacher.

1. rico	9. parra	17. arremolinarse
2. rosa	10. corro	18. arrebatar
3. ramo	11. perro	19. arreglar
4. remo	12. amarra	20. arrastrar
5. Ricardo	13. becerro	21. arraigarse
6. rabo	14. arre	22. arrogantemente
7. Roberto	15. torre	23. erróneamente
8. Roma	16. a Roma	24. derretirse

H   Question-Answer

Answer the questions in the affirmative with a complete sentence.

1. ¿Es usted pelirrojo (-a)?
2. ¿Es usted muy rico (-a)?
3. ¿Tiene usted carro?
4. ¿Tiene usted mucha ropa?
5. ¿Va usted a Monterrey?
6. ¿Tiene usted un perro?
7. ¿Ahorra usted mucha plata ahora?
8. ¿Corre usted a clase?
9. ¿Conoce usted a Ricardo Rondón Rodríguez?
10. ¿Miraba usted "Zorro" en la televisión?

I   Read Aloud (books open)

Read the following sentence aloud.

Ere con ere cigarro, ere con ere barril, rápido corren los carros cargados de azúcar del ferrocarril.

J   "Live" Transcription

20.10 Exercises

A

Give an articulatory description for [r], *for* [ɹ], *for* [r̄]. *Then check your answers in Section* 20.2.

B

Sketch a facial diagram for [r], *for* [ř]. *Then check your diagrams in Section* 20.3.

C

Make a PHONETIC *transcription of the following passage. Then check your transcription in* Appendix D.

Roberto y Enrique paseaban alrededor de la reja. Querían entregar el recado, pero la cosa estaba tan enredada que optaron por esperar una hora más. No estaban enterados de que estaba enterrado el rico que había residido en ese barrio de Roma.

D

Now make a PHONETIC *transcription of the same passage.* Use only [p t k b b̵ d d̵ g g̵ w ĉ f s z h y ŷ x m m̩ ṇ n ñ ŋ ḷ l ḻ r ř]. *Then check your transcription in* Appendix D.

21

SOUNDS REPRESENTED BY THE LETTER X

21.1 Phonemes

/s/ **extraño** /es-trá-ño/, **exacto** /e-sák-to/
/ks/ **extraño** /eks-trá-ño/
/gs/ **examen** /eg-sá-men/
/ks/ **examen** /ek-sá-men/

21.2 Allophones

[s] **extraño** [es-trá-ño]
   exacto [e-sák-to]
[ks] **extraño** [ęks-trá-ño]
[gs] **examen** [ęg-sá-męn]
[ks] **examen** [ęk-sá-męn]

21.3 Facial Diagrams

For [s] see Section 14.3.
For [k] see Section 8.3.
For [g] see Section 11.3.

21.4 Articulation

For [s] see Section 14.4. For [k] see Section 8.4. For [g] see Section 11.4.

21.5 Allophonic Distribution

The sounds represented by the letter x depend to a large extent on both dialect and phonetic environment. When x is followed by a consonant, as in **extraño,** it represents either [ks] or [s]. When x is intervocalic, as in **examen,** it represents [gs] or [ks] and [s] in a few words, such as **exacto.**

The rule for **x**:

$$
x \text{ represents } \left[
\begin{array}{l}
\left\{\begin{array}{l}[\text{ks}]\\ [\text{s}]\end{array}\right\} \Big/ \_\!\_ /C/ \\[6pt]
[\text{s}] \text{ in } \textbf{exacto, auxilio,} \text{ etc.} \\[6pt]
\left\{\begin{array}{l}[\text{gs}]\\ [\text{ks}]\end{array}\right\} \text{ elsewhere}
\end{array}
\right]
$$

21.6 Dialectal Variations

The most common pronunciation represented by **x** in American Spanish is [ks] or [s] before a consonant: **extraño** [ẹks-trá-ño] or [es-trá-ño], and [gs] or [ks] in the intervocalic position: **examen** [ẹg-sá-mẹn] or [ẹk-sá-mẹn]. Dialects that aspirate /s/ in syllable-final position—Cuba, Puerto Rico, Dominican Republic, Venezuela, the River Plata area of Argentina and Uruguay—also use [h] when **x** is before a consonant: **extraño** [ẹh-trá-ño].

In a few words where **x** is in the intervocalic position, many Spanish-speakers use only [s]: **exacto** [e-sák-to], **auxilio** [au̯-sí-li̯o], **taxi** [tá-si].

21.7 Contrasts with English

You have no trouble with either [ks] or [s] for **x** before consonants. However, you may incorrectly transfer your English pronunciation of intervocalic *x*, /gz/ as in *exact*, to Spanish where the sequence is [ks] or [gs], but never [gz]. Just devoice the [z] to [s] to achieve the correct Spanish pronunciation.

21.8 References

SPANISH

* Bolinger, "Evidence on *x*" (1952).
* _____, "The Pronunciation of *x* and Puristic Anti-Purism" (1952).
* _____, "That 'x' again" (1948).
* Navarro, "La *g* de 'examen' " (1962).
* _____, *Manual de pronunciación española* (1957), Section 129.
* _____, "La pronunciación de la x y la investigación fonética" (1952).
* Predmore, "One More Look at the Pronunciation of *x* Before a Consonant" (1949).
* _____, "The Pronunciation of X Before Another Consonant" (1948).
* Sáenz, "There is no 'eggs' in *examen*" (1961).

21.9 Drills

A   Repetition (books open)

Repeat the word or phrase after your teacher, following along in your books as you do. (The letter **x** *before consonants represents either* [ks] *or just* [s]; **x** *between vowels represents either* [ks] *or* [gs], *but* not [gz].)

1. extraño	9. sexto	17. existir
2. exacto [s]	10. sexual	18. exponer
3. extranjero	11. extenso	19. exigir
4. éxito	12. auxilio [s]	20. excusado
5. expansión	13. examen	21. exángüe
6. exhalar	14. exclusivo	22. excelente
7. explicar	15. examinarse	23. existencialista
8. exageración	16. expresar	24. expreso

B   Question-Answer

Answer the questions in the affirmative with a complete sentence.

1. ¿Cree usted que es muy extraño?
2. ¿Puede usted explicar eso?
3. ¿No es excelente la comida de esta universidad?
4. ¿Exagera usted de vez en cuando?
5. ¿Puede usted examinarse la semana que viene?
6. ¿Le gusta el café expreso?
7. ¿Ha tenido usted éxito?
8. ¿No es exactamente lo mismo que antes?
9. ¿Es usted existencialista?
10. ¿Es muy exigente su profesor?
11. ¿Le gustaría ir a algún país extranjero?
12. ¿Se expresa usted bien en español?

C   "Live" Transcription

21.10 Exercises

A

Give the most common phonetic sequences represented by **x** *in* **explicar.** *Then check your answers in Section 21.2.*

B

Give the two most common phonetic sequences represented by **x** *in* **existir.** *Then check your answers in Section 21.2.*

C

Make a PHONEMIC *transcription of the following passage. Then check your transcription in* Appendix D.

Es extraño que no existan esas cosas en este país. Los extranjeros se sorprenden y no pueden explicarlo. Pero después de examinar bien la situación, se dan cuenta de que es exactamente lo mismo en otros países también.

D

Now make a PHONETIC *transcription of the same passage. Use only* [p t k b ƀ d đ g g w ĉ f s z h y ŷ x m m̪ ŋ̪ n ñ ŋ ļ l ḷ r r̄]. *Then check your transcription in* Appendix D.

22

REVIEW OF NASALS /m n ñ/, *LATERALS* /l ļ/,
TAP /r/, *TRILL* /r̄/, *AND THE LETTER* X̰

22.1 Phonemes

	Bilabial				Alveo-lar	Palatal	
NASALS	m				n	ñ	
LATERALS					l	ļ	
TAP					r		
TRILL					r̄		

22.2 Allophones

	Bilabial	Labio-dental		Dental	Alveo-lar	Palatal	Velar
SLIT FRICATIVES					ɟ̡ / ɹ		
NASALS	m	ɱ		n̪	n	ñ	ŋ
LATERALS				ļ	l	ļ	
TAP					r		
TRILLS					r̡ / r̄		Ŗ / R

139

22.3 Facial Diagrams

See Sections 18.3, 19.3, and 20.3.

22.4 Articulation

/m/ $\begin{cases} \text{[m] voiced, bilabial nasal} \\ \text{[m̦] voiced, labio-dental nasal} \end{cases}$

/n/ $\begin{cases} \text{[n̪] voiced, dental nasal} \\ \text{[n] voiced, alveolar nasal} \\ \text{[ŋ] voiced, velar nasal} \end{cases}$

/ñ/ $\{$ [ñ] voiced, palatal nasal

/l/ $\begin{cases} \text{[l̪] voiced, dental lateral} \\ \text{[l] voiced, alveolar lateral} \end{cases}$
/ļ/ $\{$ [ļ] voiced, palatal lateral

/r/ $\begin{cases} \text{[r] voiced, alveolar tap} \\ \text{[ɹ] voiced, alveolar slit fricative} \\ \text{[ɹ̥] voiceless, alveolar slit fricative} \end{cases}$

/r̄/ $\begin{cases} \text{[r̄] voiced, alveolar trill} \\ \text{[r̥̄] voiceless, alveolar trill} \\ \text{[R] voiced, velar or uvular trill} \\ \text{[R̥] voiceless, velar or uvular trill} \end{cases}$

22.5 Allophonic Distribution

There are three nasal phonemes /m n ñ/, all of which contrast in syllable-initial position. /n/ and /ñ/ neutralize in syllable-final position. Only /n/ occurs in word-final position.

In syllable-final position the nasals assimilate to the following consonant. Thus [m] precedes the bilabials [p b], [m̦] precedes the labiodental [f], [n̪] precedes the dentals [t d], [n] precedes the alveolars [s r̄ l], [ñ] precedes the palatals [ĉ y ŷ ļ], and [ŋ] precedes the velars [k g x] and the bilabio-velar [w]. Spelling often does not coincide with the phonetic reality: **un peso** [um-pé-so], **enfermo** [em̦-fér-mo], **álbum** [ál-ƀun], etc.

Velar [ŋ] often alternates with [n] in word-final position and replaces it in some dialects, thereby assuming phonemic status.

/l/ is similar to the nasals in that it assimilates to the following consonant, although there are fewer allophones of /l/ than there are of the nasals. [l̪] precedes the dentals [t d], [ļ] precedes the palatals [ĉ y ŷ ñ ļ], and [l] precedes all other sounds.

When /l̯/ exists as a phoneme, it contrasts with /y/ in syllable-initial position, as in **calló-cayó**. Only /l/ occurs in word-final position.

/r/ and /r̄/ are phonemes but contrast only in word-medial, syllable-initial position. Only /r̄/ occurs in word-initial position. /r/ usually occurs in all other positions, but /r̄/ replaces /r/ after [n l]. The digraph **-rr-** is always used in word-medial position to represent /r̄/ (except in a few compounds, such as **subrayar**), but in word-initial position the single letter **r-** is always used.

The letter **x** represents either /ks/ or /s/ before a consonant and either /gs/ or /ks/ between vowels. In some words, such as **exacto,** intervocalic **-x-** represents /s/.

See Appendix A for the rules for allophonic distribution and corresponding examples.

22.6 Dialectal Variations

In most dialects of American Spanish the allophonic distributions discussed in the previous section are typical.

In the **yeísta** dialects palatal [l̯] is only a pre-palatal allophone of /l/, as in **colcha**. In **lleísta** dialects, which are few in number, it is a phoneme, of course. Some speakers—particularly in the Caribbean area—replace syllable-final [l] with [r] and vice versa, as in **carne** [kál-ne] or **alma** [ár-ma].

In much of Spanish America the fricatives [ɹ ɻ] alternate with or replace the tap [r] and, doubled, they alternate with or replace the trill [r̄]. In Puerto Rico and other limited sections of the Caribbean area the velars [R R̯] are heard instead of the alveolar [r̄].

Pre-consonantal letter **x** in American Spanish represents [ks] or [s], and intervocalic letter **x** represents [gs] or [ks]. Dialects that aspirate /s/ in syllable-final position also use [h] when **x** is before a consonant.

22.7 Contrasts with English

Although English has neither palatal /ñ/ nor palatal /l̯/, the sequences /ny/ and /ly/ are close enough to make these palatal sounds quite easy for you.

Nasals do not always assimilate to following consonants in English as they do in Spanish.

English syllable-final or pre-consonantal [ɫ], as in *bell*, is quite different in sound from Spanish [l], and its use in Spanish creates a conspicuous foreign accent, perhaps as much as any other single sound.

The Spanish trill /r̄/ may cause you trouble since it does not exist in English, but the tap /r/ is easy once you realize that it is really the same sound as English tap [d̮] or [t̮], as in *muddy* or *butter*. The English retroflex [r̠] sounds unpleasant in Spanish and should not be used at all. The English voiceless fricative [ɹ] after an alveolar consonant, as in *try*, should also be avoided in Spanish in such words as **entre, tres, otro.**

Intervocalic letter **x** in Spanish represents [gs] or [ks] rather than [gz] as it does in English.

22.8 References

See Sections 18.8, 19.8, 20.8, and 21.8.

22.9 Drills

A   Read Aloud (books open)

Read the words and phrases aloud.

1. enfático	16. enviar	31. un vaso
2. sol	17. gol	32. loco
3. será	18. en casa	33. juro
4. convertir	19. lira	34. infiel
5. cal	20. extranjero	35. al
6. ancho	21. ingerir	36. cuerpo
7. hora	22. luz	37. gancho
8. remo	23. confiar	38. lid
9. con hielo	24. jugar	39. arrebatar
10. hotel	25. explicar	40. un palo
11. perro	26. estanco	41. Alvaro
12. invierno	27. tul	42. exigente
13. mal	28. verde	43. delgado
14. arrastrar	29. arreglar	44. muerte
15. examen	30. exótico	45. raro

B   Repetition

Repeat the sentences after your teacher.

1. Te puedo prestar un peso.
2. Esa señorita delgada es loca.
3. El carro es verde.
4. Ayer compré un coche.
5. ¡Qué tal!
6. Un experto siempre tiene éxito.
7. El perro se tragó la perla.
8. Creo que hablan francés.
9. Este valle no vale mucho.
10. Recuerde que Rosa es rica.
11. ¿Necesitas un jarro?

12. Voy a llevarme el libro y la pluma.
13. Es extraño que exagere tanto.
14. Un vaso de agua, por favor.
15. ¿Tienen col en el Brasil?

¢ Question-Answer

Answer the questions in the affirmative with a complete sentence.

1. ¿Tiene usted un coche?
2. ¿Va usted a comer en el hotel?
3. ¿Tiene usted un carro?
4. ¿Tiene usted un examen esta semana?
5. ¿Estaba usted enfermo (-a) la semana pasada?
6. ¿Va usted a tomar el sol?
7. ¿Recuerda usted todos los datos?
8. ¿Vive usted al extremo de la calle?
9. ¿Le gusta el invierno?
10. ¿Quería usted contemplar la luna?

D "Live" Transcription

22.10 Exercises

A

Give an articulatory description for [m], *for* [ñ], *for* [ḷ], *for* [r]. *Then check your answers in Section* 22.4.

B

Sketch a facial diagram for [m̥], *for* [ŋ], *for* [l], *for* [r̄]. *Then check your diagrams in Sections* 18.3, 19.3, *and* 20.3, *respectively.*

C

Make a PHONEMIC *transcription of the following phrases. Then check your transcription in* Appendix D.

1. No confundas un peso con un beso.
2. Le puso una inyección al chico a quien había mordido el perro rabioso.
3. Es extraño y aun raro que los exámenes no encanten a los estudiantes.
4. ¡Allá en el rancho grande donde viven los chanchos, las gallinas, las ratas y los ñandúes!

D

Now make a PHONETIC *transcription of the same phrases. Use only* [p t k b ƀ d đ g g w ĉ f s z h y ŷ x m m̥ ņ n ñ ŋ ļ l ḷ r r̄]. *Since you have now studied all the consonants, these symbols will no longer be underlined.*

22.11 Questions

Write your answers on a separate sheet of paper and check them in Appendix D.

1. What consonant does [m̥] precede?
2. What is the most important characteristic of Spanish nasals in syllable-final position?
3. What distributional restrictions do /m/ and /ñ/ have in Spanish?
4. In Costa Rican Spanish [ŋ] is used in word-final position and creates such contrasts as **en hojas** vs. **enojas.** We are then justified in saying that [ŋ] is really ＿＿ in this dialect.
5. When it comes to representing nasal sounds, Spanish orthography is completely "phonetic." TRUE/FALSE
6. There are MORE/FEWER lateral allophones than nasal allophones in Spanish.
7. Most dialects of Spanish are **yeísta/lleísta.**
8. In **yeísmo,** ＿＿ does not exist as a phoneme.
9. If you use the /l/ of *mill* in the Spanish word **mil,** it is close enough to be completely acceptable to the Spanish ear. TRUE/FALSE.
10. Spanish alveolar [l] is often impressionistically called the ＿＿ **l.**
11. /r/ and /r̄/ contrast only in ＿＿ position in Spanish.
12. Both /r/ and /r̄/ occur in word-initial position in Spanish. TRUE/FALSE.
13. Although the tap /r/ and trilled /r̄/ are more common, the ＿＿ are also very common in American Spanish.
14. One of the most difficult English sounds for non-English-speakers to master is the ＿＿.
15. There is no equivalent of the Spanish tap [r] in English. TRUE/FALSE.
16. Although Americans often mistakenly use it, the phonetic sequence ＿＿ is *not* represented in Spanish by **x.**
17. In General American Spanish, **x** before a consonant represents ＿＿ or ＿＿.
18. **X** before a consonant is realized as [h] in dialects that ＿＿.
19. One common word where intervocalic **x** usually represents [s] is ＿＿.
20. The **x** in bold-face type means that ＿＿.

23

~~~~~~

CONSONANT COMBINATIONS

Consonant combinations or sequences in Spanish are composed of two to four contiguous consonants. Consonant sequences in the *same* syllable are referred to as consonant clusters. Only 12 clusters appear at the beginning of a phonemic phrase, word, or syllable: /pr br tr dr kr gr fr pl bl kl gl fl/. Two-consonant clusters (the second consonant is always /s/) can occur at the end of a syllable, but *no* clusters occur at the end of a phonemic phrase or word, except in a few foreign words, like *clubs*, which is sometimes [klúbz] but just as often [klú-ƀes]. In fact, the only single consonants that occur in this word-final or absolute-final position are /d s n l r r̄/.

In word-medial position as many as four consonants can form a sequence in Spanish. In this case two cluster in the first syllable and two in the next: **transcribir** /trans-kri-bír/, **explicar** /eks-pli-kár/. However, many Spanish-speakers eliminate the first consonant of these four-consonant sequences: /tras-kri-bír/, /es-pli-kár/.

In the case of three-consonant sequences, if the second *two* are one of the twelve possible word-initial clusters, listed above, the first consonant goes in the first syllable and the second pair in the second: **hombre** /óm-bre/. Otherwise, the first two consonants cluster in the first syllable and the third one in the next: **perspicaz** /pers-pi-kás/, **constituir** /kons-ti-tuír/.

In the case of two-consonant sequences, if they are one of the twelve possible word-initial clusters, they go in one syllable: **agradable** /a-gra-dá-ble/. Otherwise, one goes in each syllable: **perla** /pér-la/.

Across word boundaries only three-consonant sequences are possible since Spanish words end with no more than one consonant and they begin with no more than two: **el blanco** /el-blán-ko/, **hablan francés** /á-blam-fran-sés/.

Certain Spanish consonant sequences are troublesome to English-speakers, usually because of one difficult consonant, whose difficulty is increased by the presence of a contiguous consonant. Consonant (represented hereafter by C) + /r/ is usually difficult because the second element, the tap /r/, occurs in

English only in an intervocalic position (as an allophone of /t/ or /d/). You may be able to master these /Cr/ clusters more quickly if you insert a vocalic element, such as the schwa /ə/ (as in _appear_), between /C/ and /r/: **brisa** */bə-rí-sa/, **grande** */gə-rán-de/. Such pronunciations, of course, are incorrect in Spanish, but when you find you can produce the tap /r/ with ease, you can then proceed to eliminate the /ə/ gradually and pronounce /Cr/ as a true cluster.

Also difficult are word-medial clusters with the fricatives [b d g] as the first element and [r] or [l] as the second, as in **abrir, podrá, agrio, hablar, siglo,** etc. Since these fricatives alone cause some trouble, their combination with [r] and [l] requires even more concentrated practice for mastery.

Other medial two-consonant sequences in Spanish can be represented as follows: bilabial + consonant /BC/ (B is /p b/), dental + consonant /DC/ (D is /t d/), velar + consonant /GC/ (G is /k g/), nasal + consonant /NC/ (N is /m n ñ/), lateral + consonant /LC/ (L is /l l̠/), vibrant + consonant /RC/ /R is /r r̄/), sibilant + consonant /SC/ (S is /s/). In all these cases, the first consonant, since it is in the syllable-final position, often undergoes certain modifications due to assimilation. Sometimes phonemic contrasts disappear or are neutralized here, and it does not matter which consonant phoneme is used: **apto** is either [áp-to] or [áb-to], **puerta** is either [pu̯ér-ta] or [pu̯ér̄-ta]. In other cases, a certain phoneme or allophone must be used to achieve native-like pronunciation: **blanco** is [bláŋ-ko] rather than *[blán-ko], **rasgar** is [r̄az-gár] rather than *[r̄as-gár].

A particularly difficult sequence of this type for English-speakers is /RC/, as in **perla, ardor, mármol.** Again, sometimes the insertion of schwa /ə/ between the two consonants will help. Essentially the same thing is the very rapid pronunciation of certain English combinations, which approximate the Spanish sequence. For example, _better they_, pronounced rapidly, is close to **verde,** _potter though_ to **pardo,** _otter doór_ (with heavy stress on _door_) to **ardor,** at least as far as the /rd/ are concerned. If you can pronounce the trilled /r̄/, you can use it here also since either /r/ or /r̄/ can be used in this position in Spanish, although /r/ is more common. Notice that the same sequences, with the same problems, occur across word boundaries: **hablar danés, oír voces,** etc.

Other medial sequences which require special attention are /NC/, where the nasal always assimilates to C. This sometimes happens in English, too: _income_ is either /ín + kəm/ or /íŋkəm/, but it always does in Spanish: **incompleto** is always [iŋ-kom-plé-to]. You must remember that the same sequences occur across boundaries: **en casa, en Francia, un peso,** etc.

This assimilation also occurs with /LC/, but this causes English-speakers little difficulty: **alto** [ál-to], **el tomo** [el̠-tó-mo], **salchicha** [sal̠-ĉí-ĉa], **el chico** [el̠-ĉí-ko].

/SC/ also functions this way, although, in this case, assimilation causes voicing rather than a change in the place of articulation, as it does with /NC/

and /LC/. You must learn to voice [s] to [z] in such combinations as **rasgar** [r̄az-gár] and **desde** [déz-de] and also **es grande** [éz-grán̠-de] and **es de** [éz-de]. A particularly difficult sequence is /s-r̄/, but this is also a bit troublesome to Spanish-speakers, who often change /s/ to [h] in rapid conversation: **los ricos** [loh-r̄í-kos]. You can safely imitate this.

In sequences of /BC/, /DC/, and /GC/, "neutralization" takes place and either the voiceless or the voiced phoneme is used: **obtener** is [op-te-nér] or [ob-te-nér], **ritmo** is [r̄ít-mo] or [r̄íd-mo], **actor** is [ak-tór] or [ag-tór].

Medial sequences of three and four consonants generally cause English-speakers little trouble since English has frequent groups of this type in word-final as well as word-medial position: *glimpsed, texts, extreme*, etc. However, these sequences can be troublesome when they contain the combinations described above.

All the sequences discussed so far contain different consonants, but identical consonants also group together in Spanish. Identical-consonant-sequences should not be confused with double *letters*, which, in the case of **ll** and **rr,** represent *single* sounds: /y/ and /r̄/.

Identical-consonant-sequences within a word are very rare in Spanish: **innato** /in-ná-to/, **obvio** /ób-bio/, but fairly common across word boundaries: /ll/ **el libro** /el-lí-bro/, /nn/ **son nombres** /són-nóm-bres/, /ss/ **más suave** /más-suá-be/, /dd/ **libertad de** /li-ber-tád-de/, /l̠l̠/ **el llano** /el̠-l̠á-no/ (in **lleísta** dialects). /rr̄/ theoretically can occur, but they really are pronounced as one /r̄/: **hablar ruso** /a-blá-r̄ú-so/.

Actually all these pairs of identical consonants are realized as one long one (and sometimes just a single one), but it is better and more economical to analyze them as two consonants. Otherwise, we would have to add more consonant phonemes to our inventory, a long /n:/, a long /l:/, etc. Some languages, like Italian, do have single and double or "long" consonant phonemes, but it is simpler in Spanish to use the concept of two consonants since the sequences rarely occur within a word and are usually a feature of word or morpheme juncture.

In rapid conversation these identical-consonant-sequences usually telescope into one, but Spanish-speakers can make a phonemic distinction between a single and two identical consonants if they wish to:

el oro /e-ló-ro/   vs. **el loro** /el-ló-ro/
son hombres /só-nóm-bres/   vs. **son nombres** /són-nóm-bres/
vi dejada /bí-de-xá-da/   vs. **vid dejada** /bíd-de-xá-da/
de llano /de-l̠á-no/   vs. **del llano** /del̠-l̠á-no/

The case is different with /rr̄/ since it is quite difficult to distinguish three taps or vibrations of the tongue from four or five. Thus **ve ríos** and **ver ríos** are both pronounced /bé-r̄í-os/. Phonetically, there may be a slight difference between the vowels in the verbs: [bé-r̄í-os] or [bę-r̄í-os], but Spanish-speakers cannot easily distinguish between a closed [e] and an open [ę], so for all practical purposes the two phrases are the same. A single /s/ is also difficult to distinguish from /ss/ as in **más aves** /má-sá-bes/ vs. **más sabes** /más-sá-bes/.

References

SPANISH

Alarcos Llorach, *Fonología española* (1965), Part II: Chapter V.
Anderson, "Repetitions of Phonetic Change in Spanish" (1966).
* Bowen and Stockwell, *Patterns of Spanish Pronunciation* (1960), Chapter 3.
* Cárdenas, *Introducción a una comparación fonológica del español y del inglés* (1960), "Comparación de los sonidos del español y del inglés".
Malmberg, *Estudios de fonética hispánica* (1965), Chapters I, II.
* Navarro, *Manual de pronunciación española* (1957), Sections 154–56.
Quilis, "La juntura en español" (1964).
* Stockwell and Bowen, *The Sounds of English and Spanish* (1965), Chapter 6.

ENGLISH AND GENERAL

* Buchanan (1963), Chapter VI.
* Heffner, *General Phonetics* (1949), Chapter VII.
Hill, *Introduction to Linguistic Structures* (1958), Chapter 6.
Pulgram, "Consonant Cluster, Consonant Sequence, and the Syllable" (1965).

Drills

A   Repetition (books open)

Repeat the words, which contain the clusters /Cr/ or /Cl/, after your teacher.

1. abrir	17. contrario	33. hiedra
2. abrigo	18. copla	34. ingresar
3. acre	19. criado	35. letra
4. admirable	20. crítico	36. madre
5. aflicción	21. cruz	37. mueble
6. afrentar	22. cuadro	38. ofrecer
7. agradable	23. doble	39. otro
8. ágrio	24. drama	40. padre
9. anclar	25. flor	41. patria
10. atrás	26. flúido	42. peligro
11. biblioteca	27. francés	43. placer
12. brazo	28. frente	44. pregunta
13. breve	29. fruta	45. programa
14. broma	30. gloria	46. regla
15. capricho	31. gracias	47. sidra
16. cifrar	32. grado	48. teatro
	49. tecla 50. vidrio	

B   Repetition (books open)

Repeat the words, which contain the sequences /rC/ or /lC/, after your teacher.

1. acertar	17. corbata	33. observar
2. acercar	18. cordero	34. olvidar
3. acordarse	19. culto	35. palco
4. adulto	20. cuerpo	36. palma
5. alba	21. curso	37. pulgada
6. alcalde	22. reformar	38. charlar
7. aldea	23. dulce	39. silbido
8. alfalfa	24. ejercicio	40. borla
9. alma	25. enfermo	41. urgente
10. árbol	26. espalda	42. alfombra
11. calcetín	27. garganta	43. algo
12. carne	28. guardar	44. torpe
13. carta	29. largo	45. horchata
14. cercado	30. marcharse	46. Barja
15. cerdo	31. moderno	47. perder
16. colgar	32. morder	48. pardo

C   Repetition (books open)

Repeat the words, which contain three- and four-consonant sequences, after your teacher.

1. abstener	14. disfrutar	27. semblante
2. administración	15. empleado	28. suscribir
3. ampliación	16. encontrar	29. transformar
4. astro	17. enfrente	30. transmitir
5. centro	18. esclavo	31. abstracción
6. complemento	19. estrecho	32. abstracto
7. comprometerse	20. fieltro	33. constructor
8. concluir	21. manuscrito	34. exclamar
9. conflicto	22. mezclar	35. explicar
10. constante	23. mientras	36. expresión
11. constituir	24. mostrar	37. extranjero
12. describir	25. pulcro	38. transporte
13. desgracia	26. ristre	39. transcribir
	40. transplantar	

D   Read Aloud (books open)

Read the sentences aloud.

1. El criado declaró su amor por la familia.
2. Es increíble que no pueda hablar ruso.

3. Pero creo que podrá hablar danés.
4. Es verdad que es rojo, sí, es rojísimo.
5. Saldrá antes que tenga tiempo para terminar su transcripción.
6. ¿Cuál es el modo favorito de transporte en las ciudades argentinas?
7. Se ha cortado la electricidad y, por eso, no funcionará el refrigerador.
8. Los árboles se pondrán verdes dentro de poco.
9. Las ardillitas están corriendo por los céspedes, entre la hojarasca.
10. Es imprescindible que se su(b)scriba usted a esas revistas guatemaltecas.

24

INTRODUCING THE VOWELS OF SPANISH

Vowels are distinguished from consonants by the fact that the airstream is not blocked or impeded by the upper and lower articulators. The quality of vowels is determined by the shape of the resonance chambers, i.e., the oral or buccal cavity and the pharynx. These shapes, in turn, are created by the position of the tongue on both a vertical axis and a horizontal axis (see diagrams on p. 32).

There are three vertical positions of the tongue: HIGH, where the tongue is close to the palate; MID, where it is about halfway down in the mouth; and LOW, where it is very low in the mouth. There are also three tongue positions with a front-to-back axis: FRONT, where the highest part of the tongue, the blade, is fairly close to the alveolar ridge; CENTRAL, where the highest part of the tongue is in the center of the oral cavity; and BACK, where the highest part of the tongue, the dorsum, is fairly close to the velum.

Thus, we can classify vowels in this two-dimensional fashion. In Spanish there are five meaningful positions:

1. HIGH FRONT: /i/ as in **piso.**
2. MID FRONT: /e/ as in **peso.**
3. LOW CENTRAL: /a/ as in **paso.**
4. MID BACK: /o/ as in **poso.**
5. HIGH BACK: /u/ as in **puso.**

	Front	Central	Back
High	i		u
Mid	e		o
Low		a	

The vocalic system of American English[1] is much more varied and complicated than that of Spanish. Each of the nine positions (although only eight for some dialects) is filled by a phoneme. There are also three glides, which function either as syllable-initial consonants or post-vocalic semi-vowels, i.e., the second element of a complex vowel nucleus. Thus, we have

1. HIGH FRONT: /i/ as in *pit*.
2. MID FRONT: /e/ as in *pet*.
3. LOW FRONT: /æ/ as in *pat*.
4. HIGH CENTRAL: /ɨ/ as in *just a minute*.
5. MID CENTRAL: /ə/ as in *putt*.
6. LOW CENTRAL: /a/ as in *pot*.
7. HIGH BACK: /u/ as in *put*.
8. MID BACK: /o/ as in *obey* or *"gonna."*
9. LOW BACK: /ɔ/ as in *bought*.
10. HIGH FRONT GLIDE: /y/ as in *say*.
11. HIGH BACK GLIDE: /w/ as in *now*.
12. MID CENTRAL GLIDE: /h/ as in *paw*.

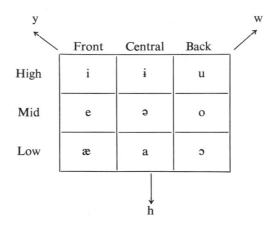

Theoretically, there are 36 possible vowel nuclei in English: nine simple vowels, plus 27 nuclei, composed of each simple vowel and one of the three glides. However, no single dialect of English has all 36 or any number even close to it.

The pronunciation differences between dialects of English are due mainly to variations in the vowels and vowel nuclei, but in Spanish such differences are due mainly to consonant variations. Spanish vowels are quite uniform from dialect to dialect. In fact, the Spanish vocalic system is simpler, more uniform, and more symmetrical than that of any other language commonly

---

[1] The vocalic system of American English presented here is the one formulated by George L. Trager and Henry Lee Smith, Jr. (1951).

studied by Americans. There are only a few allophonic modifications. /e/ has a closed [e], as in **peso** [pé-so], and a more open [ę], as in **perla** [pér-la]. This open [ę] occurs in most checked syllables, i.e., syllables which end in a consonant or consonant cluster. /i/ and /u/ each have a simple vowel allophone: [i], as in **piso** [pí-so], and [u], as in **puso** [pú-so], and a semi-vowel allophone, which is the beginning or final element of a diphthong: [i̯], as in **siete** [si̯é-te] or **seis** [sé̯is], and [u̯], as in **suave** [su̯á-ƀe] or **causa** [káu̯-sa]. Some linguists recognize other vowel allophones in Spanish, but these distinctions are minor and depend so much on phonetic environment that any English-speaker usually pronounces them automatically.

There are, however, two crucial problems that you face in learning Spanish vowels. Both, naturally, have their origin in features of the English sound system.

In English, syllables almost never end with stressed vowels, but with either a consonant or one of the three glides. Thus, the vowels which school teachers have always called "long" are in reality complex vowel nuclei composed of vowel + glide. *No* is really /nów/, *bee* is /bíy/, *high* is /háy/, *too* is /túw/.

But in Spanish stressed vowels very frequently end syllables: **no** /nó/, **vi** /bí/, **tú** /tú/, **dé** /dé/, **va** /bá/. Unaccustomed to such patterns, you tend to pronounce these Spanish words with complex vowel nuclei or diphthongs instead: **no** as */nów/, **mí** as */míy/, **tú** as */túw/, etc. Not only does this sound wrong to the Spanish-speaker, but the problem is further complicated by the fact that Spanish, too, has complex vowel nuclei or diphthongs, but *they are always represented in writing* and contrast with simple vowels. Spanish has **le** /lé/ but also **ley** /léi/, **reno** /r̄é-no/ but also **reino** /r̄éi-no/. Thus, there may be phonemic confusion as well as phonetic inaccuracy if the simple vowels in Spanish are not pronounced properly.

The other major problem concerns unstressed vowels in Spanish. In English most unstressed syllables have either /ə/ or /i̇/: *animal* /ǽnǐmə̀l/, *appear* /ə̀pír/, *atom* /ǽtǐm/, *porpoise* /pórpǐs/. Some dialects have /i̇/ instead of /ə/ and vice versa. Notice that the spelling does not correspond to the pronunciation.

You tend to substitute the vowels /ə/ or /i̇/, neither of which are Spanish sounds, for unaccented vowels in Spanish. This is completely unacceptable since it is not only incorrect phonetically, but also often destroys contrasts in gender or verbs forms. The pronunciation of **mi hermano** as */mier-má-nə/ leaves the Spanish-speaker in doubt as to whether the phrase is **mi hermano** or **mi hermana.** The pronunciation of **diría** as */di-rí-a/ may make the Spanish-speaker wonder whether it is **daría** or **diría.** Thus, neither /ə/ nor /i̇/ should ever be used in Spanish.

There are three other features of vowel articulation which are important in many languages but not in Spanish since they happen automatically with the production of each vowel. Lip-rounding is functional in a language like French, but in Spanish the lips are always rounded for the back vowels /o u/, they are always spread for the front vowels /e i/, and they are always in an intermediate or neutral position for the central vowel /a/.

Nasalization is also contrastive in such languages as Portuguese and French, but in Spanish it happens automatically. Any vowel between two nasal consonants is always nasalized: **mono** [mõ-no]. The fact that this nasalization is never used to distinguish meaning and that it is produced by the speaker without conscious attention has led us to ignore it completely in our analysis and inventory of Spanish phones.

Time length or duration is important in a language like German where long vowels are often phonemically distinct from short vowels. Long vowels also occur in Spanish, although not in a distinctive fashion, as in German. They usually occur only in stressed syllables and never contrast with short vowels.

References

SPANISH

Alarcos Llorach, *Fonología española* (1965), Part 2: Chapter III.
Cárdenas, "Acoustic Vowel Loops of Two Spanish Idiolects" (1960).
Delattre, *Comparing the Phonetic Features of English, French, German, and Spanish* (1965), Chapter III.
* Gili Gaya, *Elementos de fonética general* (1950), Chapter VIII.
* Navarro, *Estudios de fonología española* (1946), "Observaciones sobre las vocales castellanas".
* _____, *Manual de pronunciación española* (1957), Sections 33–44, 70.
* Politzer and Staubach, *Teaching Spanish: A Linguistic Orientation* (1965), Chapter VI.
* Stockwell and Bowen, *The Sounds of English and Spanish* (1965), Chapter 7.

ENGLISH AND GENERAL

* Bronstein (1960), Chapters 7, 9.
* Gleason, *An Introduction to Descriptive Linguistics* (1961), Chapter 3.
* Heffner, *General Phonetics* (1949), Chapter V.
* Hoge, "Visible Pronunciation" (1959).
Hultzén, "System Status of Obscured Vowels in English" (1961).
Ladefoged, "The Classification of Vowels" (1956).
Lane, "Acquisition and Transfer in Auditory Discrimination" (1964).
* Lloyd and Warfel, *American English in Its Cultural Setting* (1957), Chapter 18.
* Malmberg, *Phonetics* (1963), Chapter IV.
Pierce, "Spectographic Study of Vowel Nuclei" (1962).
Stetson, *Motor Phonetics* (1951), Chapter III.
Trager and Smith, *An Outline of English Structure* (1951), Part I.

25

/ e /

25.1 Phoneme

/e/ is a mid front oral vowel.

25.2 Allophones

[e] is a high or closed mid front oral vowel.
[ę] is a low or open mid front oral vowel.

25.3 Facial Diagrams

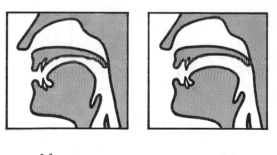

[e]   [ę]

25.4 Articulation

For [e] the velum is closed—as it is for all oral vowels—and the lips are spread—as they are for all front vowels in Spanish. The tip of the tongue rests against the lower front teeth. The highest part of the tongue dorsum is in the

front of the mouth. This [e] is very similar to the *first* part of the English vowel
nucleus in *ate*.

For [ę] everything is almost the same as for [e], except that the tongue is
slightly lower, making the oral cavity somewhat larger. This [ę] is not quite
as open, i.e., the tongue is not as low, as the English /e/ in *bet*.

25.5 Allophonic Distribution

Although [e] and [ę] can always be interchanged in Spanish, [e] occurs
most often in open syllables (those that end in vowels), as in **le** [le], **peso** [pé-so],
déme [dé-me], **en el agua** [e-ne-lá-gu̯a], or in syllables that end in [s] or [z], as
in **les** [les], **esperar** [es-pe-rár], **fresno** [fréz-no], **es de** [éz-de]. [ę] occurs most
often in syllables checked or closed by consonants other than [s] or [z], as in
entrar [ęṇ-trár], **usted** [us-tę́d], **el chico** [ęḷ-ĉí-ko], **enviar** [ęm-bi̯ár], **ver** [bę́r], as
the first element of a diphthong, as **deuda** [dę́u̯-da] and **ley** [lę́i̯], and before /r̄/,
even though in an open syllable, as in **perro** [pę́-r̄o].

The syllabic structure of words ending in a consonant is changed when
they precede words beginning with a vowel in the phonemic phrase. The final
consonant now goes with the vowel of the next word. This phenomenon of
linking or **enlace** often influences the last vowel of the first word. For example,
the **el** of **el chico** [ęḷ-ĉí-ko] forms a closed syllable because it ends with [ḷ]. But
the **el** of **el hombre** [e-lóm-bre] is a different case. The open [ę] is now replaced
by the closed [e], which occurs in most open syllables.

Many Spanish-speakers, however, vary [e] and [ę] quite freely—without
any discernible pattern of distribution. Thus, you may properly do so, too.

The rule for /e/:

$$/e/ \longrightarrow \begin{bmatrix} [ę] / - \begin{Bmatrix} /\breve{\imath}/ \\ /\breve{u}/ \\ /\bar{r}/ \\ /C_1 - C/ \\ /C_1/\# \end{Bmatrix} \\ [e] \text{ elsewhere} \end{bmatrix}$$

/ĭ/ is an unstressed /i/.

/ŭ/ is an unstressed /u/.

/C_1/ is any consonant but /s/.

25.6 Dialectal Variations

In the Caribbean area open [ę] is used frequently even in open syllables:
peso [pę́-so].

25.7 Contrasts with English

[ę] is easy for you since it matches the /e/ or *bet* and *less* quite closely. However, in English stressed /é/ almost never ends a syllable, as it does in Spanish. It is followed either by a consonant or one of the three glides. The Spanish closed [e] may sound like /ey/, to you, so you in turn, often use /ey/ for Spanish stressed [é], as in **dé** */déy/, **qué** */kéy/. Not only does this sound wrong in Spanish, but it destroys the phonemic contrast between **vente** /bén-te/ and **veinte** /béin-te/, **reno** /r̄é-no/ and **reino** /r̄éi-no/, **le** /le/ and **ley** /léi/. You must be careful to use only /e/ and not the final /y/, which is like [į] in Spanish. When the glide occurs, i.e., in a diphthong, in Spanish, it is always represented in writing: **veinte, reino, rey, me^imagino.**

25.8 References

SPANISH

* Bowen and Stockwell, *Patterns of Spanish Pronunciation* (1960), Chapter 2.
* Navarro, *Manual de pronunciación española* (1957), Sections 51–53.

ENGLISH AND GENERAL

* Bronstein (1960), Chapter 7.
* Buchanan (1963), Chapter VII.

25.9 Drills

A   Recognition

Your teacher will pronounce a series of Spanish words, some of which contain an unstressed /e/ and some unstressed /a o i u/. Identify the ones with /e/ by saying **e.**

1. besar	11. anular	21. anhelar
2. esta	12. ingleses	22. mesas
3. pesaron	13. besar	23. inglesas
4. meses	14. legaron	24. pisaron
5. visito	15. besito	25. francesas
6. este	16. esa	26. ese
7. humito	17. emito	27. cerrito
8. zorrito	18. pinar	28. penar
9. preposición	19. proposición	29. cimiento
10. ligaron	20. franceses	30. mellar

B   Recognition

Your teacher will pronounce a series of words, some of which are Spanish and contain a stressed /é/. Some are English and contain the complex vowel nucleus /éy/. Identify them by saying "Spanish" or "English."

1. *day*	9. pe	17. dé
2. *Kay*	10. dé	18. *lay*
3. le	11. le	19. *may*
4. *may*	12. me	20. *bay*
5. qué	13. *Kay*	21. le
6. *say*	14. sé	22. *pay*
7. ve	15. fe	23. sé
8. *fay*	16. *bay*	24. pe

C   Recognition

Your teacher will pronounce a series of Spanish words, some of which contain an /e/ and others the diphthong /ei/. Identify them by saying "simple vowel" or "diphthong."

1. ley	7. vente	13. tenéis
2. veinte	8. reno	14. peinado
3. penado	9. tenés	15. veis
4. reino	10. penado	16. comés
5. ves	11. pena	17. peina
6. seis	12. le	18. coméis

                   19. veinte   20. le

D   Recognition-Production

Your teacher will pronounce a series of words, some of which are Spanish and contain a stressed /é/. Some are English and contain the complex vowel nucleus /éy/. If the word is Spanish, say "Spanish" and repeat it, but if it is English, say "English" and pronounce the "corresponding" Spanish word correctly.

1. dé	9. ge	17. *day*
2. qué	10. *pay*	18. ge
3. *hay*	11. *hay*	19. me
4. me	12. *may*	20. ve
5. *Kay*	13. qué	21. *hay*
6. sé	14. *say*	22. pe
7. *bay*	15. *fay*	23. *say*
8. fe	16. ve	24. *pay*

E   Recognition-Production

*Your teacher will pronounce a series of Spanish words, some of which
contain an /e/ and others the diphthong /ei/. Pronounce the "opposite"
Spanish word in each case.*

1. le	7. veinte	13. tenés
2. vente	8. reino	14. penado
3. peinado	9. tenéis	15. ves
4. reno	10. peinado	16. coméis
5. veis	11. peina	17. pena
6. entendés	12. ley	18. comés

19. vente   20. ley

F   Repetition

Repeat the words after your teacher.

1. bebé	7. desde	13. Pepe
2. debe	8. ese	14. crece
3. prevé	9. este	15. meses
4. breve	10. leve	16. veces
5. cree	11. nene	17. eme
6. lee	12. leche	18. ele

G   Repetition

Repeat the words after your teacher.

1. aquel	8. frente	15. perro
2. aventura	9. hermano	16. errar
3. caber	10. lección	17. puerta
4. caer	11. mentir	18. cerro
5. contento	12. momento	19. servicio
6. ejemplo	13. mujer	20. término
7. envuelto	14. papel	21. verdad

H   "Live" Transcription

25.10 Exercises

A

Give an articulatory description for [e], *for* [ę]. *Then check your answers
in Section 25.2.*

B

Sketch a facial diagram for [e], *for* [ę]. *Then check your diagrams in Section* 25.3.

C

Make a PHONEMIC *transcription of the following phrases. Then check your transcription in* Appendix D.

1. ¿ Usted vive en Panamá?
2. ¿ Ves lo que hacen?
3. ¿ En qué clase piensa usted hacer ese trabajo?
4. Pienso hacerlo en esa clase.
5. El hombre y sus parientes viven en el otro pueblo.
6. Recuerden ustedes que las perlas no parecen valiosas, pero el rey las quiere para pagar la deuda en Europa.

D

Now make a PHONETIC *transcription of the same phrases. Use only the consonant allophones listed in Exercise* 22.10 D *plus* [e ę]. *Then check your transcription in* Appendix D.

26

/ a /

26.1 Phoneme

/a/ is a low central oral vowel.

26.2 Allophone

[a] is a low central oral vowel.

26.3 Facial Diagram

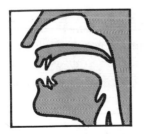

[a]

26.4 Articulation

For [a] the velum is closed, the mouth is quite open, and the lips are neither spread nor rounded but in an intermediate position. The tip of the tongue rests near the lower front teeth. The tongue itself lies low and quite level in the mouth.

This [a] is similar to the English /a/ in *hot* in most American dialects, but it is somewhat more open, tenser, and shorter in duration.

26.5 Allophonic Distribution

[a] occurs everywhere for /a/. The rule for /a/:

$$/a/ \rightarrow [a]$$

26.6 Dialectal Variations

In some areas of America, particularly central Mexico, and parts of Ecuador, unstressed /a/ in the post-tonic (after the stress) position is quite relaxed and very much like English /ɨ/ or /ə/, as the final sound in the English pronunciation of *banana*. This usually happens in very rapid speech and, even then, not in all words. The vast majority of Spanish-speakers, however, never do this.

26.7 Contrasts with English

You must be careful to place the tongue low enough for unstressed Spanish [a] and avoid English [ə] as in *[ká-sə] for **casa.** This problem exists with all unstressed Spanish vowels and can be overcome only with constant attention and diligent practice.

Also you must avoid elongating the stressed [á] as in [ká:-sa] for **casa,** as you do in *father*.

Some dialects of American English (southwestern Pennsylvania, for example) make no distinction between *cot* and *caught*, using /ɔ/ for both: /kɔt/ or /kɔht/, *pa* and *paw*, both /pɔh/. But the use of English /ɔ/ for Spanish /a/ not only sounds wrong, as in *[kɔ-sa] for **casa,** but is so close to Spanish /o/ that it can blur the distinction between such pairs as **casa** and **cosa.**

26.8 References

SPANISH

* Bowen and Stockwell, *Patterns of Spanish Pronunciation* (1960), Chapter 2.
* Navarro, *Manual de pronunciación española* (1957), Sections 54–57.

ENGLISH AND GENERAL

* Bronstein (1960), Chapters 7, 8.
* Buchanan (1963), Chapter VII.

26.9 Drills

A Repetition

Repeat the words after your teacher.

1. abierto	11. día	21. pared
2. acerca	12. esa	22. pena
3. adiós	13. español	23. poeta
4. altura	14. familia	24. prisa
5. amor	15. jardín	25. razón
6. arriba	16. manera	26. risa
7. boca	17. moza	27. ropa
8. cabeza	18. niña	28. ruina
9. cita	19. obra	29. seña
10. cura	20. papel	30. tía

31. vapor   32. zeta

B Repetition

Repeat the words after your teacher.

1. algo	11. amargo	21. cara
2. abajo	12. andar	22. grande
3. ambos	13. cárcel	23. España
4. acá	14. atrás	24. madre
5. ánimo	15. clase	25. mano
6. afán	16. daño	26. hacia
7. ave	17. casa	27. paseará
8. bajo	18. campo	28. hablará
9. allá	19. caballo	29. comprenderá
10. bondad	20. detrás	30. lisonjeará

C Repetition

Repeat the sentences after your teacher.

1. Papá va a la Habana.
2. Ana buscará la lana.
3. Alvaro está alegre ahora.
4. ¿Te quedarás en la casa, o vas al campo?
5. Hablará a mi papá.
6. Son raras y extrañas esas palabras.
7. La muchacha va a pasar por acá mañana por la mañana.
8. Celebrarán San Tomás quizás.

9. Se pasearán todas por estas calles.
10. Las damas no cazarán nada en esta semana.

D   Read Aloud (books open)

Read the words aloud.

1. Kansas	6. grande	11. español
2. absoluto	7. aspirina	12. Andrés
3. Alfredo	8. mecánico	13. barco
4. fábrica	9. taxi	14. saco
5. francamente	10. aniversario	15. Alberto

E   "Live" Transcription

26.10 Exercises

A

Give an articulatory description for [a]. *Then check your answer in Section 26.2.*

B

Sketch a facial diagram for [a]. *Then check your diagram in Section 26.3.*

C

Make a PHONEMIC *transcription of the following passage. Then check your transcription in* Appendix D.

Papá va a la Habana para hablar a Arnaldo Arana. Alvaro está alegre y quizás va a acompañar a papá cuando vaya. Buscarán regalos para toda la familia.

D

Now make a PHONETIC *transcription of the same passage. Use only the consonant allophones listed in Exercise 22.10 D, plus* [e ẹ a]. *Then check your transcription in* Appendix D.

27

/ o /

27.1 Phoneme

/o/ is a mid back oral vowel.

27.2 Allophone

[o] is a mid back oral vowel.

27.3 Facial Diagram

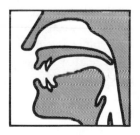

[o]

27.4 Articulation

For [o] the velum is closed, and the lips are rounded. The highest part of the tongue dorsum is in the back of the mouth. This [o] is very similar to the FIRST part of the English vowel nucleus in *so*.

27.5 Allophonic Distribution

[o] occurs everywhere for /o/. The rule for /o/:

$$/o/ \rightarrow [o]$$

27.6 Dialectal Variations

In parts of Mexico, Colombia, and Cuba, a final unstressed /o/ is often realized as [u], as in **caso** [ká-su]. However, this is done sporadically and usually does not cause any confusion, since there are very few Spanish words that normally end in unstressed /u/.

27.7 Contrasts with English

In English stressed /ó/ almost never ends a syllable, as it does in Spanish. It is rarely followed by a consonant and almost always by one of the glides, as in *boy* /bóy/, *no* /nów/, *four* /fóh/ (in "*r*-less" dialects). The Spanish /ó/ may seem to you to be the equivalent of your own /ów/, giving rise to such mispronunciations in Spanish as **no** *[nów], **yo** *[yów], **habló** *[a-ƀlów], etc. This sounds wrong in Spanish, although there are very few cases where /o/ and /ou/ contrast within a word since the Spanish diphthong /ou/ occurs mainly between words: **lo humilló** /lou-mi-yó/, **lo unieron** /lou-nié-ron/.

Many dialects of American English—mainly in the East—use /ew/ or /əw/ in place of /ow/: *no* /néw/ or /nə́w/. In Spanish /ə/ does not exist, of course, and the /eu/ diphthong, which corresponds to English /ew/, is a completely different phonemic sequence, which can contrast with /o/, as in *reuma-Roma*.

In English /ɔ/ is another back vowel phoneme, as in *caught, office, water,* etc. It is about halfway in articulation and sound between Spanish /a/ and /o/, and its use in **hombre,** for example, *[ɔm-bre], blurs the distinction between **hombre** and **hambre.** This particular problem is related to spelling, too, since the letter *o* in English is frequently written to represent both /ɔ/, as in *office,* and /a/, as in *hospital.* Depending on your own dialect, you may possibly use English /ɔ/ or /a/ for Spanish /o/. Not only can this blur the distinction between such pairs as **cantar** and **contar,** but it creates forms which do not even exist in Spanish, such as *[prán̠-to] for **pronto.**

27.8 References

SPANISH

* Bowen and Stockwell, *Patterns of Spanish Pronunciation* (1960), Chapter 2.
* Navarro, *Manual de pronunciación española* (1957), Sections 58–60.

ENGLISH AND GENERAL

* Bronstein (1960), Chapter 8.
* Buchanan (1963), Chapter VII.

27.9 Drills

A   Recognition

Your teacher will pronounce a series of words, some of which are Spanish and contain a stressed /ó/. Some are English and contain the complex vowel nucleus /ów/. Identify them by saying "Spanish" *or* "English."

1. *low*	6. *hello*	11. so
2. *sew*	7. do	12. *know*
3. lo	8. *Joe*	13. *a blow*
4. *dough*	9. no	14. *hoe*
5. habló	10. jaló	15. yo [ŷó]
	16. ¡jo!	

B   Recognition-Production

Your teacher will pronounce a series of words, some of which are Spanish and contain a stressed /ó/. Some are English and contain the complex vowel nucleus /ów/. If the word is Spanish, say "Spanish" *and repeat it, but if it is English, say* "English" *and pronounce the* "corresponding" *Spanish word.*

1. *dough*	6. no	11. *hoe*
2. habló	7. jaló	12. yo [ŷó]
3. *hello*	8. so	13. ¡jo!
4. do	9. *know*	14. *low*
5. *Joe*	10. *a blow*	15. *sew*
	16. lo	

C   Repetition

Repeat the words after your teacher.

1. acaso	6. bolsillo	11. completo
2. ajo	7. bonito	12. consejo
3. alto	8. camino	13. contento
4. año	9. claro	14. dentro
5. blanco	10. colorado	15. eso

16. fino	21. oscuro	26. puro
17. señorita	22. oficio	27. rato
18. menos	23. oído	28. río
19. mucho	24. pero	29. oficial
20. objeto	25. plato	30. honrado

D   Repetition

Repeat the words after your teacher.

1. adiós	11. hondo	21. estudió
2. ahora	12. modo	22. coloreó
3. alcoba	13. mozo	23. ocasión
4. color	14. nosotros	24. propósito
5. corazón	15. ladrón	25. tesoro
6. calor	16. nota	26. mono
7. esposo	17. obra	27. moro
8. glorioso	18. once	28. monopolio
9. gracioso	19. habló	29. sonoro
10. cosa	20. pasó	30. oloroso

E   Read Aloud (books open)

Read the words and phrases aloud.

1. oficina	8. conferencia	15. dólares
2. doctor	9. Honduras	16. costo
3. hospital	10. conversación	17. pronto
4. don Quijote	11. responsabilidad	18. monstruo
5. producto	12. contrato	19. Roberto
6. oportunidad	13. fósforo	20. operación
7. chocolate	14. dólar	21. honesto

F   Transformation (books open)

Read the sentences the way they are; then repeat them, changing the verb to the preterit.

1. El joven pasa por el Prado.
2. El loro habla español.
3. Roberto encuentra mucho oro.
4. Tiene el mismo color y el mismo olor.
5. Mi primo estudia odontología.
6. El coro canta primero.
7. El oficial juega a los bolos.

   8. El doctor se queda en el hospital.
   9. El vapor sale a las dos.
  10. Conversa conmigo en la oficina.

G   "Live" Transcription

27.10 Exercises

A

Give an articulatory description for [o]. *Then check your answer in Section* 27.2.

B

Sketch a facial diagram for [o]. *Then check your diagram in Section* 27.3.

C

Make a PHONEMIC *transcription of the following phrases. Then check your transcription in* Appendix D.

1. El doctor que busco no está en la oficina sino en el hospital.
2. Pronto lo tomó.
3. El Congreso de Honduras completó todo lo posible.
4. En el trópico lo humillaron con el oro y los fósforos que robó.

D

Now make a PHONETIC *transcription of the same phrases. Use only the consonant allophones listed in Exercise* 22.10 D, *plus* [e ę a o]. *Then check your transcription in* Appendix D.

28

/i/ *AND CONSONANT* /y/

28.1 Phonemes

/i/ is a high front oral vowel.
/y/ is a voiced, palatal slit fricative.

28.2 Allophones

[i] is a high front oral vowel, allophone of /i/.
[i̯] is a high front oral semi-vowel, allophone of /i/.
[y] is a voiced, palatal slit fricative, allophone of /y/.

28.3 Facial Diagram

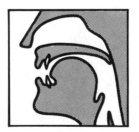

[i] [i̯]

28.4 Articulation

For [i] the velum is closed, and the lips are spread. The tip of the tongue rests against the lower front teeth. The highest part of the tongue dorsum is in the front of the mouth and very close to the alveolar ridge and front palate. This [i] is very similar to the *first* part of the English vowel nucleus in *see*.

For [i̯] everything is almost the same as for [i], except that the sound is much shorter in duration. The tongue is always in the process of going up from a lower vowel or going down to one. It is shorter and higher than the English glide /y/ in *bay*, *bee*, *boy*.

The tongue position for [y] is similar to that for [i], except that for [y] it comes so close to the alveolar ridge and palate that there is usually friction. Sometimes the tongue even touches, producing [ŷ] or [ž] (see Section 15.4). This friction or occlusion is one of the reasons that [y] is best analyzed as a consonant rather than a vowel or semi-vowel.

28.5 Allophonic Distribution

The phoneme /i/ has two principal allophones: the vowel [i] and the semi-vowel [i̯]. /i/ also is sometimes replaced by the consonant /y/.

When /í/ is stressed,[1] it is realized as the allophone [i] and can occur in any phonetic environment: V̆C **ir** [ír], CV̆C **bis** [bís], CV̆ **sí** [sí], V̆V **vía** [bí-a], V̆V̆V **veía** [be-í-a], VV̆ **país** [pa-ís]. Except for the word **y**, and a few proper names, the letter **i** represents [i]. Notice also that in most cases stressed [í], like all stressed vowels, does not have a written accent: **iba, vi, fino,** etc.

When /ǐ/ is unstressed, it is realized either as [i] or [i̯], depending on its phonetic environment. When bounded by a consonant or consonants, it is [i]: V̆C **imponer** [im-po-nér], CV̆C **pintar** [piṇ-tár], CV̆ **cursi** [kúr-si]. Except for the word **y**, the letter **i** represents [i].

But when unstressed /ǐ/ is next to a vowel, it is usually realized as [i̯]: V̆V **tiene** [ti̯é-ne], VV̆ **paisano** [pai̯-sá-no]. The letter **i** also represents [i]: **seis** [séi̯s], except for word-final position where **y** is used: **hay** [ái̯].

However, unstressed /ǐ/ never occurs between two vowels and is replaced by the consonant /y/. So VV̆V becomes VCV: **rey** [r̄ei̯], but **reyes** [r̄é-yes], **leía** [le-í-a], but **leyó** [le-yó]. Spanish orthography always indicates this. In many cases, under heavy stress, /ie/ replaces /e/ in Spanish: **pensar-pienso**. In the few cases where this happens at the beginning of a word /ye/ replaces /e/ and is spelled **ye-: errar-yerro**. Notice that [i̯], when it PRECEDES a vowel, always follows a consonant as well: **pienso** [pi̯én-so]. If there is no preceding consonant, [i̯] is replaced by [y], as in **yerro** [yé-r̄o].

---

[1] See pp. 214-15 for a listing of all the parts of speech which are ordinarily stressed in the stream of speech in Spanish.

The rule for stressed /í/:

$$/í/ \rightarrow [i]$$

The rule for unstressed /ĭ/:

$$
/ĭ/ \longrightarrow
\begin{bmatrix}
[i̯] & \Big/ \begin{Bmatrix} /C/\_\_/V/ \\ /V_1/\_\_ \end{Bmatrix} \\[2em]
[y] & \Big/ \begin{Bmatrix} /V\_\_V/ \\ \#\_\_/V/ \end{Bmatrix} \\[2em]
[i] \text{ elsewhere}
\end{bmatrix}
$$

V_1 is /a o e/. [i̯] does not follow /u/ or /i/.

28.6 Dialectal Variations

/i/ has no important dialectal variations.

/y/, of course, has several, which are discussed in Sections 15.5 and 15.6.
Leyes, for example, is pronounced three different ways by Spanish-speakers:
[lé-yes], [lé-ŷes], or [lé-žes]. But **ley** is pronounced the same way all over the
Spanish-speaking world: [léi̯].

28.7 Contrasts with English

Spanish /í/ presents a problem since in English stressed /i/ almost never ends
a syllable as it does in Spanish. It is followed by a consonant or one of the three
glides. The Spanish stressed [i] may sound like /iy/, to you, so you, in turn,
often use /iy/ for it, as in **di** *[díy]*, **sí** *[síy]*. Although there is no phonemic
confusion here since Spanish has no diphthong *[ii̯], the glide in place of a
single vowel is foreign sounding.

Also, English /i/, as in *sin*, is lower than Spanish [i] and cannot be substituted for it. The vowel in Spanish **sin** is not only higher than that of *sin*,
but is never followed by a glide as in *seen*.

Another problem is presented by the unstressed Spanish [i]. In its place
many English-speakers use /ɨ/, which does not exist in Spanish. The pronunciation of **diría** as *[dɨ-rí-a] causes confusion between **daría** and **diría.** /ɨ/ can also
be mistaken for /e/ in Spanish, and the Spanish-speaker does not know whether
*[pɨ-só] is **pisó** or **pesó.**

The Spanish semi-vowel [i̯] is higher than the English /y/ in post-vocalic
position, as in *say, see, boy*. Thus, **voy** has a much shorter and tenser sound
than *boy*.

The semi-vowel [i̯] presents other problems, too. In Spanish the pattern of [Cᵢ̯V], as in **tiene, piojo, diario,** is quite common. However, in English the corresponding pattern of /CyV/, as in *few* /fyúw/, rarely occurs with vowels other than /u/, and /CVyV/ is used instead, as in *fiesta* /fȋyéstă/, *idiot* /ídȋyȋt/, etc. This extra vowel sounds wrong in Spanish, and you must make an effort to use [Cᵢ̯V], as in **fiesta** [fᵢ̯és-ta], **idiota** [i-dᵢ̯ó-ta], **patio** [pá-tᵢ̯o], etc.

28.8 References

SPANISH

Alarcos Llorach, *Fonología española* (1965), Part II: Chapter II.
* Bowen and Stockwell, "A Further Note on Spanish Semivowels" (1956).
* ———, *Patterns of Spanish Pronunciation* (1960), Chapters 2, 3.
* ———, "The Phonemic Interpretation of Semivowels in Spanish" (1955).
* Foster, "A Note on the /ŷ/ Phoneme of *Porteño* Spanish" (1967).
* Navarro, *Manual de pronunciación española* (1957), Sections 45–50.
* Saporta, "A Note on Spanish Semivowels" (1956).
* Stockwell, Bowen, and Silva-Fuenzalida, "Spanish Juncture and Intonation" (1956).

ENGLISH AND GENERAL

* Bronstein (1960), Chapter 7.
* Buchanan (1963), Chapter VII.

28.9 Drills

A   Recognition

Your teacher will pronounce a series of Spanish words, some of which contain an unstressed /i/. Identify the ones with /i/ by saying **i.**

1. pinar	11. pesada	21. humito
2. pesado	12. imite	22. pisado
3. imito	13. seseo	23. siseo
4. pudiendo	14. omito	24. descante
5. discante	15. rimar	25. mirón
6. penar	16. ligar	26. emito
7. emite	17. murón	27. fusión
8. lugar	18. pisada	28. peñita
9. fisión	19. novelar	29. nivelar
10. piñita	20. pidiendo	30. remar

B   Recognition

Your teacher will pronounce a series of words, some of which are Spanish and contain /í/. Some are English and contain the complex vowel nucleus /iy/. Identify them by saying "Spanish" or "English."

1. mi	7. ni	13. *bee*
2. *tea*	8. *me*	14. *see*
3. ni	9. ti	15. di
4. sí	10. *knee*	16. *knee*
5. vi	11. *Dee*	17. mí
6. *me*	12. *tea*	18. ti

C   Recognition-Production

Your teacher will pronounce a series of words, some of which are Spanish and contain a stressed /í/. Some are English and contain the complex vowel nucleus /iy/. If the word is Spanish, say "Spanish" and repeat it, but if it is English, say "English" and pronounce the "corresponding" Spanish word.

1. sí	6. *knee*	11. sí
2. vi	7. *Dee*	12. di
3. *me*	8. *tea*	13. *knee*
4. ni	9. *see*	14. *bee*
5. ti	10. vi	15. ni

D   Repetition

Repeat the words after your teacher.

1. accidente	11. mérito	21. hábil
2. adivinar	12. milagro	22. idea
3. ágil	13. niñez	23. igual
4. alfiler	14. discreto	24. imagen
5. americano	15. civilización	25. individuo
6. cantidad	16. divinísimo	26. lágrima
7. casi	17. enérgico	27. lástima
8. comodidad	18. éxito	28. magnitud
9. cristal	19. fácil	29. sutileza
10. débil	20. frágil	30. útil

E   Repetition

Repeat the words after your teacher.

1. carril	11. aquí	21. país
2. castigo	12. así	22. pico
3. civil	13. bizco	23. río
4. chico	14. brío	24. viví
5. día	15. calcetín	25. entendí
6. escribir	16. camino	26. salí
7. hijo	17. iris	27. volví
8. fino	18. jira	28. comí
9. gallina	19. Lili	29. sentí
10. ahí	20. lío	30. sí, sí

F   Read Aloud (books open)

Read the words aloud.

1. diplomático	9. disgusto	17. ministro
2. firmar	10. solicitar	18. Timoteo
3. interno	11. imaginarse	19. ir
4. interesante	12. sin	20. salir
5. inteligente	13. linda	21. preferir
6. intenso	14. circo	22. invitar
7. oficina	15. décimo	23. aspirina
8. fábrica	16. interior	24. Ricardo

G   "Live" Transcription

28.10 Exercises

A

Give an articulatory description for [i], *for* [j]. *Then check your answers in Section* 28.2.

B

Sketch a facial diagram for [i]. *Then check your diagram in Section* 28.3.

C

Make a PHONEMIC *transcription of the following passage. Then check your transcription in* Appendix D.

Ignacio es un paisano mío. Vivíamos en el mismo país—Bolivia—hace dieciséis o diecisiete años. Y eso es como se interesó en los asuntos de mi amigo Zoilo. Y   lo importante es que viene a la ciudad a ayudarle en la farmacia.

D

Now make a PHONETIC *transcription of the same passage. Use only the consonant allophones listed in Exercise* 22.10 D, *plus* [e ę a o i i̯]. *Then check your transcription in* Appendix D.

29

/ u / *AND CONSONANT* / w /

29.1 Phonemes

/u/ is a high back oral vowel.
/w/ is a voiced, bilabio-velar slit fricative.

29.2 Allophones

[u] is a high back oral vowel, allophone of /u/.
[u̯] is a high back oral semi-vowel, allophone of /u/.
[w] is a voiced, bilabio-velar slit fricative, allophone of /w/.

29.3 Facial Diagram

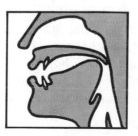

[u] [u̯]

29.4 Articulation

For [u] the velum is closed, and the lips are very rounded or pursed. The highest part of the tongue dorsum is in the back of the mouth and very close to the velum. This [u] is very similar to the *first* part of the English vowel nucleus in *suit*, although the English /u/ here is more open than Spanish [u].

For [ṷ] everything is almost the same as for [u], except that the sound is much shorter in duration. The tongue is always in the process of going up from a lower vowel or going down to one. It is shorter and higher than the English glide /w/ in *cow, low, blue.*

The tongue position for [w] is similar to that for [u] except that for [w] it comes so close to the velum that there is friction although not as much as for the fricative [g]. Sometimes the tongue touches and [gṷ] results (see Sections 11.4 and 11.5). This friction is one of the reasons that [w] is best analyzed as a consonant rather than a vowel or semi-vowel.

29.5 Allophonic Distribution

The phoneme /u/ has two principal allophones: the vowel [u] and the semi-vowel [ṷ]. /u/ also is sometimes replaced by the consonant /w/.

When /ú/ is stressed,[1] it is realized as the allophone [u] and can occur in almost any phonetic environment: V́C **último** [úl̯-ti-mo], CV́C **justo** [xús-to], CV́ **tú** [tú], V́V **actúa** [ak-tú-a], VV́V (rarely or never), VV́ **baúl** [ba-úl]. The letter *u* represents [ú]. Notice also that in most cases stressed [ú], like all stressed vowels, does not have a written accent: **puso, une, humo,** etc.

When /ŭ/ is unstressed, it is realized either as [u] or [ṷ], depending on its phonetic environment. When bounded by a consonant or consonants, it is [u]: V̆C **usted** [us-tḛ́d], CV̆C **apuntar** [a-puṇ-tár], CV̆ **espíritu** [es-pí-ri-tu]. The letter **u** represents [u].

But when unstressed /ŭ/ is next to a vowel, it is usually realized as [ṷ]: V̆V **suave** [sṷá-ƀe], VV̆ **causa** [káṷ-sa]. The letter **u** also represents [ṷ].

However, unstressed /ŭ/ never occurs between two vowels and is replaced by the consonant /w/. So VV̆V becomes VCV: **siete u ocho** [si̯é-te-wó-ĉo].

In many cases, under heavy stress, /ue/ replaces /o/ in Spanish: **poder-puedo.** In the few cases where this happens at the beginning of a word /we/ replaces /o/ and is spelled **hue-: oler-huelo.** Notice that [ṷ], when it PRECEDES a vowel, always follows a consonant as well: **puedo** [pṷé-đo]. If there is no preceding consonant, [ṷ] is replaced by [w], as in **huelo** [wé-lo].

The rule for stressed /ú/:

$$/ú/ \rightarrow [u]$$

[1] See pp. 214-15 for a listing of all the parts of speech which are ordinarily stressed in the stream of speech in Spanish.

The rule for unstressed /ŭ/:

$$
/ŭ/ \longrightarrow
\begin{bmatrix}
[\underset{\cdot}{u}] \Big/ \begin{Bmatrix} \{/C/\_\_/V/\} \\ /V_1/\_\_ \end{Bmatrix} \\[2ex]
[w] \Big/ \begin{Bmatrix} \{/V/\_\_/V/\} \\ \# \_\_/V/ \end{Bmatrix} \\[2ex]
[u] \text{ elsewhere}
\end{bmatrix}
$$

V₁ is /a o e/. [u̯] does not follow /u/ or /i/.

29.6 Dialectal Variation

/u/ has no important dialectal variations. However, in certain dialects the stress in the diphthong /ui/ shifts from the /i/ to the /u/ and changes the semi-vowel [u̯] to the full vowel [u]. Thus, **muy** [mu̯í] becomes [múi̯], a diphthong which does not exist in most dialects. The first pronunciation is much more common. Also, some speakers in some words change /iu/ to /ui/: **ciudad** [su̯i-dád] or [su̯i-dád].

/w/, of course, has several variations, which are discussed in Sections 11.5 and 11.6.

29.7 Contrasts with English

Spanish /ú/ presents a problem since in English stressed /ú/ almost never ends a syllable as it does in Spanish. It is followed by a consonant or one of the three glides. The Spanish stressed [ú] may sound like English /úw/, to you, so you, in turn, often use /uw/ for it, as in **tú** *[túw], **según** *[sey-gúwn]. Although there is no phonemic confusion since Spanish has no diphthong *[uu̯], the glide in place of a single vowel is foreign sounding.

Many dialects of English also use /ɨw/ instead of /úw/, as in *food* /fɨwd/, *you* /yɨw/. Such pronunciations as *[lɨú-na] for **luna** or *[mɨú-row] for **muro** are incorrect in Spanish, although there is little chance for phonemic confusion since the Spanish diphthong /iu/ rarely contrasts with /u/.

Also, English /u/, as in *soot*, is lower than Spanish /u/ and cannot be substituted for it. The vowel in Spanish **sus** is not only higher than that of *soot* but never is followed by a glide as in *sues*.

Another problem is presented by the unstressed Spanish [u]. Many English-speakers use in its place /ɨ/ or /ə/, neither of which exist in Spanish. The pronunciation of **humito** as */ə-mí-to/ or */ɨ-mí-to/ causes confusion between **imito, emito, omito,** and **humito.**

The Spanish semi-vowel [u̯] is higher than English /w/ in post-vocalic position as in *cow, how.* Thus, the first syllables of **causa** and **jaula** have a much shorter and tenser sound than *cow* and *how.* Also many dialects of English (particularly on the East coast and in the South) have /æw/ instead of /aw/. Since /æ/ does not exist in Spanish, such pronunciations as *[kǽw-sa] for **causa** and *[ǽwŋ-ke] for **aunque** sound very strange.

The semi-vowel [u̯] presents other problems, too, for you. In Spanish the pattern of [Cu̯V], as in **bueno, cuota, agua,** is quite common with most consonants. However, in English the corresponding pattern of /CwV/ has certain restrictions. C is rarely /b f č m n l p y/, although it is /k/ as in *quilt,* /t/ as in *twice,* and a few other consonants, too. Thus, such Spanish words as **bueno, fuera, chueco, mueca, nuera, luego, pues, llueve** cause you to split these diphthongs into two syllables, add an extra sound, or change one as in *[bu-é-no] or *[bɨ-wé-no], *[fu-é-ra] or [fɨ-wé-ra], etc. This is even done in Spanish words that have combinations that are used in English, such as *[si-ti-wár] or *[si-tu-ár] or *[si-ĉi-wár] for **situar,** even though English has the corresponding sequence in *twice, twine,* etc.

These pronunciations sound wrong in Spanish, and you must make an effort to use [Cu̯V] rather than *[Cu-V] or *[Cu-wV] or *[Cɨ-wV] in these words.

Many English-speakers also have the tendency to replace syllable-final [u̯] with stressed [ú] as in **deuda** *[de-ú-ða] instead of [déu̯-ða] or *[a-úŋ-ke] instead of [áu̯ŋ-ke]. Even speakers whose dialect of English has the diphthong /ew/, as in *no* /néw/ or *go* /géw/, seem to have trouble transferring it to Spanish, as in **deuda.** However, if you keep the stress on the FIRST vowel, you will be able to pronounce the combination as a diphthong, i.e., as only one syllable.

The final problem with Spanish /u/ has a lexical aspect. Many words spelled with *u* in English are pronounced with /yu/ or /yɨ/, depending on where the stress is: *ridiculous, peculiar, particular,* etc. Many of you carry this pronunciation over into Spanish cognate words and even some that are not cognates: *[r̄i-ðí-kyu-lo], *[pe-kyu-lyár], *[pe-lí-kyu-la] or *[pe-lí-kyɨ-la] for **película,** etc. The habit is strong, and many of you will have to work hard to pronounce only [u] instead of [yu] or [yɨ] in these words.

29.8 References

SPANISH

Alarcos Llorach, *Fonología española* (1965), Part II: Chapter II.
* Bowen and Stockwell, "A Further Note on Spanish Semivowels" (1956).
* _____, *Patterns of Spanish Pronunciation* (1960), Chapters 2, 3.
* _____ , "The Phonemic Interpretation of Semivowels in Spanish" (1955).
* Navarro, *Manual de pronunciación española* (1957), Sections 61–65.
* Saporta, "A Note on Spanish Semivowels" (1956).
* Stockwell, Bowen, and Silva-Fuenzalida, "Spanish Juncture and Intonation" (1956).

* Bronstein (1960), Chapter 8.
* Buchanan (1963), Chapter VII.

29.9 Drills

A ·Recognition

Your teacher will pronounce a series of Spanish words, some of which contain an unstressed /u/. Identify the ones with /u/ by saying **u.**

1. tumor	10. anular	19. plumero
2. troncar	11. vocal	20. porito
3. luchar	12. omito	21. sociedad
4. bucal	13. temor	22. succión
5. acosar	14. acusar	23. motilar
6. mutilar	15. plomero	24. purita
7. lechar	16. truncar	25. soplico
8. humito	17. perita	26. suciedad
9. sección	18. anhelar	27. purito
	28. suplico	

B Recognition

Your teacher will pronounce a series of words, some of which are Spanish and contain a stressed /ú/. Some are English and contain the complex vowel nucleus /úw/. Identify them by saying "Spanish" *or* "English."

1. *two*	7. *néw low*	13. tabú
2. su	8. *bay túne*	14. *tool*
3. *chew*	9. jugo	15. *Whó go?*
4. *taboo*	10. *say goón*	16. chu
5. según	11. tú	17. tul
6. *suc*	12. betún	18. nulo

C Recognition-Production

Your teacher will pronounce a series of words, some of which are Spanish and contain a stressed /ú/. Some are English and contain the complex vowel nucleus /úw/. If the word is Spanish, say "Spanish" *and repeat it, but if it is English, say* "English" *and pronounce the* "corresponding" *Spanish word.*

1. según
2. *sue*
3. *néw low*
4. *bay túne*
5. jugo
6. *say goón*

7. tú
8. betún
9. tabú
10. *tool*
11. *Whó go ?*
12. chu

13. tul
14. nulo
15. *two*
16. su
17. *chew*
18. *taboo*

D   Repetition

Repeat the words after your teacher.

1. adular
2. afortunado
3. agujero
4. apuntar
5. asegurar
6. butaca
7. calcular
8. chuchería
9. circular
10. descubrir

11. desocupado
12. disfrutar
13. documento
14. entumecido
15. espíritu
16. estupendo
17. hondureño
18. inundación
19. juramento
20. lucir

21. lugar
22. minutero
23. se murió
24. pudiste
25. puntualidad
26. rumor
28. suspenso
28. título
29. tripulación
30. utilidad

E   Repetition

Repeat the words after your teacher.

1. aguja
2. agudo
3. altura
4. anchura
5. baúl
6. seguro
7. brújula
8. buque
9. buho
10. turno

11. cintura
12. desayuno
13. descubre
14. me preocupo
15. disculpa
16. disimulo
17. dulce
18. estuvo
19. factura
20. frescura

21. Honduras
22. insinúo
23. junta
24. literatura
25. luz
26. menudo
27. muro
28. nube
29. punto
30. rudo

F   Read Aloud (books open)

Read the words aloud.

1. Cuba
2. puro
3. fumo
4. puridad
5. comunica

6. película
7. ridículo
8. regular
9. buró
10. particular

11. simular
12. museo
13. cura
14. ocupado
15. saludar

16. furioso	21. puntual	26. pubertad
17. popular	22. puntuación	27. mula
18. pútrido	23. figura	28. música
19. butano	24. figúrese	29. funeral
20. mutuo	25. furia	30. preocupado

G   "Live" Transcription

29.10 Exercises

A

Give an articulatory description for [u], *for* [u̯]. *Then check your answers in Section* 29.2.

B

Sketch a facial diagram for [u]. *Then check your diagram in Section* 29.3.

C

Make a PHONEMIC *transcription of the following phrases. Then check your transcription in* Appendix D.

1. Aunque no sea la causa de la deuda, lo humilla mucho.
2. La película aun está en el cine Europa.
3. Vamos a tomar el auto, Hugo.
4. Bueno, puse el agua aquí, y huele a humo.
5. Cuidado, aquí hubo un accidente de guaguas hace unos días.
6. ¿Cuántos quieres? ¿Siete u ocho?
7. Pues, no es ni bueno ni fuerte ni suave ni útil.

D

Now make a PHONETIC *transcription of the same phrases. Use only the consonant allophones listed in Exercise* 22.10 D, *plus* [e ẹ a o i i̯ u u̯]. *Then check your transcription in* Appendix D.

30

VOWEL COMBINATIONS

In all languages very often the sounds of a given word or morpheme (grammatical unit of meaning) are changed, modified, or even eliminated when the word or morpheme is juxtaposed with certain other words or morphemes. For example, in English when the word *won't* /wównt/ precedes the word *you* /yúw/ in normal conversation, the final /t/ of *won't* and the initial /y/ of *you* combine and turn into /č/: /wównčûw/. In Spanish when the word **mi** /mi/ precedes the word **hijo** /í-xo/, the /i/ of **mi** disappears or combines with the /i/ of **hijo**, giving /mí-xo/.

Such changes are called MORPHOPHONEMIC CHANGES because the phonemic shape or structure of words and morphemes is altered when these words and morphemes come into contact with other ones.

Most of the morphophonemic changes present in the Spanish consonantal system are due to assimilation and have already been described. They are relatively simple, however, when compared with the morphophonemic changes in the vocalic system, especially in view of the fact that single Spanish vowels are so relatively simple.

Theoretically, in Spanish any number of vowels grouping together is possible, but in actuality usually no more than three come together. They can occur anywhere in the phonemic phrase.

One of the most important considerations with these vowel combinations is the matter of syllables. Do the vowels remain in separate syllables, or do they combine into one? This question, in turn, depends mainly on stress.[1] Also, in our analysis two styles of speech will have to be recognized—slow, careful, formal and fast, conversational, informal.

Contiguous vowels undergo five different types of modifications in Spanish, although the first one is rare in fast, conversational speech.

---

[1] See pp. 214-15 for a listing of all the parts of speech which are ordinarily stressed in the stream of speech in Spanish.

1. SEPARATED. There can be a complete break between the two vowels. This pause, called a *glottal stop* [ʔ], is very short but quite prominent. The vocal bands catch abruptly, as in *cotton* or *button* in English or the first sounds made in English when one is warning a child not to touch something: *Uh-uh-uh-uhhhh!*. This glottal stop occurs frequently in English, German, and other languages and is even a segmental phoneme in some of them. In English it is sometimes placed before a word beginning with a vowel to indicate great emphasis: *It's my own!* /îts + mày ʔ ówn/. English-speakers often mistakenly use the glottal stop just to separate Spanish vowels which belong to different syllables and words: **de él** *[de ʔél], **va a comer** *[bá ʔa-ko-mér]. Glottal stops are rarely used in Spanish, however, and never just to indicate word- or syllable-boundaries.

2. LINKED. In normal conversation Spanish vowels in separate syllables within one phonemic phrase are never separated by a pause or a glottal stop. Even though they are in different syllables the transition between them is smooth and unbroken. The vocal bands never stop vibrating even though muscular action in the vocal tract is such that separate syllables are being created. Such expressions as **de él** and **va a comer** can be pronounced without any break in the sound even though syllable division is taking place: [de-él], [bá-a-ko-mér].

In the following vowel combinations, the vowels are in separate syllables but nevertheless *linked* in the sense that there is no pause or glottal stop between them: Identical vowels, one or both of which are stressed (in careful speech): **creer** [kre-ér], **lo odio** [lo-ó-d̦io], **mi hijo** [mi-í-xo], **no odio** [nó-ó-d̦io], **vi hilo** [bí-í-lo]; Any combination of /a o e/, whether or not any stress is present (in both careful and rapid speech): **pasear** [pa-se-ár], **le hablo** [le-á-blo], **pasearemos** [pa-se-a-ré-mos], **le hablaré** [le-a-bla-ré]; Stressed /i ú/ + vowel, or vowel + stressed /í ú/, that is /íV úV Ví Vú/ (in both careful and rapid speech): **vía** [bí-a], **lo vi ayer** [lo-bí-a-yér], **actúa** [ak-tú-a], **tú hablabas** [tú-a-blá-bas], **leíste** [le-ís-te], **me iba** [me-í-ba], **reúne** [r̃e-ú-ne], **se une** [se-ú-ne].

Notice that word boundaries have nothing to do with whether the vowels are linked and also that stressed /í ú/ can not always be identified by written accents.

3. FUSED. The term "fused" means "forming a diphthong" or a cluster of *two* vowels which go in one *single* syllable: **seis** [séis], **aun** [áu̯n]. "Fused" can also refer to a "triphthong" or a cluster of *three* vowels which form a single syllable: **buey** [bu̯éi̯]. One element of a FUSED group is always an unstressed /i u/, which is realized as a semi-vowel [i̯ u̯]. If either the /i/ or /u/ is stressed, the combination is *not* fused, thus *not* a diphthong, but a group of LINKED vowels (see group 2 above), which are in separate syllables: **mío** [mí-o], **baúl** [ba-úl].

Diphthongs and triphthongs, or fused vowels, occur across word boundaries, too: **me imagino** [mé̞i-ma-xí-no], **tome usted** [tó-me̞u̞s-té̞d], **mi amigo** [mi̞a-mí-go], **su ave** [su̞á-b̞e], **estudió historia** [es-tu-d̞i̞ó̞i̞s-tó-ri̞a], **fue humilde** [fu̞é̞u̞-mí̞l-de]. There is normally no difference between fused vowels within a word and across word boundaries: **suave** and **su ave** are both pronounced [su̞á-b̞e], although a speaker, if he wanted to make a distinction, could use *linked* vowels in the second phrase to show that it is two words: [su-á-b̞e]. Context, however, almost always makes such rather artificial pronunciations unnecessary.

4. ELIMINATED. Identical vowels, both of which are *unstressed*, are usually realized as just one short vowel both in careful and rapid speech: **la abriré** [la-b̞ri-ré], **creeré** [kre-ré], **lo odiaba** [lo-d̞iá-b̞a].

Also identical vowels, one of which is *stressed*, are realized as just one short vowel in rapid speech: **creer** [kré̞r], **lo odio** [ló-d̞i̞o], **mi hijo** [mí-xo]. In careful speech they are linked (see group 2 above): [kre-é̞r], [lo-ó-d̞i̞o], [mi-í-xo].

Unstressed /a o e/ are also often eliminated in rapid speech in certain combinations. This is most common at word boundaries, especially where the first word precedes another word beginning with a vowel one step higher on the same side of the vowel triangle (either side for /a/). For example, unstressed /a/ is often eliminated before /o/ and /e/, as in **la hora** [ló-ra] and **la esposa** [les-pó-sa]. Unstressed /e/ is eliminated before /i/, as in **este interés** [és-ti̞n-te-rés] and **me imagino** [mi-ma-xí-no]. Unstressed /o/ is often eliminated before /u/, as in **tengo uno** [té̞ŋ-gú-no] or **lo único** [lú-ni-ko].

/a/ also sometimes is eliminated before unstressed /i/, as in **la hijita** [li-xí-ta], and unstressed /u/, as in **la unión** [lu-ni̞ón]. This is not as frequent, however, as when /a/ precedes /e/ and /o/.

5. REPLACED. When different vowels come together in rapid speech, one phoneme is often REPLACED by another. /e/ is replaced by /i/: **teatro** [ti̞á-tro], **me habló** [mi̞a-b̞ló].   /o/ is replaced by /u/: **poeta** [pu̞é-ta], **ahorita** [au̞-rí-ta]. This is common in rapid speech all over the Spanish-speaking world.

Unstressed /i/ does not occur between full vowels[2] and is replaced by the consonant /y/: **rey** [r̄é̞i̞], but **reyes** [r̄é-yes], **voy** [bó̞i̞], but **voy a comer** [bó-ya-ko-mé̞r]. Similarly, unstressed /u/ between full vowels is replaced by the consonant /w/: **siete u ocho** [si̞é-te-wó-ĉo].[3]

In summary, a phrase like **la oficina** has three pronunciations as far as vowels are concerned: in careful speech LINKED [la-o-fi-sí-na], and in rapid speech either ELIMINATED [lo-fi-sí-na] or REPLACED [lau̞-fi-sí-na], where [u̞] replaces [o]. **La esposa** also has three pronunciations: in careful speech LINKED

---

[2] Unstressed /i/, however, can occur between a semi-vowel and a vowel, as in **muy alto** [mu̞i-á̞l-to]. Another possible pronunciation for this phrase would be [mu-yá̞l-to].

[3] There is actually another modification—LENGTHENED—where two equal vowels, one of which is stressed, combine in the same syllable into one long vowel: **de él** becomes [dé̞:l] rather than [dé̞l] or [de-é̞l]. However, the difference between *linked* [de-é̞l] and *lengthened* can be very slight. Thus, the latter phenomenon has been eliminated in our analysis in the interests of simplicity.

[la-es-pó-sa], and in rapid speech either ELIMINATED [les-pó-sa] or REPLACED [lai̯s-pó-sa], where [i̯] replaces [e].

The rules for vowel combinations:[4]

IDENTICAL VOWELS

$$/\breve{V}_1\ \acute{V}_1/ \longrightarrow \begin{Bmatrix} [\breve{V}_1 - \acute{V}_1] \\ [\acute{V}_1] \end{Bmatrix}$$

$$/\acute{V}_1\ \breve{V}_1/ \longrightarrow \begin{Bmatrix} [\acute{V}_1 - \breve{V}_1] \\ [\acute{V}_1] \end{Bmatrix}$$

$$/\acute{V}_1\ \acute{V}_1/ \longrightarrow [\acute{V}_1 - \acute{V}_1]$$

$$/\breve{V}_1\ \breve{V}_1/ \longrightarrow [\breve{V}_1]$$

$/V_1\ V_1/$ or $[V_1 - V_1]$ means that both vowels are the same.

DIFFERENT VOWELS

$$/\acute{a}/ \longrightarrow \left[[a] \Big/ \begin{Bmatrix} \underline{\quad}/V/ \\ /V/\underline{\quad} \end{Bmatrix} \right]$$

$$/\breve{a}/ \longrightarrow \left[\begin{matrix} \begin{Bmatrix} [a] \\ [\emptyset] \end{Bmatrix} \Big/ \underline{\quad} + /V/ \\ [a] \quad \text{elsewhere} \end{matrix} \right]$$

+ means word-boundary, as in *la esposa*, which is either [la-es-pó-sa] or [les-pó-sa].

$$/\acute{e}/ \longrightarrow \left[[e] \Big/ \begin{Bmatrix} \underline{\quad}/V/ \\ /V/\underline{\quad} \end{Bmatrix} \right]$$

$$/\breve{e}/ \longrightarrow \left[\begin{matrix} \begin{Bmatrix} [i] \\ [e]^{\ddagger} \end{Bmatrix} \Big/ \begin{Bmatrix} \underline{\quad}/V_1/ \\ /V_1/\underline{\quad} \end{Bmatrix} \\ \begin{Bmatrix} [e] \\ [\emptyset] \end{Bmatrix} \underline{\quad} + /i/ \end{matrix} \right]$$

‡ [e] can also be [ẹ] if it occurs in a syllable checked by a consonant other than /s/, as in *lo envió* [lo-ẹm-bi̯ó].

$/V_1/$ is /a o u/. + means word-boundary.

[4] The difference between careful and rapid speech is represented by the free variation in the braces. Thus $/\breve{V}_1\ \acute{V}_1/ \rightarrow \begin{Bmatrix} [\breve{V}_1 - \acute{V}_1] \\ [\acute{V}_1] \end{Bmatrix}$ means that in careful speech **mi hijo**, for example, is [mi-í-xo] and in rapid speech [mí-xo].

$$\text{/ó/} \longrightarrow \left[\text{[o]} \Big/ \left\{ \begin{array}{c} \underline{\quad}/\text{V}/ \\ /\text{V}/\underline{\quad} \end{array} \right\} \right]$$

$$\text{/ŏ/} \longrightarrow \left[\begin{array}{l} \left\{ \begin{array}{c} \text{[u̯]} \\ \text{[o]} \end{array} \right\} \Big/ \left\{ \begin{array}{c} \underline{\quad}/\text{V}_1/ \\ /\text{V}_1/\underline{\quad} \end{array} \right\} \\[12pt] \left\{ \begin{array}{c} \text{[o]} \\ \text{[Ø]} \end{array} \right\} \Big/ \underline{\quad} + /\text{u}/ \end{array} \right]$$

/V₁/ is /e a i/. + means word-boundary.

$$\text{/í/} \longrightarrow \left[\text{[i]} \Big/ \left\{ \begin{array}{c} \underline{\quad}/\text{V}/ \\ /\text{V}/\underline{\quad} \end{array} \right\} \right]$$

$$\text{/ĭ/} \longrightarrow \left[\begin{array}{l} \text{[i̯]} \Big/ \left\{ \begin{array}{c} /\text{C}/\underline{\quad}/\text{V}/ \\ /\text{V}_1/\underline{\quad} \end{array} \right\} \\[12pt] \text{[y]} \Big/ \left\{ \begin{array}{c} /\text{V}_2\underline{\quad}\text{V}/ \\ \#\underline{\quad}/\text{V}/ \end{array} \right\} \end{array} \right]$$

/V₁/ is /a e o/. /V₂/ is a full vowel and *not* a semi-vowel.

$$\text{/ú/} \longrightarrow \left[\text{[u]} \Big/ \left\{ \begin{array}{c} \underline{\quad}/\text{V}/ \\ /\text{V}/\underline{\quad} \end{array} \right\} \right]$$

$$\text{/ŭ/} \longrightarrow \left[\begin{array}{l} \text{[u̯]} \Big/ \left\{ \begin{array}{c} /\text{C}/\underline{\quad}/\text{V}/ \\ /\text{V}_1/\underline{\quad} \end{array} \right\} \\[12pt] \text{[w]} \Big/ \left\{ \begin{array}{c} /\text{V}_2/\underline{\quad}/\text{V}/ \\ \#\underline{\quad}/\text{V}/ \end{array} \right\} \end{array} \right]$$

/V₁/ is /a e o/. /V₂/ is a full vowel and *not* a semi-vowel.

There are some exceptions to the five vowel-combination phenomena: SEPARATED, LINKED, FUSED, ELIMINATED, and REPLACED. The pattern of words ending in **-uir, -uido, -uida,** etc. alternates between diphthong and separate syllables, i.e., between fused and linked: **destruir** [des-tru̯ír] or [des-tru-ír], **construido** [kons-tru̯í-đo] or [kons-tru-í-đo]. The diphthong is more common in ordinary conversation.

Many compounds are also sometimes pronounced with linked rather than fused vowels, revealing the morphemic boundaries: **veintiuno** [bei̯n-ti-ú-no] instead of [bẹịn-tịú-no], **cariancho** [ka-ri-áñ-ĉo] instead of [ka-rịáñ-ĉo]. Again the diphthong is more common in ordinary conversation.

Many verb forms are also pronounced with linked rather than fused vowels due to analogy with other forms in the conjugation that have linked vowels in separate syllables. For example, many verbs ending in **-iar** and **-uar** have a stress irregularity in the present tense, producing forms like **fío** [fí-o] and **actúan** [ak-tú-an]. Although the first-person plural forms and the infinitives are usually pronounced with diphthongs: **fiamos** [fịá-mos], **actuar** [ak-tụár], they are sometimes pronounced with separate syllables through analogy with the other verb forms: [fi-á-mos], [ak-tu-ár].

The following charts summarize the types of vowel combinations and modifications discussed above and provide examples (first see pp. 190-91):

EXCEPTIONS

Vowel Combinations	Linked (careful speech)	Fused (rapid speech)
Words ending in /uiC-/	**destruir** [des-tru-ír] **construido** [kons-tru-í- đo]	**destruir** [des-trụír] **construido** [kons-trụí-đo]
Compounds	**veintiuno** [bẹịn-ti-ú-no] **cariancho** [ka-ri-áñ-ĉo]	**veintiuno** [bẹịn-tịú-no] **cariancho** [ka-rịáñ-ĉo]
Analogous forms	**fiamos** [fi-á-mos] **actuar** [ak-tu-ár]	**fiamos** [fịá-mos] **actuar** [ak-tụár]

The problems that English-speakers have with these vowels and vowel combinations have already been discussed in Chapters 24–29.

References

SPANISH

Agard, "Stress in Four Romance Languages" (1967).
* Beberfall, "The Qualitative Aspect of Spanish Diphthongs" (1964).
* Bowen, "Sequences of Vowels in Spanish" (1956–57).
* _____, "Teaching Spanish Diphthongs" (1963).
* _____ and Stockwell, "A Further Note on Spanish Semivowels" (1956).
* _____, *Patterns of Spanish Pronunciation* (1960), Chapters 2, 3.
* _____, "The Phonemic Interpretation of Semivowels in Spanish" (1955).
Malmberg, *Estudios de fonética hispánica* (1965), Chapter I.

TYPES OF VOWEL COMBINATIONS

VOWEL COMBINATIONS	SEPARATED	LINKED	FUSED	ELIMINATED	REPLACED
Identical vowels, both stressed /$\acute{V}_1\,\acute{V}_1$/	NEVER	(careful and rapid speech) vi hilo [bí-í-lo] no odio [nó-ó-ðjo] dé esto [dé-és-to]			
Identical vowels, both unstressed /$\breve{V}_1\,\breve{V}_1$/	IN				
Identical vowels, one of which is stressed /$\acute{V}_1\,\breve{V}_1$/ /$\breve{V}_1\,\acute{V}_1$/	NORMAL	(careful speech) creer [kre-ér] lo odio [lo-ó-ðjo] mi hijo [mi-í-xo]		(careful and rapid speech) la abriré [la-bri-ré] creeré [kre-ré] (rapid speech) creer [kreér̥] lo odio [ló-ðjo] mi hijo [mí-xo]	
Stressed /i/ and /u/ with another unstressed vowel /íV̆ úV̆/ /V̆í V̆ú/	SPEECH	(careful and rapid speech) vía [bí-a] tú hablabas [tú-a-ßlá-ßas] me iba [me-í-ba] reúne [ře-ú-ne]			
Unstressed /i/ and /u/ with other vowels, stressed or unstressed /iV̆ úV̆/ Vi Vu			(careful and rapid speech) siete [sjé-te] su ave [suá-ße] reina [řéj-na] deuda [déu̯-ða]		(rapid speech) [pa-sjár̥] [lja-ßla-ré] [pué-ta] [lués] (from last column on p. 191)

Environment		careful and rapid speech	careful and rapid speech	rapid speech at word boundaries	rapid speech
íVi íVǔ / ǔVí ǔVǔ /	NEVER		cambiáis [kam-bjáḭs] buey [bu̯éḭ] (diphthongs and triphthongs)		(careful and rapid speech) **voy a comer** [bó-ya-ko-méɾ] **siete u ocho** [sjé-te-wó-čo]
Unstressed /i/ and /u/ between other full vowels /ViV/ /VǔV/	IN			(rapid speech at word boundaries) **la esposa** [les-pó-sa] **la hora** [ló-ra]	(rapid speech) **pasear** **le hablaré** **poeta** **lo es** (see last column on p. 190)
Any combination of /a o e/ whether or not stress is present	NORMAL	(careful and rapid speech) **pasear** [pa-se-á-̯] **le hablaré** [le-a-bla-ré̯] **poeta** [po-é-ta] **lo es** [lo-és]			
Unstressed /a e o/ before /i/ and /u/	SPEECH	(careful and rapid speech) **me iba** [me-í-ba] **lo único** [lo-ú-ri-ko]	(careful and rapid speech) **me imagino** [me̯-ma-xí-no] **la hijita** [laḭ-xí-ta] **lo unieron** [loṵ-njé-ron]	(rapid speech at word boundaries) **me iba** [mí-ba] **me imagino** [mi-ma-xí-no] **la hija** [lí-xa] **la hijita** [li-xí-ta] **lo único** [lú-ni-ko] **lo unieron** [lu-njé-ron]	

* Navarro, *Manual de pronunciación española* (1957), Sections 66–69, 134–51.
  Quilis, "La juntura en español" (1964).
  ———, "Phonologie de la quantité en espagnol" (1965).
* Saporta, "A Note on Spanish Semivowels" (1956).
  ——— and Cohen, "The Distribution and Relative Frequency of Spanish Diphthongs" (1957–58).
* Silva-Fuenzalida, "Spanish Section" in *Manual and Anthology of Applied Linguistics* (1960), "Some Aspects of Spanish Phoneme Substitution (Morphophonemics)."

ENGLISH AND GENERAL

* Bronstein (1960), Chapter 10.
* Buchanan (1963), Chapter VII.
* Heffner, *General Phonetics* (1949), Chapter V.
  Hill, *Introduction to Linguistic Structures* (1958), Chapter 5.
* Lloyd and Warfel, *American English in Its Cultural Setting* (1957), Chapter 18.
* Smalley, *Manual of Articulatory Phonetics* (1964), Chapter 12.
  Trager and Smith, *An Outline of English Structure* (1951), Part I.

Drills

A   Repetition (books open)

Your teacher will pronounce a series of Spanish words and phrases containing identical vowels, one or both of which are stressed. They are in separate syllables although not *separated by any sort of pause. Thus, they are* LINKED. *The style is* careful *speech. Repeat them after your teacher, following along in the book as you do.*

1. creer	11. va Ana	21. hablé español
2. leer	12. tú únicamente	22. estudié esto
3. de él	13. tú unes	23. di hilo
4. le era fácil	14. tu único libro	24. di indicios
5. loor	15. tome eso	25. vi islas
6. lo odio	16. tomé eso	26. vi islitas
7. alcohol	17. tomé el otro	27. su humo
8. no otro	18. la abre	28. lo hondo
9. azahar	19. da a Pedro	29. estudia algo
10. va a hablar	20. yo honro	30. aprende esto

B   Repetition (books open)

Your teacher will pronounce a series of Spanish words and phrases containing a stressed /í/ or a stressed /ú/ next to another vowel. They are in separate syllables although not *separated by any sort of pause.*

Thus, they are LINKED. *The style is either* careful or rapid *speech. Repeat them after your teacher, following along in the book as you do.*

1. mío	11. me iba	21. pía
2. aún	12. saúco	22. reúne
3. se ríe	13. la única	23. se une
4. di otra cosa	14. egoísmo	24. la hija
5. la última	15. lo hice	25. país
6. vía	16. continúe	26. buho
7. vi a Roberto	17. la uva	27. leíste
8. grúa	18. actúo	28. le hizo la cosa
9. tú hablas	19. tú entras primero	29. salía
10. leí	20. comí el pan	30. salí a verlo

C   Repetition (books open)

Your teacher will pronounce a series of Spanish words and phrases containing combinations of /a e o/. *They are in separate syllables although not separated by any sort of pause. Thus, they are* LINKED. *The style is careful speech. Repeat them after your teacher, following along in the book as you do.*

1. crear	11. caen	21. me habló
2. león	12. ahogo	22. de otro
3. le abre	13. toalla	23. cohete
4. me honra	14. la ostra	24. lo hecho
5. teatro	15. toma ésa	25. lo abre
6. peor	16. ahogado	26. saeta
7. no entró	17. caerán	27. aldea
8. poeta	18. moaré	28. peor
9. roer	19. la honra	29. empeorar
10. lo abrió	20. la heredó	30. yo abro

D   Repetition (books open)

Your teacher will pronounce a series of Spanish words and phrases containing combinations of unstressed /i/ *and* /u/ *with other vowels. They are* FUSED *into one syllable. The style is either* careful or rapid *speech. Repeat them after your teacher, following along in the book as you do.*

1. actual	5. cuidado	9. causa
2. tu amigo	6. su hijo	10. la humilla
3. abuela	7. continuo	11. deuda
4. su enemigo	8. su obra	12. de usted

13. bou
14. lo humilla
15. novia
16. cursi a todos
17. siete
18. mi enemigo
19. piojo
20. mi ojo
21. ciudad
22. mi único libro
23. paisano
24. la hijita
25. seis

26. le informó
27. hoy
28. lo histórico
29. labio
30. mi otro labio
31. veinte
32. le interesaba
33. triunfal
34. farmacia
35. me humillaron
36. homogeneidad
37. tome usted
38. presuntuoso

39. augusto
40. su ave
41. continúe historia
42. estudia historia
43. estudia usted
44. estudió historia
45. fue humilde
46. estatua inmóvil
47. antigua usanza
48. antiguo y rancio
49. antiguo uniforme
50. fue interesante
51. antigua historia

52. continuo interés

E   Repetition (books open)

Your teacher will pronounce a series of Spanish words and phrases containing identical vowels, one of which is stressed. The unstressed vowels are ELIMINATED. *The style here is* rapid *speech, as opposed to the careful speech of drill* **A,** *where both vowels were linked. Repeat the words and phrases after your teacher, following along in the book as you do.*

1. creer
2. leer
3. de él
4. le era fácil
5. loor
6. lo odio
7. alcohol
8. azahar
9. va a hablar
10. tome eso

11. tomé el otro
12. la abre
13. da a Pedro
14. hablé español
15. di indicios
16. vi islitas
17. su humo
18. lo hondo
19. estudia algo
20. aprende esto

21. mi hijo
22. no le entra
23. lo honra
24. la abre
25. lo otro
26. su último libro
27. habla a Álvaro
28. esta hacha
29. este héroe
30. va a abrirla

F   Repetition (books open)

Your teacher will pronounce a series of Spanish words and phrases containing identical vowels, neither of which is stressed. One vowel is ELIMINATED. *The style here is either* careful *or* rapid *speech. Repeat them after your teacher, following along in the book as you do.*

1. creeré
2. leeré
3. la abriré

4. lo honraron
5. entiende español
6. nuestro obrero

7. nuestra amiga
8. leeremos
9. creerán

10. mi hijito   13. lo horrible   16. mi interés
11. le envió   14. te engañó   17. de español
12. su unión   15. a América   18. esta amiga
            19. este enemigo   20. esto originó

G   Repetition (books open)

*Your teacher will pronounce a series of Spanish words and phrases
containing combinations of vowels and unstressed /i/ and /u/, which are
REPLACED by /y/ and /w/, respectively. The style is either* careful *or*
rapid *speech. Repeat them after your teacher, following along in your
book as you do.*

1. voy a comer   6. hoy o mañana   11. se cayó
2. siete u ocho   7. éste u otro   12. ayer por la tarde u hoy
3. no hay animales 8. Pablo y Enrique   13. esto y eso
4. lo leyó   9. se calla y escucha 14. eso y aquello
5. no lo creyó   10. pluma y escritorio 15. minuto u hora

H   Repetition (books open)

*Your teacher will pronounce a series of Spanish words and phrases
containing combinations of vowels and unstressed /e/ and /o/, which are
REPLACED by [i̯] and [u̯], respectively. The style is* rapid *speech. Repeat
them after your teacher, following along in your book as you do.*

1. Bilbao   11. lo envió   21. esto es
2. cae   12. poeta   22. lo es
3. lealtad   13. lo hice   23. de Honorato
4. lo abrió   14. traen   24. se untó
5. lo invitó   15. toalla   25. la heredó
6. me honraron   16. me humilló   26. de otro
7. león   17. ahogado   27. cohete
8. real   18. caerán   28. lo hecho
9. teatro   19. moaré   29. lo abre
10. peor   20. me habló   30. empeorar

I   Read Aloud (books open)

*Read the words, phrases, and sentences aloud, being careful to pronounce
the correct form of the vowel combination—LINKED, FUSED, ELIMINATED,
or REPLACED—for the style* careful *speech. Some combinations may
have more than one acceptable pronunciation even in careful speech.*

1. creer
2. de él
3. di otra cosa
4. tú hablas
5. león
6. peor
7. no entró
8. tu amigo
9. su hijo
10. creeré
11. nuestro obrero
12. entiende español
13. lo horrible
14. no hay animales
15. siete u ocho
16. No quería beber
    el alcohol.

17. Va a hablar sobre la guerra.
18. Estudia algo, pero no sé exactamente qué.
19. Lo hice a pesar mío
20. Tú entras primero, yo después.
21. Lo abrió y descubrió una sorpresa.
22. Lo hecho es lo hecho—y no hay remedio.
23. Estudié eso, pero no lo aprendí.
24. Le interesaba la historia de su marcha
    triunfal.
25. Se veía tan augusto y presuntuoso.
26. Siguió mostrando continuo interés.
27. Estudió historia cuando estaba en la
    universidad.
28. En este momento mi interés está en este
    libro de español.
29. Pablo y Eduardo vieron lo horrible de
    la situación.

30. León siempre se calla y escucha.

Read Aloud (books open)

*Read the words, phrases, and sentences aloud, being careful to pronounce the correct form of the vowel combination—*LINKED, FUSED, ELIMINATED, *or* REPLACED—*for the style* rapid *speech. Some combinations may have more than one acceptable pronunciation even in rapid speech.*

1. creer
2. se ríe
3. la última
4. vía
5. vi a Roberto
6. tu amigo
7. su hijo
8. lo humilla
9. estatua inmóvil
10. de él
11. alcohol
12. va a hablar
13. la abre
14. hablé español
15. nuestro obrero
16. entiende español
17. mi interés
18. lealtad
19. lo hice

20. ahogado
21. En ese momento me iba para la casa.
22. Salí a verlo, pero no pude ver nada.
23. Lo hice a pesar mío.
24. Lo hecho es lo hecho—y no hay remedio.
25. Me era fácil creerlo.
26. Hablé español todos los días que estuve
    en Bilbao.
27. Mi hijo tiene dificultad con la historia—
    no le entra.
28. Lo otro no le gusta tampoco a este
    héroe.
29. Te engañó cuando te dijo que podía ir a
    España.
30. Pablo y Eduardo vieron lo horrible de la
    situación.
31. —León, ¿qué estás madurando ahí?
32. Lo abrió y no encontró nada.
33. Me honraron cuando me invitaron al teatro.

34. Sabe él que la cosa no puede menos de empeorar.

35. Se untó con la crema, y después se limpió con una toalla.

36. Dice él que lo es, pero no es.

K "Live" Transcription

Exercises

A

Transcribe phonetically one Spanish word or phrase to illustrate each of these four vowel combinations and modifications: LINKED, FUSED, ELIMINATED, *and* REPLACED.

B

Transcribe phonetically any Spanish word or phrase in two different ways: first, to illustrate LINKED *vowels; second, an* ELIMINATED *vowel.*

C

Make a PHONEMIC *transcription of the following phrases. The speaker is using* careful speech. *Then check your transcriptions in* Appendix D.

1. La ama con toda su alma.
2. No creo que los poetas se paseen por esta avenida.
3. Me siento ahogado.
4. Me imagino que te ibas a la Unión.
5. Quería dieciséis o diecisiete, pero no hay aquí más que quince.
6. Pienso que es de España.
7. Su ave es suave.
8. Y eso no es yeso.
9. Si entras, lo sientes.
10. Sabe él que la cosa no puede menos de empeorar.

D

Now make a PHONETIC *transcription of the same phrases, but now in the style of* rapid speech. *Then check your transcriptions in* Appendix D.

31

~~~~~~

CONSONANT + VOWEL COMBINATIONS

The most important consonant + vowel (CV) combination is the one which occurs across word boundaries, forming linking, or **enlace.** A consonant between two vowels always goes with the next vowel to form the next syllable whether it is within a word: **pelo** [pé-lo] or between words: **el oro** [e-ló-ro]. In normal speech, no break of any kind occurs unless the word ends the phonemic phrase and is followed, naturally, by a pause. Thus, the two phrases **la sabes** and **las aves** are both [la-sá-ƀes].

The most important feature of **enlace** is the fact that it obscures word boundaries in normal speech. English-speakers often put in glottal stops or pauses to try to indicate word boundaries, and this chops up the smooth flow of sound within the phonemic phrase: **Los alumnos estaban en el aula** *[losʔa-lúm-nos es-tá-ƀanʔ ɛnʔɛlʔáu̯-la] instead of [lo-sa-lúm-no-ses-tá-ƀa-ne-ne-láu̯-la]. This unbroken flow of sound, even at a relatively slow speed, is one of the reasons that Spanish seems so fast to the beginning English-speaking student.

The only cases where word boundaries are observed as such are with /s/ and /n/ in certain dialects. When /s/ is aspirated in syllable-final position as [h], it often occurs at the end of words even between vowels. Thus, the word **los** is [loh] in **los tengo** [loh-tɛ́ŋ-go] and also in **los he tenido** [lo-hé-te-ní-do]. When /n/ is realized as the velar [ŋ] in word-final position, the [ŋ] often becomes intervocalic. Thus, the word **hablan** is [á-ƀlaŋ] in **no hablan** [nó-á-ƀlaŋ] and also in **no hablan español** [nó-á-ƀla-ŋes-pa-ñól]. However, even here, although word boundaries are observed in a sense, the resulting consonant still goes with the following vowel to form **enlace.**

Within the phonemic phrase the same phenomenon occurs even with words containing prefixes: **inoportuno** [i-no-por-tú-no], **desagradable** [de-sa-gra-dá-ƀle], **inhumano** [i-nu-má-no], **aborigen** [a-ƀo-rí-xɛn], **bienestar** [bi̯e-nes-tár].

Other CV combinations in Spanish may cause you difficulty because of contrasts with corresponding combinations in English. Some of these have already been discussed in Chapters 28 and 29, but they bear repeating here.

English combinations of /CyV/ usually have /u/ as the V, as in *few*. Some consonants, however, rarely occur in this /CyV/ combination. When confronted with one of these combinations in Spanish you may use /CVyV/ instead, as in **fiesta** *[fi̯-yés-ta], **idiota** *[i-di̯-yó-ta], **ocio** [ó-si̯-yo]. This extra vowel sounds wrong in Spanish, and the English-speaker must make an effort to use [Ci̯V] instead of /CVyV/.

Spanish combinations of [CCi̯V] are even more difficult. The second consonant of the cluster is always /l/ or /r/: **pliego** [pli̯é-go], **criada** [kri̯á-da]. The tendency for you to break these combinations into two syllables is even stronger: *[pli̯-yé-go], *[kri̯-yá-da].

English has many cognate words with palatal sounds, which are non-palatal C + [i̯] in Spanish: *delicious* -**delicioso**, *question* -**cuestión**, *cordial* -**cordial**. The temptation is strong to follow the English pattern and pronounce the Spanish words as *[de-li-ši̯ó-so], *[ku̯es-ĉón], *[kor-ǰál] instead of [de-li-si̯ó-so], [ku̯es-ti̯ón], [kor-di̯ál], respectively.

English has a limited distribution of the pattern /CwV/. C is usually /t/ *twenty*, /k/ *quit*, /d/ *dwell*, or /s/ *swim*. But in the corresponding Spanish pattern of [Cu̯V], C can be almost any consonant: **bueno, fuera, mueca, nuera, luego, pues, llueve**, etc. English-speakers often split these diphthongs into two syllables: *[bu-é-no], *[fu-é-ra], etc.

Spanish combinations of [CCu̯V] are even more difficult. The second consonant of the cluster is always /l/ or /r/: **fluir** [flu̯ír], **prueba** [pru̯é-ba]. The tendency for you to break these combinations into two syllables is even stronger: *[flu-ír], *[pru-é-ba].

You may also have trouble with the Spanish combination of [Cu̯] that occurs in cognate words that correspond to English words with /Cyu/: **ridículo, regular, museo**, and say *[ri̯-dí-ki̯u-lo], *[re-gi̯u-lár], *[mi̯u-sé-o], instead of [ri-dí-ku-lo], [re-gu-lár], [mu-sé-o], respectively.

English has many cognate words with palatal C + /uw/, which have non-palatal C + [u̯] in Spanish: *usually* -**usualmente**, *actual* -**actual**, *graduate* -**graduar**. It is difficult for many English-speakers to avoid *[u-žu̯al-mén̩-te] or *[u-ži-wal-mén̩-te], *[ak-ĉu̯ál] or *[ak-ĉi-wál], *[gra-ǰu̯ár] or *[gra-ǰi-wár] instead of [u-su̯ál-mén̩-te], [ak-tu̯ál], [gra-du̯ár], respectively.

References

SPANISH

Agard, "Stress in Four Romance Languages" (1967).
* Bowen and Stockwell, *Patterns of Spanish Pronunciation* (1960), Chapter 3.
Fernández, Joseph A., "La anticipación vocálica en español" (1963).
* Stockwell and Bowen, *The Sounds of English and Spanish* (1965), Chapter 6.

ENGLISH AND GENERAL

* Heffner, *General Phonetics* (1949), Chapter VII.

Drills

A   Repetition (books open)

Your teacher will pronounce a series of Spanish phrases which have **enlace**. *Repeat them after your teacher, following along in your book as you do.*

1. es un hombre
2. es un águila
3. hablan español
4. están aquí
5. los alumnos están aquí
6. los alumnos están en el aula
7. el hijo
8. El hijo dijo: —Elijo.
9. las uvas
10. las otras uvas
11. las otras uvas azules
12. usted es un artista
13. ustedes son artistas
14. usted es un amigo suyo
15. ustedes son amigos íntimos de él
16. nosotros hablamos español en esta clase
17. en hojas
18. lo pone en hojas
19. te enojas cuando lo pone en hojas
20. los obreros están enfermos
21. el color es muy amarillo
22. ver es creer
23. "Ver rojo" es una expresión inglesa.
24. "Ver ojo" no es una expresión inglesa.
25. El helado no tiene nada que ver con el hado.

B   Repetition

Your teacher will pronounce a series of Spanish words and phrases beginning with [CiV] *or* [CuV]. *Repeat them.*

1. tiene
2. fuera
3. piojo
4. cuota
5. piano
6. cuidar
7. ciudad
8. suave
9. siento
10. mueca
11. patio
12. antiguo
13. fiar
14. buitre
15. Miura
16. cuajar
17. pienso
18. luego
19. Rioja
20. su honor
21. liar
22. fuimos
23. ciudadano
24. ruana
25. riego
26. llueve
27. mi honor
28. mi amigo
29. tu interés
30. mi humor

C Repetition

Your teacher · will pronounce a series of Spanish words or phrases beginning with [CC̯V] *or* [CC̯V]. *Repeat them.*

1. pliego	10. clueco	19. griego
2. prueba	11. criollismo	20. fruición
3. criollo	12. cruórico	21. triunfo
4. fluorita	13. triángulo	22. truhán
5. criado	14. fluidez	23. grieta
6. fluir	15. friego	24. trueno
7. prior	16. cliente	25. prior
8. grueso	17. grueso	26. triar
9. prieto	18. friolera	27. druida

D Repetition (books open)

Your teacher will pronounce a series of Spanish words and phrases that do not have palatal C + /i/ *or palatal* C + /u/ *in Spanish although their cognates in English do. Repeat them after your teacher, following along in your book as you do.*

1. delicioso	11. nació	21. puntual
2. usual	12. residual	22. visión
3. cordial	13. pidió	23. ilusión
4. situar	14. gradual	24. perpetuo
5. cuestión	15. especial	25. discusión
6. graduarse	16. eventual	26. actual
7. gracias	17. casual	27. actualmente
8. natural	18. malicioso	28. composición
9. ambición	19. apreciar	29. nacional
10. situación	20. confusión	30. bestial

E Repetition (books open)

Your teacher will pronounce a series of Spanish words and phrases that have [Cu̯] *and not* /Cyu/ *as most of their cognates in English do. Repeat them after your teacher, following along in your book as you do.*

1. película	8. puro	15. buró
2. ridículo	9. cura	16. musical
3. museo	10. funeral	17. vehicular
4. música	11. pubertad	18. espurio
5. futuro	12. immune	19. furia
6. butano	13. curioso	20. pútrido
7. regular	14. punitivo	21. furioso

22. Cuba	25. municipal	28. simular
23. figura	26. monumento	29. curioso
24. mula	27. salutaciones	30. granular

F Read Aloud (books open)

Read the sentences aloud.

1. Voy a ver una película.
2. Es ridículo que sea tan grueso.
3. Muchas gracias por la ruana.
4. Es una cuestión de graduarse.
5. Figúrese qué puntualidad.
6. El trueno asustó al griego.
7. Es especialmente ambicioso.
8. Hizo una mueca por lo de la prueba.
9. Naturalmente, lo riego.
10. El cura visitó todos los monumentos nacionales.

G "Live" Transcription

Exercises

A

Why does **enlace** *occur in Spanish? Find an example of two phrases in Spanish which mean different things but which are pronounced exactly alike because of* **enlace**—*such as* **la sabes** *and* **las aves.**

B

Make a PHONEMIC *transcription of the following phrases. The speaker is using* careful *speech. Then check your transcription in* Appendix D.

1. El hombre iba a desatar el oso.
2. El heno está seco; por eso, vamos a ponerlo en el pajar.
3. Las acciones de los alumnos son inaplicables en este caso.
4. Los subordinados son bienaventurados.
5. Te enojas cuando lo pongo en hojas.
6. El hado no me permite comer helado.
7. El hijo dijo: —Elijo.

C

Now make a PHONETIC *transcription of the same phrases. The speaker is using* careful *speech. Use only the consonant allophones listed in Exercise 22.10 D, plus all eight vowel allophones. Then check your transcriptions in* Appendix D.

32

REVIEW OF VOWELS /e a o i u/, CONSONANTS
/y w/, VOWEL COMBINATIONS, AND
CONSONANT + VOWEL COMBINATIONS

32.1 Phonemes

	Front	Central	Back
High	i		u
Mid	e		o
Low		a	

	Palatal		Bilabio-velar
SLIT FRICATIVES	y		w

32.2 Allophones

	Front	Central	Back
High	i̥ i		u̥ u
Mid	e ę		o
Low		a	

	Palatal		Bilabio-velar
SLIT FRICATIVES	y		w

32.3 Facial Diagrams

See Sections 25.3, 26.3, 27.3, 28.3, 29.3.

32.4 Articulation

/e/   {[e] closed mid front oral vowel
    {[ę] open mid front oral vowel

/a/   {[a] low central oral vowel

/o/   {[o] mid back oral vowel

/i/   {[i] high front oral vowel
    {[i̯] high front oral semi-vowel

/u/   {[u] high back oral vowel
    {[u̯] high back oral semi-vowel

/y/   {[y] voiced palatal slit fricative consonant

/w/   {[w] voiced bilabio-velar slit fricative consonant

32.5 Allophonic Distribution

[e] usually occurs when /e/ is in an open syllable, as in **peso** [pé-so], or in syllables closed by [s] or [z], as in **ves** [bés] or **desde** [déz-de]. [ę] usually occurs when /e/ is in a syllable checked by consonants other than [s] or [z], as in **entrar** [ęn-trár], **papel** [pa-pę́l], before /r̄/, as in **perro** [pę́-r̄o], and also as the first element of a diphthong, as in **ley** [lę́i̯] and **deuda** [dę́u̯-da].

[a] occurs everywhere for /a/.

[o] occurs everywhere for /o/.

[i] occurs when /í/ is stressed, as in **mío** [mí-o] or **vino** [bí-no], or when it is bounded by a consonant or consonants, whether stressed or not, as in **ir** [ír] and **pintar** [piŋ-tár]. [i̯] occurs when unstressed /ĭ/ is bounded by a vowel or vowels, as in **tiene** [ti̯é-ne] and **hay** [ái̯]. [i̯] is the non-syllabic element of a diphthong or triphthong. Notice that when [i̯] precedes the vowel, it also follows a consonant. If there is no consonant, [i̯] is replaced by [y]. /y/ also replaces unstressed /ĭ/ between vowels, as in **leyo** [le-yó].

[u] occurs when /ú/ is stressed, as in **actúa** [ak-tú-a] and **puso** [pú-so], or

when it is bounded by a consonant or consonants, whether stressed or not, as
in **bus** [bús] and **apuntar** [a-puṇ-tár]. [u] occurs when unstressed /ŭ/ is bounded
by a vowel or vowels, as in **suave** [su̯á-ƀe] and **causa** [káu̯-sa]. [u̯] is the non-
syllabic element of a diphthong or triphthong. Notice that when [u̯] precedes
the vowel, it also follows a consonant. If there is no consonant, [u̯] is replaced
by [w]. /w/ also replaces unstressed /ŭ/ between vowels, as in **siete u ocho** [sié-
te-wó-ĉo].

/i/ and /u/ can FUSE in the same syllable with a vowel to create the following
fourteen diphthongs and twelve triphthongs:

/ie/	**tiene** [ti̯é-ne]
/ia/	**criada** [kri̯á-ɗa]
/io/	**odio** [ó-ɗi̯o]
/iu/	**ciudad** [si̯u-ɗáɗ]
/ei/	**seis** [séi̯s]
/ai/	**hay** [ái̯]
/oi/	**hoy** [ói̯]
/ui/	**cuidar** [ku̯i-ɗár]
/ue/	**bueno** [bu̯é-no]
/ua/	**cuarto** [ku̯ár-to]
/uo/	**cuota** [ku̯ó-ta]
/eu/	**deuda** [déu̯-da]
/au/	**causa** [káu̯-sa]
/ou/	**bou** [bóu̯] (This diphthong usually occurs across word boundaries, as **lo humano** [lou̯-má-no].)
/iei/	**estudie historia** [es-tú-ɗi̯ei̯s-tó-ri̯a]
/ieu/	**estudie usted** [es-tú-ɗi̯eu̯s-téɗ]
/iai/	**estudia historia** [es-tú-ɗi̯ai̯s-tó-ri̯a]
/iau/	**estudia usted** [es-tú-ɗi̯au̯s-téɗ]
/ioi/	**estudio historia** [es-tu-ɗi̯ói̯s-tó-ri̯a]
/iou/	**estudió utilitarismo** [es-tu-ɗi̯óu̯-ti-li-ta-ríz-mo]
/uei/	**buey** [bu̯éi̯]
/ueu/	**fue humilde** [fu̯éu̯-mí̯]-de]
/uai/	**estatua inmóvil** [es-tá-tu̯ai̯m-mó-ƀil]
/uau/	**antigua usanza** [aṇ-tí-gu̯au̯-sán-sa]
/uoi/	**antiguo y vetusto** [aṇ-tí-gu̯oi̯-ƀe-tús-to]
/uou/	**antiguo uniforme** [aṇ-tí-gu̯ou̯-ni-fór-me]

Triphthongs are rare in Spanish, and the above combinations sometimes
break into two syllables, especially when the middle vowel is stressed: **fue
humilde** [fu̯éu̯-mí̯-de] or [fu̯é-u-mí̯-de]

Other vowel combinations also occur. If the vowels are identical and one
or both are stressed, they are LINKED but remain in separate syllables in careful
speech: **lo odio** [lo-ó-ɗi̯o], **no odio** [nó-ó-ɗi̯o]. In rapid speech the combination

of two stressed vowels remains the same, but in the combination of stressed and unstressed, the unstressed is eliminated: [ló-d̪i̯o].

If neither one of a group of identical vowels is stressed, they become one in both careful and rapid speech: **la abriré** [la-b̪ri-ré].

Any combination of /a o e/, whether or not any stress is present, is LINKED but in separate syllables in both careful and rapid speech: **pasear** [pa-se-ár]. In many dialects in rapid speech unstressed /e/ and /o/ are REPLACED by /i/ and /u/: **teatro** [t̪i̯á-tro], **poeta** [pu̯é-ta], and all three unstressed vowels /a o e/ are eliminated at the end of a word, particularly when they precede a word beginning with a vowel one step higher on the same side of the vowel triangle (either side for /a/): **la hora** [ló-ra], **la esposa** [les-pó-sa], **me imagino** [mi-ma-xí-no], **lo único** [lú-ni-ko].

Exceptions to these patterns are words ending in /uiC–/, compounds, and analogous forms.

It should be pointed out that contiguous Spanish vowels within a phonemic phrase are rarely separated by pauses or glottal stops in natural speech, even when they are in separate words.

The most important CV combinations for you to observe occur across word boundaries and are called linking or **enlace: ellos hablan español** [é-yo-sá-b̪la-nes-pa-ñól].

See Appendix A for the rules for allophonic distribution and corresponding examples of single vowel phonemes. See pp. 187–88 for the rules for vowel combinations and pp. 189–91 for the charts with examples.

32.6 Dialectal Variations

Except for the elimination and replacement of vowels in certain combinations, single Spanish vowels have few dialectal variations. This is just the reverse of the situation in American English where dialectal pronunciation differences are due mainly to variations in the vowels and the vowel nuclei.

32.7 Contrasts with English

The two most important differences between Spanish vowels and English vowels are these: (1) Spanish syllables and words frequently end with stressed vowels, but in English stressed vowels are followed by consonants or one of the three glides /y w h/; (2) the majority of unstressed syllables in English contain either /ɨ/ or /ə/, neither of which exist in Spanish. Thus, you have the tendency to place a glide—usually /y/ or /w/—after Spanish stressed vowels: **yo** *[yów]*, **sí** *[síy]* and to substitute either /ɨ/ or /ə/ for Spanish unstressed vowels: **naturalmente** *[na-tə-rɨl-mén̪-te]*, **señorita** *[se-ñɨ-rí-ta]*. Both these errors can not only cause phonemic confusion, but sound improper in Spanish in all cases.

There are other problems, too, but the above two are the most serious and formidable for you. Even long after you become fluent in Spanish, you must continue to be on guard against the intrusion of these English sound features.

32.8 References

See references for Chapters 24–31.

32.9 Drills

(*Repeat selected drills from Chapters 25–31.*)

32.10 Exercises

A

Give an articulatory description for [e], *for* [a], *for* [o], *for* [u̯], *for* [i̯]. *Then check your answers in Section* 32.4.

B

Sketch a facial diagram for [e̞], *for* [i], *for* [u]. *Then check your diagrams with those in Sections* 25.3, 28.3, *and* 29.3, *respectively.*

C

Make a PHONEMIC *transcription of the following phrases. The speaker is using* careful *speech. Then check your transcriptions in Appendix D.*

1. Papá va a la Habana a hablar a Arnaldo Arana, que es de España.
2. Vi la estatua inmóvil.
3. Es un monstruo humano.
4. Dame uno u otro.
5. Pero no hay aquí ninguno.
6. ¿Estudia usted historia?
7. Estudie usted esto.
8. Ya estudió utilitarismo.
9. Llevaba su antiguo uniforme a la antigua usanza.
10. Es ocio inútil.

D

Now make a PHONETIC *transcription of the same phrases. The speaker is again using* careful *speech. Then check your transcriptions in Appendix D.*

32.11 Questions

Five Questions

Write your answers on a separate sheet of paper and check them in Appendix D.

1. Vowels are determined by ____.
2. Glides in English can function either as ____ or as ____.
3. In English stressed vowels rarely ____.
4. When it comes to diphthongs, Spanish writing ____.
5. Spanish vowels are never nasalized. TRUE/FALSE
6. There are no English vowels that even resemble Spanish [e] and [ę]. TRUE/FALSE
7. The terms "closed" and "open" with vowels mean that ____.
8. Spanish [ę] occurs mainly in syllables that are ____.
9. **Vente** and **veinte** are often pronounced the same way by English-speaking students. TRUE/FALSE.
10. / / replaces unstressed /i/ between vowels in Spanish.
11. The tongue is lowest for the Spanish vowel / /.
12. English-speakers who do not distinguish between *caller* and *collar* sometimes substitute English / / for Spanish / /.
13. The lips are more rounded for Spanish /o/ than for the Spanish vowels / /.
14. Other than the fact that it sounds wrong, what is one reason for which those of you who pronounce stressed English *o* as /ew/ should not substitute this pronunciation for Spanish /o/?
15. The use of English /ɔ/ for Spanish /a/ can not only cause phonemic confusion but also ____.
16. English-speakers often pronounce Spanish stressed /i/ as / /.
17. Give one restriction on the distribution of /i/ in Spanish.
18. English /i/ as in *bit* is not the same as the Spanish /i/ of **bis** because it is ____.
19. English *beat* does not have the same vowel sounds as Spanish **bis** because ____.
20. When the combination [CiV] occurs in Spanish, English-speakers often use [   ] instead.
21. In the writing system, Spanish stressed /ú/ does not always ____.
22. One common English-speaker's mispronunciation of Spanish stressed /ú/ is [   ].
23. If you do not bring your tongue back far enough in the mouth for Spanish unstressed /u/, [ɨ] is the result.
24. When a Spanish word has a [CüV] combination which does not occur in English, you often pronounce [   ] instead.

25. Give a Spanish word often mispronounced by English-speakers with [i̯u] instead of [u].

26. English-speakers sometimes incorrectly separate contiguous Spanish vowels with a pause or a ____.

27. They usually do this to try to indicate ____.

28. The correct pronunciation of vowel combinations in Spanish depends on both ____ and ____.

29. "Fused" vowels form a ____.

30. Spanish-speakers themselves sometimes pronounce the word **enviamos** with four syllables. Why?

31. You may be reluctant to use **enlace** because you think that ____ must be indicated in your pronunciation.

32. In most dialects of Spanish **en aguas** and **enaguas** are pronounced ____ .

33. One of the only exceptions to the "rule" that a consonant between two vowels is pronounced with the next vowel to form a syllable are words containing prefixes, like **malestar.** TRUE/FALSE

34. Why may **clueco** be a particularly difficult word for you to pronounce?

35. Give two potential diphthongs which do NOT occur in Spanish: / / and / / .

36. If **hay** has a diphthong [ái̯], does the phrase **hay animales** contain a triphthong? Why or why not?

ortografia - spanish spelling system

33

INTRODUCING THE SUPRASEGMENTALS OF SPANISH

The individual sounds—vowels and consonants—are referred to as segmental phonemes. These segments of sound can be influenced in several important ways by other phonological features, which are called suprasegmental or intonational phonemes.

These suprasegmentals are so important in many languages, including Spanish and English, that the listener often pays more attention to them than to the individual sound segments. For example, you can answer the question, "What do you think of it?" with the words, "It's just great!" If your voice starts quite high on the first part of "great" and drops very low within the word, you really mean what the words arranged in this sequence seem to mean. But if your voice starts low on the first part of "great" and drops slightly lower within the word, you are being sarcastic or at any rate mean just about the opposite of what these words seem to mean.

The common English expression, "It's not what you say but the way you say it" is soundly based on a linguistic reality—the complicated and subtle (for a foreign speaker) but essential suprasegmental system of the language. Spanish, too, has these same features, but the system is somewhat simpler since there are fewer suprasegmental phonemes than in English.

The first suprasegmental is STRESS, which is loudness or volume. The manipulation of this feature is what enables you to distinguish between *import* (the noun) and *import* (the verb) on the word level and between "I'm not going" and "I'm not going" on the sentence level. Stress also enables Spanish-speakers to distinguish between **libro** (the noun) and **libró** (the verb form) on the word level. Stress is not manipulated on the sentence level in Spanish the same way it is in English, however.

The second suprasegmental is PITCH, which is musical tone. In music pitch is absolute and must be exact, but in language it is relative and operates within ranges rather than on a precise scale of proportionally distant notes. Pitch is what enables you to distinguish between *What?* with a rise in the voice ("I didn't hear you; please repeat") and *What?* with a drop in the voice ("What do you want?" or "Give me more information"). Pitch also enables Spanish-speakers to distinguish between **Va a casa** (statement) and **¿Va a casa?** (question).

The third suprasegmental feature is TERMINAL JUNCTURE, a type of pause which involves a slight change in pitch, volume, and tempo. You can lower the pitch and trail away rapidly into silence to indicate finality, completion of the utterance. You can raise the pitch and cut off the volume sharply to indicate doubt or a question. Or you can sustain the pitch on a level, prolonging the last syllable, and diminish the volume slightly to indicate hesitation or incompletion. These junctures, often called clause or phonemic-phrase terminals, operate in almost the same way in both Spanish and English.

The last suprasegmental feature, rhythm, is not really part of the phonemic system of either Spanish or English, since it cannot be used to regulate or change meaning as the other suprasegmentals can. But rhythm is extremely important since it works in close conjunction with certain features that are phonemic, such as stress and the selection and quality of the vowels. Rhythm depends to a large extent on syllable- or vowel-length, neither of which are phonemic in Spanish or English but both of which are crucial in the acquisition of an authentic accent.

Language texts, until quite recently, have generally ignored the area of suprasegmentals. This is partly because linguistic studies on stress, pitch, and juncture were few in number and tentative in nature but mainly because few language teachers were convinced of the real importance of these features. Even today, when linguistic studies on these subjects are becoming more numerous and teachers are becoming more aware of their role in learning a foreign language, textbooks still devote far too little space to the suprasegmentals. It is true that these features are not as orderly and easy to analyze as the vowels and consonants, but they can be systematized and presented for learning.

Even though your Spanish grammar is perfect, your vocabulary extensive, and your individual sounds accurate, you will retain a noticeable foreign accent until you master the suprasegmental system of Spanish.

34

~~~~~~

STRESS

The force with which the air is expelled from the lungs through the larynx determines the volume or loudness of the sound. Sound waves have both a frequency, i.e., the number of vibrations or cycles per second, and an amplitude, i.e., the size of the waves. If there is more force, the amplitude of the waves is greater and the acoustic effect is that of more volume (see Diagram 2 on p. 27).

Since the vibrations of sound waves are caused by the movement of the vocal bands, stress (loudness, volume, intensity) is perceived to some extent in the voiced consonants but mainly in the vowels. Stress actually functions phonemically in the vowels, which are the syllable carriers. In some words certain vowels or vowel nuclei are pronounced louder, and this enables the speaker to make certain distinctions. For example, *import* (noun) and *import* (verb) in English or **libro** (noun) and **libró** (verb) in Spanish. These prominent syllables can also enable the speaker to make distinctions on the sentence level. For example, "I'm not going", "I'm not going", and "I'm not going" in English or *C'est impossible* (normal) and *C'est impossible* (emphatic) in French.

Stress is found in language for several reasons: the speaker's natural way of talking (idiolect) causes him to pronounce certain words and syllables louder than others; he stresses certain words because of their grammatical function in the sentence; and he stresses certain syllables automatically because the words either sound wrong otherwise or even turn into other words.

This last reason is extremely important in Spanish and English where we say that stress is *phonemic* since it can change or destroy meaning. In English, for example, it would be ludicrous for the lawyer to jump to his feet and shout, "I object!", nor would it make sense for him to say "This object was used to commit the foul crime". *Object* and *object* are two different words in English principally because of differing stress patterns.[1] In Spanish **continuo,**

---

[1] There is also a phonemic difference in the first vowel of the two words. *Object,* the noun, is /ábjèkt/, and *object,* the verb, is /ɔbjèkt/. However, this vocalic difference is due primarily to the stress pattern of the two words, /ə/ being one of the characteristic vowels of weak-stressed syllables in English.

continúo, and **continuó** cannot be interchanged, although they all have exactly the same consonant and vowel phonemes.

The varying degrees of stress in English and Spanish can be classified into a phonemic hierarchy. However, the stress phonemes, rather than being individual segments or stretches of sound, are imposed directly over or upon the vowels. Thus, they are *suprasegmental* phonemes which occur simultaneously with the *segmental* phonemes.

English, compared with Spanish, has a relatively complicated stress system. There are four stress phonemes: ′ primary, ^ secondary, ` tertiary, and ˘ weak or non-stress.[2] Some examples of simple patterns are ˘ ′ *the rest, a book, some ink*; ` ′ *my pen, lie down, New York*; ^ ′ *high time, two years, call home*; ′ ˘ *mother, coffee*; ′ ` *pie tin, baseball, White House*; ′ ^ **that** *book,* **my** *tin,* **this** *ball*; ` ^ ′ *much less time, four good books*; ′ ` ^ **don't** *go home, baseball bats.*

The Spanish stress system is less complicated because there are only two stress phonemes: ′ primary and ˘ weak, which is left unmarked in transcription. Some examples of simple patterns are ˘ ′ **está, mi voz, la sal**; ′ ˘ **ésta, mía, casa**; ˘ ˘ ′ **el sofá, animal, visitó**; ˘ ′ ˘ **la casa, mi padre, hablamos**; ′ ˘ ˘ **rápido, dígame.** Spanish weak stress is louder than English weak stress and really corresponds acoustically more closely to English tertiary stress.

Some linguists analyze the Spanish stress system as having three phonemes. What they call "secondary" occurs mainly in adverbs like **naturalmente** and certain compounds like **bienvenida.** However, the analysis presented in this book considers that the first element of such words has either a normal primary stress or a weaker *allophone* of primary stress. Moreover, since there are no words or phrases which are distinguished from each other by primary vs. this so-called "secondary" stress, it is linguistically valid, in addition to being simpler, to posit only two degrees of stress in Spanish.

In English almost all vowels in weak-stressed syllables are replaced by /ə/ or /ɨ/. Not only are these two vowels non-existent in Spanish, but unstressed or weak-stressed syllables in Spanish are rarely as weak in volume as they are in English.

All words in isolation are considered to have at least one primary stress, but in the stream of speech many of these words are unstressed or weak-stressed. For example, in *isolation* the Spanish verb form **para** and the preposition **para** both have a strong or primary stress on the first syllable and are pronounced [pá-ra]. But within the phonemic phrase, the verb form always has a primary stress, and the preposition rarely does. The phrase "Stop the car" is **Para el coche** [pá-ra-ẹl-kó-ĉe], but the phrase "for the car" is [pa-ra-ẹl-kó-ĉe].

In English there are words which are also normally unstressed or weak-stressed in the phonemic phrase, such as *him, her, the.* But for emphasis or

---

[2] The four-stress system of American English presented here is the one formulated by George L. Trager and Henry Lee Smith, Jr. (1951).

grammatical contrast, we frequently place heavy stress on these forms: "It's not her car." Spanish does this far less than English and relies instead on grammatical or lexical devices to convey such meanings: **No es el coche de ella.** English-speakers, however, tend to carry over their own stress patterns and emphasize Spanish words which do not normally have heavy stress: **No es su coche** *[nó-es-sú-kó-ĉe] for "It's not her car."

This problem is a double one. First, you must learn which words do not normally carry heavy stress in Spanish in the phonemic phrase, and, secondly, you must learn the grammatical and lexical devices which are used instead to convey the desired emphasis. This second consideration is purely grammatical and does not concern us here, but the first one is both grammatical and phonological and does.

In Spanish there are certain words which are considered "minimal free forms," i.e., they can be uttered alone and the resulting utterance is acceptable and grammatical even though it may be a sentence "fragment" by traditional standards. For example, one can say in isolation each of these words, **hombre, habla, lindo,** or **aquí.** However, one *cannot* say in isolation such words as **con, le,** or **las** (except, of course, as answers to questions on grammar, such as— **¿ Cuál se usa más, le o lo?—Le.**)

Such forms as nouns, verbs, adjectives, and adverbs are considered syntactically "free" in the sense that they can occur alone without the support of another grammatical form. But definite articles, prepositions, subordinating conjunctions, and with-verb pronouns are "non-free" or "phrase-bound" in the sense that they always occur in natural speech in a phrase with some other supporting grammatical form. Definite articles are followed by nouns, prepositions by nouns or nominalized forms or noun phrases, subordinating conjunctions by verbs, and with-verb pronouns precede or follow verb forms.

Although there are exceptions, a handy rule-of-thumb is that "free" forms are always stressed in the phonemic phrase in Spanish and "phrase-bound" forms rarely are. Thus, such phrases as **con ella** *[kó-né-ya], **le hablaron** *[lé-a-ƀlá-ron], and **las muchachas** *[láz-mu-ĉá-ĉas] do not occur in Spanish with these stress patterns.

The following list shows which words are normally stressed in Spanish in the phonemic phrase:

	STRESSED
NOUNS	**El SEÑOR me habló.** [ęl-se-ñór-me-a-ƀló]
NOMINALIZED FORMS (any form that functions as or replaces a noun)	**LO de ayer es increíble.** [ló-đe-a-yé-re-siŋ-kre-í-ƀle]
	El OTRO me gusta más. [e-ló-tro-me-gús-ta-más]

VERBS	El señor me HABLÓ. [ęl-se-ñór-me-a-ƀló]
	No lo TENEMOS. [nó-lo-te-né-mos]
ADJECTIVES	El hombre ALTO me habló. [e-lóm-bre-ál-to-me-a-bló]
ADVERBS	Lee BIEN. [lé-e-ƀįén]
WITHOUT-VERB	EL se va. [ęl-se-ƀá]
PRONOUNS	Es para MÍ. [és-pa-ra-mí]
NUMERALS	Tiene UN libro. [tįé-ne-ún-lí-ƀro] *one book*
(cardinal and	Tiene el PRIMER libro. [tįé-nęl-pri-męr-lí-ƀro]
ordinal)	
NEGATIVES	NO viene NADIE. [nó-ƀįé-ne-ná-dįe]
POSSESSIVES	Es un amigo MÍO. [é-su-na-mí-go-mí-o]
(*post*-posed and	Es el SUYO. [é-sęl-sú-yo]
pronouns)	
DEMONSTRATIVES	Quiero ESTE libro. [kįé-ro-és-te-lí-ƀro]
INTERROGATIVES	¿CUÁNDO viene? [kųáŋ-do-ƀįé-ne]
EXCLAMATIVES	¡QUÉ bien! [ké-ƀįén]
MOST	Tengo mi PROPIA casa. [téŋ-go-mi-pró-pįa-ká-sa]
DETERMINERS	CUALQUIER libro está bien. [kųal-kįęr-lí-bro-es-tá-ƀįén]
(sometimes	Viene TODOS los días. [bįé-ne-tó-doz-loz- đí-as]
called "limiting	
adjectives")	
TITLES	EL SEÑOR Martínez [ęl-se-ñór-mar-tí-nes]
(with last names)	

UNSTRESSED

SIMPLE	Habla CON ella. [á-ƀla-ko-né-ya]
PREPOSITIONS	
RELATIVES	Es el hombre QUE vimos. [é-se-lóm-bre-ke-ƀí-mos]
ARTICLES	Tiene EL libro. [tįó nęl-lí-ƀro]
(definite and	Tiene UN libro. [tįé-nęun-lí-ƀro] (see NUMERALS above)
indefinite)	*a book*
WITH-VERB	LO ve. [lo-ƀé]
PRONOUNS	SE va. [se-ƀá]
CONJUNCTIONS	papel Y pluma [pa-pé-li-plú-ma]
(coordinating and	Quiere ir, PERO no puede. [kįé-re-ír pe-ro-nó-pųé-đe]
subordinating)	CUANDO venga, se lo diré. [kųaŋ-do-ƀéŋ-ga se-lo-đi-ré]
POSSESSIVE	Es MI amigo. [és-mįa-mí-go]
DETERMINERS	

EITHER STRESSED OR UNSTRESSED
(depending on various factors)

INTENSIFIERS   **Es MAS bonita que María.** [és-máz-ɓo-ní-ta-ke-ma-rí-a] or
[és-maz-ɓo-ní-ta-ke-ma-rí-a]
Es MUY bonita. [és-mu̯í-ɓo-ní-ta] or [és-mu̯i-ɓo-ní-ta]

UNOS (-AS)   **Tiene UNOS libros.** [ti̯é-ne-ú-noz-lí-ɓros] or
[ti̯é-ne̯u̯-noz-lí-ɓros]

HABER   **Lo HA dicho.** [lo-á-ɗí-ĉo] or [lo-a-ɗí-ĉo]

ES   **Rodrigo ES de Costa Rica.** [r̄o-ɗrí-go-éz-ɗe-kós-ta-r̄í-ka] or
[r̄o-ɗrí-go-ez-ɗe-kós-ta-r̄í-ka]

FIRST ELEMENT   **CAMPOsanto** [kám-po-sáŋ-to] or [kam-po-sáŋ-to]
OF A COMPOUND   **BIENvenida** [bi̯ém-be-ní-ɗa] or [bi̯em-be-ní-ɗa]
VEINTIdós [béi̯ŋ-ti-ɗós] or [bei̯ŋ-ti-ɗós]

There are, of course, exceptions to these categories, depending on such
factors as syntactical groupings, intonation, idiolect, unusual emphasis, etc.

In Spanish a group of unstressed syllables clustered around one stressed
syllable is called a stress phrase. These phrases in themselves are relatively
insignificant in Spanish phonology since there are no pauses between them as
there are between phonemic phrases. A sentence like **Los hombres que vimos
van a Panamá** has four stress phrases but only one breath group or phonemic
phrase: [lo-sóm-bres ¦ -ke-ɓí-mos ¦ -ɓá ¦ -na-pa-na-má]. As you can see, most
stress phrases (except for long words) are relatively short in Spanish since there
are so many word classes that have primary stress. These stressed syllables are
not normally accompanied by a great many unstressed syllables in the phonemic
phrase, although long words do have such patterns: **agriculturización, constitucionalidad.**

English is quite different. It is normal for many syllables—with weak,
tertiary, and secondary stresses—to cluster around one primary stress. The sentence, "He's a very good basketball player," said normally, has only one primary
stress, on *bas-*. Nine other syllables—none with heavy stress—complete the
phrase. This is because in English each phonemic phrase has only one primary
stress. If a primary stress were placed on *he* (with the verb as a separate word—
is) there would be two phonemic phrases: "He," followed by a type of pause called
terminal juncture, and "is a very good basketball player." Thus, stress phrases
and phonemic phrases are really the same thing in English. But this is not true in
Spanish. A phonemic phrase can have a half dozen or more heavy stresses with
a relatively few unstressed syllables or even none between them. The sentence,
El es un jugador de básketbol muy bueno, is only one phonemic phrase—if it is
said without any pauses—but it has six stress phrases (if **es** is stressed), i.e., six

heavy-stressed syllables and seven unstressed syllables: [é-lé-suŋ-xu-ga-dór-de-bás-ke-bol-mu̧í-bu̧é-no].

This feature of the Spanish stress system helps to create the so-called staccato rhythm, which is so difficult for most English-speakers to acquire. This problem is discussed further in Chapters 35, "Intonation," and 36, "Rhythm."

We can also classify Spanish words according to the position of the stress:

LAST-SYLLABLE-STRESSED (agudas)—**hablar, estás, nación, habló**

PENULT-STRESSED (llanas)—**lápiz, estas, pasan, hablo**

ANTEPENULT-STRESSED (esdrújulas)—**lápices, rápido, dígame**

PRE-ANTEPENULT-STRESSED (sobresdrújulas)—**dígamelo, muéstremela**

Notice that all words in the last two categories have a written accent, but only certain words in the first two have one. The rules governing the use of the written accent are discussed in Chapter 39, "Spanish Orthography."

Spanish nouns are stressed on the same syllable in both singular and plural forms, with a few common exceptions: **carácter** [ka-rák-te̞r] but **caracteres** [ka-rak-té-res] and **régimen** [ře-xi-me̞n] but **regímenes** [ře-xí-me-nes].

Some Spanish words with two contiguous vowels have two pronunciations: a formal and less common pronunciation where the first vowel is stressed and an informal and more common pronunciation where the second one is stressed. In this latter case sometimes the first vowel is realized as a semi-vowel: **océano**— sometimes [o-sé-a-no], but more often [o-se-á-no] or [o-si̧á-no], **período**— sometimes [pe-rí-o-d̞o], but more often [pe-ri̧ó-d̞o], **psiquíatra** or **psiquiatra**— sometimes [si-kí-a-tra], but more often [si-ki̧á-tra].

Adverbs ending in **-mente** have two strong stresses: **igualmente** [i-gu̧ál-mé̞n-te], **rápidamente** [řá-pi-d̞a-mé̞n-te]. Some compounds, also: **veintidós** [bé̞in-ti-dós], **tocadiscos** [tó-ka-d̞ís-kos], **pelirrojo** [pé-li-ró-xo], although these latter forms are just as frequently pronounced without strong stress on the first element.

In English phrases long sequences of weak-stressed syllables do not occur between the primary stresses. There is usually an alternation of weak stresses with secondary and tertiary stresses: ă nêcĕssàry stép. In long Spanish words, however, as many as five or six consecutive unstressed syllables can occur: **constitucionalidad.** In such words you have a tendency to place either a secondary or tertiary stress on certain syllables because of the way the cognate words in English are pronounced: *responsibility* /rĭspânsĭbílĭtĭy/, thus **responsabilidad** *[řes-pôn-sa-bi-li-d̞ád].

Another serious stress problem for you are the great number of cognate words that have contrasting patterns of primary stress: *acrobat* **-acróbata,** *telephone* **-teléfono,** *communicate* **-comunica,** *democrat* **-demócrata,** etc. This problem, however, is more easily overcome than the preceding one. The correct positioning of Spanish primary stress is probably easier for you than the avoidance of secondary and tertiary stresses in Spanish, which requires constant effort.

References

SPANISH

Agard, "Stress in Four Romance Languages" (1967).
Bolinger, " 'Secondary Stress' in Spanish" (1962).
* _____, "Stress on Normally Unstressed Elements" (1956).
* Bowen and Stockwell, *Patterns of Spanish Pronunciation* (1960), Chapters 1, 4.
* Cárdenas, *Introducción a una comparación fonológica del español y del inglés* (1960), "Acento prosódico".
Contreras, "The Neutralization of Stress in Chilean Spanish" (1965).
_____, "Sobre el acento en español" (1963).
_____, "¿Tiene el español un acento de intensidad?" (1964).
Delattre, *Comparing the Phonetic Features of English, French, German, and Spanish* (1965), Chapter II.
* Fernández, Salvador, "Para la futura gramática" (1964).
* Gili Gaya, *Elementos de fonética general* (1950), Chapter II.
* Lado, *Linguistics Across Cultures* (1957), Chapter 2.
* Matluck, "Entonación hispánica" (1965).
* Navarro, *Estudios de fonología española* (1946), "Grupos de intensidad".
* _____, *Manual de pronunciación española* (1957), Sections 152, 157–73.
_____, "La medida de intensidad" (1964).
* Sacks, "The Pattern Drill and the Rationale of the Prosodic and Orthographic Accents in Spanish" (1963).
* Silva-Fuenzalida, "Spanish Section" in *Manual and Anthology of Applied Linguistics* (1960), "Stress".
* Stockwell and Bowen, *The Sounds of English and Spanish* (1965), Chapter 3.
* Wallis and Bull, "Spanish Adjective Position: Phonetic Stress and Emphasis" (1950).

ENGLISH AND GENERAL

* Bronstein (1960), Chapter 13.
* Buchanan (1963), Chapter VIII.
* Gleason, *An Introduction to Descriptive Linguistics* (1961), Chapter 4.
* Heffner, *General Phonetics* (1949), Chapter VII.
Hill, *Introduction to Linguistic Structures* (1958), Chapter 2.
* Hockett, *A Course in Modern Linguistics* (1958), Chapter 5.
* Malmberg, *Phonetics* (1963), Chapter IX.
Stetson, *Motor Phonetics* (1951), Chapter VI.
Trager and Smith, *An Outline of English Structure* (1951), Part I.

Drills

A   Repetition

Your teacher will pronounce a series of pairs of Spanish words and phrases, which are phonemically distinct only because of contrasting stress patterns. Repeat each pair.

1. la calle — la callé
2. baño — bañó
3. estudio — estudió
4. la corte — la corté
5. corto — cortó
6. dólar — dolar
7. lástima — lastima
8. la ópera — la opera
9. presente — presenté
10. tarde — tardé
11. viaje — viajé
12. ténder — tender
13. la vera — la verá
14. el paleto — el paletó
15. la sábana — la sabana
16. refresco — refrescó
17. celebro — celebró
18. célebre — celebre
19. celebre — celebré
20. ¿yo filósofo? — ¿yo filosofo?
21. fijo — fijó
22. seria — sería
23. tenia — tenía
24. baja — bajá
25. domino — dominó
26. papa — papá
27. abra — habrá
28. ara — hará
29. peso — pesó
30. esta — está

B   Repetition

Your teacher will pronounce a series of Spanish words which are all **agudas.** *Repeat them.*

1. está
2. atrás
3. atención
4. botó
5. caminar
6. comunicar
7. construcción
8. solicitar
9. imaginar
10. telefonear
11. depositar
12. preocupar
13. oportunidad
14. declarar
15. enderezar
16. firmar
17. glotón
18. figurar
19. honradez
20. internacional
21. irá
22. juvenil
23. león
24. mamá

C   Repetition

Your teacher will pronounce a series of Spanish words which are all **llanas.** *Repeat them.*

1. esta
2. animo
3. avergüenzo
4. boxeadores
5. campeonato
6. conferencia
7. desperdicio
8. enderezo
9. femenino
10. figura
11. golondrina
12. insignificancia
13. inverosímil
14. leones
15. manifestaciones
16. obsequio
17. imagino
18. telefoneo
19. deposito
20. preocupo
21. oportuno
22. solicito
23. felicito
24. partidario

D   Repetition

Your teacher will pronounce a series of Spanish words which are all
esdrújulas. *Repeat them.*

1. ánimo	11. fábrica	21. número
2. análisis	12. frenético	22. órdenes
3. cáscara	13. huérfano	23. pálido
4. catálogo	14. ídolo	24. párrafo
5. céntimo	15. indígena	25. pésame
6. décimo	16. lámpara	26. pútrido
7. dentífrico	17. lóbrego	27. quirúrgico
8. dispénseme	18. máquina	28. régimen
9. época	19. mismísimo	29. salíamos
10. estilográfica	20. monárquico	30. teléfono

E   Repetition

Your teacher will pronounce a series of Spanish words which are all
sobresdrújulas. *Repeat them.*

1. cuénteselo	6. dígamelo	11. llévatelo
2. devuélvamelo	7. impídeselo	12. mándenselas
3. guárdamelo	8. impónganselos	13. muéstreselo
4. échemela	9. juguémonoslas	14. dándoselo
5. enséñamelo	10. lústramelos	15. diciéndomela

F   Repetition (books open)

Your teacher will pronounce a series of long Spanish words with only
one heavy stress. Repeat them, following along in your book as you do.

1. norteamericano	9. estacionamiento	17. alfabetización
2. matemático	10. responsabilidad	18. homogeneidad
3. manifestación	11. permeabilidad	19. cristalización
4. refrigerador	12. abandonamiento	20. anterioridad
5. laboratorio	13. identificación	21. supernaturalidad
6. institucionalidad	14. constitucionalidad	22. impersonalización
7. permutabilidad	15. nacionalidad	23. impresionabilidad
8. generalización	16. conversaciones	24. agriculturización

G   Repetition (books open)

Your teacher will pronounce a series of long Spanish words and phrases
with two *or more heavy stresses. Repeat them, following along in your*

book as you do. Remember that some of these compounds are also pronounced with only one heavy stress.

1. igualmente	11. enhorabuena	21. informalmente
2. lícitamente	12. calle abajo	22. regularmente
3. especialmente	13. mar adentro	23. el color verde
4. generalmente	14. anglosajón	24. reloj pulsera
5. políticorreligioso	15. hazmerreír	25. naturalmente
6. ágilmente	16. quitanieve	26. casa cuna
7. limpiabotas	17. rompecabezas	27. cante jondo
8. guardiacivil	18. salvavidas	28. cochecamas
9. camposanto	19. plumafuente	29. cumpleaños
10. bienvenida	20. literalmente	30. hermanos Quintero

H   Read Aloud (books open)

The following Spanish words and phrases have difficult stress patterns because of a partial correspondence to English. Read them aloud.

1. permanente	9. anécdota	17. comunica
2. acróbata	10. versátil	18. teléfono
3. oportunidad	11. carácter	19. felicito
4. antídoto	12. caracteres	20. refrigerador
5. preocupo	13. régimen	21. imagínese
6. solicito	14. regímenes	22. me imagino
7. autócrata	15. democracia	23. se imaginaba
8. demócrata	16. deposito	24. homófono

I   Read Aloud (books open)

Read the following phrases and sentences, being careful to place heavy stresses only where they belong.

1. Vivo aquí.	15. Lo de ayer es increíble.
2. Está allí.	16. Pedro va a casa mañana.
3. casa de campo	17. Pedro y su esposa van a
4. Tiene sólo una casa de campo.	visitarnos el mes que viene.
5. No vino nadie.	18. conmigo
6. No vino ninguno.	19. estuvo conmigo
7. No tiene ninguno.	20. Quiere ir conmigo.
8. Es mi amigo.	21. Es para mí.
9. Es un amigo mío.	22. Es para él y para ti.
10. Pero no quiere.	23. para el coche
11. Y no quiere.	24. ¡Para el coche!
12. Sin embargo, va.	25. Lo ve.
13. ¿Tiene dos libros?	26. No lo ve.
14. No, tiene un libro.	27. Se va.

Exercises

Using CONVENTIONAL ORTHOGRAPHY, *indicate the primary stresses by placing
' over the proper vowel. Written accents have deliberately been left off all
words. Then check the sentences in Appendix D.*

1. Se comunica con los ingleses por medio del telefono.
2. Si, es lo que llaman ustedes un caracter, pero tenemos muchos caracteres
   como el por aqui.
3. Imaginese que ya se va la señora Martinez.
4. El chico cuyo padre era el candidato democrata el año pasado es alumno
   mio.
5. —¿Tienes suficiente papel? —Si, esta caja me basta.
6. —Figurese, me conto la anecdota en que no pudieron encontrar el
   antidoto a tiempo.
7. —Solicito ayuda de unos alumnos que sean muy, muy diligentes, con
   mucha responsabilidad. —¿Los has encontrado? —Todavia no y
   francamente no me lo explico.
8. —Celebre usted la llegada de un hombre tan celebre. —Ya lo celebre.

35

~~~~~~

INTONATION: PITCH AND JUNCTURE

Each language has its own melody or accent, which is so fundamental to the language that children usually learn it long before they have mastered all the segmental phonemes. When the grammatical patterns of the language and these intonational patterns seemingly contradict each other, it is the latter which hold greater importance for the listener, giving rise to the cliché, "It's not what you say but the way you say it."

Intonation is so important in language that it not only controls grammatical meaning to a large extent, but it also conveys the attitude of the speaker even more effectively than the words he chooses. If you consistently use the wrong intonation in Spanish, the meaning of what you are trying to say may be misunderstood, but your intentions and attitudes most certainly will be. This problem is perhaps the most crucial one in language learning since it is virtually impossible at first for the learner to avoid carrying over the intonational patterns of his own language into the target language. Even after you have mastered the segmental phonemes and allophones, you must exert consistent and conscientious effort to acquire the melody of Spanish.

Intonation involves several factors. One—stress—has already been taken up. The most important one, however, is PITCH. Pitch is determined by the frequency of the sound waves, i.e., the number of vibrations or cycles per second (see Diagram 1 on p. 27). This frequency is, in turn, determined by the tension of the vocal bands. The tighter they are, the faster the sound waves vibrate, and the higher the resulting pitch. The purely musical aspects of pitch are not very important in linguistics, however, where we are much more concerned with the way pitch functions to control or determine meaning. Thus, we are more interested in *relative* pitch than absolute or musical pitch.

Pitch in this respect can be analyzed as a system of relative but contrasting levels. These levels are manipulated in two general ways—either within words or from word to word within phrases, clauses, and sentences. Some languages, like Chinese, Thai, and Vietnamese, use pitch on the word level. Languages that do this are called TONE languages. The same sequence of segmental phonemes has a different *lexical* meaning according to the way the pitch changes from syllable to syllable or even within the same syllable. For example, in Vietnamese the phonemic sequence /ma/ means *cheek* if the pitch starts high and rises even higher; it means *ghost* if the pitch starts high but remains on the same level; it means *tomb* if the pitch starts at a mid point and rises; it means *rice plant* if the pitch starts low and rises to a mid point; and it means *but* if the pitch starts at a mid point and drops.[1] The African language, Hottentot, manipulates six pitch levels or tones in a similar fashion.[2]

Languages like English and Spanish, however, use pitch to control grammatical rather than lexical meaning on the phrase, clause, and sentence level and for this reason, are called INTONATION languages. For example, both of these languages generally use a final pitch drop to indicate a statement and a final pitch rise to indicate a yes-or-no question: "He lives here." **Vive aquí.** "He lives here?" or "Does he live here?" ¿**Vive aquí?**

There are cases in both English and Spanish where pitch seems to be significant on the word level, but this is because the phrase in this case happens to consist of only one word. For example, in English, you can say to your room-mate, "I brought something back for you." Your room-mate, busy studying, doesn't hear the whole utterance and says, "What?", with a rising pitch. You repeat, "I said I brought something back for you." And this time your room-mate says, "What?", with a falling pitch. You now say, "That record you've been looking for."

In this case, however, the two "What?'s" are functioning as two different questions, meaning first "What did you say?" and then "What did you bring back for me?" Neither English nor Spanish changes the lexical meaning of a sequence of segmental phonemes by changing the pitch as Vietnamese does with /ma/, for example. Some languages, however, like Norwegian and Swedish, are considered to be both TONE and INTONATION languages.

In English there are four phonemic pitch levels: low/1/, mid or normal/2/, high/3/, and extra-high or emphatic/4/.[3] In Spanish there are only three: low/1/, mid/2/, and high or emphatic/3/. Speakers of both languages can lower the pitch of their voices below level/1/ and can raise them above level/4/, but such extremes are considered "extra-linguistic" or paralinguistic and seem to resist systematic analysis. This aspect of intonation is taken up in Chapter 36, "Rhythm and Extra-Linguistic Features."

---

[1] William A. Smalley, *Manual of Articulatory Phonetics* (1964), p. 89.
[2] Bertil Malmberg, *Phonetics* (1963), p. 85.
[3] The four-level analysis of English pitch presented here is the one formulated independently by Kenneth L. Pike (1945) and Rulon S. Wells (1945) and accepted by such linguists as George L. Trager and Henry Lee Smith, Jr. (1951), Archibald A. Hill (1958), Charles F. Hockett (1958), and H. A. Gleason, Jr. (1961).

The pitch levels of both languages are relative and vary on a musical scale from speaker to speaker. All pitch levels of a child, for example, are ordinarily higher than those of an adult, and those of a woman are higher than those of a man. But each speaker of English and Spanish manipulates the same system of levels to determine grammatical meaning. In English the same sentence, "He lives in Newark," can be said with at least four different intonation or pitch patterns, depending on what the speaker means or on the previous question or statement to which he is responding.

SPEAKER A: Where does he live?

                                                 3

SPEAKER B: He lives in ⌐Newark.   2

                                                 1

SPEAKER A: Does he work or live in Newark?

                                                 3

SPEAKER B: He ⌐lives⌐in Newark.   2

                                                 1

SPEAKER A: Who lives in Newark?

                                                 3

SPEAKER B: He⌐lives in Newark.   2

                                                 1

SPEAKER A: No, I think he lives in New York, doesn't he?

                                                 4

                                                 3

SPEAKER B: He lives in ⌐Newark   2

                                                 1

Notice that if you give the last response (using pitch level /4/) for the question "Where does he live?", you sound annoyed or overbearing. Likewise, any one of the above responses given for a different question sounds equally wrong or meaningless.

Here intonation will be marked for both English and Spanish as it is in the above examples. Level /2/ is always right under the letters or the phonetic symbols. Level /3/ is right above them. Level /4/ is a space above level /3/, and level /1/ is a space below level /2/.

A phonological feature closely related to pitch is JUNCTURE, a type of pause which often involves a slight change in pitch, volume, and tempo. When a Spanish-speaker or an English-speaker comes to the end of a phonemic phrase, he can terminate it in one of three ways: by lowering the pitch of his voice slightly and rapidly trailing away into silence /↓/; by raising the pitch slightly and cutting off the volume rather sharply /↑/; by sustaining the pitch, prolonging the last syllable of the phrase, and diminishing the volume slightly /→/.[4]

These ways of ending a phonemic phrase in both Spanish and English are called TERMINAL JUNCTURES (**terminaciones**), and they are phonemic in both languages. They represent a change in pitch—but not enough to reach the next pitch level—and also a change in volume or phonation and tempo.

Since these pitch and juncture patterns are superimposed, so to speak, on syntactical constructions—phrases and clauses—we can refer to them as suprasegmental or intonational MORPHEMES. Observe that in these patterns, the pitch phonemes or levels are usually marked in at least three places: the first number within the slash bars refers to the level up to but not including the last stressed syllable, the second number represents the pitch level of the last stressed syllable itself; and the last number refers to the syllables following the last stressed syllable of the phonemic phrase. If the phrase ends in a stressed syllable, the pitch changes within that syllable and is indicated by the last two numbers. There are variations to this system, of course. For example, vocatives and tag phrases, since they are usually so short, are marked with only two numbers. Following are some basic intonational morphemes in American English:

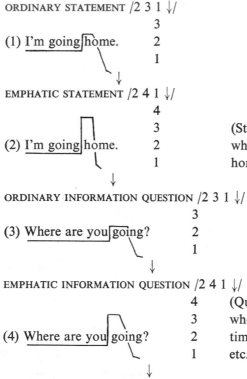

ORDINARY STATEMENT /2 3 1 ↓/

3
(1) I'm going home.   2
1

EMPHATIC STATEMENT /2 4 1 ↓/

4
3   (Statement repeated to someone
(2) I'm going home.   2   who thought you were not going
1   home or repeated the question.)

ORDINARY INFORMATION QUESTION /2 3 1 ↓/

3
(3) Where are you going?   2
1

EMPHATIC INFORMATION QUESTION /2 4 1 ↓/

4   (Question repeated to someone
3   who has failed to answer the first
(4) Where are you going?   2   time, refused to give information,
1   etc.)

[4] The analysis of English terminal junctures presented here is the one formulated by George L. Trager and Henry Lee Smith, Jr. (1951). In their original system, however, /↓/ is represented as /#/, /↑/ as /|||/, and /→/ as /||/.

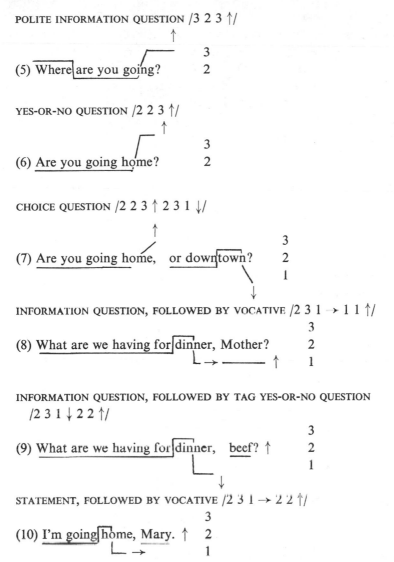

POLITE INFORMATION QUESTION /3 2 3 ↑/

(5) Where are you going?   3   2

YES-OR-NO QUESTION /2 2 3 ↑/

(6) Are you going home?   3   2

CHOICE QUESTION /2 2 3 ↑ 2 3 1 ↓/

(7) Are you going home,   or downtown?   3   2   1

INFORMATION QUESTION, FOLLOWED BY VOCATIVE /2 3 1 → 1 1 ↑/

(8) What are we having for dinner, Mother?   3   2   1

INFORMATION QUESTION, FOLLOWED BY TAG YES-OR-NO QUESTION
/2 3 1 ↓ 2 2 ↑/

(9) What are we having for dinner,   beef? ↑   3   2   1

STATEMENT, FOLLOWED BY VOCATIVE /2 3 1 → 2 2 ↑/

(10) I'm going home, Mary. ↑   3   2   1

Notice that the normal patterns for matter-of-fact statements and information questions in English are /2 3 1 ↓/ (1, 3). Emphasis is achieved with /2 4 1 ↓/ (2, 4).

Following are examples of some basic pitch and juncture patterns or morphemes in Spanish.[5] Just as with English, three pitch levels are marked—unless the phrase has only one or two syllables, in which case two levels are marked. The first number within slash bars refers to the level up to but not

[5] The analysis of pitch and juncture presented here generally follows that of J. Donald Bowen (1956), Bowen and Robert P. Stockwell (1960, 1965), and Stockwell, Bowen, and Ismael Silva-Fuenzalida (1956). Several important modifications have been made, however.

including the last stressed syllable, the second number represents the pitch level of the last stressed syllable itself, and the last number refers to the syllables following the last stressed syllable of the phonemic phrase. If the phrase ends on a stressed syllable, the pitch changes within that syllable and is indicated by the last two numbers. Vocatives and tag phrases are marked with only two numbers. Many of the following intonational patterns or morphemes have variations, which we can refer to as *intonational allomorphs*. Thus, the two patterns are in a type of free variation, and you may use either one in your own Spanish.[6]

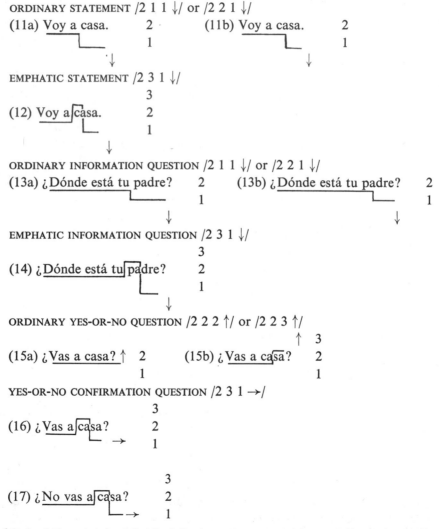

ORDINARY STATEMENT /2 1 1 ↓/ or /2 2 1 ↓/

(11a) Voy a casa.   2

                      1

(11b) Voy a casa.   2

                      1

EMPHATIC STATEMENT /2 3 1 ↓/

                3

(12) Voy a casa.   2

                   1

ORDINARY INFORMATION QUESTION /2 1 1 ↓/ or /2 2 1 ↓/

(13a) ¿Dónde está tu padre?   2

                                         1

(13b) ¿Dónde está tu padre?   2

                                          1

EMPHATIC INFORMATION QUESTION /2 3 1 ↓/

                              3

(14) ¿Dónde está tu padre?   2

                               1

ORDINARY YES-OR-NO QUESTION /2 2 2 ↑/ or /2 2 3 ↑/

                                         ↑   3

(15a) ¿Vas a casa? ↑   2

                  1

(15b) ¿Vas a casa?   2

                                 1

YES-OR-NO CONFIRMATION QUESTION /2 3 1 →/

                      3

(16) ¿Vas a casa?   2

                   →   1

                       3

(17) ¿No vas a casa?   2

                     →   1

---

[6] It should be pointed out that the following patterns are merely among the most common in Spanish. You will hear native-speakers use others. However, if you begin by mastering the ones presented here, your Spanish intonation will be authentic, and you can eventually imitate other patterns you may hear.

This type of question is used to request confirmation of information that one is already fairly sure of. In example 16 the listener is expected to answer affirmatively, but in example 15a the speaker does not know what the answer will be. Likewise, in example 17 the listener is expected to answer negatively. Notice that the only difference between this confirmation question pattern and that of an emphatic statement or emphatic information question is the final sustained terminal juncture rather than a fall.

CHOICE QUESTION /2 2 2 ↑ 2 1 1 ↓/

(18) ¿Vas a casa, ↑ o al centro?   2
                                    1
                                  ↓

Notice that this pattern is simply the combination of the ordinary yes-or-no question pattern and a normal statement pattern.

INFORMATION QUESTION, FOLLOWED BY VOCATIVE

/2 1 1 → 1 1 ↓/ or /2 2 1 → 1 1 ↓/

(19a) ¿Qué hay de postre,   mamá?   2
                                     1
                                   ↓

(19b) ¿Qué hay de postre,   mamá?   2
                                     1
                                   ↓

INFORMATION QUESTION, FOLLOWED BY TAG YES-OR-NO QUESTION

/2 1 1 → 2 2 ↑/ or /2 2 1 → 2 2 ↑/

(20a) ¿Qué hay de postre,   helado? ↑   2
                                         1

(20b) ¿Qué hay de postre,   helado? ↑   2
                                         1

STATEMENT, FOLLOWED BY VOCATIVE /2 1 1 → 1 1 ↓/ or /2 2 1 → 1 1 ↓/

(21a) Voy a casa, María.   2   (21b) Voy a casa, María.   2
                             1   1
                           ↓   ↓

Notice that the normal patterns or allomorphs for matter-of-fact statements and information questions in Spanish are either /2 1 1 ↓/ or /2 2 1 ↓/ (11, 13). Emphasis is achieved with /2 3 1 ↓/ (12, 14).

Usually in Spanish the voice starts the phonemic phrase on pitch level /1/ if the first syllable of the phrase is unstressed and on pitch level /2/ if it is stressed. This fact, however, seems a very natural thing for anyone to do in either Spanish or English and is of little real significance. The grammatical messages listed above (yes-or-no question, emphatic statement, etc.) are conveyed, as far as intonation goes, by the voice pitch on the last stressed syllable of the phrase and the following unstressed ones. Thus, for the sake of convenience, we have marked all intonation patterns or morphemes as beginning on pitch level /2/, even though both levels /3/ and /1/ are possible and frequently used for various extralinguistic reasons.

Several observations should now be made about juncture. Punctuation, in a very general way, is an indication of the terminal junctures. A period usually corresponds to /↓/, a question mark in yes-or-no questions to /↑/, and a comma, dash, colon, or semi-colon to /→/. However, there are many cases in both languages where punctuation is not an accurate indication of terminal junctures. One good example is the information question, which always starts with an interrogative word, such as *when*, *why*, **dónde, cómo,** etc. A question mark is used to end these questions, but the intonation is really the same as that of matter-of-fact statements, which end with periods in both languages.

In most cases Spanish terminal junctures will offer no particular problem to you since they correspond fairly closely to English terminal junctures. The most important contrasts between Spanish and English intonation come from the use of different pitch levels to convey the same meaning.

Before illustrating these contrasts, we must examine the relationship between pitch and stress. In English pitch generally rises with stress: the heavier the stress, the higher the pitch. In Spanish pitch rises with stress mainly at the beginning of the phonemic phrase. But at the end of the phonemic phrase in Spanish the pitch normally drops either at the last stressed syllable or the last syllable of the phrase (whether stressed or not). In the most common pattern of normal statements and information questions, the pitch drops from /2/ to /1/ on the *last stressed syllable* and stays there until the terminal juncture on the last syllable when it drops even a little more (11a, 13a). In emphatic Spanish statements and information questions the pitch rises from /2/ to /3/ on the *last stressed syllable* and drops down to /1/ on the following unstressed syllables and stays there until the terminal juncture on the last syllable when it drops even a little more (12, 14). To be sure, slight pitch changes can always be perceived on what is supposed to be one pitch level, but since they are not contrastive, we can refer to them as non-distinctive pitch *allophones* rather than pitch phonemes.

As we have said, in normal statements, if the phrase ends on a stressed syllable, that syllable starts pitch level /1/:

(22) Lo habla muy bien.   2
                                                     1

But in emphatic statements, if the phrase ends on a stressed syllable, the pitch drops *within* that syllable:

(23) Lo habla muy bien.
```
                    3
                    2
                    1
```

The same is true of information questions.

In the most normal pattern of yes-or-no questions, however, the pitch rises on the last syllable, whether stressed or not, and usually the rise is *only* a terminal juncture:

(24) ¿Habla ruso? ↑   2

Sometimes, however, the rise is to the next *level*, with a terminal rise:

(25) ¿Habla ruso?   ↑   3
                         2

Whether or not the pitch rises to level /3/ in these questions seems to depend on idiolect. You can safely use either of these intonational allomorphs in this case.

Following are several more of the most common intonation patterns in Spanish:

GREETING /2 3 1 ↓/

(26) Buenos días.
```
                3
                2
                1
```

GREETING, FOLLOWED BY VOCATIVE /2 3 1 → 1 1 ↓/

(27) Buenos días, señora
```
                3
                2
                1
```

Notice that the level juncture /→/ at the end of an utterance usually indicates that more is coming, such as a vocative, a tag phrase, another clause, etc.

LEAVE-TAKING /2 2 2 ↓/

(28) Hasta mañana.   2
                    ↓   1

Notice that leave-takings have a lower intonation pattern than greetings. This is sometimes the only linguistic element that distinguishes between the two as in

(greeting) Buenas noches.
```
                3
                2
                1
```
and

(leave-taking) Buenas noches.
```
                2
              ↓  1
```

VOCATIVE AND TAG PHRASE /1 1 ↓/

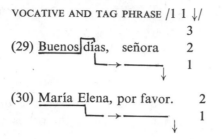

(29) <u>Buenos</u> días, señora   3
                                   2
                                   1

(30) <u>María Elena</u>, por favor.   2
                                       1

The intonation pattern /1 1 ↓/ refers, of course, only to the last phonemic phrase in each case—the vocative **señora** and the tag phrase **por favor.** The phrase **gracias** is an exception in that it does not have the intonation pattern of a typical tag phrase. It is usually said with the intonation of a greeting:

<u>No,</u> → <u>grácias.</u>   3
                               2
                               1

STATEMENT WITH LONG SUBJECT OR PREDICATE
   /2 2 2 → 2 1 1 ↓/ or /2 2 2 ↑ 2 1 1 ↓/
(31) <u>Todos los chicos que conozco</u> → <u>han entrado en el ejército.</u>   2
                                                                                1

(32) <u>Juan prepara todas sus tareas de matemática</u> ↑ <u>con mucho cuidado.</u>   2
                                                                                      1

STATEMENT WITH COORDINATED ELEMENTS
   /2 2 2 → 2 1 1 ↓/ or /2 2 2 ↑ 2 1 1 ↓/
(33a) <u>Lo habla muy bien</u> → <u>y lo entiende muy bien.</u>   2
                                                                  1

(33b) <u>Lo habla muy bien</u> ↑ <u>y lo entiende muy bien.</u>   2
                                                                  1

STATEMENT WITH SUBORDINATED ELEMENT /2 2 2 ↑ 2 1 1 ↓/
(34) <u>Si mañana no recibo noticia</u> ↑ <u>le escribiré de nuevo.</u>   2
                                                                          1

In sentences 31–34, the last phonemic phrase could also have the intonational allomorph /2 2 1 ↓/.

HESITATION AND INTERRUPTION /2 2 →/ and /2 1 →/
(35) <u>Sí,</u> → <u>pero</u> → . . . <u>bueno</u>   . . . <u>lo admito.</u>   2
                                                                              1

Exclamations are not presented here for two reasons. First, most of them have similar intonation patterns in both English and Spanish, making frequent use, as we might expect, of pitch levels /3/ and /4/. Second, many of them use tones which are extra-linguistic, i.e., above level /4/ for English and above level /3/ for Spanish. This is the area of paralanguage, which includes many extra-linguistic factors that are difficult to classify and analyze.

In summation, there are several important contrasts between Spanish intonation and English intonation. The normal English pattern for statements and information questions is /2 3 1 ↓/, but the normal pattern in Spanish is /2 1 1 ↓/. The use of pitch level /3/ in Spanish sounds insistent and emphatic since it usually has this meaning. To the English-speaker, the Spanish pattern often sounds too gruff, displeased, bored, uninterested, etc.

The normal English pattern for yes-or-no questions is /2 3 3 ↑/, but the normal pattern in Spanish is /2 2 2 ↑/. Once again the English-speaker's tendency to use pitch level /3/ sounds over-emphatic and too emotional to many Spanish speakers, and the Spanish pattern (15a) sounds rather casual and uninterested to the English-speaker.

Another problem is the fact that even though /2 3 3 ↑/ is the most normal pattern for these questions in English, /2 3 1 ↓/ is also possible since the reversed interrogative word-order in English always signals a question regardless of the intonation:

(36) Are you going home?
              3
              2
              1 ↓

Sometimes if the Spanish yes-or-no question is long, the English-speaker fails to raise the pitch at the end, thereby converting the question into a statement since the relatively flexible Spanish word-order permits the verb to precede the subject even in statements. Thus, with the intonation /2 1 1 ↓/, the following utterance has to be a statement in Spanish:

(37) Hay muchos alumnos en esta clase.
              2
              1 ↓

The pattern must be /2 2 2 ↑/ to be interrogative in Spanish. But in English the pitch can rise or fall at the end since the phrase *are there* as opposed to *there are* carries the interrogative signal:

(38) Are there many students in this class?
              3
              2
              1 ↓

Two normal English patterns for leave-takings are /2 3 2 ↑/ or /2 3 3 ↓/ (when the person is not very close to the speaker):

(39a) Good-bye ↑ or (39b) Good-bye ↓   3 / 2

The normal pattern in Spanish is /2 2 2 ↓/ (28). The English-speaker's tendency to use pitch level /3/ with a terminal rise as in the first pattern makes the Spanish expression sound too eager and ingratiating:

(40a) * Adiós ↑ or (40b) * Adiós ↓   3 / 2

The normal English pattern for vocatives and tag phrases is /2 2 ↑/ or /1 1 ↑/:

(41) Good morning, → Mrs. Smith.↑   3 / 2

but the normal pattern in Spanish is /1 1 ↓/ (29, 30). The English-speaker's tendency to use a terminal rise makes the name or tag phrase sound too ingratiating, eager, or even sarcastic:

(42) * Buenos días, señora.↑   3 / 2 / 1
       └ →

(43) * María Elena,   por favor.↗   2 / 1
       └ → ── ↑

The only case where this is natural in Spanish is after a yes-or-no question. This is for two reasons. Either there is no terminal juncture after the question, which is ended by the vocative itself:
(44) ¿Vas a casa, Pedro? ↑   2 / 1
or the vocative seems to echo the rising intonation of the question:
(45) ¿Vas a casa,↑ Pedro ↑   2 / 1

References

SPANISH

* Bowen, "A Comparison of the Intonation Patterns of English and Spanish" (1956).
* ――― and Stockwell, *Patterns of Spanish Pronunciation* (1960), Chapters 1, 4.
* Cárdenas, *Applied Linguistics: Spanish* (1961), Chapter III.
* ―――, *Introducción a una comparación fonológica del español y del inglés* (1960), "Entonación española e inglesa," "Patrones de entonación española e inglesa".
Delattre, *Comparing the Phonetic Features of English, French, German, and Spanish* (1965), Chapter II.

* _____, Olsen, and Poenack, "A Comparative Study of Declarative Intonation in American English and Spanish" (1962).
* Lado, *Linguistics Across Cultures* (1957), Chapter 2.
* Matluck, "Entonación hispánica" (1965).
* Navarro, *Estudios de fonología española* (1946), "Grupos de entonación".
  _____, *Manual de entonación española* (1948).
* _____, *Manual de pronunciación española* (1957), Sections 181–92.
* Quilis and Fernández, *Curso de fonética y fonología españolas para estudiantes angloamericanos* (1966).
  Sapon, "Étude instrumentale de quelques contours mélodiques fondamentaux dans les langues romanes" (1958–59).
* Silva-Fuenzalida, "La entonación en el español y su morfología" (1956–57).
* Stockwell and Bowen, *The Sounds of English and Spanish* (1965), Chapter 3.
* _____, _____, and Silva-Fuenzalida, "Spanish Juncture and Intonation" (1956).
* Wallis, "Intonational Stress Patterns of Contemporary Spanish" (1951).
* _____ and Bull, "Spanish Adjective Position: Phonetic Stress and Emphasis" (1950).

ENGLISH AND GENERAL

* Bronstein (1960), Chapter 14.
* Buchanan (1963), Chapter VIII.
  Buiten and Lane, "A Self-Instructional Device for Conditioning Accurate Prosody" (1965).
* Gleason, *An Introduction to Descriptive Linguistics* (1961), Chapter 4.
* Heffner, *General Phonetics* (1949), Chapter VII.
  Hill, *Introduction to Linguistic Structures* (1958), Chapter 2.
  _____, "Suprasegmentals, Prosodies, Prosodemes. Comparison and Discussion" (1961).
* Hockett, *A Course in Modern Linguistics* (1958), Chapters 4, 6.
* Lloyd and Warfel, *American English in Its Cultural Setting* (1957), Chapter 18.
  Pike, *The Intonation of American English* (1945).
  Siertsema, "Timbre, Pitch and Intonation" (1962).
  Trager and Smith, *An Outline of English Structure* (1951), Part I.
* Wells, "The Pitch Phonemes of English" (1945).

Drills

A   Repetition

Your teacher will read a series of Spanish STATEMENTS, *all of which have the intonation pattern* /2 1 1 ↓/. *Repeat them.*

1. Voy a casa.	6. Voy a faltar a esa clase.
2. Mi amigo habla español.	7. Tengo que estudiar esta noche.
3. Está lloviendo.	8. Preferimos no hacer nada.
4. Dice que es verdad.	9. Lo sabemos muy bien.
5. Creo que la quiere.	10. Tú siempre dices eso.

B   Repetition

Your teacher will read a series of Spanish EMPHATIC STATEMENTS, *all of which will have the intonation pattern* /2 3 1 ↓/. *Repeat them.*
(*Read sentences of Drill* **A**.)

C   Repetition

Your teacher will read a series of Spanish INFORMATION QUESTIONS, *all of which will have the intonation pattern* /2 1 1 ↓/. *Repeat them.*

1. ¿Cómo se llama?   6. ¿Dónde vive ese señor?
2. ¿Para dónde vas?   7. ¿Quién dice eso?
3. ¿Qué quieres?   8. ¿Quiénes lo habían visto?
4. ¿Por qué me lo preguntas?   9. ¿Para qué trabajas tanto?
5. ¿Cuándo sale el tren?   10. ¿Qué tal te gusta el vino?

D   Repetition

Your teacher will read a series of Spanish EMPHATIC INFORMATION QUESTIONS, *all of which will have the intonation pattern* /2 3 1 ↓/. *Repeat them.*
(*Read questions of Drill* **C**.)

E   Repetition

Your teacher will read a series of Spanish ORDINARY YES-OR-NO QUESTIONS, *all of which have the intonation pattern* /2 2 2 ↑/. *Repeat them.*

1. ¿Empezaron a trabajar?
2. ¿Van mañana?
3. ¿Son las doce?
4. ¿Usa usted espejuelos?
5. ¿Es éste el libro que perdiste?
6. ¿Sabe usted la dirección?
7. ¿Esperamos hasta que vengan los demás?
8. ¿Han terminado de construir el nuevo edificio?
9. ¿Sabes que todos los que habíamos visto fueron comprados?
10. ¿Hay veinticinco alumnos en cada una de las clases avanzadas de español?

F   Repetition

Your teacher will read a series of Spanish YES-OR-NO CONFIRMATION QUESTIONS, *all of which have the intonation pattern* /2 3 1 →/. *Repeat them.*

1. ¿Empezaron a trabajar?
2. ¿Van mañana?
3. ¿Son las doce?
4. ¿Prefiere usted el rojo?
5. ¿Te gusta el café instante?
6. ¿No quiere usted tomar más cerveza?
7. ¿No le importa que fume?
8. ¿No comprenden lo que les ha dicho?
9. ¿No te estorba la máquina?
10. ¿No has visto esa película?

G Repetition

Your teacher will read a series of Spanish CHOICE QUESTIONS, *all of which have the intonation pattern /2 2 2 ↑ 2 1 1 ↓/. Repeat them.*

1. ¿Quieres café or té?
2. ¿Es ésta la casa o es la otra?
3. ¿Es poesía épica o lírica?
4. ¿Prefiere usted las rosas o los claveles?
5. ¿Lo hizo él o su hermano?
6. ¿Fuiste ayer o anteayer?
7. ¿Se compró usted los zapatos o el traje?
8. ¿Vio usted la tanda de las siete o la de las nueve?
9. ¿Quiere ir a México o a Puerto Rico para sus vacaciones?
10. ¿Te vas a quedar aquí con los chicos o quieres salir de paseo con nosotros?

H Repetition

Your teacher will read a series of Spanish sentences with VOCATIVES *or* TAG PHRASES, *all of which have the intonation pattern /1 1 ↓/. Repeat them.*

1. ¿Cómo estás, chico?
2. Sí, sí, en seguida, señor.
3. ¡Hola, guapa!
4. ¿Cómo van las cosas, Pedro?
5. Hasta luego, Manolo.
6. María Elena, por favor.
7. Estoy muy bien, padre.
8. Por ahora, no.
9. Tráigame ese paquete, si me hace el favor.
10. Es el primero, creo.

I Repetition

Your teacher will read a series of Spanish GREETINGS, *all of which have the intonation pattern /2 3 1 ↓/. Repeat them.*

1. ¡Qué tal!
2. ¡Buenos días!
3. ¡Qué hubo! (the /e/ of *qué* is replaced by an unstressed /i/).
4. ¡Hola!
5. ¡Felicitaciones!
6. ¿Cómo te va?
7. ¡Buenas tardes!
8. ¡Buenas noches!
9. ¡Mucho gusto!
10. ¡Qué gusto de verte!

J Repetition

Your teacher will read a series of Spanish GREETINGS, *followed by*
VOCATIVES, *all of which have the intonation pattern* /2 3 1 → 1 1 ↓/.
Repeat them.

1. ¡Qué tal, chico!   6. ¿Cómo te va, Rodrigo?
2. ¡Buenos días, señor!   7. ¡Buenas tardes, profesor!
3. ¡Qué hubo, Diego!   8. ¡Buenas noches, señores!
4. ¡Hola, guapa!   9. ¡Mucho gusto, doctor!
5. ¡Felicitaciones, señorita! 10. ¡Qué gusto de verte, Teresita!

K Repetition

Your teacher will read a series of Spanish LEAVE-TAKINGS, *all of which*
have the intonation pattern /2 2 2 ↓/. *Repeat them.*

1. Adiós   7. Te veré.
2. Hasta luego.   8. Chao.
3. Hasta pronto.   9. Cuídate.
4. Hasta ahora.   10. Que lo pase bien.
5. Buenas noches.   11. Que Dios te acompañe.
6. No te mates.   12. Llévala suave.

L Repetition (books open)

Your teacher will read a series of Spanish STATEMENTS WITH LONG
SUBJECT OR PREDICATE, *all of which have either the intonation allomorph*
/2 2 2 → 2 1 1 ↓/ *or* /2 2 2 ↑ 2 1 1 ↓/. *Repeat them.*

1. Julio y todos los chicos vendrán después.
2. Lo que sí es preciso para criticar es un vocabulario bastante grande.
3. Esto de ir al café todos los días es el colmo.
4. La frescura y sobriedad de los diálogos constituyen un raro acierto.

5. Sí, pero las intrigas y los distintos intereses políticos impidieron la realización del gran proyecto de Bolívar.
6. Por eso siempre se están peleando mamá y abuelita.
7. En este momento se escapa del toril un inmenso toro negro de mil libras.
8. Se dicen cada vez más esas cosas.

M   Repetition (books open)

Your teacher will read a series of Spanish STATEMENTS WITH COORDIN-ATED ELEMENTS, *all of which have either the intonation allomorph* /2 2 2 → 2 1 1 ↓/ *or* /2 2 2 ↑ 2 1 1 ↓/. *Repeat them.*

1. Vino ayer y le trajo una pintura.
2. La visitó y le regaló flores también.
3. No es española pero habla español divinamente.
4. No es carpintero sino ebanista.
5. Todavía no es profesor pero piensa serlo.
6. Pensaba quedarse en casa, pero salió con nosotros.
7. Es de México, sin embargo, no está de acuerdo con esa política.
8. No sólo la visitó sino que le regaló unas flores también.

N   Repetition (books open)

Your teacher will read a series of Spanish STATEMENTS WITH SUBORDIN-ATED ELEMENTS, *all of which have the intonation pattern* /2 2 2 ↑ 2 1 1 ↓/. *Repeat them.*

1. Cuando yo llegué, todavía no había venido.
2. Si no hay nada allí, ¿qué van a hacer?
3. Cuando sonó el teléfono, María estaba comiendo.
4. Por sabrosa que sea la comida, por bueno que sea el servicio, no dejo nada.
5. Si hubiera tenido la plata, habría ido a España.
6. Si lo hubiera sabido, no hubiera ido.
7. Por su mala conducta, no le permitieron ir a la comida.
8. Para mantenerte en buenas condiciones, hay que hacer ejercicio.

O   Read Aloud (books open)

Read the following sentences aloud, being careful to use the proper intonation pattern.

1. Debiera comprar esa azul.
2. Debiera comprar esa **azul**. (*emphatic*)

3. Tengo que hacerlo ahora.
4. Tengo que hacerlo **ahora**. (*emphatic*)
5. ¿Dónde vive usted?
6. ¿Dónde vive **usted**? (*emphatic-contrastive*)
7. ¿Por qué trabaja usted tanto?
8. ¿Por qué trabaja usted **tanto**? (*emphatic*)
9. ¿Dijo usted algo?
10. ¿No vas a estudiar más? (*expected answer is* no)
11. ¿Hay muchos alumnos en sus clases?
12. ¿Te quedas o te vas?
13. ¿Prefiere usted que guarde estos blancos para usted o va a llevárselos ahora?
14. Buen trabajo, muchacho.
15. Lo acepto, gracias.
16. Buenos días.
17. ¿Le gusta mi nueva corbata? (*expected answer is* yes)
18. ¡Qué tal!
19. ¡Qué tal, Fernando!
20. Buenos días, Pedro.
21. Nos vemos.
22. Hasta luego.
23. La policía con todas sus armas no pudieron prenderlo.
24. Hablan francés, italiano y español todos los mozos que trabajan en el restorán.
25. Hablan francés y entienden alemán.
26. No quería comprarlo, sin embargo, no pude resistir.
27. Si hubiera resistido, no lo habría comprado.
28. Después de haberlo comprado, me pregunté si había hecho bien.

P   Read Aloud "Meditaciones en una calurosa tarde de verano"[7]

MANOLO: (*Haciéndose el torero, y con el pañuelo, girando el brazo en un perfecto y simétrico pase natural.*) Ale . . . toro . . . ya, ya, toro . . .

QUINO: (*Tumbado boca arriba en la hierba.*) Te llaman Manolo, que no Manolete.

MANOLO: ¿Qué dices?

QUINO: Nada . . . Ese Fernando Ramos viene a visitar a tu hermana Matilde, ¿no?

MANOLO: Ha venido a casa ya como una docena de veces.

QUINO: ¿Se quedan solos los novios?

MANOLO: Algunas veces. Por eso siempre se están peleando mamá y abuelita.

QUINO: (*curioso*) ¿Y qué pasa entonces, con los novios a solitas?

[7] Dialog II of John B. Dalbor and H. Tracy Sturcken, *Oral Spanish Review* (New York: Holt, Rinehart and Winston, 1965), p. 23.

MANOLO: *(Con un bostezo de aburrimiento.)* Hablan nada más. Horas enteras.

QUNIO: ¿De qué?

MANOLO: De . . . ¡qué sé yo!

QUINO: ¿Tú has estado alguna vez con ellos?

MANOLO: Eso nunca. Matilde se pone bastante enfadada. Tiene poca paciencia.

QUINO: *(Después de una pausa.)* A tu hermana, ¿por qué la visitan tantos muchachos?

MANOLO: *(Meditando brevemente.)* . . . ¡Qué sé yo!

QUINO: *(Otra pausa.)* Manolo, creo que hay mucho que no nos han dicho.

MANOLO: Eso mismo pensaba yo. Le pregunté a cierto muchacho si a él le gustaba Matilde.

QUINO: ¿Qué dijo?

MANOLO: Nada. Hizo una mueca . . . así. Qué bobo ése.

QUINO: Así son los enamorados. Eso lo sabe cualquier cristiano.

MANOLO: *(Ya agotado el tema, se enfrenta otra vez con el toro bravo. Gira la simulada muleta con gran simetría en un perfecto natural.)* Ale . . . toro . . . ya, toro, toro . . .

Q "Live" Transcription

Exercise

A

Using CONVENTIONAL ORTHOGRAPHY, *indicate the intonation of the following sentences and questions. Use horizontal lines, terminal junctures, and numbers at the right for pitch levels. Then check your answers in Appendix D.*

1. ¿Cuándo tienen que comenzar?
2. Quiere sacar este libro por dos semanas.
3. ¿Cómo te va, hombre?
4. ¿Sabe usted el número de su habitación? *(expected answer is* yes)
5. Tengo que irme mañana **mismo**. *(emphatic)*
6. Adiós, señorita.
7. Buenas tardes, señores.
8. Antes que todos vengan, distribuya las sillas.
9. Lo estudio mucho y me gusta más.
10. ¿Lees el *Diario* o el *Universal*?
11. ¿Dónde dejo estos **libros**? *(emphatic)*
12. ¿Cómo estás, Federico?
13. Quisiera hablar con el doctor Rodríguez, por favor.
14. ¿Sabes si se pueden comprar en aquella tienda?
15. Llueve en el trópico todos los días, ¿verdad?

36

RHYTHM AND EXTRA-LINGUISTIC FEATURES

Despite the fact that syllable length is not phonemic in either English or Spanish, it is extremely important in the acquisition of a good accent in both languages since it is one of the two main elements of rhythm, the other being stress.

When you use the rhythm of English in speaking Spanish, you retain a strong accent even though you handle all the segmental phonemes and perhaps even the intonational (suprasegmental) phonemes perfectly. Before you understood Spanish, you were probably struck by the fact that it seemed faster than English. Yet Spanish-speakers often make the very same observation about English. Speakers of both languages feel this way principally because of the fundamentally different rhythms of the two languages.

English is a STRESS-TIMED language. This means the flow of the language is determined by the recurrence of heavy stresses rather than by the number of syllables. In English it takes roughly the same length of time to get from one primary stressed syllable to the next in speaking at a steady overall tempo, whether there are few syllables between the stresses or many. If there are few, you slow down; if there are many, you squeeze them in. The "squeezing" takes place mainly because, instead of changing your tongue position from that of /o/ to /i/ to /u/ to /a/ and so on, you save time, so to speak, by keeping your tongue in a relatively neutral position for most unstressed syllables and pronouncing /ɨ/ and /ə/ instead of the other vowels.

This delaying over the heavy stresses, shortening the unstressed syllables, and substituting /ɨ/ and /ə/ for other vowels creates what might be described impressionistically as a "galloping" rhythm. The sentence "Bill is going to a party at his friend's house", for example, might have the following rhythm:

"BILL is going to a PARTY at his FRIEND's house tomorrow."

This sentence has 15 syllables, but you can easily add quite a few more in different places without creating a *corresponding* increase in the amount of time it takes to say the new sentence:

"My little brother BILL'S going to a big PARTY at his best FRIEND'S house tomorrow NIGHT."

The sentence now has 22 syllables. These extra syllables are added by saying them quite rapidly, by using /ɨ/ or /ə/ in *my* /mɨ/ and *tomorrow* /tɨmárə/, by contracting *Bill is* to *Bill's,* and by saying *best* with a shorter /e/ than it would have in another context.

Obviously it is not normal speech to say the second sentence in exactly the same time as the first (although you can quite easily do it). Nevertheless, the average speaker does not take half again as long to say the second sentence just because it has about half again as many syllables. One can experiment with a stop watch to see this. The author took about two-and-a-half seconds to say the first sentence normally and about three seconds to say the second one.

This particular aspect of the English sound system forms the basis for the rhythm of traditional English verse, which is very often written and most always read with a certain number of accents or "beats" per line. Although a great deal of modern poetry in English does not have this strong and steady rhythm, most traditional, popular, and folk poetry does. You probably tend to read poetry with this type of rhythm, and children especially love to hear nursery rimes, limericks, etc. read to them in this fashion. In the popular mind, at least, this stress-timed rhythm is one of the essential ingredients of all poetry. In fact, the average English-speaker who is not trained in literary study is often reluctant to believe that poetry without such rhythm is really poetry.

Let us examine part of a well known poem in American literature, Henry Wadsworth Longfellow's *Paul Revere's Ride.* In the following selection heavy stresses are marked with ´ and the number of syllables in each line appears at the right.

Lísten, my chíldren, and yóu shall héar	(9)
Of the mídnight ríde of Pául Revére,	(9)
On the éighteenth of Ápril, in Séventy-fíve;	(12)
Hárdly a mán is nów alíve	(8)
Who remémbers that fámous dáy and yéar.	(10)
He sáid to his friénd, 'If the Brítish márch	(10)
By lánd or séa from the tówn to-níght,	(9)
Hang a lántern alóft in the bélfrey árch	(11)
Of the Nórth Church tówer as a sígnal líght, —	(10)
Óne, if by lánd, and twó, if by séa;	(9)
And Í on the ópposite shóre will bé,	(10)
Réady to ríde and spréad the alárm	(9)
Through évery Míddlesex víllage and fárm,	(10)
For the cóuntry fólk to be úp and to árm.'	(11)

Even though it might be argued that this is not the best or the only way to read this poem, the average English-speaker almost always reads it that way and feels that this is the best, if not the only way, to read it.

Notice that if, for some unknown reason, we wished to change the poem, we could add syllables here and there without disturbing the rhythm in the slightest. Suppose we took the first line and made it "Now listen, my children, and you shall hear" or "Now listen, all my children, and you shall hear" or even "Now listen, all my good children, and you shall hear", the rhythm of four heavy stresses or beats would remain the same. We could also change the seventh line to "By land or by sea from the town tonight," or "By land or by the sea from the town tonight" or "By the land or by the sea from the town tonight" without altering the fundamental rhythm.

These syllables could only be added, of course, by shortening the time needed to say them and by using /i/ and /ə/ in place of most of the vowels which these added words have when pronounced in isolation.

Now let us look at Spanish, a SYLLABLE-TIMED language. This means that the flow of the language is determined much more by the number of syllables rather than the number and location of the heavy stresses. In Spanish it takes proportionately longer to say an utterance of 20 syllables than it does to say one of ten syllables. There is little squeezing of the unstressed syllables, although it is true that they are very slightly shorter than stressed ones. But all vowels in all syllables are pronounced more or less the same whether the syllables are stressed or not. The unstressed vowels, /i/ and /ə/, do not even exist in Spanish.

Instead of a "galloping" rhythm, Spanish has what might be termed impressionistically a staccato or "machine-gun-like" rhythm. The Spanish equivalent of our sample sentence in English, **Mañana Bill va a una fiesta a la casa de su amigo,** has the following rhythm:

Ma-ña-na-Bill-vau-na-fies-ta-la-ca-sa-de-sua-mi-go.

The sentence has 15 syllables. The preposition **a** is eliminated both times because it follows another /a/ sound, and **va** and the **u-** of **una** and **su** and the **a-** of **amigo** fuse into diphthongs. If the Spanish-speaker adds more syllables, there will be a corresponding increase in the amount of time it takes him to say the new sentence:

Mañana mi hermanito Bill va a una gran fiesta a la casa de su mejor amigo.

The sentence now has 23 syllables as compared to 15 for the first, and it takes about half again as long to say it for this reason. A native-speaker of General American Spanish took about two-and-a-half seconds to say the first sentence normally and about three-and-a-half seconds to say the second one. Recall that the timings were about two-and-a-half and three seconds for the author to read the English versions. This difference may seem insignificant in these examples, but it is not hard to see how it could become quite noticeable in even a short series of utterances.

The point, however, is that syllable-length fluctuates in English according to the stress system; in Spanish syllable-length changes very little. If you carry over your typical rhythm from a sentence like, "He said that he knew it very well, that he was sure of it, but that he really couldn't do much about it under the circumstances" to the corresponding Spanish sentence, **Dijo que lo sabía muy bien, que estaba seguro de ello, pero que en realidad no podía remediarlo bajo esas circunstancias,** it will come out something like this:

Dijo quelosabíamuy BIEN, questabase GU rodello, peroquenreali DAD, nopo Dí a reme DIAR lo bajoesas circun STAN cias.

A Spanish-speaker will say the sentence with four or five pauses, i.e., four or five terminal junctures, but within each phonemic phrase, all syllables will have more or less the same duration. Failure to use this rhythm creates a very heavy foreign accent which will certainly draw attention away from what may be otherwise acceptable pronunciation.

This particular aspect of the Spanish sound system also forms the basis for the rhythm of Spanish verse, which is usually written and read in lines of a stipulated number of syllables. Although the rhythm of Spanish poetry is also partially regulated by the stresses, it is not nearly as heavy and regular as that of English poetry. When you first heard Spanish poetry, you probably felt that it didn't particularly sound like poetry—even though it may have had rime and obvious lyrical qualities. The English-speaker seems to miss the heavy beats of stress-timed rhythm and even mistakenly tries to put them in as he reads the Spanish poem.

Let us examine part of a well known poem in Spanish literature, Jorge Manrique's *Coplas.*[1] In the following selection, the long lines all have eight syllables and the short lines four. When a line ends with an **aguda** word, another "psychological" or "ghost" syllable is counted although not sounded:

> Recuerde el alma dormida,
> avive el seso y despierte
> contemplando
> cómo se pasa la vida,
> cómo se viene la muerte
> tan callando:
> cuán presto se va el placer (+1),
> cómo después, de acordado
> da dolor (+1),
> cómo a nuestro parecer (+1)
> cualquiera tiempo pasado
> fue mejor (+1).

[1] Jorge Manrique, "A la muerte del maestre de Santiago don Rodrigo Manrique, su padre," *Las mil mejores poesías de la lengua castellana,* ed. José Bergua (Madrid: Ediciones Ibéricas, 1962), pp. 45–46.

An English-speaker has the tendency to over-emphasize the primary stresses in the poem and shorten the unstressed syllables, but such a reading of the poem is very unpleasant to the Spanish ear. This galloping rhythm is also much harder to maintain in Spanish than it is in English. Observe now Longfellow's excellent translation of the *Coplas*.[2] Not only is the language equally beautiful but the version is particularly skillful because Longfellow was able to maintain the same syllable-count in each line in English that Manrique used in Spanish. Yet when you read this English rendition of a Spanish poem you can scarcely help using your typical stress-timed rhythm of English giving the long lines three beats and the short ones two:

O, let the soul her slumbers break,
Let thought be quickened, and awake;
Awake to see
How soon this life is past and gone,
And death comes softly stealing on,
How silently!

Swiftly our pleasures glide away,
Our hearts recall the distant day
With many sighs;
The moments that are speeding fast
We heed not, but the past—the past,
More highly prize.

The other main element of rhythm—stress—has already been discussed. English has four degrees of stress, whereas Spanish has only two. English-speakers, accustomed to varied stress patterns, carry them over into Spanish. Not only does the use of secondary and tertiary stresses cause a change in syllable length but it causes a "stopping-and-starting" effect rather than the steady even flow which characterizes Spanish.

You may still find it hard to believe that the rhythms of the two languages are really so different. This is because the rhythm of each language seems so apt for that particular language and seems to fit its sounds and intonational patterns so well. But the difference between the two rhythms is most strikingly demonstrated when a speaker of one language carries his own rhythm over into the new language. Although not phonemic, rhythm is so important that you can never hope to speak Spanish with a satisfactory accent if you use English rhythm.

There are other extra-linguistic or non-phonemic aspects to pronunciation, but they are so numerous, varied, and individualized that they seem to defy

---

[2] Henry Wadsworth Longfellow, "Coplas de Manrique," *The Poetical Works of Longfellow* (London: Oxford University Press, 1961), p. 27.

systematic analysis. For example, if you go above pitch level /4/ in English, you are now in this extra-linguistic realm. Your high pitch tells us much less about the utterance itself than it does about you, how you feel, your personality, and your attitude toward the subject of your conversation and your listener. Instead of distinguishing between emphatic and normal as levels /4/ and /3/ do, tones above /4/ tell us that you are excited, upset, have a naturally high-pitched voice, are trying to persuade your listener, etc. But in Spanish using tones above pitch level /3/ has the same effect. Thus, when you use pitch level /4/ for emphasis in Spanish as you do in your own language, the Spanish-speaking listener interprets this as a manifestation of emotion rather than a feature of linguistic communication.

These extra-linguistic VOCAL QUALIFIERS or features of PARALANGUAGE are not really part of the linguistic structure and cannot be analyzed in the same way as vowels, consonants, pitch, and stress. In this sense they are not discrete; i.e., they cannot be, or, at least, as of yet, have not been organized into "-emic" units. It is even possible—although difficult—for one to speak without using these vocal qualifiers, but the resultant speech sounds artificial and colorless. Nevertheless, the meaning of the message itself is conveyed.

Some examples of vocal qualifiers are overloudness (shouting), over-softness, overhigh, overlow, overtense (rasping), overfast, overslow, drawling, clipping, devoicing (whispering), crying, breaking (laughing, giggling, quavering, tremolo), chanting, nasalization, falsetto, and glottal stops. One of the most difficult problems in phonological analysis is separating the phonemic features of pitch, juncture, and stress from these features of paralanguage, since in ordinary conversation they are almost always present to a great degree. The only non-phonemic or extra-linguistic feature that has been analyzed profitably for mastery by the student is rhythm. The others seems quite similar in all languages and are very easily imitated in themselves, although it is difficult to use them in the proper context. This, however, really has psychological and cultural implications rather than linguistic ones.

References

SPANISH

* Bowen and Stockwell, *Patterns of Spanish Pronunciation* (1960), Chapter 1.
  Delattre, *Comparing the Phonetic Features of English, French, German, and Spanish* (1965), Chapters III, IV.
  ———, "A Comparison of Syllable Length Conditioning Among Languages" (1966).
* Gili Gaya, *Elementos de fonética general* (1950), Chapter III.
* Lado, *Linguistics Across Cultures* (1957), Chapter 2.
* Navarro, *Estudios de fonología española* (1946), "Papel de la cantidad".

* ———, *Manual de pronunciación española* (1957), Sections 174–80.
* Stockwell, Bowen, and Silva-Fuenzalida, "Spanish Juncture and Intonation" (1956).
* Wallis, "Intonational Stress Patterns of Contemporary Spanish" (1951).

ENGLISH AND GENERAL

Austin, "Some Social Aspects of Paralanguage" (1965).
* Malmberg, *Phonetics* (1963), Chapter VIII.
Pike, *The Intonation of American English* (1945).
Siertsema, "Timbre, Pitch and Intonation" (1962).
* Smalley, *Manual of Articulatory Phonetics* (1964), Chapter 10.
Trager, "Paralanguage: a First Approximation" (1958).
———, "The Typology of Paralanguage" (1961).

Drills

A   Repetition

Your teacher will pronounce a series of Spanish words and phrases. Repeat them, maintaining the typical syllable-timed "staccato" rhythm of Spanish. Remember that the time taken to say an utterance in Spanish is increased proportionately when more syllables are added to it.

1. bien
2. preparaste
3. te preparaste
4. te preparaste bien
5. no te preparaste bien
6. porque no te preparaste bien
7. sido
8. habrá sido
9. Habrá sido porque no te preparaste bien.
10. todas
11. contestarlas todas
12. para contestarlas todas
13. tiempo para contestarlas todas
14. hora
15. una hora
16. una hora de tiempo
17. una hora de tiempo para contestarlas todas
18. tuvimos
19. tuvimos una hora de tiempo para contestarlas todas
20. apenas
21. apenas tuvimos una hora de tiempo para contestarlas todas
22. que apenas tuvimos una hora de tiempo para contestarlas todas

23. fue
24. fue que apenas tuvimos una hora de tiempo para contestarlas todas
25. peor
26. lo peor
27. Lo peor fue que apenas tuvimos una hora de tiempo para contestarlas todas
28. calificación
29. buena calificación
30. una buena calificación
31. saco una buena calificación
32. como saco una buena calificación
33. verás como saco una buena calificación
34. y verás como saco una buena calificación
35. examen
36. examen final
37. el examen final
38. para el examen final
39. para el examen final y verás como saco una buena calificación
40. loco
41. un loco
42. un loco para el examen final y verás como saco una buena calificación
43. estudiar
44. estudiar como un loco
45. estudiar como un loco para el examen final y verás como saco una buena calificación
46. pongo
47. me pongo
48. me pongo a estudiar
49. me pongo a estudiar como un loco para el examen final y verás como saco una buena calificación
50. noche
51. esta noche
52. esta noche me pongo a estudiar como un loco para el examen final y verás como saco una buena calificación
53. empezando
54. empezando esta noche
55. Empezando esta noche, me pongo a estudiar como un loco para el examen final y verás como saco una buena calificación.

B   Read Aloud (books open)

Read any one of the dialogs in Appendix C. *Be careful to maintain the proper rhythm.*

C   Read Aloud (books open)

Read the following poem aloud. Be careful not to give it the typical stress-timed rhythm of English, but rather the syllable-timed rhythm of Spanish. Each line has eight syllables; thus, certain vowels must be REPLACED *by* /i/ *or* /u/ *or* ELIMINATED *to cause what would be two syllables to fuse into one. For example,* **se oye** *becomes* [sịó-ye], **pero el** *becomes* [pe-rųẹl], **una hoja** *becomes* [u-nó-xa], *etc. These places are all marked in the poem. In poetry this fusing, replacement, and elimination of vowels is called* **sinalefa** *and normally occurs everywhere contiguous vowels are found (except for stressed* /í/ *and* /ú/). *However, in some cases to maintain the proper syllable count linking occurs where one would find fusing in normal conversation. Thus* **como | una** *is* [ko-mo-u-na] *rather than* [ko-moụ-na]. *In poetry this type of linking is called* **hiato** *and occurs only where necessary to maintain the syllable count.*

A un libro

En el medio de la noche
se oye el grito agonizante
de un dilapidado libro
moribundo en el estante;

cubierta su piel de tierra,
su juventud ya reseca
como | una hoja de otoño,
como | una antigua rueca;

pero el grito es persistente:
gime y llora en agonía
por el ojo dulce y suave
que en antaño le leía.

—Enrique Grönlund

37

REVIEW OF SUPRASEGMENTALS: STRESS,
INTONATION, AND RHYTHM

Suprasegmental features are those which are superimposed, so to speak, directly on the segments of sound, i.e., the consonants and vowels. Three main features are involved: volume of the phonation (stress), pitch of the phonation (pitch), and time of the units of phonation (rhythm). The first two features are discrete in the sense that they can be systematically analyzed and organized into meaningful units or phonemes.

In Spanish stress occurs in two contrasting degrees: primary /ˊ/ and weak / / (unmarked). Pitch occurs on three contrasting levels: low /1/, normal /2/, and high /3/. Phonation, before pauses, behaves in three ways: the pitch rises slightly /↑/, it drops slightly /↓/, or it remains on the same level /→/. These ways of ending the phonation are the terminal junctures. Syllable length, although not phonemic in Spanish, plays the major role in determining rhythm.

Vocal qualifiers or extra-linguistic features, i.e., paralanguage, are, strictly speaking, not part of the linguistic structure of a language and reveal more about the speaker, his attitudes, emotional state, etc. than they do about the message itself. They are extremely varied and cannot be analyzed in the same way as the suprasegmentals. They also seem to be more or less the same or at least quite similar from language to language.

Returning to the first suprasegmental feature, stress, we find that it is frequently used to determine meaning in Spanish: **hablo** vs. **habló**. Spanish stress patterns are relatively simple when compared with those of English, where four stress phonemes are utilized. Spanish vowels in unstressed syllables have the same value that they do in stressed syllables. In most English unstressed syllables, however, /ɨ/ or /ə/ replace the other vowels.

In the phonemic phrase certain classes of words in Spanish normally have heavy stress. These are words which are syntactically free in the sense that they can occur alone, without the support of other grammatical forms. These are nouns, nominalized forms, verbs, adjectives, adverbs, without-verb pronouns, numerals, negatives, post-posed possessives, possessive pronouns, demonstratives, interrogatives, exclamatives, most determiners, titles, and sometimes intensifiers, **es,** and forms of **unos** and **haber** (see pp. 214–16).

In English, stress phrases and phonemic phrases are one and the same thing since there is always a terminal juncture somewhere between successive primary stresses. In Spanish, however, several stress phrases can occur within one phonemic phrase, and they have little importance as such in Spanish phonology.

Spanish words have traditionally been classified according to their stress patterns: **agudas** (last-syllable-stressed), **llanas** (penult-stressed), **esdrújulas** (antepenult-stressed), **sobresdrújulas** (pre-antepenult-stressed). Examples of each of these are **sofá, casa, rápido,** and **dígamelo.** Written accents, while based on these classifications, are not always present to represent voice stress. They appear over only certain stressed vowels because of spelling rules which are discussed in Chapter 39, "Spanish Orthography."

English-speakers have trouble with long Spanish words since they have only one heavy stress (except for adverbs ending in **-mente** and some compounds) and several weak stresses, whereas long English words usually have several varying degrees of stress. There are also many cognate words with different stress patterns which cause difficulty: **teléfono, acróbata,** etc.

Intonation patterns are responsible for what we call the melody or accent of a language, and speakers often rely more on these patterns for the meaning of the message than they do on the arrangement of the segmental phonemes themselves.

Spanish is classified as an intonation language because it uses pitch on the phrase and sentence level rather than on the word level as tone languages, like Chinese and Vietnamese, do.

Terminal junctures are features of tempo, volume, and pitch at one and the same time. However, the most obvious aspect of these terminals is the direction in which the pitch goes. For /↓/ and /↑/ the voice goes about a half pitch level down or up, and for /→/ it maintains the same pitch. The most common English patterns are /2 3 1 ↓/ for normal statements and information questions, /2 4 1 ↓/ for emphatic statements and information questions, /2 3 3 ↑/ for yes-or-no questions, and /1 1 ↑/ or /2 2 ↑/ for vocatives and tag phrases. The most common corresponding Spanish patterns are /2 1 1 ↓/, /2 3 1 ↓/, /2 2 2 ↑/, and /1 1 ↓/, respectively.

Pitch level /4/ is extra-linguistic and over-emphatic in Spanish, and pitch level /3/, although normal in English, is emphatic in Spanish. Thus, the use of these high pitch levels in Spanish makes you sound excited, dramatic, affected. The most important contrasts between English and Spanish intonation patterns are presented on pp. 233–34.

In both Spanish and English the most important places in the phonemic phrase for pitch levels are the last stressed syllable and any syllables following it. Any slight variations in pitch between the beginning and the last stressed syllable of the phrase are usually allophonic and unimportant. For most types of phrases the pitch either rises or falls on the last stressed syllable. The principal exception is yes-or-no questions, where in the most common pattern the pitch remains on level /2/ until the last syllable, whether stressed or not, where it rises slightly /↑/ to give the interrogative signal.

Although syllable length is not phonemic in Spanish, it is one of the two main elements of rhythm, the other being stress. Even if you handle all the segmental phonemes properly, you will not have a good Spanish accent until you master the Spanish syllable-timed rhythm, which is markedly different from English stress-timed rhythm. In English we squeeze and reduce unstressed syllables, using the vowels /ɨ/ and /ə/, but in Spanish all syllables have much more nearly the same duration, causing them to have a more steady and staccato rhythm. The vowels remain the same in both stressed and unstressed syllables.

The different rhythms of the two languages are dramatically revealed in the metrical systems. English poetry is usually written and read according to the number and position of stresses in the line; Spanish poetry according to the number of syllables in the line.

References

See references for Chapters 34–36.

Drills

(Repeat selected drills from Chapters 34–36.)

Exercises

Make a phonetic transcription of each of the following sentences. Indicate segmental allophones, stresses, pitch, and terminal junctures. Use horizontal lines for intonation and put numbers for the pitch levels to the right. Consider that the speaker is using rapid speech. Then check your transcriptions in Appendix D.

1. Eso es cosa tuya.
2. ¿Te refieres a mi padre?
3. Y tú me lo das, Teresa.
4. ¡Buenos días!
5. ¡Mis hijos grandes!
6. ¡Cómo te va, chico!
7. Pero, ¿dónde está? *(emphatic)*

8. Tu padre quiere que vuelvas temprano.
9. Las casas de los hombres que trabajan en esa fábrica cuestan menos de veinte mil.
10. ¡El, tan bueno, capaz de semejantes atrocidades!
11. Lo más probable es que lo aceptaran y entonces mi hijo comenzaría a estudiar y se pasaría la vida matándose en ese trabajo.
12. ¿Te vas ahora?
13. Nos vemos. *(leave-taking)*
14. ¿Desde cuándo estás en Costa Rica?
15. ¡Qué tal!
16. ¿Quieres comer algo más, o estás satisfecho?
17. ¿Va usted a consultarles o sabe todo lo que necesita saber?
18. Pero adonde vaya, recuérdenlo siempre.
19. ¿Y cómo piensa obtenerlo?
20. Ya me siento mejor, gracias.
21. Eso mismo que tú tienes es lo que queremos hoy los jóvenes.
22. ¿Por qué nos niega el derecho de vivir como deseamos? *(emphatic)*
23. Pancho y yo hemos vivido tan unidos, que estos meses sin él casi me parecía no vivir.
24. Buenas noches. *(greeting)*
25. Buenas noches. *(leave-taking)*
26. Hola, señor Ramírez.
27. ¿Su mamá podría permitir que saliera temprano con los demás chicos?
28. Los profesores decidieron suspender las clases en vista de los desórdenes y Pepito aprovechó para irse a su casa.
29. Hasta luego.
30. ¿Conoce usted a este señor? (*expected answer is* yes)

Questions

Write your answers on a separate sheet of paper and check them in Appendix D.

1. Stress or volume is determined by the _____ of the sound waves.
2. The pair **célebre** and **celebré** shows that stress is _____ in Spanish.
3. Spanish weak stress corresponds most to _____ stress in English.
4. Why is the word **le** not syntactically "free" in Spanish?
5. Stress phrases and phonemic phrases are the same thing in Spanish. TRUE/FALSE.
6. In linguistics we are more interested in _____ pitch than in exact musical pitch.
7. In English heavy-stressed syllables in the phonemic phrase are normally on pitch level _____.
8. Terminal junctures involve a slight change in _____, _____, and _____.

9. In Spanish yes-or-no questions the pitch rises slightly on the _____ syllable.

10. The pitch level of the voice is grammatically significant at the beginning of the phonemic phrase as well as at the end. TRUE/FALSE.

11. The main difference between the intonation patterns of English and Spanish expressions for taking leave is _____.

12. In English unstressed syllables usually are _____ and contain _____ because of the basic rhythm of the language.

13. But in Spanish, because of its basic rhythm, all syllables have more or less _____.

14. Spanish poetry, as far as rhythm is concerned, is based on lines of a certain number of _____, while English poetical rhythm is based on lines of a certain number of _____.

15. Vocal qualifiers cannot easily be _____. Thus, we say they are not discrete.

16. According to its stress pattern, the word **verdad** is a(n) _____ word.

38

~~~~~~

PROBLEMS IN LEARNING THE SOUND SYSTEM
OF A SECOND LANGUAGE

Learning the sound system of a new language is difficult for several reasons. One important one is that the sounds of the target language are almost all different in quality from those of the native language. Another important one is that even the same or similar sounds are distributed differently or function differently. The phonemic sets of the two languages just do not match up neatly. Six areas of difference can be shown:

I The Sounds of the Target Language Do Not Exist in the Native Language

1. Spanish fricative [b̸] does not exist in English. English-speakers usually substitute [v] or [b], but [v] is much less common than [b̸] in Spanish and [b] is distributed differently than [b̸].
2. Spanish [x] does not exist in English, and English-speakers usually substitute what they feel is the "nearest" sound. If they choose [h] or [ç] there is no problem since both are acceptable allophones of /x/ in Spanish. But if they choose [k], phonemic confusion results: **vaca** is not **baja**, etc.
3. Spanish "light" alveolar [l] does not exist in English. The "dark" or velar [ł] of English sounds wrong in Spanish although no phonemic confusion results.
4. Spanish [r̄] does not exist in English. English-speakers often substitute either the English retroflex [r̠], which sounds very wrong in Spanish, or the tap [r], which is an allophone of a different phoneme, causing confusion between such words as **caro** and **carro**.

II   The Sounds of the Native Language Do Not Exist in the Target
      Language

1. English aspirated stops [p' t' k'] do not exist in Spanish and sound
   wrong.
2. English "dark" [ł] does not exist in Spanish and sounds wrong.
3. English retroflex [r̠] does not exist in Spanish and sounds wrong.
4. English /ɨ/ and /ə/ do not exist in Spanish and make it difficult for
   the Spanish-speaker to decide which one of the five vowels of
   Spanish should have been pronounced.
5. English /ɔ/ does not exist in Spanish, and its use obscures the
   difference between Spanish /a/ and /o/, as in **hambre** and **hombre**.
6. English words are often separated or marked in the stream of speech
   with a slight pause or pause-like feature called plus juncture /+/.
   But in Spanish phonology word-boundaries are usually meaningless.
   Enlace or linking joins a final consonant of one word with the initial
   vowel of the next: **los hombres** [lo-sóm-bres]. English-speakers tend
   to try to separate words in Spanish with a slight pause or even a
   glottal stop [ʔ], both of which sound unnatural in Spanish.

III   Phonemes in the Native Language are Only Allophones in the
      Target Language

1. English /b/ and /v/ are phonemes, but Spanish [b] and [ƀ] or [v]
   are allophones. This causes the English-speaker to over-differentiate
   and try to distinguish between **tuvo** and **tubo,** for example, which are
   pronounced exactly the same in Spanish.
2. English /d/ and /ð/ are phonemes, but Spanish [d] and [đ] (a close
   equivalent to /ð/) are allophones. The English-speaker is reluctant
   to use [đ] and substitutes [d] or [d̂], both of which sound more like
   Spanish [r], thus creating phonemic confusion between **cada** and
   cara, for example.
3. English /y/ and /ǰ/ are different phonemes, but Spanish [y] and [ŷ]
   are allophones of the same phoneme. The English-speaker is thus
   reluctant to use [ŷ] where a native Spanish-speaker uses it because he
   (the English-speaker) feels it must mean something different than
   [y] does.
4. English /ž/ is a phoneme, but Spanish [ž] is just an allophone of /y/.
   The English-speaker is reluctant to use it, as Argentinians do, for
   example, because he feels that it must be significantly different from
   [y].
5. English has four stress phonemes /′ ^ ` ˇ/, but Spanish has only

two / ´ ˘/. Use of all four stresses in Spanish destroys the rhythm of the language, making phrases sound uneven and choppy.

6. English has four pitch phonemes /1 2 3 4/, but Spanish has only three /1 2 3/. Pitch level /4/ is extra-linguistic in Spanish and is not used to control meaning the same way as it is in English.

IV Allophones in the Native Language Are Phonemes in the Target Language

1. English flap [t̂] and [d̂] are allophones of the stops /t/ and /d/, respectively, but both flap sounds are also practically the same as the Spanish tap /r/. This sound, however, contrasts in Spanish with both stops /t/ and /d/. This situation causes English-speakers to confuse both in hearing and speaking: **pata** and **para**, **cada** and **cara**, etc.

V Some Phonemes and Allophones Which Exist in Both Languages Have Different Distributions

1. English /s/ and /z/ are phonemes and therefore contrast, but Spanish [s] and [z] are allophones in complementary distribution with each other. English-speakers often use [z] in syllable-initial position, where it never occurs in Spanish. This is particularly done with words that are spelled with **z**, as **zapato**: *[za-pá-to].

2. Sometimes consonants in English combine without assimilating, that is, they are separated by the feature called plus juncture: *tan goat* /tǽn+gówt/. These same sequences are assimilated in Spanish: **tan gordo** [taŋ-gór-đo]. Failure to assimilate them in Spanish sounds unnatural: *[tan-gór-đo], **tan bonita** *[tan-bo-ní-ta], etc.

3. English does not have stressed vowels in syllable-final position; they are followed by a consonant or glide. Thus, English-speakers usually add /y/ to syllable-final stressed /í/ and /é/ in Spanish: **mí** *[míy], **qué** *[kéy], and /w/ to syllable-final stressed /ó/ and /ú/: **yo** *[yów], **tú** *[túw]. This not only sounds very bad in Spanish, but in some cases it causes phonemic confusion, as in **le-ley**.

4. The English pattern of /CwV/, as in *swim*, is restricted in the sense that only certain consonants occur in it. However, almost any consonant can occur in the corresponding Spanish pattern of /CuV/. If the Spanish sequence has a consonant which does not occur in English, the English-speaker sometimes inserts a vowel between /C/ and /w/: **fuera** *[fu-wé-ra].

VI Miscellaneous Influences of the Native Language on the Target Language

1. The pronunciation of cognate words in Spanish is influenced by their English counterparts. An /i/ is inserted between the /C/ and the /u/ of such words as **ridículo** and **peculiar** because of *ridiculous* and *peculiar* in English. Palatal sounds are used in such words as **gracias** and **situar** because of *gracious* and *situate* in English. /a/ is sometimes used in the first syllables of such words as **oficina** and **hospital** because of the pronunciation of *office* and *hospital* in certain dialects of English. The stress is misplaced in such words as **teléfono** and **comunica** because of *telephone* and *communicate* in English.
2. English pitch level /4/, which is used merely for emphasis, is transferred over to Spanish, where it is extra-linguistic and part of the paralinguistic system. English pitch level /3/, which is normal, is transferred over to Spanish, where it is emphatic.
3. English stress-timed rhythm is transferred over to Spanish, which has a staccato syllable-timed rhythm. A concomitant feature is the incorrect substitution of /i/ and /ə/ for unstressed vowels in Spanish since this usually happens in English in unstressed syllables.

Following are the most common pronounciation errors made by the average English-speaker learning Spanish:

A Consonants

1. The use of the occlusives [b d g] instead of the fricatives [b d g], particularly in the intervocalic position. Even more serious is the use of the English flap [ɖ] instead of [d], since this [d] sounds exactly like Spanish [r] and makes **cada** sound like **cara**.
2. The use of the English aspirated stops [p' t' k'], especially in word-initial position.
3. Confusion of /θ/ and /s/. This happens typically when a student learns the use of /θ/ in high school and then encounters the **seseo** pronunciation in college or elsewhere. It would be best if American teachers taught **seseo** pronunciation for this and other reasons already discussed in Chapter 14, "/s/ (and /θ/)."
4. The use of English retroflex [ɹ] in place of both /r/ and /r̄/ in Spanish.
5. The use of Spanish /r/ for /r̄/, thus destroying the contrast between **caro-carro**, **quería-querría**, etc.
6. The use of English velar or "dark" [ł] in place of Spanish alveolar or "light" [l], especially in word-final position: **tal, hotel, sal**, etc.

7. The failure to assimilate nasals to the following consonants, as in **un peso, enfermo, en casa**, etc.

8. The use of [s] instead of [z] before voiced consonants, thus confusing such pairs as **este-es de, de este-desde, rascar-rasgar**, etc.

B   Vowels and Vowel Combinations

1. Adding the English glides /y w/ to all stressed vowels, as in **sí, qué, yo, tú**, etc. This not only sounds wrong but destroys the contrast between **pena-peina, le-ley**, etc.

2. Substituting the English central vowels /ɨ ə/ for unstressed Spanish vowels. This often destroys grammatical and lexical contrasts: **este-esta, sociedad-suciedad, pesó-pisó**, etc.

3. The use of wrong vowels and vowel nuclei or even vowels and vowel nuclei that do not exist in Spanish. An example of the first is /ew/ instead of /o/, as in **yo** *[yéw]. An example of the second is /æ/ as in *español* *[es-pæ-ñól] or /æw/, as in *causa* *[kǽw-sa]. These errors are made, of course, by the speakers of the American English dialects where /æw/ replaces /aw/ and /ew/ replaces /ow/, as in *house* and *road*, for example.

4. Elongating all stressed vowels, particularly /a/, as in **casa** *[ká:-sa], **hablar** *[a-ƀlá:r].

5. Making a syllabic division between vowels which should fuse into one: **adiós** *[a-ɖi-ós], **aunque** *[a-úŋ-ke].

6. Using a glottal stop or making an artificial division to show word boundaries, such as **va a casa** *[báʔa-ká-sa] or **de España** *[de-es-pá-ña].

C   Suprasegmentals

1. The use of all four English stresses, especially in long words, such as **responsabilidad** and **generalización**.

2. Misplacing the stress in cognate words, such as **imagino, comunica, acróbata, antídoto**, etc.

3. Stressing phrase-bound unstressed forms to show contrast or emphasis. English-speakers, thinking of such a sentence in English as "He didn't ask YOU, he asked ME," try to say *No TE lo preguntó, ME lo preguntó. Spanish uses other constructions with stressed forms to convey these meanings: **No te lo preguntó a TI, me lo preguntó a MÍ.**

4. The use of wrong pitch levels. Pitch level /4/—emphatic in English—is extra-linguistic or paralinguistic in Spanish. Pitch level /3/—

normal for ending a phrase in English—is emphatic in Spanish. In general, Americans use pitch levels /3/ and /4/ too much in Spanish, giving their speech an excited, overly enthusiastic, affected tone.

5. Failure to use the terminal rise /↑/ at the end of an ordinary yes-or-no question, especially a long one. This is because English word-order immediately signals such a question and, even though the voice more often rises, it can also drop: "Were there many people at the party when you were there?" /↓/ But in Spanish the interrogative signal is carried completely in the final rise: **¿ Había muchas personas en la fiesta cuando estabas allí?** /↑/ Failure to use the terminal rise converts the question into a statement.

6. The use of terminal rise /↑/ and too high a pitch level for certain types of phrases, particularly tag phrases, vocatives, and farewells: **María Elena, por favor; Buenos días, Fernando; adiós.** These phrases are usually said with lower pitch levels and the terminal fall /↓/ in Spanish.

7. The use of stressed-timed rhythm—elongation of stressed syllables, shortening of unstressed syllables, and using /i ə/ in most unstressed syllables. Spanish syllables are almost the same length—regardless of stress—and all vowels have the same value—regardless of stress.

References

SPANISH

Fischer, "Verification of a Suggested Hierarchy of Problems Encountered by English Speakers Learning Spanish Phonology: Dialectical Case Studies" (1966).
* Stockwell and Bowen, *The Sounds of English and Spanish* (1965), Chapter 2, "Appendix: The Teaching of Pronunciation".

ENGLISH AND GENERAL

Buiten and Lane, "A Self-Instructional Device for Conditioning Accurate Prosody" (1965).
* Chreist, *Foreign Accent* (1964).
* Hall, *New Ways to Learn a Foreign Language* (1966), Chapter 14.
* Hockett, "Learning Pronunciation" (1950).
* Lado, *Linguistics Across Cultures* (1957), Chapter 2.
* León, "Teaching Pronunciation" (1966).
* Wolff, "Phonemic Structure and the Teaching of Pronunciation" (1956).

39

~~~~~~

SPANISH ORTHOGRAPHY

Although Spanish orthography is far more regular and informative than that of English and that of most languages Americans commonly study, it does have certain inconsistencies. These irregularities sometimes cause you to mispronounce words that you are unfamiliar with and also to misspell them.

Spanish has one so-called "silent letter", **h**, which, except as a part of the digraph **ch,** always represents silence: **honor** [o-nór]. When you began your study of Spanish, you may have allowed the letter **h** to draw you into such pronunciations as *[há-ƀlo] for **hablo** and *[hí-xo] or *[hí-ho] for **hijo**.

The letter **p** in a few words like **psicología** and **psicólogo** also represents silence, but this seems to cause little trouble since most of these words are cognates of English words in which the letter *p* also represents silence. There is also a growing tendency in some areas of the Spanish-speaking world to spell these words without the **p**: **sicología**.

Spanish has three digraphs, i.e., two-letter combinations which stand for only one sound: **ch** as in **chico** [ĉí-ko], **ll** as in **llevar** [ye-ƀár], [le-ƀár], [ŷe-ƀár], or [že-ƀár], and **rr** as in **corro** [kó-r̄o]. The only irregularity here is the fact that /r̄/ is represented by the single letter **r** only at the beginning of words. When a word beginning with **r-,** such as **rojo** [r̄ó-xo], is used as the second element of a compound, if the first element ends in a vowel, the digraph **-rr-** is used, just as it is anywhere within a word to represent /r̄/: **pelirrojo**. Single **-r-** is used, however, if the first element ends in a consonant: **subrayar, subrogar.**

Other contiguous identical letters sometimes represent two sounds, particularly in careful speech: **innato** [in-ná-to], **creer** [kre-ér]. However, in rapid speech only one sound is usually heard: [i-ná-to], [kr̯ér]. Thus, the writing system in this case reflects careful speech much more faithfully than rapid speech.

The vowel letter **u** is often used merely to indicate the pronunciation of the preceding consonant. When it stands between the letters **g** and **e** or **i**, it means that the letter **g** stands for /g/ rather than /x/: **llegué** [ye-gé], **seguí** [se-gí].

Beginning students often think that this letter **u** represents the vowel sound /u/ and are drawn into such incorrect pronunciations as *[ye-gué] and *[se-guí]. More often, however, this is a spelling problem, causing students to write *llegé and *segí. You may have been led to believe that "the word would be [ye-xé] if it weren't for the **u**," but, of course, no Spanish-speaker would ever say the word this way even if he read *llegé on paper.

A dieresis ¨ is always placed over the letter **u** to indicate that it represents /u/ rather than silence when it follows **g**. This happens in the sequences /gue/ and /gui/: **vergüenza, lingüística**. However, these are not very common sequences in Spanish, and you have learned to spell the few that exist correctly without a great deal of trouble.

The case of **cu** and **qu** is related to **gu** and **gü**, but is somewhat more complicated. The letters **qu** are always used before **e** and **i** to represent /k/: **busqué** [bus-ké], **aquí** [a-kí]. This is because in Spanish the letter **c** before **e** and **i** always represents /s/ in American Spanish and /θ/ in Castilian. Beginning students often think that the letter **u** in these combinations represents the vowel sound /u/ and are drawn into such incorrect pronunciations as *[bus-kué] and *[a-kuí]. More often, however, they forget to use **qu** when they write these words: *buscé, *chicito, because they are usually related to or derived from other words that have the letter **c**: buscó, chico.

The most serious problem with regard to these combinations is the fact that students are not sure that **c** + **e** and **i** stands for /s/ (or /θ/), that **qu** + **c** and **i** stands for /k/, and that **cu** *everywhere* stands for [ku]. They, therefore, confuse such words as **ciudad, quedar, quitar, cuidado, cuento,** etc., mainly because they are not sure of the function of the letter **u**.

Sometimes students spell [ku] with **qu** as in *quando, *questa, *quota. But the sound sequence [ku] is *always* represented in Spanish with **cu**: **cuando, cuesta, cuidado, cuota,** and /k/ before /e/ and /i/ is always represented with **qu**: **que, quitar** (except in a very few foreign words like **kilo** and **kerosina**).

The **seseo** of non-Castilian Spanish undeniably brings with it some rather minor orthographical problems. Certain words, which must be learned by observation, have **c** before **e** and **i** rather than **s** to represent /s/. This is no problem in Castilian where **c** in these cases always represents /θ/, a different sound. The student of American Spanish, for example, must simply remember that [sí-ma] is spelled **cima** when it means *summit* or *top* and **sima** when it means *abyss* or *chasm*. The student of Castilian Spanish, of course, is helped by the fact that the former word is pronounced [θí-ma]. The letter **z** is almost never used before **e** or **i**, with a very few exceptions, such as **zeta** and **zinc.**

Those who advocate teaching American students Castilian Spanish often cite as one advantage the fact that **c** + **e** and **i** and **z** always represent /θ/ and **s** always represents /s/. Thus, there is no confusion between **cima** and **sima, cierra** and **sierra, cazar** and **casar,** etc. To be sure, this is one of the most serious irregularities in Spanish orthography, at least as far as American Spanish is concerned. However, there are many other irregularities in Spanish orthography, which Spanish-speaking children both in Spain and Spanish-America have to learn, so the argument is not a convincing one.

Two glaring examples of such spelling irregularities in all dialects of Spanish are the letter **v**, which always represents the phoneme /b/, and the digraph **ll**, which represents the phoneme /y/ in the majority of Spanish dialects, including those of Spain. Spanish-speaking children and semi-literate Spanish-speakers often confuse **b** and **v** and **ll** and **y** in spelling. In fact, since the words for the letters **b** and **v** are both pronounced [bé], Spanish-speaking children have to learn such terms as **"b" de burro, "b" grande,** and **"b" alta** for **b,** and **"b" de vaca, "b" chica,** and **"b" corta** for **v,** to distinguish between the two.

One other spelling problem in Spanish is the use of the orthographic accent ´, which is used only in certain words to indicate the position of the primary stress. The use of the accent mark is governed by rules originally formulated and since revised by the Spanish Academy. These rules are observed by educated people in *formal* writing only and widely disregarded by all Spanish-speaking people in informal writing. The accent mark, of course, is most useful to show foreigners the correct pronunciation of unfamiliar words. Other than that, it is simply a convention of the spelling system.

The written accent ´ occurs only over vowel letters and only in the following cases:

1. In **aguda** words that end in a vowel *letter* or the *letters* **n** or **s**: **sofá, razón, después.**
2. In **llana** words that end in a consonant *letter* other than the *letters* **n** or **s**: **débil, carácter, lápiz.** Notice that although the word **lápiz** has the sound [s], it falls under this rule because it is not spelled with the letter **s**.
3. In all **esdrújula** and **sobresdrújula** words: **rápido, dígamelo.**
4. In all words containing a stressed /í/ or /ú/ in contact with another vowel: **río, país, actúa, baúl,** indicating, of course, that the vowels are linked rather than fused.
5. In many syntactically free words (stressed in the phonemic phrase) that are homophones of phrase-bound words (unstressed in the phonemic phrase):
   sé (*verb*) – **se** (*with-verb pronoun*)
   dé (*verb*) – **de** (*preposition*)
   tú (*without-verb pronoun*) – **tu** (*pre-posed possessive determiner*)
6. In all interrogative and exclamative words: **dónde, cuándo, ¡Qué lindo!, ¡Cuánto me alegro!** The accent mark is used even when the interrogative word is used in a statement: **No sé cuándo vuelve.**
7. In a few words, which are syntactically free and which have homophones

which are also syntactically free. Both have primary stress in the same place, but only one carries a written accent:

sólo (*adverb*) – **solo** (*adjective*)

él (*without-verb pronoun*) – **el** (*nominalized determiner, as in* **el de Juan**)

There are relatively few words in categories 5, 6, and 7. Adverbs in **-mente** with accent marks really fit into categories 1, 2, or 3 since they are considered to be two-word compounds with one heavy stress on the first element (adjective) and one on the **-mente.** For example, **cortésmente** is covered in category 1, **fácilmente** in category 2, and **rápidamente** in category 3.

These rules are rigidly applied in formal writing, even in cases of singular and plural forms of nouns, which change classification because of the stress patterns. For example, **joven** is a **llana** word and has no written accent because it ends in **n** (Rule 2), but **jóvenes** is an **esdrújula** word and therefore has a written accent (Rule 3). **Razón** is an **aguda** word ending in the letter **n,** so it has an accent (Rule 1), but **razones** is now a **llana** word and does not have a written accent since only **llana** words ending in a consonant letter *other* than **n** or **s** have written accents (Rule 2).

It is obvious that the Academy excepted the letters **n** and **s** to reduce the number of words in which written accents would be necessary. These two letters represent phonemes which so often cause a change from singular to plural in verbs, adjectives, and nouns, or in the person of verbs, yet words whose stress patterns remain the same: **habla-hablan, alto-altos, muchacho-muchachos, tiene-tienes,** etc.

The written accent is also frequently omitted from capital letters for typographical reasons: **Éste** or **Este.** Some type fonts have capital letters with accents over them, and others do not. The dieresis ¨ and tilde ˜, however, are rarely omitted over capital letters, since they always indicate a phonemic difference: **BILINGUE** /bi-lín-gue/ (no minimal pair) or **SAÑA** /sá-ña/ *anger* vs. **SANA** /sá-na/ *healthy.*

Despite these irregularities and problems, Spanish orthography is very good compared to that of most European languages. The very regularity of most of Spanish spelling, in a paradoxical fashion, seemingly causes irregularities, which, in truth, are simply the logical consequences of the application of rules. One example is the use of the written accent, already discussed, and another is the "orthographical-changing" verbs.

One must distinguish very carefully between real irregular verbs, such as **conocer, concluir, enviar,** where *sounds* change or are added in certain forms: **conozco, concluyo, envío,** for example, and orthographical-changing verbs, where only the *letters* change. The very regularity of Spanish spelling causes letter-changes in such verbs as **buscar (busqué), llegar (llegué), empezar (empecé), coger (cojo), seguir (sigo), vencer (venzo), averiguar (averigüé).** All of these changes are due to spelling rules, which, as we have said, are applied with great regularity in Spanish: the letter **c** represents /k/ before the letters **a, o,** and **u** (**buscar, busco, cura**), but /s/ (or /θ/) before the letters **e** and **i** (**cena, cinta**), so /k/ before /e/ and /i/ must be represented with the letters **qu (busqué, chiquito)**; the letter **g** represents /x/ before the letters **e** and **i** (**gente, gitano**), but /g/ before the letters **ue** and **ui** (**guerra, seguir, Dieguito**), so we have **llegar** but **llegué**; the letter **z** is replaced by **c** to represent /s/ (or /θ/) before **e** and **i** (**empecé, mocito**); etc.

There are still other "irregularities" which are really the result of a regular application of spelling rules: the letter sequences **ue** and **ie** never begin words in Spanish. In the first case **h** is always prefixed: **oler,** but **huelo.** In the second case **y** replaces **i: errar,** but **yerro** (actually /i/ is also replaced by /y/ phonemically). Also, a vowel letter + **i** never ends words in Spanish. The letter **i** is always replaced by **y: ley, hay,** etc.

Spanish spelling, despite these inconsistencies, is much more nearly phonemic than that of English. The majority of the sounds of Spanish have not changed appreciably in the last several hundred years, but even so, Spanish orthography has been periodically revised to represent the sounds as faithfully as possible and practical. The pronunciation of English has changed more than that of Spanish since the early 17th century, but the spelling has changed relatively little. In essence, then, English orthography is practically three centuries behind in comparison with the actual spoken language, but that of Spanish is quite up to date.

The task of revising English orthography extensively is now practically hopeless, although it is possible to employ respelling for a temporary period, such as in the teaching of reading in elementary schools. But even here the transition to regular orthography must always be made, sooner or later. Not only that, but the question of spelling revision raises many other serious problems. It is hard to combat the strong public prejudice against tampering with deep-rooted traditions. Changing the orthography would also necessitate a vast amount of reprinting. Choices of what to reprint and what to leave in the old spelling would have tremendous political and ideological implications. Either all children would have to be taught both orthographies, or everything existing would have to be reprinted, or certain things would have to be left to eventually become archaic and unreadable documents. Despite the fact that major orthographical revisions have been carried out successfully in several languages—such as Russian and Portuguese—in this century, the prospects for this in English are indeed dim.

In the case of Spanish, there is much less need for major revision. Even so, it would also present serious problems. One would be the question of morphophonemics, i.e., the sound changes which result from the juxtaposition of certain grammatical forms. For example, in a completely phonemic orthography the masculine singular form of the indefinite article, **un,** would have to be spelled three different ways: **um, un,** and **uñ,** as in **um péso, un árbol,** or **uñ ĉíko.** A verb form like **hablan** would likewise have three different spellings, as in **áblam poláko, áblan r̄úso,** or **áblañ ĉíno.** Some decision would have to be made about spaces between words, which are so often phonetically unreal in Spanish but visually necessary or at least helpful in reading.

Spanish orthography, despite the irregularities mentioned above, is at present quite sound pedagogically. It is in large part responsible for the reputation Spanish enjoys as being such an "easy" language. Phonemic or phonetic respelling of languages like English or French in elementary texts for pedagogical purposes is very helpful, but for Spanish it seems quite superfluous.

Spelling correctly, fortunately or unfortunately, as one views it, is one of the standards that society in most civilized countries uses to determine who is educated and cultured. Spelling Spanish correctly is relatively easy for the average American student of second-year Spanish. In fact, you, with even more study behind you, can probably spell Spanish better than your own language. Nevertheless, pronouncing the language correctly remains a major problem for you or a student of any level. The majority of you can succeed only with systematic and concerted effort, since the sound system of Spanish is really as inherently difficult as that of any other language spoken on the face of the earth.

References

SPANISH

Agard, "Stress in Four Romance Languages" (1967).
* Alonso, María, *Apuntes de ortografía para uso de principiantes* (1965).
* Beberfall, "The 'Indispensable' Accent Mark in the Spanish Language" (1959).
* _____, "A Note on the *Nuevas normas*" (1962).
* Bowen and Stockwell, "Orthography and Respelling in Teaching Spanish" (1957).
* Bull, *Spanish for Teachers: Applied Linguistics* (1965), Chapters 3–5.
* Casares, "Las *Nuevas normas de prosodia y ortografía*" (1958).
* _____, "Las *Nuevas normas de prosodia y ortografía* y su repercusión en América" (1955).
* Delattre, " 'Spanish is a Phonetic Language' " (1945).
* Fernández, Salvador, "Para la futura gramática" (1964).
* Politzer and Staubach, *Teaching Spanish: A Linguistic Orientation* (1965).
* Real Academia, "Nuevas normas de prosodia y ortografía" (1958).
* Rosenblat, *Las nuevas normas ortográficas y prosódicas de la Academia Española* (1953).
* Sacks, "The Pattern Drill and the Rationale of the Prosodic and Orthographic Accents in Spanish" (1963).

ENGLISH AND GENERAL

* Gelb, *A Study of Writing* (1952).
* Gleason, *An Introduction to Descriptive Linguistics* (1961), Chapter 25.

* Hall, *Linguistics and Your Language* (1962), Chapter 3.
* Hockett, *A Course in Modern Linguistics* (1958), Chapter 62.
Hoenigswald, *Language Change and Linguistic Reconstruction* (1960), Chapter 2.
* Hughes, *The Science of Language* (1962), Chapter VII.
* Lado, *Linguistics Across Cultures* (1957), Chapter 5.
* Lloyd and Warfel, *American English in Its Cultural Setting* (1957), Chapters 20, 21.
Pulgram, "Graphic and Phonic Systems: Figurae and Signs" (1965).
———, "Phoneme and Grapheme: a Parallel" (1951).
* Schlauch, *The Gift of Language* (1955), Chapter 2.

Exercises

A

Write an accent ′ on the words that require it, according to the rules of Spanish orthography. The correct pronunciation is indicated to the right. In the case of words with an accent mark, list the number of the rule (see pp. 264–65) *that governs the use of the written accent.*

1. imagino [i-ma-xí-no]
2. virgen [bír-xẹn]
3. jovenes [xó-b̶e-nes]
4. riquisimo [r̄i-kí-si-mo]
5. animal [a-ni-mál]
6. facil [fá-sil]
7. dificiles [di-fí-si-les]
8. angel [áŋ-xẹl]
9. solo (*adj.*) [só-lo]
10. nacar [ná-kar]
11. ingleses [iŋ-glé-ses]
12. farmacia [far-má-sịa]
13. analisis [a-ná-li-sis]
14. matiz [ma-tís]
15. rapidamente [r̄á-pi-d̶a-mẹ̄n-te]
16. oiste [o-ís-te]
17. teologo [te-ó-lo-g̶o]
18. den [dẹ́n]
19. fui [fụí]
20. lapiz [lá-pis]
21. preve [pre-b̶é]
22. pien [pí-ẹn]
23. piececitos [pịe-se-sí-tos]
24. maizal [maị-sál]
25. capaz [ka-pás]

(From here on you may have to look up a few unfamiliar words in the Vocabulary, Appendix F. *However, continue to cite the number of the rule which governs the use of the written accent.)*

26. ¿Para donde vas?
27. Deme el primero.
28. Para el coche, quiero bajar.
29. Solo quiere jugar al domino.
30. Quiere jugar solo.
31. Levantandote temprano, podras llegar a tiempo.
32. Podremos llamar a la policia.
33. Aunque llueva, quiero quedarme aqui.
34. No se cuando llega.
35. El dia cuando llegue, no estare alli yo.
36. No sabre que hacer.
37. Si que lo sabras.
38. Continuamos leyendo.
39. Prefiero ese que tienes tu.
40. Y esta es para ti, Periquito.
41. Cuando llego el psicologo, me hizo una serie de preguntas tontisimas.
42. El acrobata llamo por telefono, se comunico con el farmaceutico y le pidio el antidoto.
43. Los ingleses y los franceses discutiran la hegemonia de Rusia.
44. La cancion se titula "Melodia de melancolia."
45. No te dire como lo hizo pero lo completo en veintiuna horas.

APPENDIX

A. RULES FOR THE DISTRIBUTION OF SPANISH ALLOPHONES AND EXAMPLES

(The rules are listed in alphabetical order of the phonemes for easy reference. Only the single-phoneme rules are listed here. See pp. 187–91 for vowel combinations and examples.)

/a/ ⟶ [a]   **casa** [ká-sa]

$$
\text{/b/} \longrightarrow
\begin{bmatrix}
[b] \Big/ \begin{Bmatrix} \# \\ /m/ \end{Bmatrix} - \\[2ex]
[\emptyset] \Big/ \begin{Bmatrix} /o\underline{b}\text{-}/ \\ /su\underline{b}\text{-}/ \end{Bmatrix} \\[2ex]
[ƀ] \text{ elsewhere}
\end{bmatrix}
$$

voy [bói̯]
un vaso [um-bá-so]

obstáculo [os-tá-ku-lo]
subjetivo [su-xe-tí-ƀo]

yo voy [yó-ƀói̯]
alba [ál-ƀa]

/ĉ/ ⟶ [ĉ]   **chico** [ĉí-ko]

$$
\text{/d/} \longrightarrow
\begin{bmatrix}
[d] \Big/ \begin{Bmatrix} \# \\ /n/ \\ /l/ \end{Bmatrix} - \\[2ex]
\begin{Bmatrix} [đ] \\ [\emptyset] \end{Bmatrix} \Big/ \begin{Bmatrix} \text{word-final} \\ /\text{-a}\underline{d}o/ \end{Bmatrix} \\[2ex]
[đ] \text{ elsewhere}
\end{bmatrix}
$$

dámelo [dá-me-lo]
andar [an̪-dár]
aldea [al̪-dé-a]

verdad [bệr-dád] *or* [beṛ-dá]
tomado [to-má-đo] *or* [to-má-o]

nada [ná-đa]
verde [bệr-đe]
va a dármelo [bá-đár-me-lo]

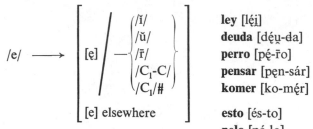

$$/e/ \longrightarrow \left[\begin{array}{l} [\text{ę}] \ / \ - \left\{\begin{array}{l} /\breve{\text{i}}/ \\ /\breve{\text{u}}/ \\ /\bar{\text{r}}/ \\ /C_1\text{-}C/ \\ /C_1/\# \end{array}\right\} \\ [\text{e}] \ \text{elsewhere} \end{array}\right]$$

ley [lę́i̯]
deuda [dę́u̯-đa]
perro [pę́-r̄o]
pensar [pęn-sár]
komer [ko-mę́r]

esto [és-to]
pelo [pé-lo]

/ĭ/ is an unstressed /i/.
/ŭ/ is an unstressed /u/.
/C₁/ is any consonant but /s/.

/f/ $\longrightarrow$ [f]   **fino** [fí-no]

$$/g/ \longrightarrow \left[\begin{array}{l} [\text{g}] \ / \left\{\begin{array}{l} \# \\ /\text{n}/ \end{array}\right\} - \\ \left\{\begin{array}{l} [\text{g}] \\ [\emptyset] \end{array}\right\} / \left\{\begin{array}{l} \# \\ /\text{n}/ \end{array}\right\} \_\_/\text{uV}/ \\ \left\{\begin{array}{l} [\text{g}] \\ [\emptyset] \end{array}\right\} / \left\{\begin{array}{l} /C_1/\_\_/\text{uV}/ \\ /V/\_\_/\text{uV}/ \end{array}\right\} \\ [\text{g}] \ \text{elsewhere} \end{array}\right]$$

gané [ga-né]
tengo [tę́ŋ-go]
guardo [gu̯ár-đo] *or* [wár-đo]
un hueso [uŋ-gu̯é-so] *or*
    [uŋ-wé-so]
los guardo [loz-gu̯ár-đo] *or*
    [loz-wár-đo]
lo guardo [lo-gu̯ár-đo] *or*
    [lo-wár-đo]
lo gané [lo-ga-né]

/C₁/ is any consonant but /n/.

/h/ $\longrightarrow$ [h]   **girar** [hi-rár]
               gente [hę́n-te]
               jardín [har-đín]

/í/ $\longrightarrow$ [i]   **fino** [fí-no]
               isla [ís-la]
               vía [bí-a]
               país [pa-ís]

$$/\breve{\text{i}}/ \longrightarrow \left[\begin{array}{l} [\text{i̯}] \ / \left\{\begin{array}{l} /C/\_\_/V/ \\ /V_1/\_\_ \end{array}\right\} \\ [\text{y}] \ / \left\{\begin{array}{l} /V\_\_V/ \\ \#\_\_/V/ \end{array}\right\} \\ [\text{i}] \ \text{elsewhere} \end{array}\right]$$

tiene [ti̯é-ne]
ley [lę́i̯]

leyó [le-yó]
y eso [yé-so]

pintar [piṇ-tár]
cursi [kúr-si]

V₁ is /a o e/. [i̯] does not follow /u/ or /i/.

/k/ $\longrightarrow$ $\begin{bmatrix} \begin{Bmatrix} [k] \\ [g] \end{Bmatrix} / \underline{} /C/ \\ \\ [k] \text{ elsewhere} \end{bmatrix}$

actor [ak-tór] *or* [ag-tór]

casa [ká-sa]

/l/ $\longrightarrow$ $\begin{bmatrix} [l̪] / \underline{} \begin{Bmatrix} /t/ \\ /d/ \end{Bmatrix} \\ \\ [l̟] / \underline{} \begin{Bmatrix} /ĉ/ \\ /y/ \\ /ñ/ \end{Bmatrix} \\ \\ [l] \text{ elsewhere} \end{bmatrix}$

alto [ál̪-to]
aldea [al̪-dé-a]

salchicha [sal̟-ĉí-ĉa]
el yerno [el̟-ŷér-no]
el ñoclo [el̟-ñó-klo]

los [los]
calma [kál-ma]

/m/ $\longrightarrow$ $\begin{bmatrix} [m̩] / \underline{} /f/ \\ \\ \begin{Bmatrix} [n] \\ [ŋ] \end{Bmatrix} / \text{word-final} \\ \\ [m] \text{ elsewhere} \end{bmatrix}$

enfermo [e̞m̩-fé̞r-mo]

álbum [ál-ƀun] *or* [ál-ƀuŋ]

cama [ká-ma]
mismo [míz-mo]

/n/ $\longrightarrow$ $\begin{bmatrix} [m] / \underline{} \begin{Bmatrix} /p/ \\ /b/ \end{Bmatrix} \\ \\ [m̩] / \underline{} /f/ \\ \\ \begin{Bmatrix} [ɱ] \\ [ɱ̩] \end{Bmatrix} / \underline{} /m/ \\ \\ [ṇ] / \underline{} \begin{Bmatrix} /t/ \\ /d/ \end{Bmatrix} \\ \\ [ñ] / \underline{} \begin{Bmatrix} /ĉ/ \\ /y/ \end{Bmatrix} \\ \\ [ŋ] / \underline{} \begin{Bmatrix} /k/ \\ /g/ \\ /x/ \\ /w/ \end{Bmatrix} \\ \\ \begin{Bmatrix} [n] \\ [ŋ] \end{Bmatrix} / \text{word-final} \\ \\ [n] \text{ elsewhere} \end{bmatrix}$

un peso [um-pé-so]
un vaso [um-bá-so]

enfermo [e̞m̩-fé̞r-mo]

conmigo [kon-mí-go] *or* [kom-mí-go]

antes [án̪-tes]
andar [an̪-dár]

ancho [áñ-ĉo]
inyección [iñ-ŷe̞k-si̞ón]

en casa [e̞ŋ-ká-sa]
tengo [té̞ŋ-go]
franja [fráŋ-xa]
un hueso [uŋ-wé-so]

se van [se-ƀán] *or* [se-ƀáŋ]

no [nó]
pensar [pe̞n-sár]

/ñ/ ⟶ [ñ]   **caña** [ká-ña]
              inyección [iñ-ŷęk-sįón]

/o/ ⟶ [o]   **oro** [ó-ro]
              color [ko-lór]
              pongo [póŋ-go]

/p/ ⟶
$$\begin{bmatrix} \begin{Bmatrix} [p] \\ [\emptyset] \end{Bmatrix} \Big/ \begin{array}{l} \text{in } \textbf{séptimo,} \\ \textbf{se(p)tiembre} \end{array} \\[2ex] [p] \text{ elsewhere} \end{bmatrix}$$
              séptimo [sęp-ti-mo] *or* [sę-ti-mo]

              palo [pá-lo]

/r/ ⟶
$$\begin{bmatrix} \begin{Bmatrix} [r] \\ [\bar{r}] \end{Bmatrix} \Big/ - \begin{Bmatrix} /C/ \\ \# \end{Bmatrix} \\[2ex] [\bar{r}] \Big/ \begin{Bmatrix} /n/ \\ /l/ \end{Bmatrix} - \\[2ex] [r] \text{ elsewhere} \end{bmatrix}$$
              puerta [pų ę r-ta] *or* [pų ę ṟ-ta]
              comer [ko-męr] *or* [ko-męṟ]

              enredar [ęn-ṟe-dár]
              alrededar [al-ṟe-đe-đór]

              pero [pé-ro]

/ṟ/ ⟶
$$\begin{Bmatrix} [\bar{r}] \\ [\bar{r}] \end{Bmatrix}$$
              rico [ṟí-ko] *or* [ṟí-ko]
              perro [pé-ṟo] *or* [pé-ṟo]

/s/ ⟶
$$\begin{bmatrix} \begin{Bmatrix} [s] \\ [z] \end{Bmatrix} \Big/ \_\_/C_l/ \\[2ex] [z] \quad /\_\_/d/ \\[2ex] \begin{Bmatrix} [s] \\ [h] \\ [\emptyset] \end{Bmatrix} \Big/ \_\_/\bar{r}/ \\[3ex] [s] \text{ elsewhere} \end{bmatrix}$$
              mismo [mís-mo] *or* [míz-mo]

              desde [déz-đe]

              los ricos [los-ṟí-kos] *or*
                        [loh-ṟí-kos] *or*
                        [lo-ṟí-kos]

              zapato [sa-pá-to]

/C_l/ is any voiced consonant but /d/ and /ṟ/.

/t/ ⟶
$$\begin{bmatrix} \begin{Bmatrix} [t] \\ [d] \end{Bmatrix} \Big/ \_\_/C_v/ \\[2ex] [t] \text{ elsewhere} \end{bmatrix}$$
              ritmo [ṟít-mo] *or* [ṟiđ-mo]

              tomar [to-már]

/C_v/ is any voiced consonant.

/ú/ ⟶ [ú]   **puso** [pú-so]
              último [úļ-ti-mo]
              actúa [ak-tú-a]
              baúl [ba-úl]

$$/\breve{u}/ \longrightarrow \begin{bmatrix} [\underset{\sim}{u}] / \begin{Bmatrix} /C/\_/V/ \\ /V_1/\_ \end{Bmatrix} \\[2ex] [w] / \begin{Bmatrix} /V/\_/V/ \\ \#\_/V/ \end{Bmatrix} \\[2ex] [u] \text{ elsewhere} \end{bmatrix}$$

pues [pu̯és]
deuda [de̯u̯-đa]

siete u ocho [si̯é-te-wó-ĉo]
huelo [wé-lo]

usted [us-té̯d]
espíritu [es-pí-ri-tu]

V₁ is /a o e/. [u̯] does not follow /u/ or /i/.

$$/w/ \longrightarrow \begin{bmatrix} \begin{Bmatrix} [w] \\ [gu̯] \end{Bmatrix} / \begin{Bmatrix} \# \\ /n/ \end{Bmatrix}\_ \\[3ex] \begin{Bmatrix} [w] \\ [gu̯] \end{Bmatrix} \text{ elsewhere} \end{bmatrix}$$

hueso [wé-so] *or* [gu̯é-so]
un hueso [uŋ-wé-so] *or* [uŋ-gu̯é-so]

la huerta [la-wé̯r-ta] *or* [la-gu̯é̯r-ta]

$$/x/ \longrightarrow \begin{bmatrix} \begin{Bmatrix} [x] \\ [ç] \end{Bmatrix} / \_ \begin{Bmatrix} /i/ \\ /e/ \end{Bmatrix} \\[3ex] [x] \text{ elsewhere} \end{bmatrix}$$

girar [xi-rár] *or* [çi-rár]
gente [xé̯ŋ-te] *or* [çé̯ŋ-te]

jardin [xar-đín]

$$\text{x represents} \begin{bmatrix} \begin{Bmatrix} [ks] \\ [s] \end{Bmatrix} / \_/C/ \\[2ex] [s] \text{ in } \textbf{exacto, auxilio, } \text{etc.} \\[2ex] \begin{Bmatrix} [gs] \\ [ks] \end{Bmatrix} \text{ elsewhere} \end{bmatrix}$$

extraño [e̯ks-trá-ño] *or* [es-trá-ño]
exacto [e-sák-to]

examen [e̯g-sá-me̯n] *or* [e̯k-sá-me̯n]

$$/y/ \longrightarrow \begin{bmatrix} \begin{Bmatrix} [y] \\ [ŷ] \end{Bmatrix} / \begin{Bmatrix} \# \\ /n/ \\ /l/ \end{Bmatrix}\_ \\[3ex] [y] \text{ elsewhere} \end{bmatrix}$$

yo lo vi [yó-lo-ɓí] *or* [ŷó-lo-ɓí]
inyección [iñ-ye̯k-si̯ón] *or* [iñ-ŷé̯k-si̯ón]
el hielo [e̯l-yé-lo] *or* [e̯l-ŷé-lo]

mayo [má-yo]
calle [ká-ye]

B. PHONEME AND ALLOPHONE CHARTS

CONSONANT PHONEMES OF SPANISH

POINTS OF ARTICULATION

MANNERS OF ARTICULATION	Bilabial	Labio-dental	Inter-dental	Dental	Alveolar	Palatal	Velar	Bilabio-velar	Glottal
STOPS	p b			t d			k g		
SLIT FRICATIVES		f	θ			y	x	w	(h)
GROOVE FRICATIVES					s				
AFFRICATES						ĉ			
NASALS	m				n	ñ			
LATERALS					l	ļ			
TAP					r				
TRILL					r̄				

(The symbols in the upper part of the boxes represent voiceless phonemes, those in the lower part, voiced ones.)

Most dialects of American Spanish have only 18 consonant phonemes, lacking both /θ/ and /ļ/. In some dialects /h/ replaces /x/, thus the parentheses on the chart.

Vowel Phonemes of Spanish

	Front	Central	Back
High	i		u
Mid	e		o
Low		a	

Suprasegmental phonemes of Spanish

STRESS   primary /ˊ/   weak / / (unmarked)

PITCH   /3/ high ⎯   /2/ normal ___   /1/ low ___

TERMINAL JUNCTURES   rise /↑/   fall /↓/   sustained /→/

Consonant Phonemes of English

POINTS OF ARTICULATION

MANNERS OF ARTICULATION	Bilabial	Labio-dental	Inter-dental	Alveolar	Palatal	Velar	Glottal
STOPS	p b			t d		k g	
SLIT FRICATIVES		f v	θ ð				h
GROOVE FRICATIVES				s z	š ž		
AFFRICATES					č ǰ		
NASALS	m			n		ŋ	
LATERAL				l			
MEDIAN				r			
SEMI-VOWELS (GLIDES)	w				y		(h)

Semi-vowels function both as consonants and vowels. /h/ is sometimes a fricative consonant and sometimes a semi-vowel or glide, thus the parentheses on the chart.

VOWEL PHONEMES OF ENGLISH

	Front	Central	Back
High	i	ɨ	u
Mid	e	ə	o
Low	æ	a	ɔ

SUPRASEGMENTAL PHONEMES OF ENGLISH

STRESS   primary /ˊ/   secondary /ˆ/   tertiary /ˋ/   weak /˜/

PITCH   /4/ extra high ‾   /3/ high ‾   /2/ normal ___   /1/ low ___

PLUS JUNCTURE   /+/

TERMINAL JUNCTURES   rise /↑/   fall /↓/   sustained /→/

CONSONANT ALLOPHONES OF SPANISH

POINTS OF ARTICULATION

MANNERS OF ARTICULATION	Bilabial	Labio-dental	Inter-dental	Dental	Alveolar	Palatal	Velar	Bilabio-velar	Glottal
STOPS	p / b			t / d			k / g		
SLIT FRICATIVES	ꝑ / ƀ	f / v	θ / ð	đ	ɟ / ɹ	ç / y	x / ǥ	w	h
GROOVE FRICATIVES					s ś / z ż	š / ž			
AFFRICATES						ĉ / ŷ			
NASALS	m	m̦		ṇ	n	ñ	ŋ		
LATERALS				ḷ	l	ļ			
TAP					r				
TRILLS					r̃ / r̄		Ŗ / R		

[s] and [z] are made with the tongue relatively level or convex. [ś] and [ż] are made with the tip of the tongue retroflexed, giving the entire tongue a concave shape.

VOWEL ALLOPHONES OF SPANISH

	Front	Central	Back
High	i̧ i		u̧ u
Mid	e ę		o
Low		a	

C. PRACTICE READINGS

Dialog 1

RUPERTO: ¡Qué barbaridad! ¡Mira cómo llueve, Honorato! Es mejor que cojamos un taxi. ¡Taxi! ¡Taxi!

HONORATO: Pero ¿de veras piensas que vas a encontrar uno en un día como éste?

RUPERTO: ¿Por qué no? En esta ciudad hay miles de taxis.

HONORATO: Sí. Pero también es cierto que en cuanto comienza a llover a cántaros, no puedes conseguir uno ni de milagro.

RUPERTO: ¡Qué le vamos a hacer! Paciencia y a esperar.

HONORATO: Mira aquel pobre viejito en la acera de enfrente. No tiene paraguas y se va a empapar.

RUPERTO: Y lo peor es que camina tan despacio. El pobre es tan viejo que ya arrastra los pies.

HONORATO: Allá viene aquella chica tan guapa que estaba anoche en casa de Ernesto.

RUPERTO: Y mira qué sombrilla tan bonita trae.

HONORATO: ¡Hombre! Quién se fija en la sombrilla.

RUPERTO: Bueno, parece que ya deja de llover tan fuerte. ¿Qué te parece si empezamos a caminar?

HONORATO: Pero despacito, a ver si ella nos alcanza.

Dialog 2

DOÑA ENCARNACIÓN: ¡Dios mío! Ya son las nueve. Muchacha, mejor te vas ya al mercado o no vas a encontrar nada bueno que comprar.

PACÍFICA: Muy bien, señora. ¿Qué quiere que traiga?

DOÑA ENCARNACIÓN: A ver. Carne, pan, verduras, frutas, azúcar, arroz y frijoles. ¿Queda algo de manteca?

PACÍFICA: Sí, señora, pero muy poco.

DOÑA ENCARNACIÓN: Entonces compra una libra, pero que sea de la buena.

PACÍFICA: Sí, señora, buena y barata.

DOÑA ENCARNACIÓN: Fíjate que las naranjas no estén magulladas y que la carne sea fresca. La que trajiste antier estaba añeja.

PACÍFICA: Fue culpa del carnicero que me aseguró que acababa de recibirla.

DOÑA ENCARNACIÓN: Bueno, mejor te vas rápido porque si no . . .

PACÍFICA: ¿Y la plata?

DOÑA ENCARNACIÓN: ¡Ay sí! ¿Dónde la habré puesto?

PACÍFICA: Seguro que sobre la máquina de coser.

DOÑA ENCARNACIÓN: Sí, aquí está.

PACÍFICA: No me dé billetes muy grandes porque cuesta conseguir cambio.

DOÑA ENCARNACIÓN: No te apures. El más grande que tengo es uno de sólo cinco pesos.

Dialog 3

HIPÓLITO: Y ¿qué tal el examen?

EUSTAQUIO: Malísimo. El profesor debe de haberse puesto de acuerdo con el
diablo y nos hizo unas preguntas que ni Einstein hubiera podido
contestar.

HIPÓLITO: Habrá sido porque no te preparaste bien.

EUSTAQUIO: ¡Qué va! Si me maté estudiando.

HIPÓLITO: ¿Cuántas preguntas había?

EUSTAQUIO: Sólo diez, pero ¡qué diez!

HIPÓLITO: ¿Largas o cortas de contestar?

EUSTAQUIO: Depende. Sobre las dos últimas se podría escribir un libro. Lo
peor fue que apenas tuvimos una hora de tiempo para contestarlas
todas.

HIPÓLITO: ¿De qué preguntó más, del libro de texto o de las notas de clase?

EUSTAQUIO: Del texto, sobre todo de los capítulos que casi no discutimos en la
clase. Yo creo que ese profesor está empeñado en hacernos fracasar.

HIPÓLITO: Y los demás estudiantes, ¿qué piensan del examen?

EUSTAQUIO: No lo sé. No tuve tiempo de hablar con ninguno de ellos, pero la
mayoría salieron con una cara muy triste.

HIPÓLITO: ¿Qué va a pasar ahora?

EUSTAQUIO: Pues nada. Por dicha que en los dos exámenes anteriores no salí
tan mal. Empezando esta noche, me pongo a estudiar como un loco
para el examen final y verás como saco una buena calificación.

HIPÓLITO: ¿Esta noche? Si es cuando tenemos la fiestecita en casa de Inés.

EUSTAQUIO: Caramba, se me había olvidado.

HIPÓLITO: Entonces no vendrás a la fiesta.

EUSTAQUIO: Eso jamás. Empezaré a estudiar mañana por la noche.

Dialog 4

SEVERIANO: Hola, Anastasio, ¿qué haces por aquí?

ANASTASIO: Pues he venido a comprar unas cuatro cosas para la familia. ¿Y tú?

SEVERIANO: Voy al Ministerio de Gobernación porque tengo un asunto importante que resolver.

ANASTASIO: Y la familia, ¿qué tal?

SEVERIANO: Así, así. La menor con el sarampión y la mujer con sus benditas jaquecas. ¿Y los tuyos?

ANASTASIO: Regular. Tiburcio, el segundo, se cayó de un caballo y ahora anda con el brazo derecho enyesado. Con los niños nunca faltan problemas, ni siquiera cuando está uno de vacaciones.

SEVERIANO: A propósito, ¿cuándo regresan del veraneo?

ANASTASIO: En unas dos semanas, en cuanto abran la matrícula para las escuelas. Pero, me han dicho que piensas cambiar de empleo, ¿es cierto?

SEVERIANO: Sí, hombre. Casualmente a eso voy al Ministerio. He sabido que necesitan un secretario y quiero ver si me nombran a mí.

ANASTASIO: ¿Es que no estás contento en la oficina de don Próspero?

SEVERIANO: Contento sí lo estoy. Don Próspero es muy bueno y siempre me ha tratado bien. Pero en el Ministerio pagan mejor y no se trabaja tanto.

ANASTASIO: Comprendo. ¿Y tienes buenos padrinos que te ayuden a conseguir el puesto?

SEVERIANO: Ya lo creo. Nada menos que el cuñado de una prima de mi mujer. El es tío de la esposa de un nieto del Ministro.

ANASTASIO: Hombre, con semejante padrino es seguro que el puesto será tuyo.

SEVERIANO: Así lo espero. Pero, hablando de otra cosa, mira qué chica tan guapa la que viene allá.

ANASTASIO: ¡Qué bárbara! ¡Fíjate en la minifalda que lleva! La falda le queda por lo menos a un decímetro arriba de las rodillas.

SEVERIANO: Y ve a aquel viejito del bastón cómo se ha quedado al mirarla. Se le van a salir los ojos.

ANASTASIO: Por admirarla ya el pobre no ve ni por dónde camina.

SEVERIANO: Ni se ha dado cuenta de que ya llegó a la esquina. ¡Cuidado, señor, cuidado con ese autobús!

ANASTASIO: ¡Lo golpeó! ¡Lo golpeó! ¡Qué barbaridad! Mejor vamos a ayudarlo.

SEVERIANO: Ya lo está ayudando a levantarse aquel policía. Parece que no fue nada serio. Fue más el susto que otra cosa.

ANASTASIO: Bueno. Hasta la próxima. Mejor me voy porque si no, se me hace muy tarde y la familia se preocupa.

D. ANSWER KEY FOR EXERCISES AND REVIEW QUESTIONS

6A.
1. ho-me-na-je
2. dí-a
3. ve-re-da
4. ba-úl
5. a-gra-da-ble
6. tran-qui-li-zar
7. cau-di-llo
8. de-sas-tro-so
9. pa-ís
10. du-ran-te
11. o-í-do
12. ha-bi-tuar-se
13. ca-er
14. sub-ra-yar

15. que-brar
16. ciu-dad
17. pan-ta-lla
18. ca-os
19. ho-yue-lo
20. deu-da
21. hay
22. pa-se-ar
23. a-ho-gar
24. per-la
25. ahu-ma-do
26. le-che-ro
27. re-la-tar
28. a-ma-rrar

29. a-hí
30. em-bau-lar
31. es-pal-da
32. hom-bre
33. pai-sa-no
34. per-mi-tir
35. le-ón
36. rei-na
37. trans-plan-te
38. po-e-sí-a
39. cons-truc-ción
40. ex-tra-or-di-na-rio
41. lo-ar
42. es-pon-ta-nei-dad

6B.
1. e-lo-ro
2. ha-blar-fran-cés
3. la-shi-jas
4. ha-bla-ses-pa-ñol
5. sua-ve
6. es-ta-hi-ja
7. pa-ra-es-tehi-ji-to

8. lo-vi-a-yer
9. se-u-ne
10. se-ve-í-a-muy-bien
11. e-nEs-pa-ña
12. co-nes-te-hom-bre
13. pa-ra-es-te-hi-jo
14. la-o-dio

15. ha-bleus-ted
16. e-lho-nor
17. la-hon-ra
18. po-re-la-mo-ra-Es-
    pa-ña
19. e-nel-lo-mo
20. la-is-la

21. tan-ne-gro   22. los-sui-zos

CHAPTER 9. /b/

Drill 9.9 G[1] [kó-mo-te-b̶á   bás-pa-ra-la-ká-sa-ó-ra   te-b̶ó-ya-k̶om-pa-ñár
á-se̯um-bu̯én̠-dí-a-pa-ra̯im-b̶i̯ér-no nó]

---

[1] The phonetic transcriptions given here for the "live" transcriptions are based on the tape recordings. However, if the teacher reads them in class, you should, of course, transcribe exactly what you hear. Thus, in that case, there may be a slight difference between your phonetic transcriptions and the ones given here.

The phonemic and phonetic transcriptions for the exercises (.10 C and .10 D) are based on the allophonic distributions for General American Spanish as presented in this book. In many cases of free variation, such as [s] or [z] before any voiced consonant but /d/, both allophones

Exercise 9.10 C /bié-ne-be-ní-to-a-bér-tel-sá-ba-do nó ké-bá bá-a-bi-si-tá-ra-
pá-blo ke-bí-bem-be-ne-sué-la bá-a-bo-lár sí fué-al-bán-ko-a-kam-biá-
ruñ-ĉé-ke-pa-ra-sa-ká-rel-bo-lé-to/

Exercise 9.10 D [bi̯é-ne-ƀe-ní-to-a-ƀér-tẹl-sá-ba-ɖo nó ké-ƀá bá-a-ƀi-si-tá-
ra-pá-ƀlo ke-ƀí-ƀẹm-be-ne-su̯é-la bá-a-ƀo-lár sí fu̯é-al-ƀáŋ-ko-a-kam-bi̯á-
ruñ-ĉé-ke-pa-ra-sa-ká-rẹl-ƀo-lé-to]

CHAPTER 10. /d/

Drill 10.9 K [a-ɖóŋ-de-ƀáu̯s-té-ɖa-ó-ra dóŋ-des-tá-su-pá-ɖre le-ɖi̯óu̯s-té-ɖẹl̦-
di-né-ro-a-la-ɖá-ma o-se-lo-ƀá-maŋ-dá-ró-tro-ɖí-a ɖí-ga-me-si-ƀí-be-la-
ɖá-ma-ẹn-la-si̯u-dáɖ ó-ẹn-la]-dĉ-a]

Exercise 10.10 C /e-duár-do-me-dí-xo-ke-r̄e-nál-do-to-da-bí-a-le-de-bí-a-mú-
ĉo-di-né-ro kuan-do-me-bió me-pre-gun-tó-dón-de-an-dá-ba-r̄e-nál-do-
e-nés-tos-dí-as i-le-r̄es-pon-dí-ke-nó-sa-bí-a-ná-da/

Exercise 10.10 D [e-ɖuár-ɖo-me-ɖí-xo-kẹ-r̄e-ná]-do-to-ɖa-ƀí-a-le-ɖe-ƀí-a-mú-
ĉo-ɖi-né-ro ku̯aŋ-do-me-ƀi̯ó me-pre-gu̯ŋ-tó-ɖóŋ-de-aŋ-dá-ƀa-r̄e-ná]-do-e-
nés-toz-dí-as i-lẹ-r̄es-poŋ-dí-ke-nó-sa-ƀi-a-ná-ɖa]

CHAPTER 11. /g/ AND /w/

Drill 11.9 F [ó-ye gus-tá-bo ké-kḷé-rez-gu̯a]-té-r̦o tẹŋ-go-gá-nnaz-dc-ko-me-
ru-noz-wé-ƀos-frí-tos pu̯é-dez-gi-sár-los kom-mú-ĉo-gús-to de-sé-as-ke-
los-frí-a-ko-nés-ta-grá-sa nó wé-le-mál]

---

s
will be given, e.g. [loz-wé-sos], indicating that either one is correct in the transcription. In some
cases of free variation, however, only the most common allophone will be given in the trans-
ø
s
scription, e.g. [loh-r̄í-kos], instead of [loh-r̄í-kos]. Thus, in this case a transcription of [los-r̄í-kos]
would be equally correct, although not given here.

Exercise 11.10 C /sen-tí-a-el-frí-o-ás-ta-en-los-wé-sos ye-bá-ba-pués-tos-lo-san-tí-guos-wa-rá-ĉes i-te-ní-a-gá-nas-de-po-nér-los-piés sér-ka-del-fué-go-pa-ra-ka-len-tár-se-los a-sí-a-bá-rios-dí-as-ke-lo-so-bré-ro-ses-tá-ban-de-wél-ga se-kom-fe-sá-bain-te-riór-mén-te-ke-a-bí-a-ke-rí-do-wír pe-ro-sa-bí-a-ke-lo-ne-se-si-tá-ban-de-guár-dia guár-dia de-r̄e-pén-te-le-gri-tá-ron bén-ga/

Exercise 11.10 D [sẹṇ-tí-a-ẹl-frí-o-ás-ta-ẹn-loz-wé-sos ye-b̶á-b̶a-pu̯és-toz-lo-saṇ-tí-gu̯oz-wa-rá-ĉes i-te-ní-a-gá-naz-de-po-nẹ́r-los-pi̯és sẹ́r-k̲a-dẹl-fu̯é-go-pa-ra-ka-lẹṇ-tár-se-los a-sí-a-b̶á-ri̯oz-dí-as-ke-lo-so-b̶ré-ro-ses-tá-b̶aṇ-de-wél-ga se-koṃ-fe-sá-b̶ai̯ṇ-te-ri̯ór-mén-te-ke-a-b̶í-a-ke-rí-d̶o-wír pe-ro-sa-b̶í-a-ke-lo-ne-se-si-tá-b̶aṇ-de-gu̯ár-d̶i̯a gu̯ár-d̶i̯a dẹ-r̄e-pẹ́ṇ-te-le-gri-tá-ron b̶ẹ́ŋ-ga]

Chapter 12. REVIEW OF STOPS /p t k b d g/ AND FRICATIVE /w/

Drill 12.9 G [pu̯és pá-ko-te-d̶í-xo-ke-nó-po-d̶í-a-b̶i̯a-xá-rẹŋ-gu̯á-gu̯a por-ké-sí-ge-sin-sis-ti̯ẹ́ṇ-do-ẹŋ-ke-lo-á-ga d̶í-se-ke-le-d̶u̯é-lẹṇ-loz-wé-sos-ku̯aṇ-do-ti̯é-ne-kes-tár-sẹṇ-tá-d̶o-táṇ-to-ti̯ém-po-e-num-be-í-ku-lo-a-tes-tá-d̶o]

Exercise 12.10 C /bík-tor-dí-se-ke-yá-bo-tá-ro-nem-bo-lí-bia i-ke-nó-le-gús-tan-ná-da-los-r̄e-sul-tá-dos es-pe-rá-ba-ke-tó-do-su-bié-ran-de-kla-rá-dou-na-wél-ga-xe-ne-rál pe-ro-a-be-ri-guá-mos-ke-tó-do-sa-lió-bién i-kel-go-biér-no-sí-ge-r̄i-xién-do-deu-na-ma-né-ra-mui-es-tá-ble/

Exercise 12.10 D [bík-tor-d̶í-se-ke-yá-b̶o-tá-ro-nẹm-bo-lí-b̶i̯a i-ke-nó-le-gús-tan-ná-d̶a-loh-r̄e-sul-tá-d̶os es-pe-rá-b̶a-ke-tó-d̶o-su-b̶i̯é-raṇ-de-kla-rá-d̶ou̯-na-wél-ga-xe-ne-rál pe-ro-a-b̶e-ri-gu̯á-mos-ke-tó-d̶o-sa-li̯ó-b̶i̯ẹ́n i-kẹl-go-b̶i̯ẹ́r-no-sí-gẹ-r̄i-xi̯ẹ́ṇ-do-d̶ẹu̯-na-ma-né-ra-mu̯i-es-tá-b̶le]

12.11 Questions

1. place of articulation, manner of articulation, and function of vocal bands (voiced or voiceless)
2. consonants

3. syllable-final

4. regressive assimilation

5. [x] [ɾ̃] [ƀ]

6. one

7. aspirated, word-initial

8. **para**

9. **psicología, psicólogo,** etc.

10. /b d g/ (or) their voiced counterparts

11. slit

12. [mb]

13. free variation, hypercorrection

14. false

15. It is simply spelling carried down from Latin.

16. [ð] as in *father, this, lather,* etc.

17. end in /d/ or /-ado/

18. [đ], tap (flap)

19. dental [ṇ]

20. velar [ŋ]

21. [gṵ]

22. complementary distribution

23. sub-standard

24. the lips are rounded

CHAPTER 13. /ĉ f/

Drill 13.9 C [fran-sís-koi̯-fe-đe-rí-ko-í-ba̰ŋ-kon-loz-mu-ĉá-ĉo-sa-to-már-la-láñ-ĉa í-ba-na-ye-bár-lé-ĉe ĉo-ko-lá-te fré-sas ĉo-rí-sos i-fram-bṵé-sas sí los-ĉi-kos-te-ní-am-mṵi-bṵé-na-for-tú-na]

Exercise 13.10 C /ĉa-lí-toi̯-fran-sís-ko-í-ba-na-dá-ru-na-ĉár-la - so-bre-frán-sia pe-ro-los-mu-ĉá-ĉos-r̄e-ĉa-sá-ron-lai-dé-a em-bés-de-é-so se-fué-ron-tó-do-sa-to-már-ĉo-ko-lá-te-frí-o i-sal-ĉi-ĉas-fuér-tes/

Exercise 13.10 D [ĉa-lí-toi̯-fran-sís-ko-í-ba-na-dá-ru-na-ĉár-la- so-bre-frán-si̯a
       s
pe-ro-loz-mu-ĉá-ĉoh-r̄e-ĉa-sá-ron-lai̯-dé-a ḛm-béz-de-é-so se-fṵé-ro̰n-tó-đo-sa-to-már-ĉo-ko-lá-te-frí-o i-sal̯-ĉi-ĉas-fṵér-tes]

Chapter 14 /s/ (and /θ/)

Drill 14.9 G [ęl-pre-si-dę́ṇ-te-míz-mo-sa-l̦i̦ó-đe-su-r̄e-si-đę́n-si̦a-sin-sa-pá-tos
loh-r̄í-ko-ses-tá-ban-se-gú-roz-đe-ke-le-fa̦l-tá-ba-sáŋ-gre-a-súl   ko-mo-đí-
sęn-lo-siŋ-glé-ses   dez-đęṇ-tón-ses-se-f̦i̦á-bam-máz-đe-loz-đik-ta-đó-res-ke-
por-lo-mé-no-saṇ-đá-bam-bi̦ę́m-bes-tí-đos]

Exercise 14.10 C   /el-mó-so-dí-xo-em-bó-sál-ta-ke-nó-é-ra-ka-pás-de-r̄o-bár-
los-sa-pá-tos   bol-bió-a-la-r̄e-si-dén-sia   o-yén-do-las-le-ĉú-sas   los-tí-ros-
de-los-ka-sa-dó-res   i-las-bó-ses-de-las-si-ga-r̄é-ras   des-de-don-des-tá-ba
us-me-á-ba-las-r̄ó-sas   i-pen-sá-ba-en-los-dí-as-kuan-do-ye-gá-ron-los-gó-
do-sa-é-sas-r̄e-xió-nes/

Exercise 14.10 D   [ęl-mó-so-đí-xo-ęm-bó-sá̦l-ta-ke-nó-é-ra-ka-páz-đę-r̄o-bár-
                                                                      s
los-sa-pá-tos   bol-bi̦ó-a-la-r̄e-si-đę́n-si̦a   o-yę́ṇ-do-laz-le-ĉú-sas   los-tí-roz-
                                   s
đe-los-ka-sa-đó-res   i-laz-bó-sez-đe-las-si-ga-r̄é-ras   dez-đe-đoṇ-des-tá-ba
s
uz-me-á-ba-lah-r̄ó-sas   i-pęn-sá-ba-ęn-loz-đí-as-ku̦aṇ-do-ye-gá-ron-loz-gó-
                                                                       s
đo-sa-é-sah-r̄e-xi̦ó-nes]

Chapter 15. /y/

Drill 15.9 F [ŷó sí yó-b̦ó-ya-ya-már-lo   le-đi-ré-ke̦l-ŷér-no-pu̦é-đe-tra-é-re̦l̦-
ŷé-lo í-és-to-me-bá-yu-đár-mú-ĉo   a-yér-no-más-pęn-sá-ba-ęñ-ŷa-már-lo
yęn-se-gí-đa-lo-bo-ya-sę́r]

Exercise 15.10 C   /mi-yér-no-es-tá-ba-tra-ba-xán-do-koñ-yé-r̄oi-yé-so   se-ka-
yó-e-nel-yé-lo i-se-da-ñó-mú-ĉo í-é-ya-má-do-al-dok-tór-ga-yár-do bá-a-ye-
gár-mui-prón-to-pa-ra-po-nér-leu-naiñ-yek-sión/

                                                                         y
Exercise 15.10 D   [mi-yér-no-es-tá-ba-tra-ba-xáṇ-do-koñ-ŷé-r̄oi̦-yé-so   se-ka-
y
yó-e-ne̦l-ŷé-lo i-se-đa-ñó-mú-ĉo í-é-ya-má-đo-a̦l-dok-tór-ga-yár-đo bá-a-ye-
                                                                  y
gár-mu̦i-próṇ-to-pa-ra-po-nér-le̦u-nai̦ñ-ŷęk-si̦ón]

CHAPTER 16.   /x (h)/

Drill 16.9 F [xu̯á-neŋ-koŋ-tróu̯-na-xó-ya-e-nel̯-xar-d̯ín   doŋ-de-a-b̯í-a-nes-tá-

d̯o-xu-gáŋ-do-su-sí-xos   su̯í-xo-ma-yór   çe-rár-d̯o   xu-ró-ke-la-b̯í-a-d̯e-xá-
d̯o-e-nel̯-ka-r̄o]

Exercise 16.10 C   /el-xe-ne-rál-xu-ró-ke-r̄es-pe-ta-rí-a-las-ké-xas-de-la-mu-xér
kie-nes-tá-ba-ta-na-fli-xí-da   por-ke-la-xén-te-a-b̯í-a-r̄e-ko-xí-do-tó-do-e-lá-
xo-en-su-xar-d̯ín   los-xi-tá-nos-di-xé-ron-ke-nó-sa-b̯í-an-ni-xó-ta   el-xe-ne-
rál-por-fí-ne-li-xió-a-sér-kons-truí-ru-na-r̄é-xa-pa-ra-pro-te-xé-rel-xar-d̯ín/

Exercise 16.10 D   [e̯l-çe-ne-rál-xu-ró-ke̯-r̄es-pe-ta-rí-a-las-ké-xaz-d̯e-la-mu-çér

kie̯-nes-tá-ba-ta-na-fli-çí-da   por-ke-la-çéŋ-te-a-b̯í-a-r̄e-ko-çí-d̯o-tó-d̯o-e-lá-

xo-e̯n-su-xar-d̯ín   los-çi-tá-noz-di-çé-roŋ-ke-nó-sa-b̯í-an-ni-xó-ta   e̯l-çe-ne-

rál-por-fí-ne-li-çi̯ó-a-se̯r-kons-tru̯í-ru-na-r̄é-xa-pa-ra-pro-te-çé-rel̯-xar-d̯ín]

CHAPTER 17.   REVIEW OF AFFRICATE /ĉ/ AND FRICATIVES /f s y x (h)/

Drill 17.9 E   [mu-ĉá-ĉo   pa-ra-d̯óŋ-de-b̯ás   a-xu-gá-ral-fú-b̯ol   pe-ro-dé-xa-
mo ír por-ko b̯ó-yu-yo-gár-tár-d̯o   ĉz-d̯os-po-rár   tú-nó-yé-gaz-nún̯-ka-
ti̯ém-po   ái̯-mú-ĉa-çéŋ-te-ke-xu̯é-ge-a-yí   sí   mu-ĉí-si-moz-mu-ĉá-ĉoz-d̯e-
nu̯és-tra-es-ku̯é-la   noz-b̯é-mos]

Exercise 17.10 C   /el-mu-ĉá-ĉo-r̄as-gó-la-ó-xa-de-pa-pél   i-la-ti-ró-a-lal-fóm-
bra   se-le-ye-ná-ron-lo-só-xos-de-lá-gri-mas   yem-pe-só-a-yo-rár   tó-das-
las-dá-mas-fué-ro-na-so-la-sár-lo   pé-ro   a-ó-ra-el-ĉí-ko-se-yér-ge   se-di-rí-
xe-al-yér-no   i-le-dí-se   b̯ó-ya-ya-má-ral-pre-si-dén-te/

Exercise 17.10 D   [e̯l-mu-ĉá-ĉo-r̄az-gó-la-ó-xa-d̯e-pa-pe̯l i-la-ti-ró-a-lal-fóm-bra

se-le-ye-ná-ron-lo-só-xoz-de-lá-gri-mas   ye̯m-pe-só-a-yo-rár   tó-d̯az-laz-

dá-mas-fu̯é-ro-na-so-la-sár-lo   pé-ro   a-ó-ra-e̯l-ĉí-ko-se-yér-ge   se-di-rí-çe-

al̯-y̯e̯r-no   i-le-d̯í-se   b̯ó-ya-ya-má-ral-pre-si-d̯e̯n-te]

17.11 Questions

1. [š]
2. lower, upper front
3. groove
4. nasal
5. sub-standard
6. /θ/
7. peninsular Spanish
8. syllable-final and word-final
9. For [s] the tongue is convex or flat. For [š] the tongue tip is retroflexed and the tongue itself has a concave shape.
10. never
11. [ĉ]
12. **yeísmo**
13. false
14. /y/ and /ĵ/ are phonemes in English, but the corresponding sounds [y] and [ŷ] are only allophones in Spanish and therefore never contrast.
15. They feel that there is a significant difference between [ŷ] and [y]. (See answer no. 14.)
16. [x] does not exist in English
17. occurs in some idiolects and dialects
18. false
19. There is no closure anywhere in the vocal tract above the larynx.
20. **j, g + e, g + i**

CHAPTER 18. /m n ñ/

Drill 18.9 E [el-ní-ño-em-fér-mo-se-be-bióum-bá-so-de-á-gua-koñ-ŷé-lo   se-sin-tió-me-xó-ri-nó-ke-rí-a-ke-dár-sen-ká-sa   pen-sá-ba-en-xu-gá-raḷ-té-nis i-fuéim-me-diá-ta-mén-te-a-la-káñ-ĉa]

Exercise 18.10 C   /em-frén-te-del-kom-bén-to-de-sám-be-ní-to-a-bí-aun-xar-díñ-ŷé-no-de-na-rán-xos   um-món-xe-pa-se-á-ba-r̄e-sán-do-su-so-ra-sió-ne-sem-bós-bá-xa   uñ-ĉí-ko-es-tá-ba-xu-gán-do-ko-nun-ga-tí-to-keum-pá-dre-le-a-bí-a-em-biá-do/

Exercise 18.10 D   [ęm-frę́n-te-dȩl-kom-bę́n-to-de-sám-be-ní-to-a-bí-aųn-xar-
y
díñ-ŷé-no-de-na-rán-xos um-món-xe-pa-se-á-ba-r̄e-sán-do-su-so-ra-sı̣ó-ne-
s
sȩm-bóz-bá-xa uñ-ĉí-ko-es-tá-ba-xu-gán-do-ko-nuŋ-ga-tí-to-kȩum-pá-dre-
le-a-bí-a-ȩm-bı̣á-do]

CHAPTER 19.   /l ļ/

Drill 19.9 F [le-baṇ-tó-ȩļ-di-né-ro-e-náļ-to-kon-la-má-no   i-lo-a-r̄o-xó-aļ-ĉí-
ko-ke-se-ya-má-ba-le-o-póļ-do aļ-ye-gá-ra-dón-des-tá-ba-la-plá-ta   ȩļ-ĉí-
ko-la-r̄e-ko-xı̣ó i-se-lar-gó]

Exercise 19.10 C   /el-xe-ne-rál-ya-mó-al-sol-dá-do   i-le-dí-xo-ke-fué-ra-le-di-
fí-sio-fe-de-rál-kes-tá-ba-en-la-pár-tc-sen-trál-dc-lal-dé-a-pa-ra-bér-sia-bí-a-
ye-gá-do-la-kár-ga-de-sál kuan-do-ye-gó-al-por-tál-de-le-di-fí-sio el-guár-
dia-le-gri-tó ál-to/

x   y
Exercise 19.10 D   [ȩl-çe-ne-ráļ-ŷa-mó-al-soļ-dá-do   i-le-dí-xo-ke-fųé-ra-le-dí-
fí-sı̣o-fe-de-rál-kes-tá-ba-ȩn-la-pár-tc-sȩn-tráļ-dc-laļ-dé-a-pa-ra-bér-sı̣a-bí-a-
ye-gá-do-la-kár-ga-de-sál   kuaṇ-do-ye-gó-al-por-táļ-de-le-di-fí-sı̣o   ȩļ-
gųár-dı̣a-le-gri-tó áļ-to]

CHAPTER 20.   /r r̄/

Drill 20.9 J [pé-ro-r̄o-bér-to   nó-es-tá-sȩṇ-te-rá-do-de-ke-se-le-kor-tó-ȩl-r̄á-
bo-al-pé-r̄o-dȩn-r̄í-ke le-kos-tó-ká-ro nó ȩh-r̄á-ro-ke-nó-loı̣-r̄í-te-más]

Exercise 20.10 C   /r̄o-bér-to-yen-r̄í-ke-pa-se-á-ba-nal-r̄e-de-dór-de-la-r̄é-xa ke-
rí-a-nen-tre-gá-rel-r̄e-ká-do   pe-ro-la-kó-sa-es-tá-ba-ta-nen-r̄e-dá-da-ke-
op-tá-rom-po-res-pe-rá-ru-na-ó-ra-más   nó-es-tá-ba-nen-te-rá-dos-de-kes-
tá-ba-en-tc-r̄á-do-cl-r̄í-ko-kc-a-bí-a-r̄c-si-dí-do-c-nć-sc-bá-r̄io-dc-r̄ó-ma/

Exercise 20.10 D   [r̄o-bér-to-yȩn-r̄í-kc-pa-se-á-ba-nal-r̄e-de-dór-dc-la-r̄é-xa ke-
rí-a-nȩṇ-tre-gá-rȩl-r̄e-ká-do   pe-ro-la-kó-sa-es-tá-ba-ta-nȩn-r̄e-dá-da-ke-
op-tá-rom-po-res-pe-rá-ru-na-ó-ra-más   nó-es-tá-ba-nȩn-te-rá-doz-de-kes-
tá-ba-ȩn-tȩ-r̄á-do-ȩl-r̄í-ko-ke-a-bí-a-r̄e-si-dí-do-e-né-se-bá-r̄ı̣o-dȩ-r̄ó-ma]

CHAPTER 21.   SOUNDS REPRESENTED BY THE LETTER X

Drill 21.9 C   [ku̯aŋ-do-lo-sȩks-traŋ-xé-roz-b̶á-na-los-pa-í-se-sȩk-só-ti-kos
su̯ȩks-pe-ri̯ȩ́n-si̯a po-rȩks-tȩ́n-sa-ke-sé-a nó-le-sa-se-gú-ra-ȩ́k-si-to]

                                        ø   g
Exercise 21.10 C   /é-seks-trá-ño-ke-nó-ek-sís-ta-né-sas-kó-sa-se-nés-te-pa-ís

        ø   ø
lo-seks-tran-xé-ros-se-sor-prén-de-ni-nó-pué-de-neks-pli-kár-lo   pe-ro-des-

        g   ø
pués-dek-sa-mi-nár-bién-la-si-tua-sión   se-dán-kuén-ta-de-ké-é-sek-sák-

ta-mén-te-lo-mís-mo-e-nó-tros-pa-í-ses-tam-bién/

                                        ø   g
Exercise 21.10 D   [é-sȩks-trá-ño-ke-nó-ȩk-sís-ta-né-sas-kó-sa-se-nés-te-pa-ís

        ø   ø
lo-sȩks-traŋ-xé-ros-se-sor-prȩ́n̦-de-ni-nó-pu̯ȩ́-d̶e-nȩks-pli-kár-lo   pe-ro-d̶es-

        g   ø
pu̯ȩ́z-d̶ek-sa-mi-nár-b̶i̯ȩn-la-si-tu̯a-si̯ȩ́n   se-d̶áŋ-ku̯ȩ́n̦-ta-de-ké-é-sȩk-sák-

        s
ta-mȩ́n̦-te-lo-míz-mo-e-nó-tros-pa-í-ses-tam-b̶i̯ȩ́n]

CHAPTER 22.   REVIEW OF NASALS /m n ñ/, LATERALS /l ḷ/, TAP /r/, TRILL /r̄/,
        AND THE LETTER X

Drill 22.9 D   [ȩn-r̄í-ke-ke-rí-a-ȩm-b̶i̯á-rum-pa-ké-te-a-sus-pa-ri̯ȩ́n̦-tes ke-b̶í-b̶e-
nȩm̦-frán-si̯a pe-rou̯ñ-ĉí-ko-se-lo-r̄o-b̶ó ŷa-mó-a-la-po-li-sí-a i-ye-gá-ro-
nȩn-se-gí-da-lo-tȩ́l]

Exercise 22.10 C

1. /nó-kom-fún-da-sum-pé-so-ko-num-bé-so/
2. /le-pú-sou-naiñ-yek-sió-nal-ĉí-ko-a-kie-na-bí-a-mor-dí-do-el-pé-r̄o-r̄a-
   bió-so/
                ø   g
3. /é-seks-trá-ño yaun-r̄á-ro ke-lo-sek-sá-me-nes-nó-en-kán-te-na-lo-ses-
   tu-dián-tes/
4. /a-yá-e-nel-r̄áñ-ĉo-grán-de   don-de-bí-ben-los-ĉáñ-ĉos   las-ga-yí-nas
   las-r̄á-tas i-los-ñan-dú-es/

Exercise 22.10 D

1. [nó-koṃ-fúṇ-da-sum-pé-so-ko-num-bé-so]

2. [le-pú-soụ-naịñ-ỳẹk-sịó-naḷ-ĉí-ko-a-kịe-na-bí-a-mor-dí-do-ẹl-pẹ́-r̄o-r̄a-
bịó-so]

3. [é-sẹks-trá-ño yaụn-r̄á-ro ke-lo-sẹk-sá-me-nez-nó-ẹŋ-káṇ-te-na-lo-ses-
tu-dịáṇ-tes]

4. [a-yá-e-nẹl-r̄áñ-ĉo-gráṇ-de   doṇ-de-bí-bẹn-los-ĉáñ-ĉos   laz-ga-yí-nas
lah-r̄á-tas i-loz-ñaṇ-dú-es]

22.11 Questions

1. /f/
2. They assimilate to and thus take the point of articulation of the
following consonant.
3. Neither /m/ nor /ñ/ end words in Spanish.
4. phonemic in that dialect
5. false
6. fewer
7. **yeísta**
8. palatal /ḷ/
9. false
10. "light"
11. word-medial intervocalic
12. false. /r/ never occurs in word-initial position.
13. fricative varieties [ɹ ɻ]
14. retroflex [r̠]
15. false. The tap [t̂] and [d̂] are equivalents.
16. [gz]
17. [ks] or [s]
18. aspirate /s/ in syllable-final position
19. **exacto** or **auxilio**
20. x is a letter of the alphabet

CHAPTER 25. /e/

Drill 25.9 H [es-té-ban-sa-kó-ẹl-pé-r̄o-a-pa-se-ár-se-por-la-ká-ye se-de-tú-bo-
por-kẹŋ-koṇ-tróụ-na-pẹ́r-la pa-re-sí-a-ke-ke-rí-a-ko-mẹ́r-la pe-ro-es-té-
ban-nó-lo-de-xó-a-sẹ́r-lo]

Exercise 25.10 C

1. /us-téd-bí-bem-pa-na-má/
2. /bés-lo-ke-á-sen/
3. /en-ké-klá-se-pién-saus-té-da-sé-ré-se-tra-bá-xo/
4. /pién-so-a-sér-lo-e-né-sa-klá-se/
5. /e-lóm-brei-sus-pa-rién-tes-bí-be-ne-ne-ló-tro-pué-blo/
6. /r̄e-kuér-de-nus-té-des-ke-las-pér-las-nó-pa-ré-sem-ba-lió-sas   pe-ro-el-
   r̄éi-las-kié-re-pa-ra-pa-gár-la-déu-da-e-neu-ró-pa/

Exercise 25.10 D

1. [us-tẹ̄d-b̶í-b̶ẹm-pa-na-má]
2. [béz-lo-ke-á-sẹn]
      s
3. [ẹŋ-ké-klá-se-pi̯ẹ́n-sau̯s-té-d̶a-sé-ré-se-tra-b̶á-xo]
4. [pi̯ẹ́n-so-a-sẹ́r-lo-e-né-sa-klá-se]
5. [e-lóm-bre̯i-sus-pa-ri̯ẹ́n-tez-b̶í-be-ne-ne-ló-tro-pu̯é-b̶lo]
      s
6. [r̄e-ku̯ẹ́r-d̶e-nus-té-d̶es-ke-las-pér-laz-nó-pa-ré-sẹm-ba-li̯ó-sas   pe-ro-ẹl-
      s
   r̄ẹ́i̯-las-ki̯é-re-pa-ra-pa-gár-la-dé̯u-d̶a-e-nẹu̯-ró-pa]

CHAPTER 26.   /a/

Drill 26.9 E   [au̯ŋ-ke-tó-d̶as-laz-mu-čá-čaz-b̶ái̯-le-na-sí nó-me-gus-ta-rá-xa-más
a-ó-ra-b̶ói̯-pa-ra-la-ká-sa kẹ-r̄á-sa-kom-pa-ñár-me]

Exercise 26.10 C   /pa-pá-bá-a-la-bá-na-pa-ra-blá-rar-nál-do-a-rá-na ál-ba-ro-
es-tá-a-lé-gre i-ki-sás-bá-a-kom-pa-ñá-ra-pa-pá-kuan-do-bá-ya bus-ka-rán-
r̄e-gá-los-pa-ra-tó-da-la-fa-mí-lia/

Exercise 26.10 D   [pa-pá-b̶á-a-la-b̶á-na-pa-ra-b̶lá-rar-nái̯-do-a-rá-na ál-b̶a-ro-es-
      s
tá-a-lé-gre i-ki-sáz-b̶á -a-kom-pa-ñá-ra-pa-pá-ku̯aṇ-do-b̶á-ya bus-ka-rán-r̄e-
gá-los-pa-ra-tó-d̶a-la-fa-mí-li̯a]

Chapter 27. /o/

Drill 27.9 G [ŷó-kré-o-ke-é-bís-tou̯-no-só-xos-ko-mo-lós-ke-é-pi̯ŋ-tá-đo-e-
nés-ta-le-yéņ-da nó-sé-si̯ęn-su̯é-ños pe-ro-yó-lo-sé-bís-to de-se-gú-ro-ke-
nó-los-po-đré-đes-kri-bír-tá-les-ku̯á-le-sé-yo-sé-ran]

Exercise 27.10 C

1. /el-dok-tór-ke-bús-ko-nó-es-tá-en-la-o-fi-sí-na-si-no-e-ne-los-pi-tál/
2. /prón-to-lo-to-mó/
3. /el-kon-gré-so-de-on-dú-ras-kom-ple-tó-tó-do-lo-po-sí-ble/
4. /e-nel-tró-pi-ko-lou-mi-yá-ron-ko-ne-ló-roi-los-fós-fo-ros-ke-r̄o-bó/

Exercise 27.10 D

1. [ęl-dok-tór-ke-bús-ko-nó-es-tá-ęn-la-o-fi-sí-na-si-no-e-ne-los-pi-tál]
2. [próņ-to-lo-to-mó]
3. [ęl-koŋ-gré-so-de-oņ-dú-ras-kom-ple-tó-tó-đo-lo-po-sí-ble]
4. [e-nęl-tró-pi-ko-lou̯-mi-yá-roŋ-ko-ne-ló-roi̯-los-fós-fo-ros-kę-r̄o-bó]

Chapter 28   /i/ and consonant /y/

Drill 28.9 G [mẹi-ma-xí-no-ke-te-í-bas-pa-ra-la-o-fi-sí-na-las-séi̯s o-a-las-si̯é-te
i-le-í-la-lę́i̯ le-ís-te-tú-laz-lé-yes bi̯é-nęm-pá-blo-yęn-r̄í-ke]

Exercise 28.10 C /ig-ná-sio-é-sum-pai-sá-no-mí-o bi-bí-a-mo-se-nel-mís-mo-
pa-ís bo-lí-bia á-se-die-si-séi-so-die-si-sié-te-á-ños yé-so-és-ko-mo-sein-
te-re-só-en-lo-sa-sún-tos-de-mia-mí-go-sói-lo   i-loim-por-tán-te-és-ke-bié-
ne-a-la-siu-dá-da-yu-dár-len-la-far-má-sia/

Exercise 28.10 D   [ig-ná-si̯o-é-sum-pai̯-sá-no-mí-o bi-bí-a-mo-se-nęl-miz-mo-
pa-ís bo-lí-bi̯a á-se-đi̯e-si-séi̯-so-đi̯e-si-si̯é-te-á-ños yé-so-és-ko-mo-sęi̯ŋ-
te-re-só-ęn-lo-sa-súņ-toz-de-mi̯a-mí-go-sói̯-lo   i-loi̯m-por-táņ-te-és-ke-bi̯é-
ne-a-la-si̯u-đá-da-yu-đár-lo-ęn-la-far-má-si̯a] ^s

Chapter 29. /u/ and consonant /w/

Drill 29.9 G [es-tói̯-se-gú-ro-ke-é-se-tra-bá-xo-nó-éh-r̄i-đí-ku-lo-ni-đú-ro   tu-
bís-te-tú-ke-a-sér-lo-des-pu̯éz-đe-la-pe-lí-ku-la sí éz-la-pú-ra-bęr-đáđ]

Exercise 29.10 C

1. /aun-ke-nó-sé-a-la-káu-sa-de-la-déu-da lou-mí-ya-mú-ĉo/
2. /la-pe-lí-ku-lau-nes-tá-e-nel-sí-neu-ró-pa/
3. /bá-mo-sa-to-má-re-láu-to ú-go/
4. /bué-no pú-se-lá-gua-kí i-wé-le-a-ú-mo/
5. /kui-dá-do a-kí-ú-bou-nak-si-dén-te-de-guá-gua-sá-seu-nos-dí-as/
6. /kuán-tos-kié-res sié-te-wó-ĉo/
7. /pués nó-és-ni-bué-no-ni-fuér-te-ni-suá-be-niú-til/

Exercise 29.10 D

1. [auŋ-ke-nó-sé-a-la-káu̯-sa-de-la-déu̯-da lou̯-mí-ya-mú-ĉo]
2. [la-pe-lí-ku-lau̯-nes-tá-e-nel̯-sí-neu̯-ró-pa]
3. [bá-mo-sa-to-má-re-láu̯-to ú-go]
4. [bu̯é-no pú-se-lá-gu̯a-kí i-wé-le-a-ú-mo]
5. [ku̯i-dá-do a-kí-ú-bou̯-nak-si-déṇ-te-de-gu̯á-gu̯a-sá-seu̯-noz-dí-as]
6. [ku̯áṇ-tos-ki̯é-res si̯é-te-wó-ĉo]
7. [pu̯és nó-éz-ni-bu̯é-no-ni-fu̯ér-te-ni-su̯á-be-ni̯ú-til]

CHAPTER 30.   VOWEL COMBINATIONS

Drill 30 K [kré-o-kéz-de-é-ya la-í-xa-ęm-bi̯ó-ęl-ba-ú-la-sus-pa-ri̯éṇ-tes sói̯s-
  mu̯í-ál̯-tos pe-ke-ñu̯é-los kre-ré-ke-la̍-bri-rá-ku̯aṇ-do-lo-bé-a]

Exercise 30 C

1. /la-á-ma-kon-tó-da-suál-ma/
2. /nó-kré-o-ke-los-po-é-tas-se-pa-sé-em-po-rés-ta-be-ní-da/
3. /me-sién-to-a-o-gá-do/
4. /mei-ma-xí-no-ke-te-í-ba-sa-lau-nión/
5. /ke-rí-a-die-si-séis o-die-si-sié-te pe-ro-nó-á-ya-kí-más-ke-kín-se/
6. /pién-so-ke-és-des-pá-ña/
7. /suá-be-és-suá-be/
8. /yé-so-nó-es-yé-so/
9. /sién-tras lo-sién-tes/
10. /sa-be-él-ke-la-kó-sa-nó-pué-de-mé-nos-dem-pe-o-rár/

Exercise 30 D

1. [lá-ma-koṇ-tó-đa-su̯ál-ma]
2. [nó-kré-o-ke-los-pu̯é-tas-se-pa-sém-po-rés-ta- be-ní-đa]
3. [me-si̯éṇ-to-au̯-gá-đo]
   $\overset{u̯}{}$
4. [me̯i-ma-xí-no-ke-te-í-ba-sa-lau̯-ni̯ón]
   $\overset{øi \qquad\qquad ø}{}$
5. [ke-rí-a-di̯e-si-sé̯is o-di̯e-si-si̯é-te pe-ro-nó-a-ya-kí-más-ke-kín-se]
6. [pi̯én-so-kéz-đes-pá-ña]
7. [su̯á-bés-su̯á-be]
8. [yé-so-nói̯z-yé-so]
   $\overset{s \quad ŷ}{}$
9. [si̯éṇ-tras lo-si̯éṇ-tes]
10. [sa-bél-ke-la-kó-sa-nó-pu̯é-đe-mé-noz-đem-pi̯o-rár]

CHAPTER 31. CONSONANT + VOWEL COMBINATIONS

Drill 31 G [e-lí-xo-es-tá-ba-e-ne-lá-gua lo-sa-lúm-no-ses-tá-ne-le-láu̯-la i-bá-na-blá-res-pa-ñól-kon-lo-sar-tís-ta-ses-pa-ñó-les la-sá-bez-bí-be-nu-na-xáu̯-la]

Exercise 31 B

1. /e-lóm-bre-í-ba-de-sa-tá-re-ló-so/
2. /e-lé-no-es-tá-sé-ko po-ré-so-bá-mo-sa-po-nér-lo-e-nel-pa-xár/
3. /la-sak-sió-nes-de-lo-sa-lúm-nos-só-ni-na-pli-ká-ble-se-nés-te-ká-so/
4. /los-su-bor-di-ná-dos-som-bié-na-ben-tu-rá-dos/
5. /te-nó-xas-kuan-do-lo-pón-go-e-nó-xas/
6. /e-lá-do-nó-me-per-mí-te-ko-mé-re-lá-do/
7. /e-lí-xo-dí-xo e-lí-xo/

Exercise 31 C

1. [e-lóm-bre-í-ba-de-sa-tá-re-ló-so]
2. [e-lé-no-es-tá-sé-ko po-ré-so-bá-mo-sa-po-nér̯-lo-e-nel-pa-xár]
3. [la-sak-si̯ó-nez-đe-lo-sa-lúm-nos-só-ni-na-pli-ká-ble-se-nés-te-ká-so]
4. [los-su-bor-di-ná-đos-sóm-bi̯é-na-beṇ-tu-rá-đos]
5. [te-nó-xas-ku̯aṇ-do-lo-póŋ-go-e-nó-xas]
6. [e-lá-đo-nó-me-per̯-mí-te-ko-mé-re-lá-đo]
7. [e-lí-xo-đí-xo e-lí-xo]

CHAPTER 32.   REVIEW OF VOWELS /e a o i u/, CONSONANTS /y w/, VOWEL

COMBINATIONS, AND CONSONANT + VOWEL COMBINATIONS

Exercise 32.10 C

1. /pa-pá-bá-a-la-bá-na-blá-rar-nál-do-a-rá-na ke-és-des-pá-ña/
2. /bí-la-es-tá-tuaim-mó-bil/
3. /é-sum-móns-truou-má-no/
4. /dá-me-ú-no-wó-tro/
5. /pe-ro-nó-á-ya-kí-nin-gú-no/
6. /es-tú-diaus-té-dis-tó-ria/
7. /es-tú-dieus-té-dés-to/
8. /yá-es-tu-dióu-ti-li-ta-rís-mo/
9. /ye-bá-be-suan-tí-guou-ni-fór-me-a-lan-tí-guau-sán-sa/
10. /é-só-sioi-nú-til/

Exercise 32.10 D

1. [pa-pá-ƀá-a-la-ƀá-na-a-ƀlá-rar-náḷ-do-a-rá-na ke-éz-đes-pá-ña]
2. [bí-la-es-tá-tu̯ai̯m-mó-ƀil]
3. [é-sum-móns-tru̯ou̯-má-no]
4. [dá-me-ú-no-wó-tro]
5. [pe-ro-nó-á-ya-kí-niŋ-gú-no]
6. [es-tú-đi̯au̯s-té-dis-tó-ri̯a]
7. [es-tú-đi̯eu̯s-té-đés-to]
8. [yá-es-tu-đi̯óu̯-ti-li-ta-ríz-mo]   ŷ   s
9. [ye-ƀá-ƀa-su̯aṇ-tí-gu̯ou̯-ni-fór-me-a-laṇ-tí-gu̯au̯-sán-sa]   ŷ
10. [é-só-si̯oi̯-nú-til]

32.11 Questions

1. the shape of the resonance chambers (oral cavity and pharynx)
2. consonants, vowels
3. end syllables
4. always represents them
5 false
6 false. English /e/ resembles both of them.

7. the tongue is higher or lower in the mouth

8. checked or closed by consonants other than [s] or [z]

9. true

10. /y/

11. /a/

12. /ɔ/, /a/

13. /a/, /i/, and /e/

14. /eu/ (like English /ew/) and /o/ sometimes contrast in Spanish.

15. create forms which do not exist in Spanish

16. /iy/

17. Unstressed /i/ does not occur between vowels. It is replaced by /y/.

18. more open

19. It has the complex vowel nucleus /iy/, but Spanish **bis** has the simple vowel /i/.

20. [CVyV], as in **patio** *[pá-tɨ-yo]

21. have an accent mark

22. [uw] or [ɨw]

23. [ɨ]

24. [CVwV], as in **fuera** *[fu-wé-ra] or *[fɨ-wé-ra]

25. **película, ridículo, museo,** etc.

26. glottal stop

27. word boundaries

28. stress, style of speech

29. diphthong or triphthong

30. They pronounce the word [ęm-bi-á-mos] through analogy with **envío** [ęm-bí-o], **envía** [ęm-bí-a], etc., where the consonant plus /í/ forms a separate syllable.

31. word boundaries

32. exactly alike

33. false. The consonant is pronounced with the next vowel, although in dividing the word in *writing* the prefix may be indicated: **mal-estar.**

34. It begins with a sequence of sounds that is never used to begin words in English.

35. */ii/, */uu/

36. No. The unstressed /i/ of **hay,** now intervocalic, is replaced by the consonant /y/. This intervocalic consonant /y/ goes with the next vowel to form a separate syllable [á-ya-ni-má-les].

CHAPTER 34. STRESS

Exercise 34 A (Stresses on the words that do not carry written accents in regular writing are enclosed in parentheses.)

1. Se comun'í'ca con los ingl'é'ses por m'é'dio del teléfono.
2. Sí, 'é's lo que ll'á'man ust'é'des un carácter, pero ten'é'mos m'ú'chos caract'é'res como él por aquí.
3. Imagínese que y'á' se v'á' la señ'ó'ra Martínez.
4. El ch'í'co cuyo p'á'dre 'é'ra el candid'á'to demócrata el 'á'ño pas'á'do es al'ú'mno m'í'o.
5. —¿Ti'é'nes sufici'é'nte pap'é'l? —Sí, 'é'sta c'á'ja me b'á'sta.
6. —Figúrese, me contó la anécdota en que n'ó' pudi'é'ron encontr'á'r el antídoto a ti'é'mpo.
7. —Solic'í'to ay'ú'da de unos al'ú'mnos que s'é'an mu'ý', mu'ý' dilig'é'ntes, con m'ú'cha responsabilid'á'd. —¿Los h'á's encontr'á'do? —Todavía n'ó' y fr'á'ncam'é'nte n'ó' me lo expl'í'co.
8. —Cel'é'bre ust'é'd la lleg'á'da de un h'ó'mbre tan célebre. —Y'á' lo celebré.

CHAPTER 35. INTONATION: PITCH AND JUNCTURE

Drill 35 Q   [ku̯áṇ-to-sá-ños-ti̯é-ne̯us-té̯d

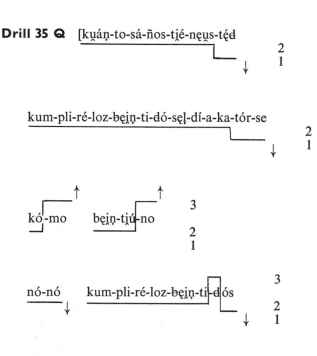

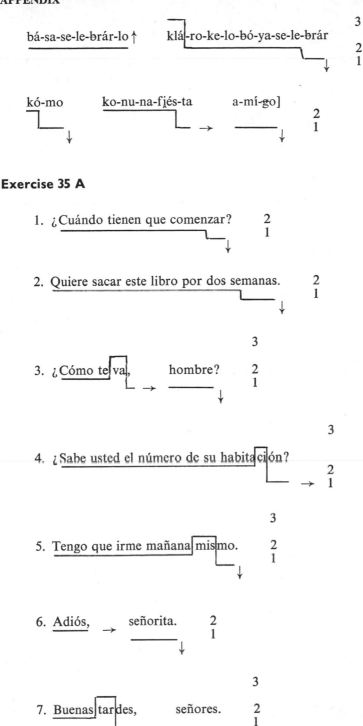

bá-sa-se-le-brár-lo ↑   klá-ro-ke-lo-bó-ya-se-le-brár   3 2 1

kó-mo   ko-nu-na-fi̯és-ta   a-mí-go]   2 1

Exercise 35 A

1. ¿Cuándo tienen que comenzar?   2 1

2. Quiere sacar este libro por dos semanas.   2 1

3. ¿Cómo te va,   hombre?   3 2 1

4. ¿Sabe usted el número de su habitación?   3 2 1

5. Tengo que irme mañana mismo.   3 2 1

6. Adiós,   señorita.   2 1

7. Buenas tardes,   señores.   3 2 1

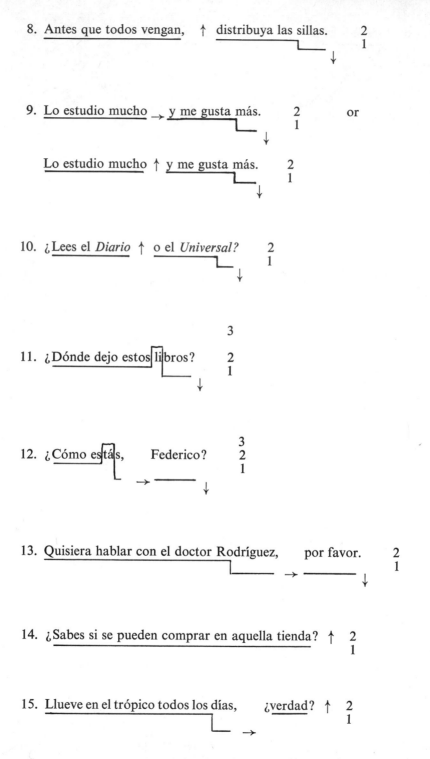

8. Antes que todos vengan, ↑ distribuya las sillas.   2
                                                       1

9. Lo estudio mucho → y me gusta más.   2   or
                                         1

   Lo estudio mucho ↑ y me gusta más.   2
                                         1

10. ¿Lees el *Diario* ↑ o el *Universal?*   2
                                             1

                                         3
11. ¿Dónde dejo estos libros?   2
                                 1

                                         3
12. ¿Cómo estás,   Federico?   2
                                 1

13. Quisiera hablar con el doctor Rodríguez,   por favor.   2
                                                             1

14. ¿Sabes si se pueden comprar en aquella tienda? ↑   2
                                                       1

15. Llueve en el trópico todos los días,   ¿verdad? ↑   2
                                                         1

CHAPTER 37   REVIEW OF SUPRASEGMENTALS: STRESS, INTONATION, AND
            RHYTHM

Exercise 37A

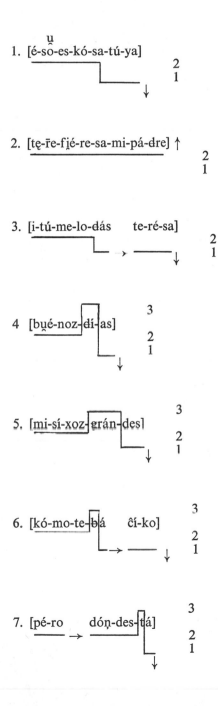

1. [é-so-es-kó-sa-tú-ya]
    2
    1

2. [tẹ-r̄e-fịé-re-sa-mi-pá-dre] ↑
    2
    1

3. [i-tú-me-lo-dás   te-ré-sa]
    2
    1

4 [bṵé-noz-dí-as]
    3
    2
    1

5. [mi-sí-xoz-grán-des]
    3
    2
    1

6. [kó-mo-te-bá   ĉí-ko]
    3
    2
    1

7. [pé-ro   dón-des-tá]
    3
    2
    1

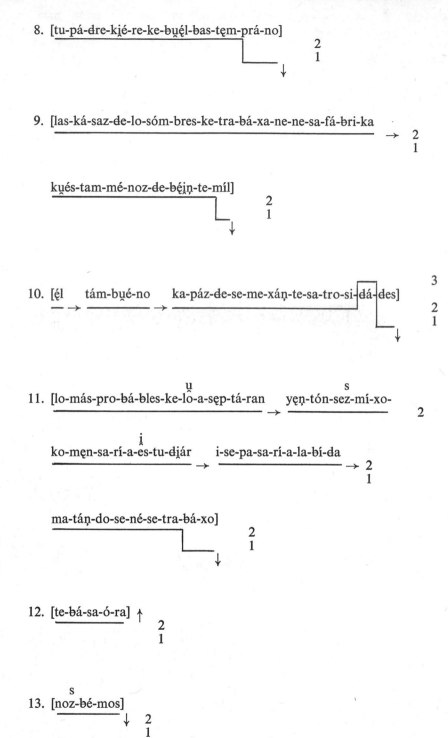

8. [tu-pá-dre-ki̯é-re-ke-bu̯él-bas-tem-prá-no]
2
1

9. [las-ká-saz-de-lo-sóm-bres-ke-tra-bá-xa-ne-ne-sa-fá-bri-ka → 2
1

ku̯és-tam-mé-noz-de-béi̯n-te-míl]
2
1

10. [él → tám-bu̯é-no → ka-páz-de-se-me-xán-te-sa-tro-si-dá-des]
3
2
1

11. [lo-más-pro-bá-bles-ke-lo-a-sep-tá-ran yen-tón-sez-mí-xo-
   u̯   s
→ 2

ko-men-sa-rí-a-es-tu-di̯ár i-se-pa-sa-rí-a-la-bí-da → 2
   i   1

ma-tán-do-se-né-se-tra-bá-xo]
2
1

12. [te-bá-sa-ó-ra] ↑
2
1

13. [noz-bé-mos]
   s
↓ 2
1

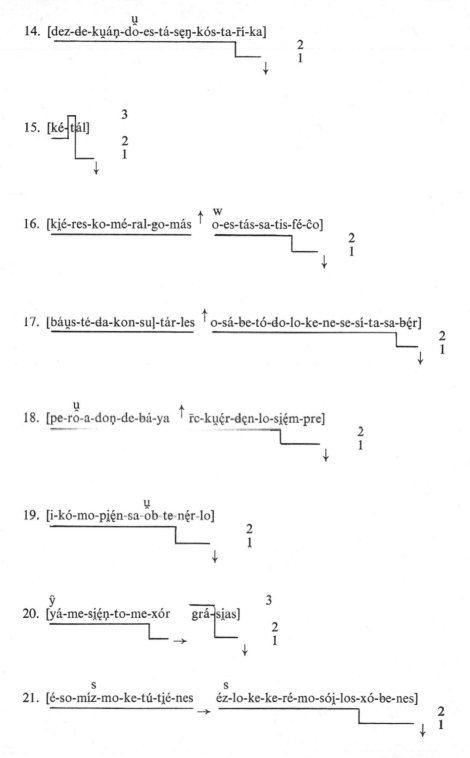

14. [dez-de-kųáṇ-dô-es-tá-sęŋ-kós-ta-r̄í-ka]

15. [ké-tál]

16. [kįé-res-ko-mé-ral-go-más ↑ ᵂo-es-tás-sa-tis-fé-ĉo]

17. [báųs-té-đa-kon-suḷ-tár-les ↑ o-sá-ƀe-tó-đo-lo-ke-ne-se-sí-ta-sa-ƀę́r]

18. [pe-rô-a-doṇ-de-ƀá-ya ↑ r̄c-kųę́r-đeṇ-lo-sįę́m-pre]

19. [i-kó-mo-pįę́n-sa-ob-te-nę́r-lo]

20. [yá-me-sįę́ṇ-to-me-xór grá-sįas]

21. [é-so-míz-mo-ke-tú-tįé-nes → ᵉz-lo-ke-ke-ré-mo-sój̦-los-xó-ƀe-nes]

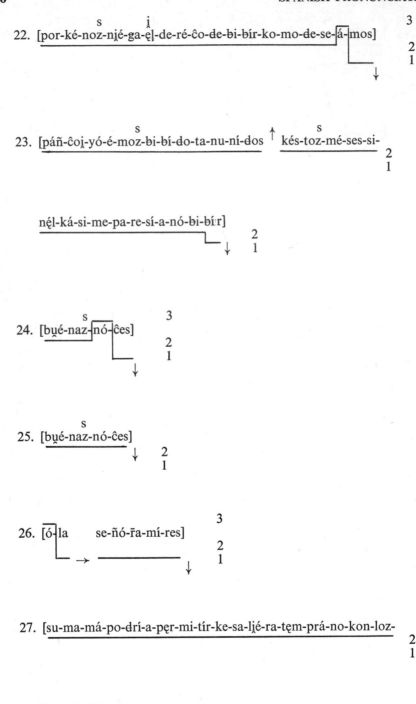

22. [por-ké-noz-nị̧é-ga-ȩ̣l-de-ré-ĉo-de-bi-bír-ko-mo-de-se-á-mos]

23. [páñ-ĉoị-yó-é-moz-bi-bí-do-ta-nu-ní-dos ↑ kés-toz-mé-ses-si-

nȩ̣l-ká-si-me-pa-re-sí-a-nó-bi-bír]

24. [bụé-naz-nó-ĉes]

25. [bụé-naz-nó-ĉes]

26. [ó-la   se-ñó-r̄a-mí-res]

27. [su-ma-má-po-đrí-a-pẹr-mi-tír-ke-sa-lị̧é-ra-tẹm-prá-no-kon-loz-

đe-más-ĉí-kos] ↑

28. [los-pro-fe-só-rez-de-si-djé-ron-sus-peŋ-dér-las-klá-se-sem-bís-

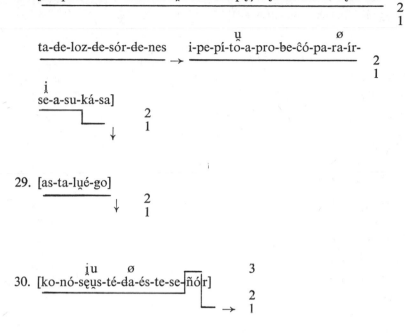

37. **Questions**

1. amplitude
2. phonemic
3. tertiary
4. It is phrase-bound since it is a form which can occur only with a verb and never in isolation.
5. false, although they are the same thing in English
6. relative
7. /3/
8. pitch, volume, and tempo
9. last
10. false
11. that in English they usually end on pitch level /2/ with a terminal rise /↑/ or on pitch level /3/ with a terminal fall /↓/ whereas in Spanish they usually end on pitch level /2/ with a terminal fall /↓/
12. shortened (compressed, squeezed), /ɨ ə/
13. the same length
14. syllables, beats (heavy stresses)

15. organized systematically (into "-emic" units)
16. **aguda** (last-syllable-stressed)

CHAPTER 39.   SPANISH ORTHOGRAPHY

Exercise 39 A

1. (no written accent)
2. (no written accent)
3. **jóvenes** (rule 3)
4. **riquísimo** (rule 3)
5. (no written accent)
6. **fácil** (rule 2)
7. **difíciles** (rule 3)
8. **ángel** (rule 2)
9. (no written accent)
10. **nácar** (rule 2)
11. (no written accent)
12. (no written accent)
13. **análisis** (rule 3)
14. (no written accent)
15. **rápidamente** (As far as stress goes, this is considered to be a compound word with two primary stresses. Rule 3 governs the use of the written accent in the first part, **rápida-**.)
16. **oíste** (rule 4)
17. **teólogo** (rule 3)
18. (no written accent)
19. (no written accent, although **fuí** had a written accent in materials published before widespread observation of the Spanish Academy's orthographical revisions of 1952.)
20. **lápiz** (rule 2)
21. **prevé** (rule 1)
22. **píen** (rule 4)
23. (no written accent)
24. (no written accent)
25. (no written accent)
26. **dónde** (rule 6)
27. **déme** (rule 5)

28. (no written accents)

29. **sólo** (rule 7), **dominó** (rule 1)

30. (no written accents)

31. **Levantándote** (rule 3), **podrás** (rule 1)

32. **policía** (rule 4)

33. **aquí** (rule 1)

34. **sé** (rule 5), **cuándo** (rule 6)

35. **día** (rule 4), **estaré** (rule 1), **allí** (rule 1)

36. **sabré** (rule 1), **qué** (rule 6)

37. **sí** (rule 5), **sabrás** (rule 1)

38. (no written accents)

39. **ése** (rule 7), **tú** (rule 5)

40. **ésta** (rule 7)

41. **llegó** (rule 1), **psicólogo** (rule 3), **tontísimas** (rule 3)

42. **acróbata** (rule 3), **llamó** (rule 1), **teléfono** (rule 3), **comunicó** (rule 1), **farmacéutico** (rule 3), **pidió** (rule 1), **antídoto** (rule 3)

43. **discutirán** (rule 1), **hegemonía** (rule 4)

44. **canción** (rule 1), **Melodía** (rule 4), **melancolía** (rule 4)

45. **diré** (rule 1), **cómo** (rule 6), **completó** (rule 1)

E. BIBLIOGRAPHY

The following references are divided into two groups: those dealing principally with Spanish phonology and those dealing with English phonology or related general linguistic areas. References marked with a * are relatively nontechnical and are recommended for beginners in Spanish linguistics. Others are best consulted by students who already have had work in linguistics. With a few exceptions, works which treat specific dialects of Spanish have been omitted.

SPANISH

* Agard, Frederick B., "Present-Day Judaeo-Spanish in the United States." *Hispania* 33 (1950): 203–10.
* ———, "Pronunciation and Spelling." *Modern Approach to Spanish.* New York: Holt, Rinehart and Winston, 1964, pp. 521–59.
  ———, "Stress in Four Romance Languages." *Glossa* 1 (1967): 150–200.
  Alarcos Llorach, Emilio, "Algunas cuestiones fonológicas del español de hoy." *Presente y futuro de la lengua española,* II: 151–61.
  ———, *Fonología española,* 4a ed. Madrid: Gredos, 1965.
  ———, "El sistema fonológico español." *Revista de Filología Española* 33 (1949): 265–96.

Allen, J. H. D., Jr., "Tense/Lax in Castilian Spanish." *Word* 20 (1964): 295–321.

Alonso, Amado, *Estudios lingüísticos: Temas hispanoamericanos.* Madrid: Gredos, 1953.

———, "Una ley fonológica del español." *Hispanic Review* 13 (1945): 91–101.

———, "Nota sobre una ley fonológica del español." *Hispanic Review* 15 (1947): 306–07.

* Alonso, María Rosa, *Apuntes de ortografía para uso de principiantes.* Mérida, Venezuela: Universidad de los Andes, 1965.

Alvar, Manual, "Estado actual de los atlas lingüísticos españoles." *Arbor* 63 (1966): 5–28.

Anderson, James M., "Repetitions of Phonetic Change in Spanish." *Phonetica* 14 (1966): 16–19.

* Ayer, George W., "An Auditory Discrimination Test Based on Spanish." *Modern Language Journal* 44 (1960): 227–30.

Bäckvall, H., "¿Es únicamente francés el fenómeno llamado *liaison?*" *Moderna Språk* 61 (1967): 283–92.

* Beberfall, Lester, "The 'Indispensable' Accent Mark in the Spanish Language." *Modern Language Journal* 43 (1959): 289–94.

* ———, "A Note on the *Nuevas normas de prosodia y ortografía* (1959)." *Hispania* 45 (1962): 504–08.

* ———, "The Qualitative Aspect of Spanish Diphthongs." *Modern Language Journal* 48 (1964): 136–41.

* ———, " 'Y' and 'll' in Relaxed Spanish Speech." *Hispania* 44 (1961): 505–09.

Bès, Gabriel G., "Examen del concepto de rehilamiento." *Thesaurus* 19 (1964): 18–42.

* Besso, Henry V., "Situación actual del judeo-español." *Presente y futuro de la lengua española,* I: 307–24.

Beym, Richard, "*Porteño* /s/ and [h] [ȟ] [s] [x] [Ø] as Variants." *Lingua* 12 (1963): 199–204.

* ———, "Practical Phonological Orientation for Effective Spoken Spanish." *Hispania* 43 (1960): 67–69.

* Bolinger, Dwight L., "Evidence on *x.*" *Hispania* 35 (1952): 49–63.

* ———, "The Pronunciation of *x* and Puristic Anti-Purism." *Hispania* 35 (1952): 442–44. [Letter to the editor.]

———, " 'Secondary Stress' in Spanish." *Romance Philology* 15 (1962): 273–79.

* ———, "Stress on Normally Unstressed Elements." *Hispania* 39 (1956): 105–06.

* ———, "That 'x' Again." *Hispania* 31 (1948): 449–50. [Letter to the editor.]

* ———, et al., *Modern Spanish.* New York: Harcourt, Brace, 1960.

* ———, Joan E. Ciruti, and Hugo H. Montero, *Modern Spanish*, 2nd ed. New York: Harcourt, Brace and World, 1966.

* Bowen, J. Donald, "A Comparison of the Intonation Patterns of English and Spanish." *Hispania* 39 (1956): 30–35.

* ———, "Sequences of Vowels in Spanish." *Boletín de Filología* 9 (1956–57): 5–14.

* ———, "Teaching Spanish Diphthongs." *Hispania* 46 (1963): 795–800.

* ———, and Robert P. Stockwell. "A Further Note on Spanish Semivowels." *Language* 32 (1956): 290–92.

* ———, and ———, "Orthography and Respelling in Teaching Spanish." *Hispania* 40 (1957): 200–05.

* ———, and ———, *Patterns of Spanish Pronunciation.* Chicago: University of Chicago Press, 1960.

* Bowen, J. Donald, and Robert P. Stockwell, "The Phonemic Interpretation of Semivowels in Spanish." *Language* 31 (1955): 236–40.
* Bull, William E., *Spanish for Teachers: Applied Linguistics.* New York: Ronald Press, 1965.
  Campbell, R. Joe, "Phonological Analyses of Spanish." *Dissertation Abstracts* 27 (1967): 2137A (U. of Illinois).
* Canfield, D. Lincoln, "Andalucismos en la pronunciación hispanoamericana." *Kentucky Foreign Language Quarterly* 8 (1961): 177–81.
  ———, "The Diachronic Dimension of 'Synchronic' Hispanic Dialectology." *Linguistics* 7 (1964): 5–9.
* ———, *La pronunciación del español en América.* Bogotá: Instituto Caro y Cuervo, 1962.
* ———, "Trends in American Castilian." *Hispania* 50 (1967): 912–18.
  Cárdenas, Daniel N., "Acoustic Vowel Loops of Two Spanish Idiolects." *Phonetica* 5 (1960): 9–34.
* ———, *Applied Linguistics: Spanish, a Guide for Teachers,* ed. Simon Belasco. Boston: D.C. Heath, 1961.
* ———, "The Geographic Distribution of the Assibilated *R, RR* in Spanish America." *Orbis* 7 (1958): 407–14.
* ———, *Introducción a una comparación fonológica del español y del inglés.* Washington: MLA Center for Applied Linguistics, 1960.
* Casares, Julio, "Las *Nuevas normas de prosodia y ortografía.*" *Boletín de la Real Academia Española* 38 (1958): 331–42.
* ———, "Las *Nuevas normas de prosodia y ortografía* y su repercusión en América." *Boletín de la Real Academia Española* 35 (1955): 321–46.
  Contreras, Heles, "The Neutralization of Stress in Chilean Spanish." *Phonetica* 13 (1965): 27–30.
  ———, "Sobre el acento en español." *Boletín de Filología* 15 (1963): 223–37.
  ———, "¿Tiene el español un acento de intensidad?" *Boletín de Filología* 16 (1964): 237–39.
* Davis, J. Cary, "*A* as in Father." *Hispania* 42 (1959): 373–76.
  Delattre, Pierre, *Comparing the Phonetic Features of English, French, German, and Spanish: An Interim Report.* Heidelberg: Julius Groos Verlag, 1965.
  ———, "A Comparison of Syllable Length Conditioning Among Languages." *International Review of Applied Linguistics* 4 (1966): 183–98.
* ———, " 'Spanish is a Phonetic Language'." *Hispania* 18 (1945): 511–16.
* ———, Carroll Olsen, and Elmer Poenack, "A Comparative Study of Declarative Intonation in American English and Spanish." *Hispania* 45 (1962): 233–41.
  Dykstra, Gerald, "Spectographic Analysis of Spanish Sibilants and its Relation to Navarro's Physiological Phonetic Description." *Dissertation Abstracts* 15 (1955): 1394 (U. of Michigan).
* Feldman, David M., "A Comparison of the Segmental Phonemes of Brazilian Portuguese and American Spanish." *Linguistics* 29 (1967): 44–57.
  Fernández, Joseph A., "La anticipación vocálica en español." *Revista de Filología Española* 46 (1963): 437–40.
* Fernández, Salvador, "Para la futura gramática." *Boletín de la Real Academia Española* 44 (1964): 431–48.
  Fischer, Milla, "Verification of a Suggested Hierarchy of Problems Encountered by English Speakers Learning Spanish Phonology: Dialectical Case Studies." *Dissertation Abstracts* 27 (1966): 758A (Georgetown).

* Foster, David W., "A Note on the /ŷ/ Phoneme of *Porteño* Spanish." *Hispania* 50 (1967): 119–21.

* García de Diego, Vicente, *Manual de dialectología española,* 2a ed. Madrid: Ediciones Cultura Hispánica, 1959.

* Gili Gaya, Samuel, *Elementos de fonética general.* Madrid: Gredos, 1950.

Gurren, Louise, "A Comparison on a Phonetic Basis of the Two Chief Languages of the Americas, English and Spanish." *Dissertation Abstracts* 15 (1955): 1849–50 (N.Y.U.).

* Hefler, Alden R., and Frank R. Thompson, "Seseo vs. θ in the Classroom." *Modern Language Journal* 27 (1943): 500–01.

Henríquez Ureña, Pedro, "Observaciones sobre el español de América." *Revista de Filología Española* 8 (1921): 357–90.

* Hoge, Henry W., "Testing in the Language Laboratory: a Laboratory Experiment in Spanish Pronunciation." *Hispania* 42 (1959): 147–52.

* Hyman, Ruth L., "[ŋ] as an Allophone Denoting Open Juncture in Several Spanish-American Dialects." *Hispania* 39 (1956): 293–99.

* Jones, Willis K., "What Spanish Pronunciation Shall We Teach?" *Hispania* 24 (1941): 253–60.

Kahane, Henry R., and Richard Beym, "Syntactical Juncture in Colloquial Mexican Spanish." *Language* 24 (1948): 388–96.

* Kiddle, Lawrence B., "On Phonemes and Allophones." *Hispania* 39 (1956): 325–27. [Letter to the editor.]

* Lado, Robert, "A Comparison of the Sound Systems of English and Spanish." *Hispania* 39 (1956): 126–29.

* _____, *Linguistics Across Cultures: Applied Linguistics for Language Teachers.* Ann Arbor: University of Michigan Press, 1957.

Lapesa, Rafael, "Sobre el ceceo y el seseo en Hispanoamérica." *Revista Ibero-americana* 21 (1956): 409–16.

* Lundeberg, Olav K., "What is *ceceo*? Inquiry and Proposal." *Hispania* 30 (1947): 368–73.

Malmberg, Bertil, "L'espagnol dans le Nouveau Monde—problème de linguistique générale." *Studia Linguistica* 1 (1947): 79–116, 2 (1948): 1–36.

_____, *Estudios de fonética hispánica,* tr. Edgardo R. Palavecino. Madrid: Consejo Superior de Investigaciones Científicas, 1965.

_____, "*Obtativo y sujuntivo:* A propósito de dos grafías." *Revista de Filología Española* 48 (1965): 185–87.

_____, "Phonèmes labio-vélaires en espagnol?" *Phonetica* 7 (1961): 85–94.

_____, "La structure syllabique de l'espagnol. Étude de phonétique." *Boletim de Filologia* 9 (1948): 99–120.

Martin, John W., "Distinctive-Feature Systems of English and Spanish," supplement in Stockwell and Bowen, *The Sounds of English and Spanish,* pp. 139–63.

* Matluck, Joseph H., "Entonación hispánica." *Anuario de Letras* (Facultad de Filosofía y Letras de la Universidad Nacional de México) 5 (1965): 5–32.

* _____, "The Presentation of Spanish Pronunciation in American Textbooks." *Modern Language Journal* 41 (1957): 219–28.

* Navarro, Tomás, *Estudios de fonología española.* Syracuse: Syracuse University Press, 1946.

* _____, "La *g* de 'examen'." *Hispania* 45 (1962): 314–16.

_____, *Manual de entonación española,* 2a ed. New York: Hispanic Institute, 1948.

* Navarro, Tomás, *Manual de pronunciación española,* 5a ed. New York: Hafner, 1957.

———, "La medida de intensidad." *Boletín de Filología* 16 (1964): 231–35.

* ———, "The Old Aspirated *h* in Spain and in the Spanish of America." *Word* 5 (1949): 166–69.

* ———, "La pronunciación de la x y la investigación fonética." *Hispania* 35 (1952): 330–31. [Letter to the editor.]

* O'Connor, Patricia, Ernest F. Haden, and Frank Durand, "Introduction to Spanish Pronunciation" in *Oral Drill in Spanish,* 2nd ed. Boston: Houghton Mifflin, 1963, pp. 155–76.

* Politzer, Robert L., and Charles N. Staubach, *Teaching Spanish: A Linguistic Orientation,* revised ed. Boston: Blaisdell, 1965.

Predmore, Richard L., "Notes on Spanish Consonant Phonemes." *Hispanic Review* 14 (1946): 169–72.

* ———, "One More Look at the Pronunciation of *x* Before a Consonant." *Hispania* 32 (1949): 344–45. [Letter to the editor.]

* ———, "The Pronunciation of X Before Another Consonant." *Hispania* 31 (1948): 196–97. [Letter to the editor.]

Presente y futuro de la lengua española, 2 vols. Madrid: Oficina Internacional de Información y Observación del Español, 1964.

Quilis, Antonio, "La juntura en español: un problema de fonología." *Presente y futuro de la lengua española,* II: 163–71.

———, "Phonologie de la quantité en espagnol." *Phonetica* 13 (1965): 82–85.

* ———, and Joseph A. Fernández, *Curso de fonética y fonología españolas para estudiantes angloamericanos,* 2a ed. Madrid: Consejo Superior de Investigaciones Cientfícas, 1966.

Rabanales, Ambrosio, "Las siglas: un problema de fonología española. *Boletín de Filología* 15 (1963): 327–42.

⁺ Real Academia, "Nuevas normas de prosodia y ortografía (nuevo texto definitivo)." *Boletín de la Real Academia Española* 38 (1958): 343–47.

Rona, José P., "El problema de la división del español americano en zonas dialectales." *Presente y futuro de la lengua española,* I: 216–26.

* Rosenblat, Angel, *Las nuevas normas ortográficas y prosódicas de la Academia Española.* Caracas: Universidad Central de Venezuela, 1953.

* Sacks, Norman P., "The Pattern Drill and the Rationale of the Prosodic and Orthographic Accents in Spanish." *Hispania* 46 (1963): 361–72.

* ———, "A Study in Spanish Pronunciation Errors." *Hispania* 45 (1962): 289–300.

* Sáenz, Gerardo, "There is no 'eggs' in *examen.*" *Hispania* 44 (1961): 510–11.

Sapon, Stanley M., "Étude instrumentale de quelques contours mélodiques fondamentaux dans les langues romanes." *Revista de Filología Española* 42 (1958–59): 167–75.

* Saporta, Sol, "A Note on Spanish Semivowels." *Language* 32 (1956): 287–90.

———, and Rita Cohen, "The Distribution and Relative Frequency of Spanish Diphthongs," *Romance Philology* 11 (1957–58): 371–77.

* Sawyer, Janet B., "The Distribution of Some Consonant Allophones in Spanish." *Language Learning* 7, iii–iv (1956–57): 89–98.

* Serís, Homero, *Bibliografía de la lingüística española.* Bogotá: Instituto Caro y Cuervo, 1964.

* Silva-Fuenzalida, Ismael, "La entonación en el español y su morfología." *Boletín de Filología* 9 (1956–57): 177–87.

* Silva-Fuenzalida, Ismael, "Spanish Section" in *Manual and Anthology of Applied Linguistics—For Use in the NDEA Foreign Language Institutes,* ed. Simon Belasco. Washington: U.S. Dept. of Health, Education, and Welfare, 1960.

Skelton, Robert B., "Phonetics, Phonemics, and Pronunciation: Dialect and Standard Language." *Applied Linguistics in Language Teaching,* ed. Ernst Pulgram. (Georgetown University Monograph Series on Languages and Linguistics 6.) Washington: Georgetown University, 1954.

* Stockwell, Robert P., "On Phonemes and Allophones." *Hispania* 39 (1956): 325–27. [Letter to the editor.]

* _____, and J. Donald Bowen, *The Sounds of English and Spanish.* Chicago: University of Chicago Press, 1965.

* _____, _____, and Ismael Silva-Fuenzalida, "Spanish Juncture and Intonation." *Language* 32 (1956): 641–65.

* Trager, George L., "The Phonemes of Castilian Spanish." *Travaux du Cercle Linguistique de Prague* 8 (1939): 217–22.

* Wallis, Ethel, "Intonational Stress Patterns of Contemporary Spanish." *Hispania* 34 (1951): 143–47.

* _____, and William E. Bull, "Spanish Adjective Position: Phonetic Stress and Emphasis." *Hispania* 33 (1950): 221–29.

* Wilkins, George W., Jr., and E. Lee Hoffman, "The Use of Cognates in Testing Pronunciation." *Language Learning* 14, i-ii (1964): 39–44.

* Wright, Leavitt O., "Five Spanish *R*'s: How to Approach Them." *Hispania* 45 (1962): 742–43.

* Zamora Vicente, Alonso, *Dialectología española.* Madrid: Gredos, 1960.

ENGLISH AND GENERAL

Abercrombie, David, *Elements of General Phonetics.* Chicago: Aldine Publishing Co., 1967.

* Albright, Robert W., *The International Phonetic Alphabet: Its Backgrounds and Development.* Bloomington: Indiana University Research Center in Anthropology, Folklore and Linguistics, no. 7, 1958.

* Anderson, Wallace L., and Norman C. Stageberg, *Introductory Readings on Language,* 2nd ed. New York: Holt, Rinehart and Winston, 1965.

Austin, William M., "Some Social Aspects of Paralanguage." *Canadian Journal of Linguistics* 11 (1965): 31–39.

Balk, Frida, "The Pronounceability of Phonemes and Its Consequences for Linguistics." *Linguistics* 9 (1964): 5–12.

* Belasco, Simon, "General Section" in *Manual and Anthology of Applied Linguistics—For Use in the NDEA Foreign Language Institutes,* ed. Simon Belasco. Washington: U.S. Dept. of Health, Education, and Welfare, 1960, pp. 1–59.

* _____, "Introduction" to *Applied Linguistics: Spanish, a Guide for Teachers,* Daniel N. Cárdenas, ed. Simon Belasco. Boston: D. C. Heath, 1961, pp. I–XLII.

* Bolinger, Dwight, *Aspects of Language.* New York: Harcourt, Brace and World, 1968.

* Bronstein, Arthur J., *The Pronunciation of American English: An Introduction to Phonetics.* New York: Appleton-Century-Crofts, 1960.

* Buchanan, Cynthia D., *A Programed Introduction to Linguistics: Phonetics and Phonemics.* Boston: D. C. Heath, 1963.

Buiten, Roger, and Harlan Lane, "A Self-Instructional Device for Conditioning Accurate Prosody." *International Review of Applied Linguistics* 3 (1965): 205–19.

* Chreist, Fred M., *Foreign Accent*. Englewood Cliffs, N.J.: Prentice-Hall, 1964.

Cohen, A., "On the Value of Experimental Phonetics for the Linguist." *Lingua* 11 (1962): 67–74.

* Delattre, Pierre, "The Physiological Interpretation of Sound Spectograms." *PMLA* 66 (1951): 864–75.

Denison, Norman, "Phonetics and Phonemics in Foreign Language Teaching." *Proceedings of the Fourth International Congress of Phonetic Sciences* (1961), eds. Antti Sovijärvi and Pentti Aalto. The Hague: Mouton, 1962, pp. 571–76.

* Fries, Charles C., *The Structure of English: An Introduction to the Construction of English Sentences*. New York: Harcourt, Brace, 1952.

* Gelb, Ignace J., *A Study of Writing: The Foundations of Grammatology*. London: Routledge and Kegan Paul, 1952.

* Gleason, H. A., Jr., *An Introduction to Descriptive Linguistics,* revised ed. New York: Holt, Rinehart and Winston, 1961.

Hala, Bohuslav, "Apical, cacuminal, rétroflexe, coronal, dorsal." *Phonetica* 11 (1964): 186–95.

———, "La syllabe, sa nature, son origine et ses transformations." *Orbis* 10 (1961): 69–143.

* Hall, Robert, *Introductory Linguistics.* Philadelphia: Chilton Books, 1964.

* ———, *Linguistics and Your Language*. Garden City, N.Y.: Doubleday, 1962.

* ———, *New Ways to Learn a Foreign Language*. New York: Bantam Books, 1966.

Halle, Morris, "On the Bases of Phonology" in *The Structure of Language,* eds. Jerry A. Fodor and Jerrold J. Katz. Englewood Cliffs, N.J.: Prentice-Hall, 1964, pp. 324–33.

———, "Phonology in Generative Grammar." *Word* 18 (1962): 54–72.

———, "The Strategy of Phonemics." *Word* 10 (1954): 197–209.

* Harris, L. S., "Programmed Learning for Phonetic Transcription." *Phonetica* 10 (1963): 42–50.

* Heffner, R-M. S., *General Phonetics*. Madison: University of Wisconsin Press, 1949.

Hill, Archibald A., *Introduction to Linguistic Structures: From Sound to Sentence in English*. New York: Harcourt, Brace, 1958.

———, "Suprasegmentals, Prosodies, Prosodemes. Comparison and Discussion." *Language* 37 (1961): 457–68.

* Hockett, Charles F., *A Course in Modern Linguistics*. New York: Macmillan, 1958.

* ———, "Learning Pronunciation." *Modern Language Journal* 34 (1950): 261–69.

———, *A Manual of Phonology*. (Indiana University Publications in Anthropology and Linguistics 11.) Baltimore: Waverly Press, 1955.

Hoenigswald, Henry M., *Language Change and Linguistic Reconstruction*. Chicago: University of Chicago Press, 1960.

———, "Phonetic Reconstruction" in *Proceedings of the Fifth International Congress of Phonetic Sciences,* eds. Eberhard Zwirner and Wolfgang Gethge. Basel: S. Karger, 1965, pp. 25–42.

* Hoge, Henry W., "Visible Pronunciation." *Hispania* 42 (1959): 559–64.

* Hughes, John P., *The Science of Language: An Introduction to Linguistics*. New York: Random House, 1962.

Hultzén, Lee S., "Free Allophones." *Language* 33 (1957): 36–41.

Hultzén, Lee S., "System Status of Obscured Vowels in English." *Language* 37 (1961): 565–69.

* International Phonetic Association, *The Principles of the International Phonetic Association*. London: IPA, 1957.

Jakobson, Roman, and Morris Halle, *Fundamentals of Language*. The Hague: Mouton, 1956.

——,C. Gunnar M. Fant, and Morris Halle, *Preliminaries to Speech Analysis: The Distinctive Features and Their Correlates*. Cambridge, Mass.: MIT Press, 1963.

Jones, Daniel, *The Phoneme: Its Nature and Use*. Cambridge: W. Heffer and Sons, 1950.

Joos, Martin, *Acoustic Phonetics*. (Language Monographs 23.) Baltimore: Linguistic Society of America, 1948.

Kaiser, L., ed., *Manual of Phonetics*. Amsterdam: North-Holland, 1957.

* Kenyon, John S., and Thomas A. Knott, *A Pronouncing Dictionary of American English*. Springfield, Mass.: G. and C. Merriam Co., 1953.

Ladefoged, Peter, "The Classification of Vowels." *Lingua* 5 (1956): 113–28.

——, *Elements of Acoustic Phonetics*. Chicago: University of Chicago Press, 1962.

——, "The Value of Phonetic Statements." *Language* 36 (1960): 387–96.

Lane, Harlan L., "Acquisition and Transfer in Auditory Discrimination." *American Journal of Psychology* 77 (1964): 240–48.

* Langacker, Ronald W., *Language and Its Structure*. New York: Harcourt, Brace and World, 1967.

* Léon, Pierre, "Teaching Pronunciation" in *Trends in Language Teaching,* ed. Albert Valdman. New York: McGraw-Hill, 1966, pp. 57–79.

* Lloyd, Donald J., and Harry R. Warfel, *American English in Its Cultural Setting*. New York: Alfred A. Knopf, 1957.

* Marckwardt, Albert H., "Regional and Social Variations," in Anderson and Stageberg, *Introductory Readings on Language,* pp. 389–406.

Malmberg, Bertil, "Análisis estructural y análisis instrumental de los sonidos del lenguaje. Forma y substancia." *Thesaurus* 18 (1963): 249–67.

* ——, *Phonetics*. New York: Dover, 1963.

——, *Structural Linguistics and Human Communication*. New York: Academic Press, Inc., 1963.

* Martinet, André, "Dialect." *Romance Philology* 8 (1954–55): 1–11.

Mol, H., "The Relation Between Phonetics and Phonemics." *Linguistics* 1 (1963): 60–74, 7 (1964): 55–62.

* Obrecht, Dean H., "A Visual Aid to Pronunciation." *Language Learning* 7, iii–iv (1956–67): 51–58.

Pierce, Joe E., "Spectographic Study of Vowel Nuclei." *Language Learning* 12, i (1962): 241–47.

Pike, Kenneth L., *The Intonation of American English*. Ann Arbor: University of Michigan Press, 1945.

——, *Phonetics*. Ann Arbor: University of Michigan Press, 1943.

* Potter, Ralph K., George A. Kopp, and Harriet C. Green, *Visible Speech*. New York: D. Van Nostrand, 1947.

* Potter, Simeon, *Modern Linguistics*. London: André Deutsch, 1957.

Pulgram, Ernst, "Consonant Cluster, Consonant Sequence, and the Syllable." *Phonetica* 13 (1965): 76–81.

Pulgram, Ernst, "Graphic and Phonic Systems: Figurae and Signs." *Word* 21 (1965): 208–24.

——, *Introduction to the Spectography of Speech,* 2nd ed. The Hague: Mouton, 1964.

——, "Phoneme and Grapheme: a Parallel." *Word* 7 (1951): 15–20.

* Quilis Morales, Antonio, "El método espectográfico." *Revista de Filología Española* 43 (1960): 415–28.

Robins, R. H., *General Linguistics: An Introductory Survey.* Bloomington: Indiana University Press, 1965.

* Schlauch, Margaret, *The Gift of Language.* New York: Dover, 1955.

* Sebeok, Thomas A., comp., "Selected Readings in General Phonemics (1925–1964)." *Studies in Linguistics* 14 (1959): 43–47, 17 (1963): 3–9.

* Shearer, William M., *Illustrated Speech Anatomy.* Springfield, Ill.: Charles C. Thomas, 1963.

Siertsema, B., "Timbre, Pitch and Intonation." *Lingua* 11 (1962): 388–98.

* Smalley, William A., *Manual of Articulatory Phonetics,* revised ed. Tarrytown, N.Y.: Practical Anthropology, 1964.

Stetson, R. H., *Motor Phonetics,* 2nd ed. Amsterdam: Published for Oberlin College by North-Holland, 1951.

* Thomas, Charles K., *An Introduction to the Phonetics of American English.* New York: Ronald Press, 1958.

* ——, "Phonetic Change: Assimilation" in Anderson and Stageberg, *Introductory Readings on Language,* pp. 310–18.

Trager, George L., "Paralanguage: a First Approximation." *Studies in Linguistics* 13 (1958): 1–12.

——, "The Typology of Paralanguage." *Anthropological Linguistics* 3 (1961): 17–21.

——, and Henry Lee Smith, Jr., *An Outline of English Structure* (*Studies in Linguistics: Occasional Papers* 3, 1951.) Washington: American Council of Learned Societies, 1957.

* Waterman, John T., *Perspectives in Linguistics.* Chicago: University of Chicago Press, 1963.

* Wells, Rulon S., "The Pitch Phonemes of English." *Language* 21 (1945): 27–39.

* Wise, Claude M., *Applied Phonetics.* Englewood Cliffs, N.J.: Prentice-Hall, 1957.

* Wolff, Hans, "Phonemic Structure and the Teaching of Pronunciation." *Language Learning* 6 (1956): 17–23.

VOCABULARY

This vocabulary includes all Spanish words in the text whose meanings a fourth-year student of Spanish might not know. In the case of verbs, only the infinitives have been included, and stem and orthographical changes are indicated with letters in parentheses: **acertar (ie), gozar (c), regir (i, i; j)**. A few exceptions are verb forms which may not be easily identified by the student, such as **yerro** from **errar**.

The gender of nouns is not listed in the case of masculine nouns ending in **-o, -l, -r**, and **-ista** and feminine nouns ending in **-a, -d, -z, -ie, -ión**, and **-umbre**. Proper nouns are listed only when it is not obvious from context that they are personal or place names. Words that are homonymous are normally listed with only the most common meanings. Also, in the case of homonyms that are both verb forms and other parts of speech, usually only the verbal meaning is given. Idiomatic expressions are listed under their principal words. All words from foreign languages other than Spanish are also given.

—A—

abajo: calle abajo down the street
aborigen indigenous, primitive
aburrimiento boredom
acera sidewalk
acertar (ie) to hit the mark, succeed, be right
acosar to pursue relentlessly, harass
acre sour
acróbata acrobat
adentro: mar adentro out to sea
adivinar to guess
afán *m.* eagerness
afligido anguished
afligir (j) to afflict
agonizante dying
agotado exhausted, run out, used up
agrio sour
aguardar to wait for

agudo sharp
águila eagle
aguja needle
agujero hole
ahijado godchild
ahogar (gu) to drown, smother, suffocate
ahora: Hasta ahora See you in a little while
ahorrar to save, economize
ahumar to smoke *(to cure in smoke)*
airoso windy; graceful
ajo garlic
alabar to praise
alba dawn
alcalde mayor, justice of the peace
aldea village
alfabetización literacy
alfiler pin
aliar (i) to ally

319

amargo bitter
amarrar to tie, fasten
ampliación enlargement
anclar to anchor
anchura width
anhelar to desire, long for
ánimo spirit, courage
antaño long ago, yesteryear
antídoto antidote
antier *also* **anteayer** day before yesterday
anular to annul, make void
añejo rancid
aprovechar to profit by, make use of
apuntar to aim; to point out; to make note of
apurarse to worry
ara altar
arder to burn *(intrans.)*
ardillita *dim. of* **ardilla** squirrel
arrastrar to drag
arre *interjection* giddyap!
arrebatar to snatch away
arremolinarse to form a crowd
arriba: boca arriba face up, on one's back
arrojar to throw
arrollar to roll (up)
arroyo stream
asamblea assembly, legislature
astro heavenly body
atestado crowded
augusto august, magnificent
auxilio help, aid
ave *f.* bird, fowl
avergonzar (üe; c) to shame
averiguar (gü) to find out; to inquire, investigate
avivar to quicken; to encourage
azahar orange blossom

—B—

Baco Bacchus *(god of wine)*
Bahn *(Ger.)* way, track
bala bullet
balón *m.* football
balsa pool, pond
Bann *(Ger.)* ban
barbudo bearded
Barja *family name*
barra bar, rod
barril barrel
barrio district of a city
bastón *m.* cane

baúl trunk
bebé *m.* baby
beca scholarship
becerro yearling calf
betún *m.* shoe polish
bienaventurado blessed; happy, fortunate
bienestar well-being
bienvenida welcome
Bilbao *city in northern Spain*
bilingüe bilingual
bizco cross-eyed
blasfemar to swear, curse
bobo fool
boca: boca arriba face up, on one's back
bocadillo sandwich, snack *(Spain)*
bol punch bowl
boleto ticket
bolos *pl.* bowling
borla tassel
borrar to erase
bostezo yawn
botar to throw away
botella bottle
bou joint casting of a fish net by two boats
bravo wild, fierce
brío vigor
brisa breeze
broma joke
brújula compass
bucal buccal, pertaining to the mouth
buey *m.* ox
buho owl
buitre *m.* vulture
bulto bundle, package
buque *m.* large boat
buena: de buena gana willingly
buró *m.* bureau; writing desk
butaca armchair
butano butane
buzón *m.* mailbox *(on the street)*

—C—

caber to fit in, be held
cabo end
cajón *m.* drawer *(desk)*
cal *f.* lime *(chem.)*
calar to penetrate, soak through
calentar (ie) to heat
calesa chaise
calificación judgment, mark
calle: calle abajo down the street

callejuela alley
camba a V-shaped piece in garments
camilla stretcher
campeonato championship
camposanto cemetery
cana gray hair
cancha tennis court
cancho boulder
canoa canoe
cántaro: llover a cántaros to pour,
  rain "cats and dogs"
cante: cante jondo Spanish Flamenco
  or gypsy "deep" singing
caña cane, reed
capaz capable
capilla chapel
* capitia (Vul. Latin) head
  (unattested form)
capricho caprice, whim
capŭt (Latin) head
careta mask
carga load
cariancho broad-faced
carirredondo round-faced
carril rail
casa: casa cuna foundling home
cáscara rind, peel, husk
castigo punishment
casualmente "it just so happens,"
  by chance
catar to sample, try by tasting
caudillo leader, chief
cazador hunter
ceja eyebrow
cercado fence
cerdo pig
cerrito dim. of cerro hill
cerveza beer
césped m. lawn
c'est (Fr.) it is, this is
cifrar to place one's hopes on
cigarrera pocket cigarcase;
  woman cigar-maker
cima summit, top
cimiento foundation
cinta ribbon
cintura waist
circo circus
clavel carnation
clueco decrepit
coca coca leaves
cochecamas m. sing. sleeping-car
codo elbow
cohete m. rocket

col cabbage
cola tail; line (of people)
colcha quilt
colmo heap; height
colorado red
comés vos form of comer
comodidad comfort, convenience
comprometerse to commit oneself;
  to become engaged
cóndor condor (bird)
confiar (í) to trust; to expect
confundir to confuse
congelar to freeze
congelador freezer
conllevar to aid; to bear with
  patience
constar to be clear, evident
cónyuge m. or f. spouse
copla couplet; popular song, ballad
cordero lamb
cordura sanity
cornada thrust with the horns, goring
coro chorus, choir
coser to sew
cota quota, share
crecer to grow
criollismo a movement or feeling
  favoring native or American elements
  as opposed to peninsular or Spanish
cruórico bloody (poet.)
cuajar to coagulate
cuerno horn (animal)
cuna: casa cuna foundling home
cuñado brother-in-law
cursi ridiculous, pompous

—CH—

chamaco little boy
chancho hog
chao good-bye, so long
charlar to chat
chavalito dim. of chaval lad
chisme m. gossip
chorizo pork sausage
chu exclamation
chuchería trinket
chueco crooked, lame

—D—

danés Danish
daño harm, damage
dato fact, item of data
decano dean

degollar (üe)   to behead, cut the throat
delgado   slender
dentífrico *adj. pertaining to* teeth *as in*
   pasta dentífrica   toothpaste
derivar   to derive
derretir (i, i)   to melt
derribar   to knock down, overthrow
desarrollar   to develop
desatar   to untie
descantar   to clear of stones
desganar   to discourage
desperdicio   waste
despertador   alarm clock
diario   daily
dicha: por dicha   luckily, fortunately
dicho   saying
digerir (ie, i)   to digest
discantar   to chant, sing; to comment
disculpar   to excuse
disfrutar   to enjoy
disgusto   displeasure
disimular   to pretend
dispensar   to excuse
do *m. first note of a diatonic scale*
dolar   to hew
domar   to tame
dominó   dominoes
donner *(Fr.)* to give; donné *masc.*
   sing. past. part.; donnés *masc. pl.*
   past part.; donnée *fem. sing. past*
   part.; données *fem. pl. past part.*;
   donnez *second pers. pl. pres. tense*
druida   druid
dueña   landlady

—E—

ea   *exclamation use to attract attention*
ebanista   cabinetmaker
eje *m.*   axle
ele *f.*   letter l
embaular   to pack in a trunk
eme *f.*   letter m
emitir   to emit, send
empapar   to soak, drench
empeñarse (en)   to insist (on)
enaguas *pl.*   petticoat
enderezar (c)   to straighten
enfadado   mad, angry
enfilar   to place in a row or line
enfocar (qu)   to focus (on)
enfrentar   to confront, face;
   enfrentarse (con)   to face, oppose
engañar   to fool, deceive
engendrar   to engender, produce, bear

enhorabuena   congratulation
enlatar   to can, put in a can
enlazar (c)   to lace, bind, join, tie, link
enredar   to entangle, snarl, complicate
enterar   to inform
enterrar (ie)   to bury
entendés   vos *form of* entender
entumecido   numb, "asleep" *(limbs)*
enyesado   in a cast
enyesar   to plaster
ere *f.*   letter r
erguirse (ye, gu)   to straighten up,
   stand erect
errar (ye)   to miss (the mark);
   to be mistaken; to wander, roam
esbozo   sketch, outline
escritorio   desk
esdrújulo   stressed on third-to-last
   syllable
esfuerzo   effort
esmalte *m.*   enamel
espejuelos *pl.*   eyeglasses
espurio   spurious, counterfeit
estacionamiento   parking
estanco   watertight, leakproof
estaros   estar + os *as in* ¿Queréis
   estaros quietos?   Will you keep still?
estilográfica: pluma estilográfica
   fountain pen
estorbar   to bother, obstruct
estufa   stove
exangüe   anemic, weak, exhausted
excusado   bathroom, toilet
exigente   demanding, strict

—F—

faca   long knife
factura   invoice, bill
facha *(colloquial)*   face, look
fait *(Fr.)* masc. sing. past part. of*
   faire   to do, make
faja   band, sash, girdle
farmacéutico *adj.*   pharmaceutical;
   n. druggist
fe *f.*   faith
fiar (i)   to trust: fiarse de   to trust
fieltro   felt *(cloth)*
figlio *(Ital.)*   son
fil: fil derecho   leapfrog *(game)*
filho *(Port.)*   son
filosofar   to philosophize
fin *(Fr.)*   end
finca   farm

firmar to sign
flojo loose
fluidez fluidity
fluir (y) to flow
fluorita fluorite *(mineral)*
foco focus; light bulb
fofo spongy, soft
foro forum
forro lining
fracasar to fail
frambuesa raspberry
franja fringe
fregar (ie) to rub; to scrub
freír (i, i) to fry
fresa strawberry
frescura freshness, coolness
fresno ash tree
friolera trifle, bauble

—G—

gabán *m.* overcoat
gafas *pl.* eyeglasses
gala ostentation; finery
gallo rooster
gama doe
gamba shrimp *(seafood)*
gana: de buena gana willingly
gancho hook
ganga bargain, good buy
ganso goose
gasa gauze
ge *f.* letter g
gemir (i, i) to moan
genial brilliant *(person)*
Ginebra Geneva
girar to spin, whirl
glotón *m.* glutton
godo Goth
gol goal *(soccer)*
gola gullet, throat
golondrina swallow *(bird)*
gordura fatness
gorrión *m.* sparrow
gota drop
gozar (c) de to enjoy
grado degree
grasa fat, grease
grieta crevice, crack
grúa crane, derrick
grueso fat, stout, thick
guagua bus *(Puerto Rico and some countries)*; baby *(other countries)*
Gualterio Walter

guante *m.* glove
guapa young-lady *(used to address young girls)*
guardiacivil *f.* body of rural police in Spain; *m.* member of this body
guisar to cook

—H—

haba bean
hacha axe
hado fate, destiny
hasta: Hasta ahora See you in a little while.
hazmerreír *m.* laughing stock
hecho: lo hecho what is done (is done)
hegemonía leadership, predominance
helado ice cream
helar (ie) to freeze
hembra female *(animals)*
henchir (i, i) to fill, stuff
heno hay
heredar to inherit
herir (ie, i) to wound, injure
hiato hiatus
hidalguía nobility
hiedra ivy
hielo ice
hiena hyena
hierba grass
hierro iron
hígado liver
hijastro step-child
hijuela *dim. of* **hija**
hilo thread
hinchar to swell
hojaldrado resembling puff paste
hojarasca dead leaves
homenaje *m.* homage
homófono homophone
homólogo proportional
hondijo sling
hondo deep
hondureño native of Honduras
honradez honesty, integrity
horchata drink made from almonds
hoyo pit
hoyuelo dimple
huaraches *(Mex.)* sandals
hubo: ¡Qué hubo! How's it going!
hueco hollow
huelga strike
huelo *lst pers. sing. of* **oler**
huella track, footprint

huérfano orphan
huerta vegetable garden
huerto orchard
hueso bone
huésped *m.* guest; host
huidizo fleeting
huir (y) to flee
humilde humble
humillar to humiliate
humito thin smoke
humo smoke
husmear to scent, smell

—I—

ich *(Ger.)* I *(pers. pro.)*
imprescindible essential, imperative
indicio indication, sign, hint
indígena native, indigenous
indigno unworthy, despicable
infiel unfaithful
ingerir (ie, i) to ingest *(food and drink)*
ingresar to enter, enroll (in)
innato innate
inoportuno untimely
inundación flood
inverosímil unlikely, improbable
ira anger, wrath
iris *m.* iris, rainbow
istmo isthmus

—J—

jalar *also* **halar** to haul, pull, tow
jama *(Hond.)* small iguana
jaqueca headache
jara small plant
jareta fold in cloth to hold belt or string
jaula cage
jema *also* **gema** gem
jira strip of cloth
jo whoa!
jornada working day
jorobado humpbacked
jondo: cante jondo Spanish Flamenco or gypsy "deep" singing
jota letter **j**; iota, "nothing"
joya jewel
junta board, council
juramento oath
jurar to swear
juzgar (gu) to judge

—K—

kilo kilogram *(2.2 lbs.)*

—L—

laca lacquer
laja flagstone
lama mud, slime
lamer to lick
lancha launch *(boat)*
Lara *family name*
largarse (gu) to leave, get out
lechar *adj.* nursing *(milk)*
lechero milkman
lechuza owl
legar (gu) to bequeath
leja *(Andalusian)* shelf for glasses
leve light *(weight)*, slight
liar (í) to tie, bind
lid contest, fight
ligar (gu) to tie, bind, fasten
lijar to sand(paper)
Lili *first name*
Lillo *family name*
limpiabotas *m. sing.* shoeshine boy, bootblack
lío fight, row, scrape
lira lyre; *Italian monetary unit*
liso smooth, even
lisonjear to flatter
litro liter *(1.06 liquid quarts)*
loar to praise
lóbrego sad, dark, gloomy
lodo mud
Loja *department (state) of Ecuador*
lomo back *(of an animal)*
lona canvas
loor praise *(poet.)*
loro parrot
lucir (zc) to shine
lustrar to polish

—LL—

llaga ulcer, sore
llama *pack animal of the Andes*
llano *n.* flatland; *adj.* flat
llevar: Llévala suave Take it easy

—M—

machen *(Ger.)* to make, do
madurar: ¿Qué estás madurando?
   What are you thinking (cooking) up?

magullado   bruised
maizal   corn field
malestar   malaise, indisposition
Mallea   *family name*
mallo   mallet
manteca   lard
mar: mar adentro   out to sea
mármol   marble
matiz *m.*   shade, tint
matrícula   registration *(academic)*
medir (i, i)   to measure
melancolía   melancholy
melodía   melody
mellar   to dent
mensual   monthly
mentir (ie, i)   to lie (tell a lie)
menudo   small, minute
mero   mere, pure, simple
meta   goal, aim
minutero   minute hand *(clock)*
mirón *m.*   spectator, onlooker
mismísimo   very same
Miura   *family name*
moaré   moiré *(watered silk)*
mocita *dim. of* **moza**   girl, lass
moco   mucus
mojo   wet
monja   nun
monje *m.*   monk
mono   monkey
morder (ue)   to bite
moribundo *adj.*   dying
moro   Moor
morro   snout
motilar   to cut the hair of
moto *f. shortened form of* **motocicleta**
   motorcycle, motorbike
moza   girl, lass
mozo   boy, lad
mueca   grimace, "face"
mueco *(colloquial)*   slap on the back
   of the neck
muleta   *red cloth used by matador in
   bullfighting*
muro   wall
murón *m.*   *augmentative of* **muro**

—N—

nabo   turnip.
nácar   mother-of-pearl
nafta   naptha; gasoline *(Arg.)*
naranjo   orange tree
nene *m.*   baby

nieto   grandson
nivelar   to level
novelar   to write novels
nuera   daughter-in-law
nuevo: de nuevo   again
nulo   null, void

—Ñ—

ñandú *m.*   *American ostrich*
ñato   pug-nosed
ñoclo   *type of cake*
ñoño   timid, shy; feeble

—O—

obsequio   gift
ocio   leisure, idleness
oda   ode
odontología   dentistry
oler (hue)   to smell *(trans. and
   intrans.)*
oloroso   fragrant
optar por   to choose to
orar   to pray, orate
oso   bear *(animal)*
ostra   oyster

—P—

paca   bale
padrino   godfather; protector
paisano   fellow countryman
paja   straw
pajar   barn
pala   shovel
palco   box *(theater)*
paleto   fallow deer
paletó   overcoat
palón *m.*   guidon; big stick
panal   honeycomb
pantalla   screen; lampshade
pañal   diaper
paño   cloth
pardo   brown; dark gray
parra   grapevine
párrafo   paragraph
partidario   supporter, backer, partisan,
   follower
pasar: Que lo pase bien   Have a good
   time
pase: pase natural   *move made by
   matador in bullfighting*

pata paw, leg *(of an animal or piece of furniture)*
pe *f.* letter **p**
peca freckle
pecar (qu) to sin
pegar (gu) to hit; to fasten, stick
peinado hairdo
peinar to comb
pelar to skin, peel
pelirrojo redhead
penado convict
penar to suffer
pender to hang
peñita *dim. of* **peña** rock, boulder
perita *dim. of* **pera** pear
perspicaz acute, clear-sighted
pésame *m.* condolence
pesar *v.* to weigh; *n.* sorrow, grief;
  a pesar mío in spite of myself, against my wishes
piar (í) to chirp, peep
pico beak; peak
piel *f.* skin
pijama pajama
pillar to pillage; to grasp, catch
pinar pine grove
piñita *dim. of* **piña** pine cone, pineapple
pío pious, holy
piojo louse
pisada footstep
pisar to step, tread
pista racetrack, course; court *(handball)*
placer *v.* to please; *n.* pleasure
plata silver; money
pliego sheet *(of paper)*
plomero plumber
plumafuente *f.* fountain pen
plumero feather duster
pocho *(colloquial)* discolored, faded
polaco Polish
policía police
porito *dim. of* **poro** pore
porra club
posar to perch, light
postre *m.* dessert
potro colt
Prado, el *art museum in Madrid*
prender to seize, grasp, turn on *(light)*
presto quick, swift, prompt
presuntuoso conceited, vain
prevé 3rd pers. sing. pres. of **prever** to foresee

prieto black, very dark
psicólogo psychologist
pulcro graceful; nice, neat
pulgada inch
pulsera: reloj (de) pulsera wrist watch
purita *dim. of* **pura** pure
purito *dim. of* **puro** pure

—Q—

quebrar (ie) to break
Quintero: los hermanos Quintero
  Spanish playwrights: Serafín (1871–1936) *and Joaquín* (1873–1944)
quirúrgico surgical
quitanieve *m.* snowplow

—R—

rabo tail
ramo branch
rana frog
rancio stale, old, antiquated
raña lowland
rascar (qu) to scratch
rasgar (gu) to tear, rip
rayar to scratch, draw lines on
recado message
rechazar (c) to reject, refuse
red *f.* net
refrescar (qu) to refresh, cool
refresco refreshment, cool drink
regar (ie; gu) to water, irrigate
régimen *m.* regime; diet
regir (i, i; j) to rule, conduct, manage
reja iron grating
reloj: reloj (de) pulsera wrist watch
remar to row
remo oar
reno reindeer
repente: de repente suddenly
reseco too dry
reuma rheumatism
reunir (ú) to gather, join
rezar (c) to pray
rimar to rhyme, make verse
Rioja *province of Argentina; also of Spain*
ristre *m.* rest or socket for lance
roer to gnaw
rompecabezas *m. sing.* riddle, brain-teaser
rot *(Ger.)* red
rouge *(Fr.)* red
rozar (c) to rub, brush against

ruana square, heavy poncho
rudo rough, unpolished
rueca spinning wheel
rumor noise; murmur; rumor
Rusia Russia

—S—

sabana grassy plain
sábana sheet *(bed)*
sabroso delicious
saeta arrow, dart
salchicha sausage
salir: Se le van a salir los ojos His
  eyes are going to pop out of his head
salpicar (qu) to spatter, sprinkle,
  splash
salvavidas *m. sing.* life preserver
sano healthy
saña anger, rage
sarampión *m.* measles
saúco elder tree
seda silk
sellar to seal, stamp
semblante *m.* countenance, look,
  expression
seña sign, mark; gesture, signal
sera large basket
serado group of baskets
serie *f.* series
serio serious
seso brain
seta bristle
sidra cider
silbido whistle
sima abyss, chasm
simular to pretend, simulate
siseo hiss, hissing
so under, below; whoa, stop!
sobresdrújulo stressed on fourth-to-
  last syllable
sobriedad sobriety
solazar (c) to comfort, cheer
solitas: a solitas alone, all alone
sombrilla parasol
sonoro sonorous, loud
soplico slight puff
sotana cassock *(clergyman's garment)*
suave soft; **Llévala suave** Take it
  easy
sublevar to incite, to cause to rebel
subrayar to underline
suciedad filth, dirt
suevo Swabian *(from a district in
  southern Germany)*

suizo Swiss
suplicar (qu) to beg, implore
susto fright, scare
sutileza subtlety

—T—

taba anklebone; gaucho game
tanda show, performance
tanza fishing line
tato *(colloquial)* little brother
teca teakwood
tecla key *(of piano, typewriter, etc.)*
teja roof tile
teléfono telephone
ténder coal tender *(railroad)*
tender (ie) to stretch, spread
tenés vos *form of* **tener**
tenia tapeworm
teólogo theologian
tillar to floor, put in a floor
Timoteo Timothy
toalla towel
tojo *leguminous plant*
tonar to thunder
torcer (ue; z) to twist
tordo thrush
toril *pen for bulls before they go into
  the ring*
torpe slow, awkward, dull
torrero lighthouse keeper
tragar (gu) to swallow; **tragarse** to
  swallow
trama plot *(of a play, novel, etc.)*
triar (i) to choose, select
trillar to thrash, beat *(agriculture)*
tripulación crew
troncar (qu) to cut off, mutilate
trueno thunder
truhán *m.* rascal, scoundrel
truncar (qu) to maim, mutilate
tuerzo *1st per. sing. pres. of* **torcer**
tul *m.* tulle *(thin, fine cloth)*
tumbar to knock down

—U—

unir to unite
untar to grease, oil
usanza usage, custom

—V—

vagar (gu) to roam, wander
vago vagrant, tramp
valioso valuable

vapor   steam; steamship
vara   stick, rod
veis 2*nd pers. pl. pres. of* **ver**
vela   vigil, wakefulness; candle; sail
venado   deer
vencer (z)   to conquer, beat
vente *fam. sing. imp.* of **venirse**   Come
   here
vera   edge, border
verdura   greenness; *pl.* greens,
   vegetables
vereda   path
vetusto   ancient
vid *f.*   vine, grapevine
vidrio   glass
viuda   widow
volar (ue)   to fly
vuelo   flight

—X—

xococo   *Mex. plant*
хорошо *(Russ.)*   good, well

—Y—

yacer   to lie, recline
yegua   mare
yema   egg-yolk
yerba   grass, weed; **yerba mate**   maté
   (Paraguayan tea)
yermo   barren, uncultivated
yerno   son-in-law
yerro 1*st pers. sing. pres. of* **errar**
yeso   plaster
yodo   iodine
yugo   yoke
yunque *m.*   anvil
yuyo   weed

—Z—

zafar   to adorn
zapoteca   *Mex. Indian tribe*
zeta   letter **z**
zorrito *dim. of* **zorro**   fox
zurdo   left-handed, clumsy
Я *(Russ.)*   I *(pers. pro.)*

INDEX

All references are either to chapter or to chapter and section. Material in the drills and exercises is not included here.